THE
GERMAN
DILEMMA

THE
GERMAN
DILEMMA

The Throes of Political Emancipation

KARL DIETRICH
BRACHER

Translated from the German
by Richard Barry

WEIDENFELD AND NICOLSON
London

Originally published in Germany by R. Piper & Co
Verlag, under the title *Das deutsche Dilemma:
Leidenswege der politischen Emanzipation* © 1971 by
R. Peper & Co. Verlag, München

English translation exluding original chapters 3, 13, 14
and 17 © 1974 by Weidenfeld and Nicolson Ltd.

Weidenfeld and Nicolson
11 St. John's Hill, London, S.W.11

ISBN 0 297 76790 3

Text set in 12/13 pt. Monotype Bembo, printed by
letterpress, and bound in Great Britain at The Pitman
Press, Bath.

Contents

Preface   vii

PART I   THE PROBLEM OF THE GERMAN STATE
1   Concept of the State and Democracy in Germany   3
2   The Old School of Liberalism – Dahlmann on
     Politics and History   30
3   Weimar in Retrospect   49
4   Unpolitical Policy – Brüning   69
5   Gravedigger of Democracy – Papen   80
6   *Gleichschaltung* of the Universities   86
7   Loyalty to the State and Resistance   104

PART II   GERMANY'S SECOND DEMOCRACY
8   Changes in Western Europe   135
   1   The Background   135
   2   Tendencies of the Post-war Period   140
   3   Problems in Individual Countries   143
   4   The Bonn Democracy   150
9   Theodor Heuss and the Foundation of the Federal Republic   156
10   Salient Features of the Adenauer Era   178
11   The Bonn Party System   211

PART III   POLITICAL CRITERIA
12   Democracy and Political Parties – Theory and Practice   235
13   Nationalism and Internationalism   253
14   Racialism and Politics   264
15   On Imperialism   270
16   Democracy and Emergency Legislation   278
17   Peace and War   287
   Notes   297
   Publication Register   316
   Index   319

Preface

This book is based upon studies originating from a critical analysis of modern German history and politics. Their start is the question of the intellectual, sociological and political turning points leading to the decisions of 1848 and 1871, 1914 and 1918, 1933 and 1945. The present-day German dilemma is not simply, as is still generally maintained, the unhappy result of external political pressures and necessities. Rather it reflects the deep contradictions which have governed the modern development of Germany in the nineteenth and twentieth centuries. The central problem was the discordance between external power policy and internal political emancipation, between economic modernization and social conservatism, between a patriarchal concept of the state and a suppressed fluctuating idea of democracy. Analysis of the historical circumstances is necessarily bound up with the search for criteria to govern the formation of political judgement. So from an account of the more important stages on Germany's *via dolorosa* towards political emancipation emerges the question of what standards history can provide for an evaluation of politics and how they can be applied.

Part I of this book deals with the background and the change in the problem of the German state brought about by its two great encumbrances: the fixation of external politics on expansion and revision; in internal politics the discordance between the state and democracy. Between 1848 and 1918 liberals, conservatives and socialists all failed to solve the problem; the attempt to do so by authoritarian methods led to totalitarian dictatorship and voluntary *Gleichschaltung*, not least of the universities; even the anti-Hitler resistance remained largely under the spell of a traditional concept of the state.

In Part II discussion turns to the development of the Federal Republic against the background of the experiences of Weimar and in the framework of the West European policy. The salient features both of internal and external politics, the development of the party system and structural problems, both long-standing and new, are examined in the context of the stability and ability to function of the second German democracy. The

vii

more promising efforts to solve the German problem of state and democracy do not, of course, depend solely on institutional reforms. The patriarchal tradition, the concentration of internal politics upon economic progress and the rise of new ideologies constitute obstacles to the formation of a political culture and to popular identification with a free democratic system.

In Part III of the book an attempt is made, starting with a discussion of critical points in the theory and practice of political behaviour, to answer the question of the standards to be applied to modern democratic politics. This is done not by abstract disquisitions but by analysis of concrete problems. The subjects dealt with here are the relationship between politics and political science, the significance of political parties for modern democracy, the conflict between the national and international attitude towards politics and finally an up to date examination of the problems of racialism and imperialism, of policy in emergency and of research into peace. These questions are of overriding importance and in the light of them the present-day German problem appears in broader perspective. It offers an opportunity to learn from history and to overcome the historic dilemma of German thinking on the subject of the state.

Part I
The Problem of the German State

I
Concept of the State and Democracy in Germany

I

Among the problems confronting political science, that of the relationship between the state and democracy in Germany is of special significance; moreover consideration of it helps to clarify both the meaning of the term politics and the relationship between the various social sciences. In the past both the 'ruling doctrine' and political opinion differentiated between the concept of the state and that of democracy; the two ideas were either regarded as incompatible or one was clearly subordinated to the other. It is this that has led to the decisive turning points in recent German history. In every case except that of 1945 the concept of the state has clearly been accorded priority over that of democracy. The decisions of 1848 and 1866-71, the formation of the 'semi-democracy' of 1918 and finally the proclamations of solidarity of 1914 and 1933 all illustrated the preference accorded to the organization and efficiency of the state over the requirements and desires of the individual and of society. Even in the post-1945 period the question still remains whether, despite a considerable effort to revise the historical picture, the general view is not coloured by this primacy of the state over democracy, whether in fact the trend is not becoming more pronounced year by year. The call for greater national consciousness, use of nationalistic terminology both in political speeches and in the nomenclature of the Federal Republic's institutions, the arguments about emergency legislation and the relationship between security of the state and the established freedoms – all this indicates that the old problem is still with us even under the new conditions of the second German democracy. This raises the question of the solidity of the new order of 1945-9 and therefore that of the whole basis of German political science. Yet the re-establishment of democracy in West Germany was accompanied by a critical

3

re-examination and revision of the relationship between the concepts of the state and of democracy.

Twenty years ago political science made a fresh start under such general and anodyne formulae as 'politics consist of the fashioning of public life.'[1] This was, of course, inadequate when more precise questions began to be asked about the structure and scale of values of the political system which was under actual concrete examination. There followed a discussion of the extent to which a science of politics should be based on empirical analysis of the processes of power or the normative view of the established order, given the fact that 'the real problem is the relationship between freedom and power, between government and the restriction of liberty.'[2] This argument, which still continues today, became too theoretical and abstract to be very fruitful as regards the specific position and tasks of our discipline in circumstances when both tradition and ideologies had been shattered.

The controversy was highlighted by the deliberate effort, based on official state doctrine to equate politics with the science of democracy. This showed that the close connection between the rise of modern democracy and the formation of a modern science of politics had been realized. Obviously this presupposes some minimal degree of political freedom and consensus; it is no accident that political science is now active even in the countries of eastern Europe; equally it is no accident that in Germany it has been in decline ever since the second half of the nineteenth century and was forced to emigrate in 1933. The science of constitutional law can obviously flourish under all sorts of regimes – to this extent political science is not 'without a scale of values'.[3] Any attempt to solve the problem of the state simply by restricting political science to a study of a single pattern or a single typology of democracy would provide no adequate answer; so truncated a science of democracy would end in substituting for a self-critical science an idealistic attempt at political education, all too easily reduced to propaganda in favour of the system. In addition to the confrontation between democratic and non-democratic systems many of the problems facing our science are to be found in the vast areas of transition, of political and social change and in forms of government which are neither one thing nor the other. The various types of underdeveloped country, communist systems in process of change, and structural crises in established parliamentary democracies also provide food for thought. In addition we have learnt that any attempt to judge political reality by the standards of a model, ideal, but unattainable, democracy carries with it both scientific and political

4

dangers; we also know how easily such a process can be twisted to produce basically anti-democratic criticism.

No very profound thought is necessary, however, to realize that the term 'science of democracy' is descriptive of only one side of the subject with which political research is concerned. The other side is more difficult to define. It is concerned with the special historical and social elements of the structure of political systems and here the main difficulties of comparative research and comparison of political cultures and systems are evident. Even so momentous an effort as Gabriel Almond's and Sidney Verba's thoughtful book makes this plain.[4] The resulting impulse to the science of democracy is particularly productive under conditions when the British and American tradition, which regards democracy as a way of life, is generally accepted. This viewpoint, however, if applied to Italian or German conditions, merely leads to a narrowing of the context in which the political culture of a 'retarded nation' should be approached;[5] this applies with even greater force to comparative analysis of the underdeveloped countries. In fact account must be taken of all those special conditions which can only be elucidated by detailed historical and sociological analysis of the antecedents of and 'built-in obstacles' to democracy in the various countries and systems.[6] This is the real problem of comparative research into systems.

This is no place to try and classify or describe the non-democratic components of the various political systems. Since comparative research is essential, the value of analysis of individual systems is obvious; it is not of value, however, if it results in self-satisfaction and self-deception on the part of the profession of history or, by taking individual cases in isolation, ends by becoming a mere apologia for the system under consideration; this was the trap into which all too many German historians, constitutional lawyers and philosophers fell for more than one hundred years. They considered only their own country in isolation; both the content and the general trend of their findings, therefore, tended towards formation of a special concept of the state and this process reached its height in the peculiar German ideologies of the First World War and then in National-socialism. Neither the history nor the decline of political science in Germany are understandable unless account is taken of the influence of the old-established doctrine of the state and its confrontation with western tradition.[7] It is said that conservative critics accuse political science of being an import from America; this is certainly untrue but the question of the relationship between the concept of the state and democracy undoubtedly holds one of the keys to any understanding of this distinctive German development –

both in German politics and in German political science. It is significant that application of this question to British, American or even French conditions produces no comparably illuminating answer. There the state has never been regarded as a sovereign entity over and above social and political groupings; alternatively the idea went into limbo as a result of successful revolution.

2

It is well known that the development of the German concept of the state in the early nineteenth century was largely influenced by argument about the significance and consequences of the French Revolution. Here was a revolutionary force, a movement bent on modernization and democratization confronting the old traditions of empire and the enlightened absolutism of the territorial state. But the revolution degenerated into Napoleonic imperialism rousing the first stirrings of German nationalism. This led to the confrontation between western democracy and the German state which was to have so great and ultimately so fateful an influence on the development of German national consciousness.[8]

Admittedly the final cleavage did not occur until after the constitutional movement had failed for the second time in 1848. But this failure was not merely the result of a series of unfortunate accidents; its background was the ambivalent posture of German liberalism which found itself caught between an unsatisfied longing for a national state and the patriarchal structures of the principalities. Leonard Krieger has given a penetrating analysis of the situation in his book *The German Idea of Freedom* published in 1957 and far too little read. He shows how, even among the majority of liberals, the German idea of freedom was constricted from the outset and increasingly by the concept of the state as the law-and-order authority standing above society, guaranteeing unity and efficiency, the powerful protector standing above party. Initially under this concept of the state a place was to be found for freedom of the individual within society but ultimately concessions were made to defensive conservative forces and so there came about that concept of the state which has increasingly governed the juridical and political thinking of the citizenry since the age of romanticism and which places an exaggerated emphasis on the theories of Hegel.

As the starting point of any consideration of the German national problem it must, of course, be realized that Germany did not reach the status of a centrally governed state with a historical and national background on the same time-scale as the western powers. In contrast to France certain of the

6

eighteenth-century German principalities developed a moderate form of enlightened absolutism and this seemed to make possible organic transition to modernity without revolutionary upheaval. It is still to be proved whether it is true to say that Germany's enlightened princes 'had anticipated western achievements as early as the eighteenth century'.[9] The other side of the coin, however, was that an absolutist doctrine of state and the doctrine of constitutional law converged; here lay the strength of German absolutism and the weakness of German constitutional law.[10] This was a far cry from the British 'rule of law' which was 'based on the vital concept of complete fusion of individual and political liberties'.[11]

It would be all too easy to lay the blame for this anti-western, anti-democratic development at Napoleon's door, but this would be too facile an explanation. The French occupation exerted a modernizing influence on the reformers and the liberals, particularly in western and southern Germany. In the Netherlands, where conditions were similar, democratization went much further. In Germany the adherence of Prussia to the cause of nationalism set the seal on the development acidly described by von der Gablentz as follows: 'We turned our backs on enlightenment.'[12]

These problems were further complicated by the historical difference between the forms of democratization adopted on the continent and by the Anglo-Saxons. In Britain and America democratization amounted to 'adoption of the state by the people'; on the continent it was 'integration of a self-governing people into a state',[13] although, as opposed to France, the state in Germany still only existed as an idea. After the failure of 1848 the liberal movement, strong though it was, gave increasing preference to foreign policy based on the ideal of national freedom and unity over internal policy based on the ideal of individual liberty and the constitution; as a result it became subject to the reactionary authority of the princely courts, the military and the bureaucracy. Bismarck and Prussia, both pillars and symbols of this reaction on the part of the old-established order, contrived to impose on the people their long-sought German nation-state by means of revolution from above.[14] The result was a Prussian authoritarian substitute for the liberal democratic nation-state which had been the object prior to 1848. It satisfied the longings of the unity movement, however, and so was able at the same time to absorb the bourgeois-liberal emancipation movement into the structure of an ostensibly constitutional, semi-absolutist state based on feudalism, the military and officialdom. Impressed by Bismarck's successes, the bourgeoisie accustomed itself to a cynical concept of *Realpolitik* in which might alone, rather than law and morality, was the only thing that mattered in politics. Politics were dominated by authoritarian ideas about established order and prestige which once led Thomas Mann to coin the sarcastic phrase: 'The state is both a professor and a general.' The opposite poles of this attitude of mind were the cult of power and the spirit of submission.[15]

From the outset, therefore, the Bismarckian empire suffered from severe strains and structural faults only barely concealed by the glitter of its formative period. These stresses and faults prevented development of an effective parliamentary system or of political parties prepared to assume responsibility. They barred the way to co-operation by the growing mass of the working class with its social-democrat and trade union organizations. There was a deep cleavage between the structure of society and a political order which took little account of the changes in the social situation resulting from the industrial revolution. There was a growing tendency, particularly after the fall of Bismarck, to neutralize the problem by diverting attention to external matters (a kind of social imperialism). As far as external affairs were concerned the new unified German Reich regarded itself as a 'retarded nation'. Both conservatives and liberals agreed that Germany must make good as soon as possible the lead gained by other world powers in terms of nationhood and empire; as a great power, they maintained, Germany had a natural claim to the hegemony of Central Europe and to participation in the colonial, economic and political penetration and partition of the world.

A vast material expansion took place giving rise to far-reaching national and imperial demands; facing this was an immobile, out of date, political regime – and nowhere was it more out of date than in Prussia which occupied far the most dominating position. The monarchy remained anchored to an historic mode of life bearing no relation to modern political and social trends. It stood in sharp contrast to the tendency of the age which was towards increasing democratization of all spheres of life. There were, of course, discerning critics, not only from the Left, who pointed out this fatal incongruity and demanded, as a minimum, adaptation of the Bismarckian system to the changed circumstances – Friedrich Naumann's idea of a democratic Kaiser, for instance. It was illusory, however, to think that, with minor modifications, the Reich of 1871 could master the problems of a great modern country and assume the leadership of 'Central Europe'. To this extent the Reichstag too failed to fulfil its function in that it did not press for reform with sufficient urgency or for the institution of a parliamentary regime. In the Kaiser's eyes and in those of Bismarck, social democracy, growing though it was, remained a movement of 'enemies of the Reich' and 'stateless fellows'. Even the liberals, the section of the population mainly responsible for economic growth, were denied full political participation at the top.

A bourgeois mentality was the hallmark of William II's Germany, strong though it was in some respects but helpless in others. Its motif was not so much a deliberately aggressive foreign policy as the worship of success. The bourgeoisie dreamed of being given a title or at least of becoming a reserve officer and this helped to condition its political ideas to 'autocratic constitutionalism'[16] and to blunt the political offensive of the emancipation movement. Socialism's egalitarian concept of democracy became an object of fear and a spectre, whether it was Lassalle's pro-national evolutionism or Marx's anti-national revolutionism which was trying to assert the rule of the majority. Democracy was regarded as an enemy, not a potential ally,[17] and its opponents closed ranks to suppress it. In the security of the Second Reich, based as it was on privilege, the bourgeoisie was absorbed in making profits and safeguarding their economic and social position; so they came to look on politics as administration and good administration as the best internal politics.

Such is the background against which must be viewed the manifestoes of the First World War, the much trumpeted ideas of 1914, the Kaiser's August proclamation with its key-note phrase 'I know no parties any more', finally the battle-cries of journalists and professors in which the antagonisms between the German state and western democracy reached their height.[18] Thomas Mann's 'Thoughts of a Non-political' give vivid expression to the fact that basically this concept of the state was non-political; similarly the notion that the state was something above party, in so far as it was not mere ideological camouflage, betrayed an unpolitical misconception of the nature and function of the state.[19]

Closely and clearly allied to all this was the German concept of the nation; initially it had been closely connected with the liberal and democratic emancipation movements, but eventually it emerged as an anti-western ideology in vogue when the nation–state (admittedly a *kleindeutsch* one) was formed. So there arose the special German concept of the nation which ultimately acquired anti-democratic overtones and was basically unpolitical. This was the concept of the ethnic nation, in existence before the formation of the state and to which a man was indissolubly bound by origin and language whether he wished it or not. There was no question of free decision by the citizen or the individual, of the 'ability to say no' in

9

Max Scheler's phrase;[20] the nation was an authority superior to the individual. Fichte, Arndt and Jahn presented it as a hope for the future, a beautiful dream; it could only too easily, however, become an object of limitless trans-political irrationalism and reach the metaphysical heights of a pseudo-religion.

The concept of 'nation' was not, as in France, Britain or America, linked to emancipation in the social, constitutional or political sense or to concrete measures of democratization; the people had not become articulate as a result of a successful revolution. According to the German scheme of things disparity between nations was not to be judged in terms of the degree of internal liberty and self-government. So the gulf between the German concept of the state and that of the West was parallelled by an increasing divergence between nationalism and democracy in the mind of the Germans. Since both thought and behaviour continued to be coloured by the customs of the patriarchal state, any attempt to lead this 'retarded nation' to identify people and state was bound to result in convulsions – all the more so because the realities of politics did not accord with theory. The conclusive struggle to produce a structure identifying the political state and the ethnical nation led to the 'natural' community and eventually to the 'popular community' (Volksgemeinschaft). The resulting strains and aberrations have both coloured and distorted the history of the German concept of the state in the nineteenth and twentieth centuries.[21]

This brought out into the open the great cleavage which ultimately destroyed any foundation, based on the communal freedoms, which the democratic national emancipation movement might have possessed; this was the cleavage between the principle of an internal political structure based on democracy and that of nationhood considered in terms of foreign policy, between the internal and external political connotations of the concept of freedom, between the rights of the citizen and the power–policy demands of the nation–state. Prior to 1918 this profound conflict was either shelved or solved at the expense of democracy. Ideas of a state based on democratic and liberal principles were naturally humanist and supranational in character; nationalism, on the other hand, postulated confrontation and battle, particularly when the nation was declared to be of overriding importance. The newly awakened national consciousness was directed primarily to the attainment of national power–policy ends and so internal liberty and organization were subordinated to the concept of external freedom. Nationalism was consequently used to further a spurious defensive ideology in the service of existing power relationships; instead of giving concrete political expression to the interest of the people it degenerated into a non-political metaphysical concept of the absolute importance of the nation. A German ideology serving the ends of reaction and the patriarchal state was able to restrain or divert the democratic tendencies inherent in the concept of the nation and even to make use of the concept in the fight against democracy. Hans Kohn, Helmut Plessner and Hermann Lübbe have all emphasized in their philosophical and historical works that 'in nineteenth-century Germany the thinking in high political places disregarded, in turn and with increasing obstinacy, political liberalism, the ideal of social justice and the technocratic ideas thrown up by positivist scientific thought';[22] they have also shown what difficulties stood in the way of 'any genuine alliance between the forces of enlightenment and the formation of the nation–state in Germany'.[23] From the sociological angle M. Rainer Lepsius has recently stated the problem as follows: there was 'a general stabilization of the political system without any further progress being made in democratization ... From the internal political point of view the symbols of the imperial period were an empty façade' – as meaningless as proclamation of the date of the battle of Sedan as a national holiday. Lepsius concludes:

'Ultimately, therefore, it was only logical and inevitable that, before its collapse, the democratically-orientated section of the German party system should have paced Hindenburg on a pedestal as their representative – Hindenburg who symbolized identification with the nation but not the desire to express it in democratic terms.'[24]

A glance back into the history of this German problem shows that in relation to democracy and the concept of the state, nationalism has always been in an ambivalent position and still is so today. The development of a national consciousness has contributed to the rise of democratic movements; it has also, however, become unpolitical and so supported and deified authoritarian regimes; on occasions it has de-politicized and diverted the demands of the masses for freedom and democracy and used them for ideological, imperialist and power–policy ends.

This applies even to American democracy;[25] it applies with particular force to the popular nationalism of central and eastern Europe.[26]

3

Against this background most pre-1945 German theorists have answered the question of the relationship between the state and democracy by subordinating one to the other – democracy has been regarded as a form of government. In some cases reference was made to the ancient theory on forms of state, the modern state being simply equated with the *polis* or *res publica*, frequently with no great historical accuracy.[27] Alternatively the reasoning was philosophical and often enough ideological. *Brockhaus** (and more recently Herbert Krüger) still say that the basis of all theories on the state must be that 'the state is no mere tool or "machine" for the pursuit of individual or group interests (the instrumentalist concept of the state); it is a phenomenon in its own right, the standing and value of which rest upon the fact that it is the manifestation of a concept of the state transcending the individual.' This idea is now being discredited: 'the leaders must be wise and the led must be intelligent if consciousness of the dignity and value of the state is to be re-established.'[28]

This amounts to a claim that the specifically German ideas to which nineteenth-century idealism and romanticism had given birth, are of general application – and this is a significant development. The plethora of small German states is contrasted with the unified state and so, extrapolating history, the state is presented as a neutral and superior entity standing above social or political parties and divisions. The attempt to substantiate this concept, pursued over the last 150 years, led from the pretensions of the Wilhelmian period to the catastrophe of the Weimar Republic. As a doctrine on forms of state the old pattern monarchy–aristocracy–democracy is not applicable to modern political systems; ever since Polybius and the Roman system of government, since Montesquieu and in the development of the British monarchy and the American presidential system, a blend of constitutional powers has been the governing idea. On the other hand, though not totally unrealistic, the notion of the state as something standing above politics and society contains much make-believe, self-deception and ideology, whether advocated on philosophical, historical or juridical grounds. The more the state came to be regarded as something greater than a mere practical instrument on the British or American model, the weaker became the impulse towards a democratic concept of the state; yet it had some roots in more distant German tradition,[29] although in the period of enlightened absolutism more thought was admittedly given to the state based on the rule of law than to democracy. This applies too to the liberal theorists of constitutionalism such as Robert von Mohl, Rudolf Gneist and Lorenz von Stein; they used a 'concept of the state based on the rule of

---

* The German equivalent of the *Encyclopaedia Britannica*.

law as a vehicle' for their democratic ideas.[30] These ideas were, however, overshadowed by the concept of a state based on power–policy particularly in post-1848 political historiography; the concept of the state based on the rule of law was also increasingly deprived of meaning by excessive juridical formalism. This left a vacuum easily filled later by authoritarian and nationalist ideas, starting with the monarchical patriarchal state and ending with Papen's and Hitler's state which worked on emergency legislation.

Naturally numerous historical reasons can be given to justify Germany's choice in the nineteenth century. Nevertheless this choice in favour of a state standing over and above society was in fact an exercise in self-deception, used and misused by the opponents of democracy, by reactionaries and authoritarians. We meet this concept again in the anti-democratic ideas current under the Weimar Republic when the state was placed on a pedestal as the guarantor of continuity and good order, standing above party and above the interplay of democratic forces. Admittedly in the constitution and external structure of Weimar some attempt was made to bridge the gap between state and democracy. However, both in the day-to-day running of the official machine and in political thinking, the actual initiation of measures of democracy remained partial only; the pre-war and wartime concept of the state, though now without its monarchical head, continued to dominate the scene, contrasting with and excluding ideas of democracy based on parliament and political parties.

The new democratic order of 1918 turned out very differently from that intended and the reason was that, even through revolution, people clung stubbornly to their ideology concerning the state. The institutional framework was, of course, changed; what hardly changed at all, however, was the confrontation between state and society, between state and democracy; in face of rapid socio-political change, the pre-war theory of the semi-constitutional, semi-patriarchal state was turned into a dogma and an ideology. This theory of the nature of the state failed to meet Georg Jellinek's demand in his pioneering book that the state be regarded as representing 'the totality of social life' within the framework of a social theory; Martin Drath has recently put forward the same view yet again. The reason lay partially in the fact that the legal profession, reared in a *status quo* attitude of mind, took small interest in socio-scientific matters; an equally important reason, however, was that the problem was looked at from a non-political standpoint, the result of political conservatism. Drath says this:

'The theories taught were inherited from the old regime; ultimately they became dogma and so were turned into a practical political concept of the state and even a dogmatic philosophy concerning the state. This is particularly likely to happen if this theory is used as an argument for or against important concrete social and political developments or postulates necessitating the elaboration or application of certain scales of values and the systematic formation of views or firm attitudes based more or less on principle.'[31]

Such a 'transformation of theory into justificatory ideology *pro vel contra*' is in fact characteristic of periods of 'rapid social change accompanied by significant social dislocation'.[32] In face of the social and political conflicts of a rapidly changing industrial society protection of the imperial Reich seemed to be the task of the state and provided convincing justification for its existing structure and character. This was the argument used by legal positivism which could thus be ostensibly 'non-political' and devote itself to exposition and application of the state's regulations. Abbreviated expressions, used systematically and dogmatically, came to have a value of their own – 'expressions which in practical terms were oversimplified such as "will of the state", "the personality of the state", "the organs of state", etc.; all these implied a special concept of the state' and were moulded 'into the pattern of an organism'.[33] In addition, however, Drath explains how this theory of the state was used by the 'ruling classes' of the time to oppose the democratization demanded by socio-political change; it became 'the rulers' theory concerning the state, used *in all spheres* to buttress the existing order both of government and society, to turn into an ideology the specifically German type of constitutional monarchy, the form of state and, to a large extent, the social order stemming from that monarchy'.[34]

The imperial period and its repercussions upon Weimar have been cited as an example; to some extent the same is true of the consolidation of a conservative and conservationist concept of the state prior to 1870 and 1848. It was regarded and defended as a shield against, and counterweight to, actual social reality, as a bulwark in face of the uncontrolled dynamism of democratic emancipation movements. With the idea of a state based on the rule of law some of the liberal demands were accepted – for example, bourgeois liberalism's need for protection was met and used as a weapon against the true democratic movement; yet the fateful cleavage between liberalism and democracy remained, leading to an even deeper rift between the political constitution and that of society. This too was a specifically German phenomenon. In Britain and America, even in France and Italy, no such cleavage occurred.

It was not only under the monarchy that the concept of the state as an ideological and juridical super-entity was the governing theory. After the disappearance of a liberal political doctrine from the universities in mid-century it was unchallenged and it survived the collapse of the monarchy and, in some people's minds, even the end of Hitler's state. Whatever the political or non-political motives, its central theme was the absolute necessity for an order and an authority, aloof from the conflicts and fluctuations of socio-political life, functioning smoothly and surely, a shield against change and upheaval, a counterweight to the democratic dynamism of a society in which barriers were falling, the guarantor of the capability to rule, to achieve and (according to Carl Schmitt) to take decisions, as opposed to the perils of pluralism and polyarchy. For the theorists such as Carl Schmitt the state had to be even more than this. Friedrich Julius Stahls'[35] was the last attempt to legitimize the state using the old theistic transcendental arguments and these were now irretrievably discredited. The democratic argument, however, did not seem to Schmitt sufficiently deep or solid and so, even in his earlier writings, he declared the modern state to be viable only if it disposed of emergency powers and was based on the possibility of dictatorship.[36] The state was therefore something both opposed to and superior to democracy; as a substitute for the monarchy its basis was the capacity to take decisions; Hobbes and Donoso Cortes were cited as its classic advocates. So, whether rightly or wrongly, the field was left open to the speciously selective interpretation of Schmitt and his school.

Kurt Sontheimer and other writers have given detailed proof of the extent to which other people gave the Weimar Republic's doctrine of state a non-democratic, or even anti-democratic, twist, though they did not draw Schmitt's extremist conclusions.[37] In general their doctrine was no mere battle-cry but any innovation was ruled out and declared non-constitutional; doubt was thrown on its legitimacy and it was treated as a mere product of defeat or a transitory interlude. Furthermore the state was presented as something either contrasting with or superior to the realities of party politics, parliamentary government and pluralist democracy. There was a further fresh factor. Under the monarchy this concept of the state had lent sanctification to the existing power structures; now it assumed the character and function of a counter-ideology founded on a broad view of history, philosophy and morality and contrasting with the short-lived, confused, crisis-ridden day-to-day democratic politics which were labelled 'dirty'. Admittedly, however, both its strength and its influence rested upon its close connection with the main props of the pre-democratic, patriarchal ruling order which had been unable to cope either with a partial revolution or the new constitution.

Franz Neumann, Arthur Rosenberg and Theodor Eschenburg have given vivid descriptions of the improvised republic of 1918 with its compromise blend of old and new;[38] continuity in the governmental machine, in the Reichswehr, in industry and in education did not produce any fundamental revision of the relationship between the state, society and democracy. Whether, from the historical point of view, acceptance of this continuity, both on the personal and institutional level, was really as essential as is generally assumed must remain questionable, particularly since Kolb and Oertzen have revived discussion of the soviet problem and since Wolfgang Sauer's investigations into the Groener–Ebert alliance; equally questionable is the habitual attempt to reduce the Weimar situation to the stark alternative – semi-democracy or bolshevism.[39] The outcome, as decided during those turbulent months, gave concrete support to the notion of a state standing above democracy – in the independent, ostensibly non-political position of the military (Seeckt openly expressed the view that the Reich and the state were entities transcending the democratic republic); in the aloof, if not hostile, attitude of the bureaucracy and judiciary who considered themselves a special caste, regarded themselves as guardians of the state against democratic politics and turned their pre-republican, above-party position into a tenet of conservative nationalist ideology; in the susceptibility of the citizenry to stab-in-the-back legends and revisionism which diverted attention from the political causes and consequences of Germany's defeat.

Finally this restorationist counter-ideology found a sheet-anchor at the highest level of the republic in the position and functions of the Reich president. A perfectionist effort, to which even Hugo Preuss and Max Weber had contributed, had been made to synthesize the Anglo-American and French forms of government and the result had been the elevation of the president to the status of counterweight to parliamentary democracy with potentially dictatorial powers; it was only too easy to regard him as a 'substitute Kaiser' and turn him into the focus of anti-parliamentary authoritarian tendencies. With so symbolic a pre-republican figure as Hindenburg in this position there was permanent risk of a relapse into the concept of non-democratic official politics, unfavourably contrasted with 'sheer' party politics. No more than a mention need be made here of the fateful role played by Article 48 of the constitution together with the right of nomination, dismissal and dissolution when lodged in the hands of such a president. The country was barely habituated to democracy and its exercise in practice was continually threatened by the seductive possibility of the *dolus eventualis*, a presidential dictatorship.[40] Premature abandonment of the task of forming a parliamentary government was only accelerated as a result. As early as 1923 and again after 1929 Carl Schmitt, together with many other propagandists of authoritarianism, seized their opportunity to point out that the dictatorial power of the Reich president gave constitutional authority to the limitation of democracy in favour of the state and ultimately provided justification for democracy's destruction. In this they were supported by the bureaucracy, the Reichswehr, industry and the professors who, each pursuing their own interests, were protagonists of the pre- or anti–democratic ideology of the state.

The position of most democrats, who were anyway only a minority, was uncertain; they vacillated between firm choice and a disinclination to abandon entirely the time-honoured concept of the state. This applied particularly to the bourgeois parties of the centre including the key Centre Party, as Rudolf Morsey has now shown.[41] The attempt to revert to 1848 did not succeed and little comfort was to be drawn from the failure of that year.[42] The republic had been born as the result of defeat; even common-sense republicans such as Troeltsch or Meinecke attempted to salvage from tradition more than it could offer. Political and democratic teaching barely had a place in school and university curricula; the fall of the republic meant the end of the promising experiment of the German Institute for Political Science (*Hochschule für Politik*) in Berlin, where so many of our more revered colleagues from both sides of the Atlantic had lectured. Moreover even such pronounced republican interpreters of the Weimar constitution as Anschütz or Radbruch clung to a positivist or relativist concept of democracy. In general they had no solid concept of democracy – of democracy as a political way of life – to set against the massive front of their opponents, the ideologists of the state, the nationalist historians and lawyers. The constitutional lawyers, who looked at matters from the point of view of the state, had largely become habituated to regarding democratic institutions merely as the mechanism for moulding the will of the people. They were ready to consider change in the substance of the constitution, even democratic change, but only if the prescribed forms were observed. Militant democrats and pioneers of our discipline, such as Hermann Heller, were branded as outsiders; during the legal proceedings 'Prussia versus the Reich' in 1932 Heller complained bitterly of 'the relationship of certain constitutional lawyers to the present Reich constitution', saying that poachers had been turned into gamekeepers.[43]

Certain of the leading brains in the social and political sciences attempted to come to terms with the new conditions but their efforts were frustrated by lack of a clear concept of democracy, due partly to formalism and partly to their view of the relationship between democracy and the concepts of government and state. To take a positive example: in a book dedicated to Max Weber one of the authors, Richard Thoma, discusses from the point of view of contemporary history, the 'concept of modern democracy in relation to that of the state'; democracy, he says, is the 'form generally accepted at present for formation of a system of national government'; it did, however – and this he considered to be the main problem – seem to postulate 'partnership' rather than government. Thoma then differentiates between extreme egalitarian and liberal democracy, between juridical, realist and sociological concepts of the state, but he characterizes the state as

'an association of people ... and a person in law; everything which normally appears as government is merely the application of the authority transferred to the various organs. In this, therefore, the personality of the state must be the sole ruling factor and this is relatively less fictional under a democracy than under any other form of government.'[44]

Thoma is opposed to a sociological withering away of the state which he finds to be implicit in marxism and also in the works of Max Weber; he refutes most convincingly, however, any tendency to range democracy and the state one against the other or to subordinate democracy as a partnership to the state as a system of government.

Although Thoma recognized democracy as 'government by majority decision', for him as well as for Max Weber democracy's real problem if it was to rule the state lay in the position occupied and the weight carried by that *corps intermediaire*, the 'administrative staff' in the broadest sense of the word;[45] owing to its stability, longevity and devotion to duty it may well come to consider itself as the hard core of the state, contrasting with the social and political dynamism of democracy. The 1918 reconstruction showed – as did subsequently the smoothness of the 1933 *Gleichschaltung*– the extent to which it is possible to count upon the pliancy of the administrative staff, upon its capacity to 'click into place' (in Max Weber's phrase) under changed governmental circumstances. For the citizen the administration manifests the state's continuity; Max Weber considers that 'real government' lies in the hands of the administration and is exercised 'not through parliamentary speeches and pronouncements by monarchs but through the day-to-day running of the administration'.[46] In the administration, however, where integration of democracy was more essential than anywhere else, the ideology of the state was at its most flourishing and its supporters most vocal.

A supposedly non-political sense of continuity and good order, therefore, lay at the root of the concept of the state; good administration was regarded as the best politics. This was of fateful significance for the Weimar Republic and its pseudo-legal transformation into the National-socialist state. The claim to stand above party still blocked the way to democratization of the concept of the state, to recognition of the party state and of parliamentary democracy – a claim described by Gustav Radbruch in his famous phrase 'the life-long deception of the patriarchal state.' Such a pre-democratic or non-democratic concept of the state was impotent or alternatively prone to illusion in face of the extremist claim to domination on the part of the Party dictatorship which proclaimed the totalitarian state but in fact used the state merely as a formal façade for an arbitrary Party dictatorship. Carl Schmitt's proposal that the Hitler regime be entitled 'a state based on the rule of law with emphasis on the state' shows how the ideology of the state or even the concept of the state based on the rule of law can be used to mislead; hardly another country on earth could provide so clear an example. Other constitutional lawyers such as Helfritz and Koellreutter made similar pronouncements until finally Hans Frank simply proclaimed 'Adolf Hitler's German state based on the rule of law'.[47]

It is not possible here to give details of all the various names and groupings, of dates and political developments which lent support and force to the anti-democratic concept of the state. The loudest trumpet call was that of Oswald Spengler who proclaimed that democratization spelt the ruin of the modern state. Any serious attempt to divorce the republic as a democracy from the old concept of the state was smothered. Even the views of so constitutionally minded a writer as Richard Thoma were disregarded; he maintained that, under modern social and political conditions, the old authoritarian, patriarchal concept of the state could not substantiate its claim to unity and superiority to party, that 'a state based on privilege could no longer cope with social stresses' and that 'the present-day method of "domesticating the masses", in other words the form of state more able to cope with present-day conditions, to save and preserve the state, was democratization with its principles of equality and majority rule'.[48] But people preferred to succumb to the illusory promises of the German-nationalists and the National-socialists rather than be forced to purchase the salvation of their state by acceptance of democracy.

4

Where do we stand today? To begin with there are two catchphrases; in numerous political speeches and leading articles these days an increasingly impatient demand is made for first, more national consciousness and second, greater state consciousness.[49] Behind this lies the accusation, openly made by many conservative critics of our post-war development, that the German social sciences, from contemporary history to political science, have spent their energies in 'demoralizing' analysis of the traditional governmental and national values. An ideologist of the state such as Ernst Forsthoff, who wrote a book entitled *The Total State* in 1933, today goes so far as to maintain that the 'political sciences', for which so much propaganda is made in western countries, are 'in some ways a counterpart' to the communist doctrines of society with their demolition of all previous concepts of the state.[50]

This implies an overestimation of the influence of our science on politics; more important still it places on the analysts the burden of proof that their facts are correct. What is meant by the terms 'nation' and 'state'? In what way are these ideas applicable to the second German democracy? In what relationship do they stand to each other both as regards meaning and importance? First there is the historical fact that, in terms of foreign policy, the state of 1871 has been destroyed; it was a state which was anyway incomplete according to the German concept of nationhood. After the experiences of the Weimar and Hitler periods we must redefine in terms of internal politics the concept of the nation–state.[51] Neither the Parliamentary Council nor the Basic Law succeeded in defining this clearly enough to exclude the possiblity of highly varied interpretations. They range from the democratic and social view of the Federal Republic through opinions with pronounced liberal overtones to the theses of the traditionalists; of the latter Herbert Krüger, for instance, sees the revival of the patriarchal state;[52] Werner Weber makes the bureaucratic state the criterion of his criticism and bewails the disintegration of the state into fractional political and social authorities.[53]

In fact the Basic Law itself seems to be founded solidly on the idea of a free, pluralist democracy and not upon some abstract concept of the state. Nevertheless the terminology of the constitution remains ambivalent; in certain cases the relationship between the concepts of democracy and the state is left hanging in the balance, although this may be thought to be simply the expression of the reciprocal limitations between democracy (politics) and the constitutional state (the institutions).[54] This applies also to the concept of democracy itself and to the argument (a much oversimplified one) between representative versus plebiscitary forms of democracy.[55] In this case the only answer can be a carefully considered 'the one as well as the other'; there can be no dogmatic 'either-or', no balancing of social reality against institutional expediency. Within the framework of the Great Coalition we may now have some possibility of installing a typical democracy based on proportional representation, but at the conclusion of his study on this subject Gerhard Lehmbruch rightly issued a warning against 'cutting the corners by setting up a certain defined type of democracy as the norm', even on the British or American model.[56]

These constitutional and political controversies were primarily a reflection of the various scales of value on which the creators of the Basic Law, who were drawn from differing camps, attempted to compromise between official traditionalism and the democratic creed. Key passages in the Basic Law set out the democratic foundation and rights of the Federation and of the *Länder*, whose functions are primarily of a democratic nature; Article 1 deals with the state as the protector of the individual, Article 2 with marriage and the family, Article 20 with the authority of the state as emanating from the sovereignty of the people, and so on. The point can legitimately be made that in the fundamental provisions on human rights and the banning of parties, democracy and not the state is the criterion.[57] Nevertheless a tendency soon developed, particularly after the Korean war and rearmament, to orientate the interpretation and execution of the provisions for safeguarding democracy and those of the code for political offences towards the protection and security of the state. It may be recalled that under the Weimar Republic the concept of protection of the republic was turned into one for the mere protection of the state and of authority. Gotthard Jasper has provided impressive proof that in this case there was too much concern for the state and too little loyalty to the constitution.[58]

This shift of accent is illustrated by the controversies concerning emergency legislation and their constitutional implications. They show the extent to which, even under the changed conditions of the Basic Law, the divergencies between a concept of politics based on democracy and one based on the primacy of the state still persist or have even increased. One of the frequently reiterated reasons is that 'the spurious revolutions of 1918 and 1945–6 left the substance of the bureaucracy basically untouched.'[59]

The really important point, however, is that lamentations about the lack of national and state consciousness all too easily leave out of account the historical elements in the German concept of the state. When the historical background is considered, the real subject of the present-day debates becomes clear, as does its longer-range significance over and above the current or electoral catchwords.

As we have seen, under the Weimar Republic tension rather than partnership, confrontation rather than identification, characterized the relationship between the state and democracy. By contrast the Basic Law has laid down as an overriding, inalienable principle that the state of the Federal Republic is a free democracy, a democratic and social federation. The part to be played by political parties is explicitly emphasized; a direct connection is established between democracy and the internal structure, financing and aims of the parties. Moreover this constitutional order is described as a militant democracy determined to preserve its existence, thus underlining the significance of new provisions designed to protect democracy against anti-democratic or pseudo-democratic tendencies.[60]

This does not mean, however, that the concrete political problems which have made this relationship so complex over the last 150 years and which have weighed so heavily against the development of democracy in Germany, have simply vanished. Application of the concepts of state and democracy is still an uncertain process today, showing that the old German dilemma still exerts a powerful influence. This may have a dubious effect on the interpretation of the constitution and of the law, on the attitude towards democracy both of the judiciary and the bureaucracy, and on the relationship between state administration and self-administration. Admittedly the Basic Law has, for the first time, unequivocally established freedom of the citizen as a fundamental right and made it the first principle of the political order. As a result and with the removal of the dualism between the authority of parliament and that of the president, the problem of the German state, which has developed in so specialized and problematical a manner and pursued such devious channels over a hundred years, seems to have found its way into the main stream of western democracy. The Federal Republic has even attempted to anticipate certain of the reforms now overdue in other quarters and to introduce them after suitable modernization and modification. Among these problems are 'political finance' (a question exercising all democracies), financing of political parties (admittedly a controversial matter) and finally the increased strength in the position of a chancellor government. The latter, however, depends more on personalities than on

22

provisions in the constitution, as the experience of three chancellors has shown.

Here, however, emerges the other aspect of a 'militant democracy' in that the principle of stabilization weighs heavily. This is understandable after the experiences of Weimar and the French republics; the result, however, is that the emphasis swings from concepts of freedom and dynamism to political conservationism. A comment by Hans Maier is of interest and deserves consideration: that the traditions of the chancellor democracy are to be sought in the enlightened absolutism of the monarchical state.[61] In any case there is an element here of the increasing tendency in all democracies to reinforce government and administration, to emphasize the governmental aspect of democracy. The effect is to complicate the problem of parliamentary political control. In Britain and America people are far more conscious and far more critical of this structural change; an erudite periodical entitled *Government and Opposition* and devoted entirely to this subject has recently appeared.[62] In Germany, on the other hand, opposition activities long carried the stigma of anti-state activities and have remained traditionally unpopular. Yet the future of any democracy depends on the existence of an effective opposition.

Germany now has a well-known periodical entitled *Der Staat* (The State) which shows much sympathy for Carl Schmitt's ideology; the words 'opposition' and 'democracy' in the sense referred to above, hardly appear. This publication came into being five years ago proclaiming that 'appreciation of the political and legal importance of the state has vanished; the state has been denigrated'—hence this 'forum for the state-conscious'.[63] Graf von Krockow has subjected this to penetrating analysis.[64] He drew attention to the peculiar concept of freedom on which the various authors (they included lawyers, historians and philosophers) based their efforts to safeguard the state. In my view this concept can be summarized as follows: only the state can guarantee freedom; therefore there is no freedom *vis-à-vis* the state. Alternatively as Forsthoff has put it: 'Freedom does not give rise to state-consciousness as the basis of a willingness to obey. Freedom isolates people and divorces them from the state. It is not a constituent factor in an order of society standing above the individual or even above ethics. It does not produce state-conscious people.'[65] This is tantamount to a specifically German concept of the state showing the traditional German passion for originality; compared to the international concept of democracy it is barely distinguishable from the elevation of the state to the status of an end in itself. Its basis is not freedom but strength, unity and efficiency at a level above that of the individual and with state-consciousness as a super-structure. This is a growing school of thought and it throws up theorists who regard administration as the essence of politics, who think that the main purpose of political science is to expand and enforce the administrative functions of the state in face of an allegedly inefficient parliamentary democracy; ultimately they maintain that the object should be, not to educate the citizen to democracy and increase the responsibilities of parliament, but to create administrative agencies and command posts at governmental level. This was the view put forward by Roman Schnur when addressing the parliament of North Rhine–Westphalia.[66]

These are horrifying portents, particularly when they appear in the name of political science. An ideology of state in which unity and efficiency are the governing factors may, in the short term, be beneficial to the technique of government and procedure. But the special feature of German development is that this notion of the state as something above politics has been carried to absurd extremes. In justification of it a highly selective view is taken of history; by arbitrary interpretation pre-revolutionary and anti-democratic philosophies of state are applied to the present day; the great divide between the state and society, between the state and democracy is perpetuated. The discussions on the theories of Hobbes, the consequences of which were so questionable, tended in the same direction; in these Roman Schnur, Reinhart Kosselleck and Bernard Willms attempted to present as the model of present-day political theory Carl Schmitt's theories of the absolute primacy of the modern state over all political and social forces.[67] Ernst Rudolf Huber took a somewhat different line; basing himself on nineteenth-century values he clings to the notion of the unitary state and in his desire to preserve the state under present-day conditions, he disregards the fact that society is changing.[68]

These efforts, which are increasingly in line with certain trends in political oratory and the publicity media, are evidence of a concept of politics and society which is partly reactionary, partly bureaucratic, non-political and technicist; it reduces political science to a science of the state and of administration; it would ultimately produce a modernized version of the patriarchal state. In these wide-ranging apologia for the state the Weimar Republic and National-socialism are largely disregarded; there is barely a place for them in the pattern. This is a revival of Schmitt's theory that, in the interests of good order and freedom (!), the citizen may not criticize the state whether on political, moral or spiritual grounds, that he must submit himself unconditionally to the wielder of authoritarian power of decision if he is not to relapse into 'the state of uncertainty preceding formation of the state.'[69] This theory may be explained, but it is also contradicted, by the failure of an intact state machine in face of the Party dictatorship of 1933. Its primary consideration is the efficient functioning of the 'state machine' (Schmitt's words), not of democracy. Democracy, one is forced to conclude, is an internal political luxury which can only be permitted, within limits, under the umbrella of the 'protective levels'[70] provided by a state machine standing above politics and society.

The protagonists of this viewpoint (who must be taken seriously since they include influential representatives of the professions as well as academic ideologists) have concerned themselves a great deal with Hobbes but little with the actual political and social realities of British and American democratic development. The system in force there is one of 'government' working in integral association with democracy and society, a system which is poles apart from the postulates of the Schmitt school and its associates. In the case of Germany the reason for the political crises of recent decades lies, not in the destruction of the old state by the bourgeois and democratic revolutions, as Kosselleck maintains;[71] it lies in the revival and persistence of an anti-democratic concept of the state which has been turned into an ideology and which postulates establishment of a patriarchal authority based on good order and technical efficiency at the price of political modernization.

Otto Kirchheimer has given us a penetrating outline of the decline of political opposition. In the light of this the trends towards renewed differentiation between the concepts of state and of democracy must be taken doubly seriously, whether their background is a selective interpretation of the Basic Law or the necessity for far-reaching changes in the constitution. The appearance of the NPD (*Neue Partei Deutschlands* – New Germany Party) seems dangerous primarily because it is both a symptom of and a stimulus to more fundamental tendencies. It has aptly been said that 'Germany's national task lies in the effort to do away with all that has traditionally been implied by the word "national".'[72] The same may be said of the necessity to dethrone the non-political concept of the state from its position as an ideology. Only then shall we be free to examine the concrete structural problems of a modern parliamentary democracy. Only then will it be possible to solve the increasingly complex problems of government and administration, of co-ordination and planning, of the balance between expertise and politics[73] by means of proposals for reform which will do justice to democracy.

I propose to give here only the headings under which reform is required: public hearings; more light to be shed on the use of influence; mixed planning groups; expansion of the information and advisory service; streamlining and updating of parliamentary procedure; activation of the democratic potential in federalism and self-government; greater accessibility, mobility and public responsibility on the part of the administration following the dismantling of those hierarchical structures in political and social life which constitute so decisive an obstacle to the inculcation and exercise of a democratic way of life. Last but not least we must have more true publicity about 'public life'; there should be a free versatile press instead of those monopolies which, in the hands of irresponsible manipulators of public opinion, may imply a threat to the formation of any true public opinion and make Article 5 of the Basic Law meaningless. The ambiguous phrase about the 'public duty' of the press and communications media is only meaningful if it implies, not mere acquiescence with official decisions, but true 'publicity', in other words critical examination and participation in the control of public affairs.

As elsewhere, therefore, even after the institution of a second and more stable democracy in Germany, there remains the problem of continuous further adaptation of democratic institutions and processes to the changing social situation. The transition from a liberal parliamentary democracy to a party democracy (G. Leibholz's phrase) is only the most obvious aspect of this development. In this, but even more clearly in the discussion on party financing, the danger could be seen that the political and social structure of the parties might become officialized; similarly the tendency to increasing institutionalization of all spheres of life throws up serious problems of the 'officialization of democracy'. This may lead to the creation of vacuum areas outside the established system and here frustrated political dynamism may take root and ultimately turn against the system itself. In view of the long 'sorry history of the civic spirit in Germany' (K. Buchheim's phrase) our main task is not to officialize democracy but to democratize the state.

Space does not allow me to deal in detail with the international decline in importance of the concept of the state in view of the interdependence of world politics – 'No state is any longer totally sovereign today; no state can now make a sovereign decision about its own destiny'[74] – not even during a state of emergency. Preservation of the peace is now considered more important than insistence on the sovereignty of the nation–state; political and ideological associations are now held to transcend loyalties to the nation–state. Gerhard Leibholz put it thus and he was not considering merely the problem of Germany alone: today the principles of the nation–state no longer in themselves possess the strength to prevent large-scale, long-term unification of Europe and thereafter of the world.[75]

It has not been possible to include as a subject of investigation the present-day question of Germany and the East German state. Many highly dogmatic utterances emerge from East Germany but, in the absence of a political science there, they are to be found in the official periodical *Staat und Recht* (State and Law). This paper has proclaimed, for instance, that 'the state as a specifically political institution will gradually become redundant';[76] this utopia of an end to politics sounds almost like a counterpart to the ideology of the non-political state. In parallel with East Germany's efforts to obtain international recognition, however, goes gradual progress in the development of its own system and its own national consciousness – not without some reliance upon a traditionalism which stands in entertaining contrast to the fundamental principle of socialist democracy. Faced with East Germany and its claim to be a state and a democracy, the Federal Republic must look to its own credibility as a democratic state as proof against the temptations both of deification of the state and of dictatorship. In the debate about the recognition problem this aspect of the German question is all too frequently obscured by the foreign policy aspects and formulae of the reunification theme.

If, therefore, we refer to an ethos of the state as something which, under all circumstances, we must have, this should be taken to mean a solidly based democracy with a proper scale of values. It should not be confined to one definite ideology (*Weltanschauung*), however; it must abide by the rules which guarantee freedom and equality of opportunity, which continually relegitimize parliament and government by means of free choice, which 'give the minority an equal chance of becoming the majority and allow freedom of choice of political purpose,'[77] which above all guarantee that the basic democratic rights remain valid and take precedence over and above those of the state. Constitutional courts should take the place of the High Court. Only on this basis, and not with its roots in a non-political official traditionalism or perfectionism, can a new tradition slowly develop which will be more than a mere amalgam of democratic and patriarchal elements.[78] Naturally democracy today cannot be direct self-government of the people by the people. A state there must be, since democracy can only function through a capable government and administration. In contrast to other systems, however, under democracy this is not the first consideration, although for a long time this notion was in the forefront in Germany and it has survived many unhappy experiences.[79] Naturally too, the state is not regarded as having a purely economic function as under the marxist system; its *raison d'être* today is a function of a more variegated democratic process. The idea is best summarized in the English word 'government' which covers both parliament and 'the government'.[80] This is the real meaning of Carl Joachim Friedrich's comment that 'strictly, under a democracy, the state does not exist'.[81] I would not therefore wish to describe government and politics as 'activities directed towards attainment of the state's aims'.[82] This seems to me to imply too little 'interpenetration of state and society'[83] and to lean too much towards the idea of the state as the embodiment of the 'common good' – which must, in any case, first be established. Moreover both experience and reasoning prove how misleading it is to 'refer to the state as such, divorced from its particular form of government'.[84]

Of course intolerant statements will still be made in the anti-pluralist tradition (which is still deep-rooted and popular) pouring scorn on minorities which have incurred official displeasure and which think differently from other people; of course the manipulators of public opinion and the unenlightened plebs can agree on some catchphrase like the 'subversive intelligentsia'. The political style proper to democratization of the state is that advocated with such eloquence by Theodor Heuss, one of the founding fathers of our federation, and practised by him as democratic representative of the state. Only then is it right to refer to the 'dignity of the state'.[85] The democratic style, however, demands that those who govern us, the so-called representatives of the state, take note of the voice of criticism as an expression of the community and do not judge it in the light of an outmoded concept of the state.

Whether political crises can be surmounted will be decided by our ability to comport ourselves politically, and not by questions of distribution of power or the design of the political structure. Admittedly the western democracies are 'not only highly complex but highly fluid creations'.[86] As Max Weber was forced to admit in 1918, however, their ability to surmount crises both in internal and external politics has disproved the popular legend of the greater efficiency and stability possessed by non-democratic states.[87] Under the social and political conditions of the modern state confidence and authority will only be assured through more, rather than less, democracy with participation by the citizenry at all levels; otherwise democracy, and with it the state, will be smothered by arbitrary dictatorial action taken in the name of some specious political order. Those who think that crises can be surmounted by emergency planning involving the suspension of democracy, the basic rights and the parliamentary and federal structure, have once more come to that fatal divide between democracy as a fair-weather system only and a trans-democratic state as fall-back. Historical and political experience show, on the other hand, that any departure from democracy, even its voluntary suicide as in 1930-3, means a crisis of the state.[88] This point of view and realization of these facts must be inculcated if we in Germany are to discard an ideology of the nation and of the state which is obsolete, misused and coloured by patriarchal thinking, and to acquire instead a concept of the state as something open to society, markedly democratic and no longer unpolitical. The contribution to this process which the work of political science can make is to criticize and enlighten. To this extent it is a science *for* democracy.

2

The Old School of Liberalism—
Dahlmann on Politics and History

I

Friedrich Christoph Dahlmann was simultaneously historian, political scientist and politician. In his famous book *Politics*, published in 1835, he explained where he stood in the intellectual life of the time together with the direction and purpose of his scientific activity. He did so as follows:

'At times one becomes conscious of legal erudition too great to be used in application of the law and pursued as an end in itself, of a present state of affairs too bad to be understood, of a science of history too lofty to concern itself with the present day. Those whose minds work in this way are impervious to a poet's advice to consolidate by long-range thinking that which now appears fluctuating.'[1]

Definitely and deliberately, therefore, he was rejecting what, in his view, was an over-quietistic and contemplative aloofness from current affairs on the part of many of his colleagues. In the foreword to the first edition of his book Dahlmann acknowledged that he had 'never for long been able to resist the powerful challenge of the present that notice be taken of it'.

This being his basic attitude to the problems of his day, Dahlmann was convinced that the scholar, the constitutional scientist or the historian cannot withdraw from participation in public life, or deny the close connection between his scientific activity and the problems of the present. Both in his writings and his actions Dahlmann gave living proof of this conviction. Dahlmann is significant because he propounded two great themes which are still actual in the best sense of the word and still have an immediate bearing on our own present-day problems. His first theme was the relationship of science, scientific research and doctrine to the great questions of the form and order of public life, in other words the relationship between intellect and power which has so frequently been upset in recent German history. His second theme was a more scientific and theoretical question but one of far greater significance than mere dispute about method – the relationship between politics and history. This question he posed not in the sense of projection into the present of the manifold links between the present and the past, but with the definite intention that the science of history should become a science of the state and of politics, should draw the two together and provide them with a systematized basis.

Dahlmann's experiment was of immediate significance in that it was both the purport and the achievement of a scholarly, but at the same time political, life lived in that vital half-century of German history from 1810 to 1860. It was a life as full of heights and depths as the history of the older school of German liberalism, to which it was devoted; it was a life intimately associated with the passions and the grandeur but also with the aberrations and the tragedy of this epoch.

Dahlmann's capabilities and activities developed in three main stages. During the first period he studied and then became professor in Kiel when the Danish–Schleswig-Holstein problem was at its height; then, with his appointment as professor in Göttingen in 1829, came the period of active participation in the constitutional movement culminating in the famous protest of the 'Göttingen Seven'* in 1837; finally from 1842[2] he became professor in Bonn, a period which includes the final culminating point of his career with his participation in the great venture of the *Paulskirche*.** It is not possible here to deal with all the implications of Dahlmann's career. A fresh appreciation of him is undoubtedly required since the earlier biographies are either outdated or – like that of the National-socialist constitutional lawyer Ernst Rudolf Huber – distorted.[3] What concerns us here is the connection which he established between politics and history, his political doctrine and doctrine of politics in its special relationship to historical experience. It is this that establishes Dahlmann's stature and importance in our day as well as his own. This can only be realized and understood, however, by applying the lessons of his career to the present day.

Dahlmann was born in 1785 in the Baltic city of Wismar; he was a Swedish subject and came of a family respected in public service. He studied classics in Copenhagen and Halle, coming into contact with the burgeoning romanticism; in an access of patriotism he made an adventurous journey with his friend Heinrich von Kleist to the battlefield of Aspern. Boldly

* *See* p. 33.
** *See* p. 44.

transferring his talents from philology to history, in 1812 he became Professor of History at the University of Kiel, then part of Denmark. Here he came in active contact with the world of politics; he wrote articles pleading for retention of the Holstein nobility's privileges but he also campaigned for some evolution of the old corporate constitution and the granting of some political responsibility to the bourgeoisie. Though not yet aged thirty, in 1814 he produced detailed ideas and proposals for the future political order in Germany. His was an original brain in the reform movement which had emerged from the wars of liberation and in which liberal constitutional and national patriotic tendencies combined.[4]

Dahlmann's campaign for Schleswig–Holstein's historical right to independence and unity was the first pointer to that peculiar combination of liberal and national thinking characteristic of the further development of the German constitutional movement. This departure from the unpolitical romanticist academic world of neo-humanism and entry on to the concrete battlefield of historical and political realities became the hallmark of Dahlmann's entire generation, but it began within a small and comparatively restricted circle. Not until his appointment to Göttingen University, which he owed to his famous elder colleague and friend Niebuhr and also to Freiherr von Stein, did Dahlmann come in contact with a wider circle, not only of intellectual but also of political life.

During the arguments over the new national order in Germany after the fall of Napoleon, Dahlmann had been torn in two directions; on the one side he saw the concrete power-policy requirement for national unity, on the other the sympathy, rooted in history, for the established forms of law and government. In Göttingen he realized and became fully conscious of the clash between the two. The latent conflict between these two components was not solved until Bismarck did so unequivocally and in his own fashion. Dahlmann's great contribution was to see the problem of unity versus constitution as an expression of the conflict between politics and history and to raise it to the level of a realistic doctrine of politics. Unlike the turbulent nationalists and equally unlike the basically unpolitical romanticists, he accorded priority to the constitutional movement over the slogans about national unity.

This was, of course, something quite different from that general, supranational line of thinking which visualized European or world citizenship and which Dahlmann and many of his contemporaries had pursued at one time. That was a phenomenon with which Friedrich Meinecke took violent issue in his *Weltbürgertum und Nationalstaat* (World Citizenship and the

National State).[5] Dahlmann too, in his earliest political analysis of 1814, had not been altogether disturbed by the dispersion of so many Germans abroad; his comment had been: 'It may perhaps be admissible to suppose that this strange process of admixture may be the starting point for a genuine European union liberated from an over-rigid and narrow-minded nationalism and based on mutual respect and recognition.'[6]

Such ideas may seem to have regained actuality today but in Dahlmann's day they were generally pushed into the background and they did not form the true starting point for Dahlmann's doctrine of politics. His basic concept was entirely in line with that held by the liberal movement until 1848; it was that the German nation in the cultural sense could become a nation in the political sense if it could create a constitutional order combining the historical with the modern constructive aspects of the principles of law and liberty.

This was the background to Dahlmann's two greatest achievements which occurred during his time in Göttingen. First, on the scientific side, was his book on *Politics*, a second enlarged edition of which was published in Bonn in 1847 on the eve of revolution; on the political side was his work on the Hannoverian constitution and the solemn protest against the *coup d'état* in 1847 by Ernst August, King of Hannover; this was taken throughout Germany as a demonstration against an authoritarian breach of the constitution. It was a protest by professors, the 'Göttingen Seven' under Dahlmann's leadership, and it resulted in his dismissal from office and banishment from the *Land* together with his friends Jakob Grimm and Gervinus – to the outside world a futile gesture but a potent symbol for the pre-March freedom movement.[7]

So a connection was established between scientific and political activity, between intellectual conviction and concrete action in public affairs, between views based on history and constructive constitutional thinking; it is this which, projected into the present, can give us much food for thought today. Admittedly we live under different conditions and are influenced by different scientific discoveries but we are nevertheless facing a new start in the conscious formation of German politics and the German constitutional order. The limited subject 'politics and history', which inevitably leaves so much else out of account, opens up a much discussed problem in the post-war debate about constitutional and political science. It is this which gives importance to the phrase about 'conquest of the past', to the question of the lessons of history, to the question of the value of historical experience and its place within a system and a doctrine of politics.

2

In the pre-March days the teaching of politics in German universities was very uneven. Practically everywhere political lectures were regularly offered but they were given, not by professors of political science but by historians, philosophers and economists. In 1819 Friedrich von Raumer from Breslau was appointed to the Chair of History and Political Science in the new University of Berlin and this combination was typical of the development of the faculty elsewhere. Raumer was still giving courses of political lectures until well into the 1860s but from 1834 Adolph Friedrich Riedel, and from 1843 Siegfried Hirsch, both historians, were also teaching the subject. In addition Johann Karl Glaser, working as a freelance lecturer, and Leopold von Henning, Professor-in-Ordinary for Political Science and Philosophy, following the tradition of Hegel, pioneered a philosophical doctrine of politics. From 1865 lectures on politics were also given by members of the legal profession and at the same time the faculty was divided into two distinct subjects – political science and history. Raumer was followed by two historians, Droysen and Treitschke.

The trend in other universities was similar. In Breslau Raumer occupied the Chair of History and Political Science from 1811 to 1819; in 1839 the Faculty of Philosophy unsuccessfully applied for the appointment of Dahlmann who had been expelled from Göttingen; from 1847 political lectures were given by Johann Ludwig Tellkampf, a lawyer and politician who had emigrated to America after the Göttingen conflict; finally in 1873 with the appointment of Lujo Brentano the professorship of political science was absorbed into the Faculty of National Economy. In Freiburg, then part of Austria, a chair of political science was set up in 1768 but only after the dismissal of the unruly senate by Joseph II. Karl von Rotteck, who had become Professor of History in Freiburg in 1798 when aged only twenty-three, assumed the office of Professor-in-Ordinary for Political Science in the Faculty of Law in 1818; he was dismissed in 1832, however, because of unorthodox activities, as was his liberal associate Karl Theodor Welcker; this was followed by a temporary closure of the university. He was succeeded by Franz Joseph Buss, whose lectures on politics bore the imprint of the catholic popular movement; from 1863 to 1866 Treitschke, as Professor for Political Science, was prominent with a course of lectures on politics.

Development was equally fluctuating in Giessen (F. J. Schmitthenner), Göttingen (Dahlmann, Gervinus, Roscher, Waitz), Halle-Wittenberg (the

34

first chair was created in 1727), Heidelberg (Mohl), Marburg (Vollgraff), Jena, Leipzig (Bülau, Roscher) and Tübingen (F. List, Mohl); in the Bavarian universities, on the other hand, progress was inhibited by political considerations. The frontiers of the discipline were in a permanent state of flux; at times it was equated with practical philosophy and at others split between the faculties of history, law and national economy. In addition to the genuine chairs of political science, some of which traced their origin back to the seventeenth century, courses of lectures on the subject were given by a wider circle drawn from the faculties of philosophy and law. The teaching of politics, however, reached its height in the pre-March days with the rise and fall of the liberal constitutional movement.

Pre-March Bonn saw the heyday of an independent doctrine of politics primarily based on history. C. G. Sturm, the first Professor of Political Science, confined himself to the subject of agrarian economy; Wilhelm Butte, his colourless successor from 1826 to 1833, accomplished little (he was only engaged as lecturer and did not occupy the chair which remained empty). The extra-curricular courses of lectures by Karl Theodor Welcker, Johann Friedrich Ferdinand Delbrück, Carl Joseph Windischmann and Max von Gagern attracted more attention. The great upsurge, however, came with the appointment of Dahlmann. His lectures on politics soon drew a numerous audience; the Great Hall of the University became known as 'Dahlmann's auditorium'; Kaiser Friedrich (as he was to be later) and Treitschke were among his listeners. As in his book *Politics*, Dahlmann laid stress on constitutional problems and historical themes; administration; foreign relations and political science clearly took second place. In addition to politics the subjects of Dahlmann's lectures were British and German, Roman and French, Scandinavian and Russian history; towards the end of his life (in 1859) he also lectured on 'The History of Politics'. Both his political and historical courses of lectures, which generally alternated, aroused equal interest.

There is no denying the fact that Dahlmann's audiences shrank after the failure of the *Paulskirche* – an illustration of the close connection between political science, history and state politics characteristic of the development of the social and political sciences in the nineteenth century. Heinrich von Sybel, Dahlmann's successor, tried to carry on the tradition; in 1860, however, with the appointment of Erwin Nasse, a national economist, the teaching of politics was in practice divided between two professorial chairs, the purely historical and the economic. The scientific presentation of politics in the Dahlmann tradition fell into desuetude. About the time of formation of the Reich the practice of giving political lectures in German universities ceased almost totally; it was left to the western democracies to carry on the tradition. This is characteristic of the whole development of German universities. Its causes are to be found in the positivist specialization of the social sciences and in the 'unpolitical', de-politicized atmosphere of the monarchical, bureaucratic, patriarchal state under which national unity was ultimately achieved.

3

The special nature and the character of Dahlmann's principal work, his book *Politics* of which only the first volume appeared, does not emerge unless its full title is given. It is: *Politics, Reduced to the Basis and Measure of Existing Conditions*. This was, therefore, no speculative philosophy of politics, no abstract theory of the state, neither was it any doctrine of state moulded to fit any normative pattern of ideas; equally, on the other hand, it was not a mere descriptive catalogue of political events and institutions. These were the two usual forms of literature on the subject of the state; by constrast here was a presentation based on an empirical and primarily historical stock-taking of 'existing conditions'; the object was to examine their 'basis' (in other words their causes) and their 'measure' (in other words their order of magnitude), and so, by comparative analysis and with the help of the author's own 'acquired experience'[8], produce a clear overall picture of the structure, the conditions and the tasks of the new post-revolutionary state; it also set out to give a picture of the correct political order, of good politics in the sense of an ethic of political values.

Significantly this historical doctrine of politics and the state took as its starting point the classic Greco–Roman classification of the forms of state; the three basic types are given as monarchy, aristocracy or democracy depending on 'the number of persons in a position to rule';[9] this is illustrated by evaluation of the Spartan, Athenian and Roman constitutions. Then, however, both in the introduction and even more so in the detailed discussion of the 'more recent state constitutions', the specialized development through history of the christian–germanic state is contrasted with these stereotyped categories of structure.[10] Special emphasis is laid on the British pattern of an aristocracy combined with a parliamentary constitution rooted in history; this serves as the model of a political order developed over the years, something that has happened instead of being designed. Following his great predecessors, especially Montesquieu and Edmund Burke, and drawing on the then current compendium of British constitutional development,[11] Dahlmann draws a somewhat idealized picture of the British constitution; this is the true starting point of his proposal for a balanced, corporate constitutional state which he regards as both the requirement and the fulfilment of politics.

Such ideas had already been foreshadowed in Dahlmann's statements during his time in Kiel and in his draft of a Hannoverian constitution – the constitutional link with England made this natural. Now, however, he looked further; the background to his *Politics* is the conviction that only if constitutional ideas could permeate Prussia could the way be open to the double objective of political reform and German unity; all labour devoted to constitutional reform in the smaller German states, he considered, would be mere tinkering so long as no one succeeded in 'introducing English liberal constitutional arrangements into the Prussian administrative state'.[12]

Here again, therefore, was the dual political starting point – the constitutional and the national, and once again emphasis was clearly placed on the former. At the same time, however, and despite the fact that his adulation of his British model is only partially justified, Dahlmann continually stresses the basic prerequisite for any doctrine of politics: it must not produce an abstract idealist system unconnected to place or time; it must seek to discover the realities and eschew mere form. The introduction to *Politics* includes a paragraph aptly describing this concrete connection between history and a realist political doctrine:

> 'Mankind has no existence other than that which implies continuous developmental struggle both in place and time and which is comprised in our history. Any representation of the state, therefore, which lacks historical foundation, can have no real instructive value and is a mere imaginative exercise. The idealist who tries to indicate what the proper form of state should be without regard to time or place, is merely solving riddles of his own making; using men who have never existed, he draws a picture of a state of affairs which can never be.'[13]

Dahlmann then gives a definition of politics which goes to the heart of the problems and tasks of this discipline; he calls it a science of reality.

> 'To be instructive politics must be the recipient, not the chooser, of its tasks; they will emerge, in the turmoil of space and time, from the elemental interplay between the healthy forces of mankind and the pernicious side which physically is termed bad and morally is termed evil. Politics is a doctrine of health, not because it can give health but because it can detect the causes of sickness and often alleviate them.'

Here and wherever basic principles must be discovered or confirmed, Dahlmann's thinking revolves around critical comparison with earlier experiments. Again and again he ends with the striking sentence: 'Let us take counsel of history.'[14] Politics, in his view, should be both teacher and taught and, if only people have the courage to ask concrete questions applicable to the present, history can provide the examples and the lessons. This, of course, is something quite different from mere examination of the historical dimension of some political order or political action. It is an attempt to make good the reduction in importance of politics in relation to history, an attempt which is once more being made in Germany today after long fateful aberrations; it is somewhat inadequately expressed in the catchphrase about 'conquest of the past' but in more concrete terms it is detectable in the renewed efforts now beginning to bring the social and political science disciplines together after a century of compartmentalization into separate technical fields.

Certain other basic ideas in Dahlmann's concept of politics also merit mention. The train of thought stemmed from his admiration of his British model, to which he accorded almost mythical adulation – as has been said, it was not quite so perfect as he thought. The old arrangements in Germany, provided that they could be freed from the superstructure of the absolutist system and be adapted to modern requirements, seemed to provide a good starting point for the perpetuation of constitutionalism. Brought up in the romanticist period and belonging to the historical school, Dahlmann thought that he could see in the universal germanic respect for law and order a sure foundation for a constitutional order which would be as effective a guarantee of smooth transition to the modern state in Germany as in England or Scandinavia. He did not believe that rationalist formulae setting out theoretical agreements or distribution of powers were necessary to guarantee control and stability under a liberal constitution. Today it is easy to see where he was subject to illusion or guilty of self-deception both in practice and in his thinking. As a result, his self-assurance led him subsequently to turn against the Western European development of democratic thought and to oppose theoretical blueprints for a state, particularly those of French revolutionary and constitutional doctrine. Undoubtedly this has much to do with the subsequent retreat of liberalism in face of the concept of the power–policy state and of that specifically German self-assertiveness *vis-à-vis* the West which governed both German history and German political science from the second half of the nineteenth century and reached its first climax during the First World War.[15]

Today all these problems have (rightly) been thought through afresh. It must, nevertheless, be remembered that, from many points of view, the old school of German liberalism remained a firm adherent of the general principle that the form of state was a matter of free choice; it is this that differentiated its thinking from the limitations and distortions stemming from nationalism and imperialism. In concise terms the objective and the limitations were determined by the priority accorded to the ideal of internal political freedom as against a nationally and externally orientated concept of freedom, the latter being based on a concept of the German state rooted in history and romanticism and a proud reliance on a special tradition of germanic legal and constitutional history. Both in his writings and his teaching Heinrich von Treitschke, Dahlmann's most famous successor, presented politics in the new, narrowly national, sense of the liberalism of the Bismarck era – with far greater immediate effect, it should be added.[16] Between his and Dahlmann's overall view of politics and history a great gulf was fixed. We shall be reverting later to this stage, if not caesura, in liberal theory;[17] it is no accident that it coincides with the end of Dahlmann's life. The fact that the political ideas of Dahlmann and his contemporaries showed many indications in this direction only makes the difference clearer. Since he concentrated primarily upon the constitutional aspect, deliberately and almost automatically he regarded politics as something transcending the state and nationality; politics was conceived as basically internal and not as a power struggle between states. Later politics in Germany were distorted until they came to be regarded as no more than a channel for and method of expansion in the game of European power conflicts. This was not Dahlmann's view.

The clearest illustration of this was his attitude to the wielders of power and makers of decisions within the constitution which he visualized. Obviously his main aim here was to convert Prussia which, in his view, could only play its true role in overall German politics by this means and not by the pursuit of sheer power policy. The King was to remain outside the various conflicts of opinion but not by virtue of occupying an absolute, isolated position superior to the state; he had a definite position within the constitution which would in the first place enable him to exert his full influence and in the second, prevent him taking action prejudicial to the state. The monarch was thus to be integrated into, in fact subordinated to, the constitution but this could not be guaranteed by mere institutional arrangements or rational structures. Civic sense on the part of his former subjects was necessary; it postulated a degree of steadiness and maturity on the part of 'public opinion' in which liberal, social and constitutional theory has always placed optimistic confidence; this public opinion was held to be the centrepiece of a modern constitutional order which Dahlmann goes so far as to call 'a concentration of the mind of the people – the only practicable method of the present day'.[18] It is one of the central features in his concept of politics, strikingly described in the phrase: the people 'will not renounce its right to square the moral account'[19] – not even *vis-à-vis* the King. Admittedly he does say that there can be no certainty that the optimistic expectations placed in public opinion will be fulfilled; they have been so often and so shatteringly disappointed in our present century and not least in Germany. He refers particularly to the threat to freedom from the 'attraction exerted by the power of great princes'[20] and to responsibility for internal liberty as against external successes which can be so temptingly misrepresented and misapplied as guaranteeing the highest form of freedom.

From this stems Dahlmann's conviction that monarchy is 'the most comprehensible form of government and that most likely to inspire affection,'[21] it must not be based on some divine right, however; a dynasty has no intrinsic right to rule if a prince has not the necessary ability or the agreement of his people. This was a viewpoint with its roots deep in the historical picture of the germanic popular monarchy. Like the popular assembly of the old days the last word now lay with the people's representatives, those persons representing the population in the larger modern state. He concludes: 'The subjects have the right, which should be guaranteed by the courts, to regard as null and void the rule of a prince who refuses recognition to the constitution of the country.'[22]

This eventually leads him to make certain very definite statements regarding the *right of resistance*. Again he relies heavily on historical tradition and experience with regard to political order and political action; he recalls the debates on resistance in which European tradition is so rich, which his successors in the patriarchal state of the Bismarck and post-Bismarck era had so largely forgotten and of which we were once more forcibly reminded by our experience under the Nazi dictatorship.[23] Dahlmann is utterly opposed to the view that 'the existence of constitutional rights is a matter for the conscience of the prince alone and that the subject must under all circumstances remain passive'; this, he says, is the road 'to arbitrary rule and anyone who reads the lessons of history would realize that such ideas, sanctimoniously presented as anti-revolutionary, will lead the German people into an upheaval which will rock this entire portion of the world'.[24] There is no need to emphasize how truly prophetic this is; for Germany it came true barely a hundred years later. In a note he adds a phrase of Pascal's which aptly illustrates the meaning and significance of the concept of resistance: 'When everyone is on the road to ruin, no one seems to be so. When someone cries halt, however, he becomes a fixed point which makes the aberrations of the others noticeable.'

Dahlmann's answer to this question was certainly not given light-heartedly; as one of the 'Göttingen Seven' he gave practical proof of his beliefs. The French definition of human rights of 1793 seemed to him too broad and indefinite; he considered that it carried with it a threat of anarchy and the destruction of all political order. Although, however, he rated the value and right to existence of the state far higher than did abstract French revolutionary theory, he insisted that the legality of the state stood or fell by the right of resistance. If the people were compelled unresistingly to obey any governmental order, even though unconstitutional, if they were under obligation 'not merely to tolerate any injustice in silence but even to help in implementing it, then any constitution is a fraud. Moral doctrine prescribes resistance to any tyranny which demands not mere toleration but actual participation in injustice.' Blind obedience blurs 'all distinction between *de facto* and *de jure* government'. As regards the biblical requirements for obedience to authority Dahlmann, a protestant, comments that all 'straightforward followers of the word of God' ('I do not include the present-day court theologians', he adds acidly) from Christ to Luther and Melanchthon had given 'far more intrepid answers'. According to Dahlmann political experience, therefore, shows that 'certain methods of resistance are permissible and should be employed to ensure that, by timely warning, other more destructive methods are not used'. Actual force and revolution, of course, are still the last resort; in a constitutionally organized state, however, emphasis should be placed on the right to refuse to do that which is illegal or unconstitutional – 'resistance by refusal', as Dahlmann once called it.[25]

On the subject of these ideas, which the most recent past has brought to our attention once again, the historian is both knowledgeable and sceptical; he concedes both to the individual and to government the right of self-defence because, being a political being himself, he has learnt the lesson of history that demolition of legal systems and constitutions, never quite carried through to the end, is part of the nature and dynamism of politics. The driving force of politics is the repeated attempt to implement the ideal of the right form of community existence in the midst of the permanent clash between differing tendencies and interests; if this is so the historian's view is also valid that 'as long as there are popular revolutions there will also be *coups d'état* by those in power'. The historian naturally hopes that the policy which he advocates will put an end both to revolution and *coups d'état*. Despite all his criticism, however, the ultimate outcome is a quietistic cult of authority and eventually an almost conservative adulation of the mature personality which contributes more to freedom than all the rambling notions of revolutionary innovators – 'The man who can master the empire of which he has been born king, that of his own soul, and who can present a picture of just rule within his own family contributes to the betterment of public morality upon which all liberal institutions rest; even under a despot he will preserve intact one area of freedom.'[26]

4

The above has been only a small selection, by way of example, of the views put forward by a man who was a prisoner of his age and yet touched on questions which were dismissed without an answer – to the detriment of our more recent history. Reference has already been made to the obvious limitations of Dahlmann's proposals. Among his great contemporaries who strove to create a science of politics, Dahlmann is certainly not the most noteworthy. Even if we disregard de Tocqueville and the English theorists of those days and consider only the impressive number of German writers from Gentz and Görres to Rotteck and Welcker, from Hegel and Savigny to Robert von Mohl, Friedrich Julius Stahl and Johann Caspar Bluntschli, it is clear that, as a systematic book, Dahlmann's *Politics* cannot lay claim to be in the first rank. In view of the decline and the exiguity of German literature on political science which, with the exception of someone like Max Weber, has continued uninterruptedly since the turn of the century, that general period appears as the classical, unchallenged age of scientific thought on the subject of politics.[27]

Dahlmann's particular importance lay in his unique linkage of politics and history. The historical school of Dahlmann's day, including Ranke, considered that history's special attribute as a science lay in the attempt to observe and understand all historical happenings, including the state as their product, without, however, evaluating the various forms of state; Dahlmann, on the other hand, worked out a series of criteria and principles by which the good state could be distinguished from the bad. The historical purist may consider it sacrilege to apply an absolute standard to historical arrangements. Inevitably, however, even this class of historian, with his ostensibly objective relativism, shows certain sympathies and antipathies in the selection and direction of his research and presentation; does he not therefore in fact apply meta-historical criteria? Would it not often be more honest to admit that use has been made of the basic values of the liberal theory regarding the state than to lay claim to absolute objectivity divorced from any scale of values? Such objectivity could never be quite complete and subsequently often became tantamount to insensitivity to the true values or alternatively resigned acceptance of the 'normative force of the factual'; both history and the doctrine of the state gave way almost unresistingly in face of this concept during the catastrophe of 1933.[28]

Although, therefore, Dahlmann owed much to the methods and knowledge of the historian, he cut straight through the relativism of history when dealing with the nature of the state and the structure of politics as such. As we have seen, in his eyes politics was a 'doctrine of health'; it postulated a capacity and a readiness to form judgements, admittedly based on history but coloured by his concept of the good state. His historical reflections start from the present and then return to the present in the light of the lessons taught and simultaneously explained by history. Dahlmann left no one in any doubt as to the fundamental position on which his thinking and teaching were based; it seems a legitimate one, more legitimate than that of his opponents since the premisses on which it rests can be verified. That the decided nature of his views did not obscure his awareness of the other side of the picture is evidenced by his evaluation of absolutism as the path-finder for the modern state,[29] not absolutism for its own sake but as a transitionary stage on the road to the good state. Invariably, however, he insisted on a concept of the state based on clear thinking, not mere emotion; here he deliberately parted company with the historical school and with romanticism, both of which tended to envelop the state in a cloud of mysticism. Herein lay the real advantage of his attempt to bring politics and history together and this was where he differed so greatly from Ranke who, in an address in 1836 on 'The relationship and difference between politics and history', tried to keep the two fields strictly separate.[30]

Dahlmann's conviction led him early in the 1840s to make a renewed attempt to link the two subjects. His inaugural address at Bonn University when, as the last of the 'Göttingen Seven', he returned to academic office, was devoted primarily to the increased interest in active politics. At the same time, however, it included an acknowledgement of the basic necessity for coupling history and politics in that he announced his conviction that the state should be

> 'the object of deeper and more serious research and understanding . . . far be it from me to maintain that the more historical method of enquiry to which my career has inclined me is the only or the best avenue for political education . . . I do, however, believe that it is the surest, particularly from the point of view of academic training. The world of events in which history deals is by no means an ideal one but even when at its worst, some traces of the ideal are to be found.'

And on the other side: 'What good does it do to draw a picture of the most perfect state imaginable . . . if in reality no structure even remotely resembling it could exist.'[31]

At the same time, however, Dahlmann laid down quite definitely the limit to which politics could be based on history: 'No one is less qualified than I to be counted among the number of those who say: This arrangement is good because it is historic.'[32] This basic viewpoint governed Dahlmann's further activity in discussion of the constitutional question; equally it coloured his two historical works of this period on the British and French revolutions (published in 1844–5), which Treitschke called 'the stormy petrels of the German revolution'.[33]

In the petition addressed to the King of Prussia by Bonn University on 8 March 1848 Dahlmann pressed for the implementation of his constitutional ideas. The result, however, was the failure of the *Paulskirche*, a failure from the point of view of both the constitutional and the unification questions. As member of the constitutional commission and of the deputation which vainly offered the imperial throne to the King of Prussia, Dahlmann was a direct participant in this tragic development. This was equally a personal failure and it brought Dahlmann's extra-curricular activities to an abrupt end. He was now aging and, like others, was condemned to that 'withdrawal from public life characteristic of the old school of liberalism as a whole.'[34] It was this withdrawal which opened the way to ideas of nationhood based on external successes and so set the seal both on the fate of the constitutional movement and on the tragedy of German liberalism, which now fell victim to a process of political corruption and internal disintegration.

Few other developments of this period illustrate so vividly the depth of the cleavage and the importance of the events of 1848–9. The consequences of this transformation of liberalism were most serious, not only for the development of the state but also for the direction in which political, constitutional and also historical thinking in Germany tended to move in the future. Any attempt to explain all this by laying it at the door of external developments alone produces only an inadequate half-truth. The reasons for the failure lie deeper. The liberal synthesis of history and politics on which hopes of an organic transition were based, had underestimated the tenacity of the existing authorities; the attempt made in subsequent decades by political historians of the *kleindeutsch* school to adapt the concept to the changed circumstances and so restore its viability led both historiography and political teaching to adopt that narrow viewpoint to which reference has already been made. Dahlmann had idealized the British constitutional state and presented it as a model; as the idea became discredited, it contributed to disillusionment and aversion to western constitutional concepts. The moderate constitutional movement was now in a position of impotence, caught between the reactionary and revolutionary fronts; in such a posture it could neither initiate the necessary measures of liberalization in good time nor master the realities of the power-policy situation.

More important still, however, is the fact that, unlike its British counterpart, German liberalism did not suceed in mastering the changed social conditions stemming from the industrial revolution and the vast increase in population. It clung to the views of the turn of the century; it remained a 'liberalism of the squirearchy', looking upon the bourgeoisie as 'the people', taking note only dimly and defensively of the rise of new social classes and attempting to exclude both from the constitution and the franchise the Fourth Estate, which it labelled 'rabble'. Even Dahlmann had failed to take adequate account of the two great factors of the time – 'the might of the princes and their governments' on one side and 'the great masses of the people' on the other.[35] The researches of Rudolf Stadelmann, for instance, have shown that the German revolution of 1848 was primarily bourgeois in character in contrast to the mythology on the subject emanating from marxist sources.[36] The disregard of the movement for social emancipation, however, the sequel to the semi-successful emancipation of the bourgeoisie, generated tensions and explosive forces which were soon pressing for some outlet. They heralded the fate of bourgeois liberalism, now faced with the choice between two alternatives only: either to be pulverized between the old authorities and the movement for socialism, now driven in upon itself, or to line up with the stronger side and so cease to be the driving force for an internal liberal order.

Dahlmann, now nearly seventy, took no further part in all this. The dilemma was set out in his book *Politics* and visible in the spirit of resignation in which he returned from the *Paulskirche*. As late as 1864 Treitschke said: 'Even today no member of our company who has not, consciously or unconsciously sat at Dahlmann's feet, says anything sensible on matters of state.'[37] The background to his political thinking, particularly in fields where system and history combined, showed not a trace of that narrowness of view resulting from a nationalistic or class-warfare, political outlook or even from anti-semitism, a trap into which his successors, even including Treitschke, fell from the start of the 1850s.[38] Dahlmann was explicit in his support for the admission of Jews to academic office.[39] He campaigned on behalf of those persecuted by the forces of reaction such as his friend Gervinus who was expelled from Leipzig University in 1855. He also opposed the narrow racial nationalism current at the time; at the assembly of Germanists in Lübeck in 1847, for instance, he disagreed violently with a proposal for a policy on Germans resident abroad; on the contrary he hoped that émigrés would quickly 'take root in their new country with German pertinacity' and to this end 'deliberately make the inevitable sacrifice' of their mother tongue; then they would 'enter upon a new full existence; otherwise their abandonment of an unhappy existence in their old home country would be no more than a half-measure'.[40]

Dahlmann's aim was the formation of a political bourgeoisie and this he hoped to achieve by his own example and through his influence in public life and in academic education. He contrasted active support of the state with the dangerous apparition of the unpolitical citizen. The state must be one, however, which, as he put it, opened the way to humanity, which placed itself at the service of humanitarian sentiment. He remained convinced that the ultimate purpose of the state lay, not in itself but outside it – 'We believe in a great communal creation of mankind, for which the existence of individual states is only the groundwork; we believe that human affairs will reach their full dimension at the end of the day.' In the matter of progress towards a supra-national order history was, in Dahlmann's view, the intermediary between the state and mankind. One of the lessons of history was 'the frailty of human affairs', a factor which politics and any constitution must take into acount.[41]

Here again was a clear, broad, vivid concept of the essential connection which should exist, to their mututal advantage, between politics and law and between politics and history. Dahlmann was convinced of the necessity of political education, of the urgency of a fresh link between education and politics and of the close relationship between intellect and power; the latter, he considered, had suffered serious distortion and after a 'via dolorosa of the civic spirit'[42] had ended in the subordination of intellect to power. Freedom within the state was to him the true value and purpose of politics, as he emphasized during the struggle for freedom of the press, which he regarded as the supreme test.[43] The purpose of foreign policy, in his view, was to serve as a guarantee of this internal freedom; only for this purpose, and not as an end in itself, was it justified in acquiring and exercising power.[44]

The great tenet of his creed, however, was that science could and should concern itself with politics before all these efforts foundered in mere positivism or the cult of the irrational and of the man of violence. Dahlmann defined politics as a science based on empirical investigation. It if could be so regarded, he maintained, this would finally put an end to the illusion that the basic human tendency to form communities, in other words politics, was 'the exception to the rule that knowledge is a better guide than ignorance'. With his eye on the universities Dahlmann added provocatively: 'The majority still think today that they must learn everything other than politics and that all political problems can be dealt with by the light of nature.'[45] In his inaugural address in Bonn in 1842 he criticized the tendency of political science either to dissolve into 'completely formal airy-fairy theory' or to deal with its problems 'with ponderous partiality ... primarily through the eyes of the policeman or the financier'; he accused it of 'evading all questions of liberty either by saying nothing or referring to christian dogma'. In this address in Bonn Dahlmann summarized the German dilemma most impressively:

> 'It almost seems as if the German wishes to learn everything else in detail and make his way slowly from the bottom up with the single exception of the doctrine of state; the state he simply wishes to accept, to love or to hate as occasion serves; in general there is little enthusiasm to observe the state or enquire into the secrets of its nature.'

Dahlmann seemed to have some premonition of the problems to which this would give rise, for he added: 'A situation has now been reached, in fact, in which, if people will not come to the state, the state will come to them with all its array of power.'[46]

In his great history of political science published in 1864, Johann Caspar Bluntschli, one of Dahlmann's younger contemporaries and a pioneer of the discipline, accorded Dahlmann a permanent place in it; despite certain criticisms of detail he emphasized that Dahlmann's ideas were 'in certain respects among the greatest and most magnificent that have ever been propounded on the subject of the state'. Discussing Dahlmann's *Politics* he is even more specific:

'The great merit of this book lies first in its method of using history; it does not, as do most others, set forth ideas on the state as abstract axioms; it gives illustrations of these ideas as embodied in historical states. Its second great merit lies partially in the high moral plane on which it seeks to harmonize the established and respected forms of constitutional order with the requirements and stirrings of popular freedom, partially in the nobility of its basic concepts.'[47]

We might add to this list the ideas and convictions for which Dahlmann staked his position. His classic declaration on the step taken by the 'Göttingen Seven' includes this:

'I consider it unworthy of a man or a christian to stand by in silence and watch the destruction of all human order, merely to pray and to sigh, when legal means are still available, or to say like some rural official: "I sign anything; we are after all mere underdogs." If I use the weapons of the law to fight something which, in a moment of aberration, a mortal king is doing in contravention of existing laws, then I am fighting for the immortal king and for the legitimate will of the government . . . I cannot bring about a revolution and I would not do so if I could; all I can do is to testify to the truth and to legality in face of a system of deception and violence and this is what I am doing.'[48]

These are words and ideas of which we should do well to take note when considering the connection between politics and history in an era when totalitarianism still threatens.

3

Weimar in Retrospect

I

Since the Second World War the debate about more recent German history and politics has primarily revolved around National-socialism. It soon became evident, however, that consideration of Nazism in isolation was inadequate and might even be misleading unless placed in the context of more distant political history. The Third Reich is not explicable as a phenomenon in itself; it is no mere unfortunate accident, as so many observers still maintain. Instead the Nazi tyranny emerged, apparently as the natural sequel, from the problems and crises of the first German republic.

This realization of the significance of the Weimar era as the antecedent and pre-condition of the rise and triumph of National-socialism in Germany is the one major reason for dealing with this past period of bankruptcy in German history. For this reason one of the most important duties both of politicians and journalists after the collapse of 1945 was to bring to light not only the crimes of National-socialism but also the weaknesses and errors of the Weimar Republic. The deliberations of the Parliamentary Council show the extent to which the founding fathers of the Basic Law and the Federal Republic's constitution looked for guidance to the experience of Weimar. Historians, sociologists and political scientists too were called upon to apply their minds to this vital question and this has meanwhile given rise to research into the period of the First World War which has had many ramifications and occasioned much debate.

There is, however, a second important aspect of this question. The Weimar Republic provides a visible instance of a democracy which, in the short space of fourteen years, passed through all the stages from formation to dissolution. Here was a state presented with all the opportunities and exposed to all the threats inherent in a democratic experiment ranging from revolution from below to *coup d'état* from above. The genesis and pathology

49

of a state have perhaps never been so clearly demonstrated except in the various phases of the French Revolution.

Much has been written either in a spirit of criticism, accusation or exculpation about the reasons for the German capitulation to the National-socialist dictatorship; the stability of the Federal Republic has often been questioned; in all this, whether admitted or not, comparison between the first and second German republics plays a major role. One may take the easy way out and say optimistically: 'Bonn is not Weimar' as did a Swiss observer (Fritz René Alleman) in 1956 in an undoubtedly penetrating analysis of the Federal Republic. It should also be remembered that discussion of the Weimar catastrophe played a definite role in the deliberations and drafts of the anti-Hitler resistance movement. Finally there is no doubt that many of those intimately involved have considered the relationship between Weimar and Bonn against the background of personal experience and constitutional comparison. So in the debate about German post-war politics constitutional, journalistic or day-to-day political arguments continue to be drawn from the fate and experiences of the Weimar state. The crisis-ridden development and the catastrophe of the first German republic provide a case history to which people turn in the first instance whether their object is admonition and warning, substantiation of German democratic tradition and affirmation that a fresh start has been made or diagnosis and prognosis of the political present.

This in itself, however, highlights the difference between the possibilities and prospects of the two democratic experiments in Germany. As far as German history was concerned the Weimar Republic could look back, if necessary, to 1848 and to numerous attempts to form a democratic state, either blocked or suppressed; the result was a carefully but highly theoretically constructed state and constitution, which soon found itself divorced from constitutional reality. Moreover the historical and constitutional thought of the time was only too inclined to look back for guidance to the semi-constitutional or indeed semi-absolutist scale of values of the past imperial period.

By contrast, today reference to our political history undeniably tends to reinforce efforts to stabilize our new democracy and make it immune to crisis. This can be seen even in the externals. Historical experience has led to institutional arrangements the object of which is to prevent any return to the more obvious structural weaknesses of the Weimar Republic, The powers of the president, for instance, have been decisively curtailed; to stabilize cabinets the 'constructive vote of no-confidence' has been introduced; the existence of the party state, as opposed to the fiction of a state based on liberal representation, has actually been written into the constitution; finally a ban has been imposed on all associations directed against the basic democratic order in an attempt to ensure that totalitarian movements will never again be tolerated or protected by democracy and so enabled to use the methods of democracy to undermine and overwhelm it.

Such constitutional reforms and safeguards, however, also indicate that the causes of the crisis and the failure of the Weimar Republic have tended to be reduced to standardized formulae. The proportional representation rule with the resulting appearance of splinter parties has also been adduced as an explanation, although on this point (the importance of which is much overestimated) it has not been possible to introduce any constitutional reform. The continuing controversy over the franchise, which in any case has become overlaid with principle and dogma, raises the old problem: how far can institutional safeguards produce the desired effect? Was the failure of the first German experiment in republican parliamentary government really due primarily to the absence of concrete safeguards or reforms? The finger is usually pointed primarily at the dictatorial authority of the Reich president and the famous Article 48 which in fact led to disastrous consequences – authoritarian presidential government and its usurpation by Hitler. In the latest discussions on emergency legislation these ideas have raised their heads once more. Over a century ago, however, Robert von Mohl, the great constitutionalist, explicitly warned against laying the blame for unhappy political developments solely at the door of errors in the structure of the constitution. In 1862 Mohl said: 'The real safeguard against governmental excesses does not lie in a refusal to grant powers which may in fact be necessary or at least extremely useful; it lies in the perception and constitutional sense of the people and their representatives which will recognize any unjustified measure as such and forcibly reject it.' In more concrete terms: the problem of the Weimar Republic is not explicable solely in terms of its constitution or institutions but must be seen in the context of historical experience. Owing to its historical political background, its economic and social structure and its intellectual and ideological contours this republic faced burdens and tasks which cannot be judged in purely constitutional terms.

The republic capitulated to abuse of an article in its constitution and it was ripe to do so because there were serious cracks in its political and social structure and because the political consciousness of the public lacked solidity. So the stark problem was raised of the 'vitality of the constitution' and its relationship to its own institutions. At the same time this raises another question: whether politics of all shades of opinion can draw comparisons with and criticize the experience of the Weimar period without running a number of risks, different though the conditions are. The danger is that political action and the capacity to deal with novel situations may be inhibited because a misconceived view of history may conjure up ostensible parallels and conclusions may be accepted too hastily if they are presented as pragmatic or can serve a purpose in the political conflict of opinion.

The fact that our political thinking tends to hark back to the Weimar Republic frequently stems from an understandable inclination to write off the breakdowns of 1933 and 1945 as the direct outcome of that Republic's failures. This, however, implies an underestimation of the importance of the 1933 breakdown and also of the powerful effect exerted by our subsequent political experiences. Total domination, its power to seduce and its frightful consequences were totally new experiences in Germany and they have largely influenced the build-up of political life since 1945 and its development since foundation of the Federal Republic – with all its repercussions on the far-reaching changes in political consciousness now in progress throughout Europe.

2

Here, in fact, we come to one important reason why the 1945 situation is comparable only on the surface with that in which the Weimar Republic started in 1918. A mere glance at the more important conditions and factors in the development of the Weimar Republic shows where comparability ends. Of course the curtain-raiser for both experiments was the fact of complete military and political defeat. From this point, however, the differences begin. The collapse of 1918 came largely unexpectedly and was then overshadowed with incredible rapidity by a no less unexpected revolution. Immediately, therefore, the beginnings of a new constitutional order were overshadowed and thrown out of gear by the venomous falsehood of the stab-in-the-back legend, a legend referred to by Theodor Litt, the philosopher, as being 'raised to the status of a national dogma'. The subsequent foreign political situation was one of bewildering complexity; it is significant, however, that the most frequently heard rallying cry, the most obvious point around which the splintered political life of the country could integrate, was a negative one – the well-nigh universal indignation over the Treaty of Versailles; its implications on the psychology of the masses were more serious than the material burdens which it imposed.

This 'peace' was never accepted and this fact could always be exploited for propaganda purposes. This was a factor always to be reckoned with by those parties and politicians who, under pressure of events or because they took a realistic view of the situation, sacrificed themselves by accepting it.

On the other side the fear, only partially justified, of attempts at a *coup* by the extreme Left had an effect no less serious. This 'red spectre' forced Ebert's revolutionary government, which possessed no armed force, into alliance with the old army; in addition, however, it led to reliance on non-republican forces, to toleration and support of the Free Corps and Self-Defence movements and later to continuously fluctuating compromises and emergency solutions – and not only in the parliamentary field. The young republic's endemic internal crisis then became more acute when the after effects of the war, the peace treaty provisions and a hesitant economic and financial policy culminated in the social crisis of inflation; finally, after a few short years of recovery, the onset of the world economic crisis seemed definitely to confirm the hopelessness of the development mapped out in 1918 and the impotence of parliamentary democracy itself.

It is therefore not enough simply to emphasize certain deficiencies of an institutional or even personal nature. Certain socio-psychological factors are no less significant; there was a widespread tendency to political bitterness and still more an inclination to stand sulkily aloof from events and reverse the relationship of cause and effect. Governing everything was the criticism, nationalistic in tone, of the ex-enemy states. The conclusion drawn by 'public opinion' from the impressions and events of these crisis years was of decisive political significance; rather than wrestle with the specifically German conditions which had produced this unhappy situation, public opinion turned against the new 'system', against parliamentary democracy and any form of international co-operation. The result was a hasty conclusion with many implications and pregnant with consequences: instead of the Kaiser, whose legacy all this was, the republican legatees were made responsible for all the disillusionments and burdens of the 1918 heritage.

Democracy has aptly been termed (by Eva Reichmann) a 'difficult ideology', meaning that authoritarian or dictatorial forms of government are more easily comprehensible to the average citizen, who looks for law, order and security, than the complex system of compromises and co-operation characteristic of parliamentary democracy. In the case of Germany, moreover, prejudiced emotional and ideological forces were at work; in some cases their object was restoration of the monarchical patriarchal state on the Wilhelmian model; others looked forward to further development of authoritarian and dictatorial tendencies. Naturally the external 'enemy', who had dictated the severe conditions of the peace treaty, was accused of incomprehension and rigidity. Even more significant, however, was the fact that all criticism of the political and social difficulties of the post-war years was directed inwards. Here was the starting point for an extremist national opposition by a militant minority hostile to parliament and democracy; it could count on the sympathy or inertia of wide sections of the population; until 1923 it manifested itself in menacing attempts at a *putsch*; finally, under the impulse of renewed crisis, it turned into an all-embracing, new-model collective movement which carried through its bloodless revolution in 1933.

Does this mean, therefore, that from the very beginning of the Weimar Republic the direction which it would take and the limits within which it could evolve were determined by factors which, with hindsight, seem almost inescapable? The first critical account of the history of this period came from the left-wing historian Arthur Rosenberg in 1935; this traced an almost determinist line of development from the ill-starred birth of the republic following the 'missed opportunity' of revolution in the socialist sense to its inevitable 'counter-revolutionary' fall; even more impartial consideration of the events surrounding the republic's end cannot avoid the conclusion that there were early and deep-rooted indications of an almost continuous process of disintegration. It is often said that the Weimar Republic was an 'improvised democracy', that historically it did not constitute a fresh start; Theodor Eschenburg considers that it was the final echo of the Wilhelmian period, painfully and abruptly ended by one last catastrophe; M. Freund regards the leading parties and politicians as 'moulded and permeated by the spirit of the Kaiser's empire'. The resigned conclusions of leading Weimar statesmen in their memoirs (Otto Braun, Carl Severing, Heinrich Brüning) also point in the same direction; their general purport is that disaster was inevitable.

In fact the failure of the Weimar state can be traced back to a series of basic historical and political facts; following each other with apparent logic, they severely restricted genuine freedom of action or decision in republican politics and any real practice of parliamentary democracy as prescribed by the Weimar National Assembly. For its political power the new state relied on a series of immature, hurriedly concluded and deceptive compromises between the old order and the new – between the imperial army and the revolutionary government, between employers bent on putting the system to the test and trade unions with increased realization of their strength, between federalist and centralist tendencies, between parties with little room for manoeuvre, divided on principle by tradition and *Weltanschauung*. A majority of the population only accepted this fragile emergency structure unwillingly and under pressure of events – as was shown in the first parliamentary election after the constitution had lapsed; compromises between the men in power on matters of state or formation of governments proved to be of short duration; their anti-republican opponents both of the Right and Left in principle adopted an obstructive attitude which after a few weeks turned to battle-cries threatening the existence of the state. From the outset the Weimar Republic was forced on to the defensive; the result was almost inconceivable caution in dealing with its declared enemies. An even more serious factor in its weakness was the fact that people wanted order and authority such as had been given them by the patriarchal, administrative state and this requirement the republic was never able to satisfy.

3

The collapse of the old order, obvious and almost uncontested though it was, was not followed by complete upheaval. One of the more remarkable aspects of the 1918 revolution was the readiness both of the military and the bureaucracy to co-operate with the new rulers. This took the form of a mutual pact : retention of the professional civil servants and respect for their 'well-earned rights' was a price the Social-democrats were prepared to pay. Initially there was much trouble with the self-assertive Workers' and Soldiers' Councils but Ebert and the *Land* governments generally succeeded quite soon in restricting them to supervisory functions and, after the convention of the National Assembly, in eliminating them altogether. In the desperate external, internal, economic and political situation of the winter 1918–19 continuity of administration seemed an essential; the reverse side of the coin, however, was that, as in the military sphere, no real clarification of the relationship between officialdom and democracy took place and the question of continuance in office of patriarchal elements was prejudged. This tendency was to be seen throughout the history of the Weimar Republic and it increased with the formation of numerous 'cabinets of experts' ending with the preponderance of bureaucratic elements in the presidential governments of 1930–3. The result was that in 1933 as in 1918 the bureaucracy and the army survived the change of government and in fact, by their support, made the National-socialist dictatorship capable of ruling.

The political configuration from which the new constitutional structure had emerged was governed by three further great compromises. The first took place in the economic and socio-political field and practically without participation by official agencies. On 15 November 1918, after negotiations between employers associations and the trades unions, the 'Central Labour Union' was formed. This recognized the exclusive right of the trades unions to represent the workers in all negotiations on wages, differentials and labour regulations. It introduced a new factor into the social and economic structure of power and it was based on arrangement between interested parties, not on any official regulations. Though it underlined the pluralist character of democracy, at the same time it endorsed maintenance of a capitalist form of economy in face of a socialist revolution.

Another important compromise was the clarification of the relationship between the *Länder* and the Reich. Contrary to most people's expectations the collapse of the Bismarckian princely association did not lead to a centralist new order. Ebert did treat the Reichstag as dissolved but he deliberately confirmed the previous Bundesrat (Upper House) in office. In face of all revolutionary demands for centralization he clung to the statement that this was a provisional regime and the final arrangement must be left to the National Assembly. The South German *Länder* in particular soon came out in favour of a federal form of constitution. Both federalist tradition and the actual decentralization which had taken place during the revolutionary period contributed to this preliminary decision. So the Republic remained a federal state but the dualism of the Prussia–Reich relationship was even further accentuated; there were now two governments functioning in Berlin with that of Prussia representing three-fifths of the entire population of Germany. No attempt was made to break down this top-heavy Prussia into normal-size provinces. The conflict between federalism and unionism and the failure to seize the opportunity to reform the Reich were destined to create further trouble for the Republic. The problem eventually became the handle for Papen's and Hitler's policy of *Gleichschaltung*.*

The most important of all these compromises, however, was that which eventually came to fruition in the co-operation between the three parties of the later 'Weimar Coalition'. The hard core of the parliamentary

* There is no precise English equivalent for the German word *Gleichschaltung*. It implies compulsory conformity. The nearest translation is perhaps 'regimentation' – translator.

majority born of the peace resolution of 1917 consisted of the Social-democrats (SPD), the Centre Party and the newly formed German Democratic Party (DDP) which had taken over the heritage of progressive liberalism; this was now joined by the bourgeois-socialist alliance which, after the defection of the USPD (*Unabhängige Sozialdemokratische Partei* – Independent Social-democrat Party) from the revolutionary government, was working for creation of true parliamentary democracy. Despite resistance from the hard-core socialist wing of the SPD and monarchist elements in the Centre Party, a further continuity factor lay in the co-operation between these parties, which in fact formed the first coalition government of the Weimar Republic. This was a genuine political compromise putting an end to the revolutionary dynamic in affairs of state and contributing to consolidation of the fragile compromises between the old and new orders. At the same time, however, it set the seal on the half-finished, incomplete character of the revolution. The old functions continued to be performed within a new framework: the pre-war distribution of powers within society, the economy and the bureaucracy was maintained with only minor alterations; although the strongest party, the SPD was unable to insist on democratization.

The new framework was the Weimar constitution. It was intended to integrate all the various forces and movements thrown up by the revolution; at the same time it was designed to institutionalize the structural principles of parliamentary democracy. Moreover this first German democratic constitution was intended to establish a system of values binding on all citizens – the first commitment binding on all because it was democratically legitimized. Disastrously, this did not succeed, although the constitution-makers aimed at perfection. The object was to substitute for the traditions of the pre-war authoritarian and patriarchal state a sense of participation in a generally valid and recognized democratic state but it proved that the political conditions did not exist and that carefully contrived systematic construction of a constitution did not suffice.

4

In his last governmental decree issued on 9 November 1918 Max von Baden had urged that general elections for a constituent national assembly be held. The people's representatives immediately took up the idea, prescribing the introduction of universal suffrage on the principle of proportional representation for all German citizens over twenty years of age, including also women for the first time (Reich electoral law of 30 November 1918).

This procedure was confirmed by the *Land* governments and the Reich Conference of Soviets, the basic theme of their decisions being firm establishment of democracy and preservation of national unity. Sovereignty was therefore to be vested in future, not in the princes as in the past, or in a single class as the left-wing extremists wanted, but in the people as a whole. Coupled with the decision in favour of the democratic principle was that for a parliamentary system of government. This was confirmed by the vast majority of votes scored by the three major parties of the new order at the elections of 19 January 1919; the SPD with 165, the Centre Party with 91 and the DDP with 75 captured 331 of the 423 seats in the National Assembly. The opposition groups (German-nationals 44 seats, German People's Party 19 and USPD 22) were largely defeated; at its inception, therefore, the Weimar Republic had a broad-based mandate to revise the constituion and the political system. Similar results emerged from the elections for constituent assemblies in the *Länder*. The vast majority of people had ranged themselves behind the decision in favour of a democratic republic.

The National Assembly met on 6 February in the theatre in Weimar – primarily to avoid the threat of revolutionary pressure in Berlin. Hopes of success were high. Moreover it was assumed that German–Austria, which had sent a representative, would join the federation; the scope of the subsequent provisions of the Versailles peace treaty could not yet be foreseen. By the time the National Assembly was dissolved in May 1920 it had done great work. In addition to accepting the constitution and the severe terms of the peace treaty it had passed a whole series of vital laws providing a basis for reconstruction. Its discussions primarily concentrated, however, on a government draft of a constitution published in the *Official Gazette* on 20 January 1919, the day after the elections.

It was clearly a good sign that a working basis for parliamentary discussion had been provided so quickly. This was primarily the work of Hugo Preuss, a constitutional lawyer whom Ebert had nominated State Secretary of the Interior on 14 November 1918 for this specific purpose. He was a left-wing liberal politician and scholar who had been campaigning for years for democratization of the German state. When the revolution began he urged that degree of co-operation between the bourgeoisie and the working class which was eventually responsible for the consolidation of the republic.

Even at this early stage two innovations were the object of special attention. The first was an attempt at far-reaching reform of the federal structure by means of plebiscites, the object of which was reorganization into a number of free states of similar size; this was tantamount to partition of Prussia. Second was the idea, put forward by Max Weber and originating from the American governmental system, that the new Reich president should be directly elected by the people and not by parliament as under the classical French parliamentary system. Plans for reform of the Reich failed in face of resistance from the *Länder*. The special position of the president, however, was ultimately written into the constitution; he was thus entitled to consider himself independent of parliament and the direct representative of the sovereignty of the people. The pregnant consequence was that the Weimar governmental system wore an air of dualism; it was a mixture of presidential and parliamentary democracy; in course of time, instead of supporting and reinforcing each other, these two principles obstructed and ultimately destroyed each other. Admittedly success was achieved in drawing up a list of 'Basic Rights of the German People', making the classical rights to freedom and ownership of property an integral part of the constitution. The vital point, however, remained the special position and function attributed to the Reich president. He was regarded as a counterweight to the Reichstag and, in his strong independent position, he seemed, particularly to left-wing critics, like a dangerous throw-back to the Wilhelmian system; there was fear of a monarchical restoration or even of dictatorship by a popularly elected president. Preuss countered this criticism with the statement that the parliamentary system contained firm guarantees against any abuse of the power of the state; nevertheless it was laid down that members of the pre-1918 ruling families were not eligible for election as president during the next fifteen years. In the constitution as finally passed, however, this provision was omitted and all further attempts to restrict the power of the president were defeated. During these discussions the full implication of the Reich president's emergency 'dictatorial power' contained in Article 48, later to become so significant (and so fateful), was clearly not realized.

A further important subject of discussion was the use to be made of the referendum or plebiscite. Preuss was sceptical of it; in so large a country (in contrast to Switzerland, for instance) it seemed to him a questionable expedient, a possibly disruptive factor in a parliamentary democracy. Here he overlooked the fact, of course, that the presidential election was basically of a plebiscitary nature. The relationship between the parliamentary representative elements in a modern democracy and the plebiscite principle, a difficult problem anyway, was never satisfactorily solved in the Weimar Republic; later, and particularly in the elections held during the closing stages of the republic, it proved to offer disastrous opportunities for encroachment to authoritarian and dictatorial tendencies. In 1919, however, it was primarily the Left which did not feel that it could forego this element of direct democracy. The referendum as a resort for a minority outvoted in parliament and popular demand as an extra-parliamentary stimulus for legislation were both written into the constitution; the SPD's more far-reaching plans, however, were rejected. Nevertheless this was an innovation more fundamental than was to be found in any other comparable constitution. No one can say that it was a great success; on this point Bonn's Basic Law has followed a different path – that of a fully fledged parliamentary representation system.

During the discussions in the National Assembly a violent dispute arose about the national flag. The Right opted for the old black–white–red and the extreme Left for the red flag of revolution. A majority was for the new colours – black–red–gold; they were the symbol of the 1848 freedom movement whereas the black–white–red signified Bismarck's *kleindeutsch* solution. Such memories proved to have faded, however; the new Reich colours never became popular in subsequent years and the Right was able to rally with increasing success behind the black–white–red symbol. This was made all the easier for them in that the National Assembly took refuge in a highly odd compromise – the mercantile flag was to be the black–white–red with a small black–red–gold ornamentation in the upper corner.

Finally the pressure of the Versailles negotiations largely contributed to the haste with which the final discussions were conducted both in committee and in plenary session. Nevertheless there were bitter arguments over such questions of detail as abolition of orders of knighthood and substitution of names for titles. It is an open question whether the Republic did not deprive itself of an effective method of popularizing democracy by its exaggerated puritanism on questions of orders and symbols. Possibly the contrast with the imperial regime and the traditional arrogance of the bearers of orders and titles was altogether too great. On the other hand efforts at large-scale liberal reform such as the abolition of the death sentence, for instance, which the SPD demanded, were defeated. The most difficult problem proved to be that of the churches and schooling; here there was an almost insuperable gulf within the Weimar Coalition between the confessional and ecclesiastical concept of education held by the Centre Party or the SPD. The result was a liberal compromise which compelled both sides to give up something.

5

The most important point, however, was that society in the Weimar Republic persisted in adhering to the traditions of the authoritarian, patriarchal state which were at variance with the new order of things. This was to be seen in the continuing debility and the rapid further emasculation of parliamentary government, also in the rapid fall, with only temporary recoveries, in the democratic vote. It was to be seen too in the pressure for a presidential system to which the Hindenburg myth gave support; this was tantamount to pressure for a substitute imperial regime and it sprang from the desire to return to Wilhelmian, authoritarian, nationalistic and dictatorial ways. The background was a lack of any desire to co-operate politically; on the parliamentary level this was made clear by the incapacity to form coalitions and the splintering of parties including even the demo-cratic groupings. As a result there was neither a reliable government majority nor a constructive opposition in parliament. Instead what was known as the 'national opposition' grew, in other words a front consisting of groups hostile to the republic on principle; this expanded vastly with the rise of extremist totalitarian mass movements (on the Left at first but then even more on the Right) until finally the formation of any working major-ity became impossible and the Centre, which stood for integration, was pulverized between these two millstones. Hand in hand with this went hectic, extra-parliamentary, anti-democratic activity on the part of militant associations and fighting formations; politics and society became 'mili-tarized'. Even in the early years of the Weimar period the Free Corps, the Stahlhelm and the SA had opened the mass demonstration era; they swept up hundreds of thousands of citizens looking for discipline and authority, primarily the young; the republic itself possessed no counter-attraction, such as the Reichsbanner's black–red–gold flag, to divert or arrest this trend towards a militaristic, authoritarian state.

Ideologically these tendencies fed on a terrorist philosophy of power which took the elementary and barbaric view that all politics were based on a clash between friend and foe; this doctrine was given a pseudo-juridical top-dressing (by Carl Schmitt) and so inevitably widespread, anti-Weimar publicity pictured politics as a pitiless struggle in which force was used and might was right; scorn was poured on the principle of tolera-tion and the ideas of co-operation or compromise inherent in a pluralist democracy. There thus arose an either-or philosophy which presented political opponents as actual enemies; it became both persuasive and explosive because the middle classes, under pressure both socially and economically, were susceptible to demagogic simplification of political problems, presenting the authoritarian or totalitarian state as the solution to all their difficulties; to this was added a readiness to renounce the rights of self-determination and self-government in favour of the alleged security provided by a 'Führer' cult and a 'popular community' (*Volksgemeinschaft*) with nationalist and ultimately national-socialist overtones and proclaimed with pseudo-religious fervour. Under the pressure of social and economic crises this seemed to provide a refuge from the overheated antagonisms and somewhat mysterious activities of political and economic interest-groups.

A process of erosion of the democratic order therefore set in; patriarchal, authoritarian and dictatorial longings persisted or were revived. Moreover this process received support from the official state machine, primarily through the equivocal 'neutralism' of the bureaucracy; it should have been the backbone and the main pillar of the democratic executive; in fact, however, its attitude to the republic was one of suspicion. This applied with even greater force to the headstrong, autonomist, independent policy of the Reichswehr *vis-à-vis* the republic. By its very nature an armed force, even more than a bureaucracy, is based upon a rigid chain of command and therefore tends to authoritarian views in the political field as well. In the case of the Weimar Reichswehr this tendency was even stronger; in the first place it had inherited an almost unbroken monarchical, military tradition; secondly, the restrictions of the Versailles treaty compelled it to be a professional, élitist army. The result was permanent suspicion of the democratic state coupled with a tendency to insulate itself from the outside world and preserve absolute, unquestioned solidarity within itself. Under these circumstances everything depended on the leadership of the army and the use made of it. As far as the leadership was concerned Seeckt initially kept the Reichswehr deliberately and consciously aloof from the civil power: during the crisis of 1930 the Reichswehr once more appeared as a political factor in its own right; finally under Blomberg it voluntarily placed itself at the service of the National-socialist state. The Reichswehr, therefore, invariably treated the republic with reserve and accepted it merely as an intermediate stage. All this makes the Reichswehr's role in the process of disintegration of the Weimar state both questionable and significant. This, of course, also implies failure on the part of the political leadership; lacking a democratic defence policy, it left the Reichswehr in this atmosphere of mistrustful independence; it did not demand that subordination which was its natural right and resigned itself to the growth of a 'state within the state'.

6

So a fateful combination of historical, political, social and ideological factors prevented the growth of that politically alert civic sense without which no democratic order can survive. The electoral results showed that primarily the protestant bourgeoisie and agricultural population were drifting away from the centre towards extremism, from the Social-democrats via the People's Party to the German-nationals and the National-socialists. How can any state survive as a democracy, however, if, like the republic from 1920 onwards, its constitutional and political core is not solid, if the preponderance of its leading strata in society, industry, culture and politics do not support it, are largely opposed to it on principle in fact? The dilemma was further aggravated by the attitude of the largest republican party. In the summer of 1920 the SPD refused to participate in government and thereafter its political self-abnegation at Reich level was a constant complicating factor in forming coalitions. The SPD was afraid that, if it participated in unpopular governments, it would lose supporters to its left-wing extremist competitors; moreover its leaders, its functionaries and its hard-core supporters found it difficult to divest themselves of the long-standing tradition of opposition inherited from the imperial period; they were barely able to muster more than half-hearted support for the compromise system of Weimar. Only with some hesitation did they address themselves to the radically changed role which devolved on political parties in 1918; those who, like Friedrich Ebert, were able to shake off the trammels of tradition and old habits of thought, were few. Initially the SPD had good prospects of breaking down class barriers and becoming a true popular majority party as in Scandinavia for instance, but the German Social-democrats remained entrenched with the support of no more than 30 per cent of the electorate.

One is tempted to say, therefore, as even so perspicacious a writer as Arnold Brecht has done, that from the outset this state was caught in an insoluble dilemma and its disastrous development was therefore pre-determined. Large sections of the population laid at the door of the new order all blame for their present difficulties despite the fact that they were actually the legacy of the monarchy, of four years of war and the harsh conditions of an unavoidable peace; people looked back longingly to the happy pre-war period; they yearned, if not for the lost Reich of the Kaiser, at least for some firmer leadership to replace this ponderous, lustreless parliamentary democracy. All this explains why, at the very first Reichstag elections held in June 1920, barely ten months after the Weimar constitution came into force, the republic's supporters were in the minority and why in succeeding years they never attained a Reichstag majority. Those faithful to the black–red–gold of the constitution faced an anti-constitutional opposition under the black–white–red and red flags, the mere existence of which inhibited the interplay between government and opposition essential to the system. Throughout the republic's existence formation of a stable democratic government was a questionable proposition; governments were either minority cabinets, unwillingly tolerated, or large, basically unstable coalitions or finally, extra- or even anti-parliamentary, presidential cabinets of an authoritarian nature. The majority of the twenty Weimar cabinets survived only for a few months – their average life was eight and a half months; the longest period (twenty-one months) was achieved by the creaking 'Great Coalition' of 1928, the fall of which ushered in the last great crisis of state.

This state of affairs was all the more serious in that the onset of the economic crisis and the rise in unemployment from 1929 onwards brought social unrest both to town and country; as in 1923 this enabled the extremist groups' propaganda to score alarming political successes. The local and *Landtag* elections of 1929 showed a shift of forces towards extremism, primarily National-socialist but secondarily communist. In addition the Hugenberg group, which exerted a powerful influence both in industrial and press circles, fell victim to illusion and lent support to National-socialism. This gave Hitler the *entrée* into new spheres of influence and, against the will of moderate conservatives, carried the German-nationals alongside the Nazis into the turbulent 'National Opposition' front, which from autumn 1929 used every available method to bring about the final downfall of the democratic republic.

An important weapon in this campaign was the 'dictatorship paragraph' (Article 48) of the Weimar constitution; it contained no adequate safeguards and empowered the Reich president to issue emergency regulations and enforce the executive authority of the Reich against recalcitrant *Land* governments. Admittedly the Reichstag could demand cancellation of such measures but, owing to his prerogative of dissolution, the president's position was stronger than that of parliament. In addition he had the right, without agreement from the Reichstag, to appoint or dismiss the chancellor and ministers; in practice, therefore, he could govern without parliamentary control. These three presidential prerogatives had been inserted by the National Assembly of 1919 in order to strengthen the republic and in Ebert's time they were in fact used to protect the democratic order. Wielded by Hindenburg, however, they were used from 1930 onwards first to eliminate the Reichstag, then to enforce the authoritarian experiments of Papen and Schleicher, to impose *Gleichschaltung* on Prussia and finally to enable a minority government under Hitler to seize power by terrorist methods.

The fall of the Great Coalition and the nomination of Brüning were deliberately engineered over the head of the Reichstag, which thus saw its obligation to pursue a constructive policy removed at the moment of crisis. A little later, when the Reichstag refused to support Brüning's authoritarian policy of emergency regulation, he dissolved it prematurely, thus finally restricting its role to one of toleration. The subsequent Reichstag elections (September 1930) produced a vast increase in National-socialist deputies (107 as against 12), demonstrating how disastrously ill-timed the decision had been. The assistance given to Hitler by Hugenberg's German-nationals in face of warnings from the more thoughtful conservatives had proved more than effective. In fact the Reichstag was now incapable of action. The presidential cabinet too, which from the outset in no way really represented the will of the people, was regarded as a bureaucratic foreign body. Admittedly it is generally considered that a crisis situation demands a cabinet of experts independent of parliament. From 1930 onwards, however, the presidential government, rooted in authoritarianism and aloof from the public at large, merely increased the trend towards extremism; the public had less opportunity than ever to exert any influence on politics through democratic parties and parliament. Searching for some methods of demonstrating their opposition, the middle classes, the peasants and the unemployed flooded into the all-embracing Nazi movement which promised everything to everybody; a smaller section turned to the communist party which for its part was doing all it could to overthrow the Republic, frequently in negative alliance with the National-socialists.

So in the spring of 1932 the democratic groups executed a political about-turn, thinking that only through the re-election of Hindenburg could they stem the onrush of the totalitarian movement. When the newly elected President of the Reich turned against his Chancellor, Brüning, only a few weeks were required before the final break; the last remnants of parliamentary responsibility disappeared when von Papen, a renegade Centre Party politician, was appointed and proceeded with the illusory experiment of a 'party-free authoritarian state'. Both the rise of the National-socialists and the series of elections to which Papen's abuse of the presidential prerogatives of emergency legislation and dissolution gave rise, produced a destructive majority for the totalitarian parties by July 1932. Three months later, however, came the first noticeable reduction in the National-socialist mass following.

General Schleicher, Papen's successor, then made a last-minute attempt to end the authoritarian experiment and avert the threatening civil war situation by splitting the NSDAP and attracting the support of all non-extremist groups. But his idea came too late. Papen, his predecessor, was offended and went to work more quickly on his own account; with frivolous overestimation of his own potentialities he hoped to implement his ambitious plans for reorganization of the state on restorationist and authoritarian lines by concluding a deal with Hitler. In alliance with the German-nationals and the Stahlhelm he opened the doors of power to the man to whom they had so far been firmly closed and of whom Hindenburg had a low opinion, calling him the 'Bohemian corporal'.

So Hitler was nominated Chancellor of the Reich and endowed with full presidential powers at a moment when his party was supported, in free elections, by little more than one-third of the electorate and appeared to be in process of crisis-ridden decline. This turns the decision of 30 January 1933 and the intrigues of the Papen–Meissner group responsible for it into one of the most momentous errors in our history; it was doubly nonsensical in that by the end of 1932 the nadir of the economic crisis and of unemployment had been passed and a far-reaching revision of the Versailles treaty was in the offing. The rewards of the recovery initiated under the republic were now reaped solely by Nazi propaganda and the 'Third Reich' with its message of salvation.

Yet although legacies of history, political errors and general lack of civic sense may have contributed to the debility and eventual paralysation of the Weimar Republic, the fact that a state based on the rule of law was overwhelmed by total dictatorship, the 'German catastrophe' in the words of Friedrich Meinecke, was not an inexorable necessity. At an unexpected moment accident, together with personal interests and intrigue, brought to power a minority party which, without the freely expressed agreement either of the people or of parliament, contrived to establish a total tyranny and annex the means to enslave and destroy both Germany and Europe.

7

In retrospect the fatal flaw seems to be that, despite all attempts at compromise, the opposing fronts were still unreconciled when the Weimar constitution was accepted on 31 July 1919. The German–nationals the German People's Party, the USPD and the Bavarian Peasants' League all voted against the constitution. Many deputies, even from the coalition parties, abstained, foreshadowing the rapid disappearance of the broad-based coalition majority. From the outset, therefore, it was easy for its opponents to lay at the republic's door the three great irritants to German national sentiment – the collapse, the revolution and the Versailles treaty. The subsequent crises, lasting until 1923, merely accentuated the divergence between the people's political consciousness and the constitutional order. Further factors were the constitution's structural complexity and certain serious structural errors.

This view, clearly put forward with the benefit of hindsight, should not obscure the fact that the Weimar constitution was a significant attempt to introduce into Germany, for the first time and with complete consistency, the concept of the modern democratic state based on liberalism and the sovereignty of the people. It took its cue deliberately from the abortive attempt of 1848 but it was at pains to come to terms with the actual distribution of power and to draw on the experience of the older-established western democracies. The constitution was faced with the duty of combining protection for the freedom and rights of the citizen with organization of a form of state capable of functioning and attracting the goodwill of the people. Accordingly the basic rights of the individual were set out in as much detail as the official institutions. It should also be noted that the part of the constitution setting out the basic rights embodied not only the old liberal thinking but a whole series of new ideas on the reorganization of society. Here was a valuable start which should have led to productive extension of the Weimar Republic and its further development on modern lines.

That this did not occur was due to the combination of external and internal factors just described. A further contributory factor was the obstructive and frequently reactionary role played by the judiciary which persisted in political error even in face of the achievements of the republic's first president. The republic did in fact succeed in weathering the fearful post-war crises and all attempts at a *putsch* whether by Right or Left. But the ideas of democracy had been suppressed for so long that the republic was never able to instil them into a large section of the population, particularly into those classes of society which remained at the head of affairs. The time was too short before, with the election of Hindenburg, a monarchist Field Marshal was endowed with the powers of Reich President and, with the onset of the great economic crises, the Nazi dictatorship movement began to overwhelm the weakened parliamentary regime. The Third Reich never formally abolished the Weimar constitution but, with its arbitrary regime it deprived the constitution of all substance. The fateful role played by the failure to solve the relationship between Prussia and the Reich and by the hypertrophy of presidential power was an ever-present warning to the founding fathers of the Bonn Basic Law. The new federal structure and the built-in parliamentary system of government in the Federal Republic constitute an attempt to learn from the experience of Weimar.

In many important respects, however, the second German democracy was able to base itself on the achievements of Weimar. The fact that the first attempt to introduce democracy in Germany was a failure was due less to the compromise character of the constitution than to the lack of prior preparation of the population and of the political parties for a form of state which cannot survive unless its citizens are prepared to play a positive part and possess the necessary political sense. The Weimar constitution's loss first of the ability to function and then of all substance was due to the grievous legacies of the 'Second Reich' and the First World War, and to the theoretical way in which the constitution was interpreted and used. Have the illusions which made the life of the Weimar Republic so difficult and which finally condemned its constitution to failure, vanished in the cataclysm of the National-socialist catastrophe? That was the question asked of the second German democracy and at the same time its hope.

4
Unpolitical Policy—Brüning

The appearance or non-appearance of the Brüning memoirs was shrouded in mystery and speculation for decades. This was clear from the obituaries published when Brüning died at the age of eighty-five on 30 March 1970, forty years to the day from his truly historic formation of a government. What is the significance at this point of their long-delayed publication (they were mostly written in 1934–5)? They have destroyed many illusions, illusions formed around the personality of Brüning, his political potentialities and aims, around the character and importance of the presidential cabinet of 1930–2, illusions which have persisted until the present day. They persist in the latest account of this period by Gottfried Treviranus, one of the ministers most closely associated with him,[1] and in the monograph published in celebration of the eightieth birthday of the former Chancellor.[2] Despite much recent research there appears here and in popular literature an estimate of Brüning which might well be termed 'the Brüning myth'. Its central theme is insistence on the inexorable necessity of the Brüning policy as the sole possibility of surmounting Weimar's crisis and saving democracy. Coupled with it is the legend of his tragic fall 'one hundred yards from the winning post', used to explain or conceal his failure.

The myth has now been largely dispelled by Brüning himself and herein lies the great importance of this book, unsensational and somewhat dry though it is, both for historiography and for political analysis of the first German democracy. The controversies over the dissolution of the Weimar Republic which raged during the 1950s and 1960s must be looked at in a new light. All the participants must now complete and alter their picture and none more than the numerous defenders of the Brüning experiment led by historians such as Werner Conze who addressed himself to my critical expose of 1955 *Auflösung der Weimarer Republik* (Dissolution of the Weimar Republic), characterizing it as unhistorical and determinist; in the process, however, he himself defended the determinist viewpoint that there was no other way out of the crisis.[3]

This is no place to give yet another historical account of the dissolution of the Weimar Republic. Equally it is not possible to take Brüning's memoirs chapter by chapter, in all their confusing detail, subject them to critical examination and if necessary refute them. The important points have already been brought out in the first major reviews.[4] These extremely comprehensive memoirs may be looked at from three main points of view:

(i) what importance should be attributed to the concrete information given and the actual disclosures of factual events and circumstances? The mass of detailed information is so great and it is poured out so unendingly that the inexperienced reader may well conclude that the book is no more than a jumble of innumerable details and that he cannot see the wood for the trees.

(ii) what light does it shed on Brüning's personality and his political style which in my view can be characterized by the somewhat paradoxical phrase 'unpolitical policy'?

(iii) what position in history does the Brüning regime occupy in the context of the Weimar Republic's progress from parliamentary democracy through presidential dictatorship to Führer state?

The Brüning memoirs are revealing from two points of view. In the first place they are a contribution – admittedly a subjective one but written by someone intimately involved – to the reconstruction of what actually happened; at the same time, however, they are the most important source for any appreciation of the historically vital presidential cabinet of 1930 and for any answer to the vexed question whether the Brüning regime was a last effort to salvage democracy, or the first stage in the transition to authoritarianism leading via Papen, to Hitler.

2

It should be said at the outset that Brüning's account of the period of his Chancellorship, occupying more than two-thirds of the memoirs, is of uniformly high informative value. There is little reason to doubt the accuracy of the factual data or the précis of conversations and they give us real insight into the activities and views of the persons and groups involved. The day-to-day reconstruction of events is naturally coloured by the author's decided views, so if Brüning's account is to be really understood, the main tenets of his political creed must be analysed first. Here is a particular difficulty for any reader who wishes to use this best-seller as a history book. The mass of detailed information is, of course, valuable in filling many gaps in research, but this should not blind us to the serious shortcomings in the book: the significance, the importance and the political context of the events described are not made clear; the most frequent explanation for the bitter impression left upon the author by these events is that they were the product of individual intrigue and plotting; Brüning does not, however, ask the self-criticizing question of how this came about, or whether the reconstruction of the government of 1930 on oligarchic and authoritarian lines was not a contributory factor. It is significant that he attributes many developments simply to failure or betrayal on the part of individuals; there is no historical consideration of constitutional or structural problems nor are the various developments in any way classified.

The background is a basically unpolitical concept of politics and, unless this is realized, neither the calligraphy of the memoirs nor the character of the Brüning regime are comprehensible. It is a concept of politics which misappreciates the conditions and potentialities of political planning and action in a modern mass society – a society in which all politics, even including authoritarian or totalitarian domination, are designed on a democratic or pseudo-democratic basis. Both Brüning's utterances during his period as Chancellor and his subsequent self-revelation show that his concept of politics followed the tradition of the German concept of the state; this differentiated qualitatively between party politics and state politics and gave precedence to the state over democracy.[5] This differentiation was characteristic of the structure of the Kaiser's empire of 1870 and of the internal tug-of-war between the state and society, between social and economic emancipation and internal political stagnation. The political truce of the First World War seemed to substantiate this specifically German myth of the state which was deliberately contrasted with the reduced importance attributed to the state by the western democracies. Such was the view of conservatives, liberals and even some social-democrats; Thomas Mann's *Creed of a Non-political* written in 1918 is striking testimony to it.

Defeat, revolution and the advent of the republic made little difference; in this respect continuity was more compelling than a fresh start. Admittedly, with the change in political structure and the rule of a state based on parliamentary democracy and political parties, the ideal of a state standing above party entered the realm of fiction; faced with the realities of republican party and coalition politics, of democracy in other words, it had had its day. Nevertheless its influence became more potent as the internal governmental problems and external vexations facing the republic apparently became more serious. The monarchy with its greater glitter became an object of romantic adulation; the yearning for security, order and efficiency in coping with problems became identified with the supra-party state; realism and politics were regarded as antithetical.

For a time the Centre Party, like democratic liberalism, suffered severely from this pre-democratic concept of the state with its authoritarian and patriarchal overtones; with its links to certain interests in social, cultural and political circles it was forced into an ambivalent position between parliamentary political practice and its trans-democratic concept of the state.[6] Among the bourgeoisie in general and even in the constitutional theory of the Weimar state, the catchphrase was 'State above party' – aptly labelled by Gustav Radbruch as 'the lifelong deception of the patriarchal state'.

Brüning is no less than a paradigm of this attitude of mind. His memoirs open with his experiences of the war and suppression of the revolution and these colour all that follows. His criterion for the future was the role he had played, or thought he had played, in guarding Hindenburg's GHQ and the Kaiser. Different though their positions were, 9 November 1918 was the neuralgic moment both for Hindenburg and Brüning. Again and again they returned to it in conversation; for both it was the horizon of their experiences.[7] Here lies the key to Brüning's concept of the state, part romantic and conservative, part realistic and ascetic. These two primary components of his thinking emerge in the two major facets of his policy as chancellor: first in the attachment, formed against his better judgement but stubbornly maintained, between the ex-officer and his Field Marshal Commander-in-Chief of 1918 whom he regarded as the embodiment of the state in its pre-democratic sense; second, in his insistence upon a regime supposedly standing above party and devoted solely to a 'realistic' solution of Germany's problems. Although his memoirs do not say so specifically, Brüning's political picture of the world and his scale of values were governed by ideas such as 'supra-party agencies', influential 'cross-channels', the 'generation of the trenches,' respect for all things military, the welfare of the community, etc. instead of politics. Transcending mere 'politics' he felt himself impelled to embark on a road leading from a parliamentary to a bureaucratic and authoritarian system. He himself acknowledged as much in a letter at the time: 'In the ultimate issue I could not refuse in face of the Reich President's appeal to my soldierly sense of duty.'[8] His readiness to express such sentiments illustrates the extent to which Brüning felt that he belonged to the 'generation of the trenches' and it also explains the deep disillusionment evidenced in his later utterances and even more in the statements and opinions given in his memoirs.

The two guiding principles of Brüning's thinking, therefore, were his devotion to the state (the result of which was that he hitched his star to Hindenburg) and his ethos of realism (which during the economic crisis dictated a tenacious policy based purely on economics). But there was a further element in Brüning's non-democratic concept of politics and the state – his conviction of the primacy of foreign policy. After the failure of 1848 and captivated by Bismarck's successes, the majority of German historians and journalists thought more in terms of external power politics than of internal politics, party squabbles or democratic parliamentary development; they applauded the idea that good administration was the best form of internal politics over which foreign policy took priority because it decided the fate of states and of peoples. During the imperial period the idea that true politics consisted of foreign policy served to divert attention from the internal tensions to external problems. Under the Weimar Republic the *idée fixe* that the Treaty of Versailles was the root of all evil cast a shadow over internal democratic politics and fostered radical revisionism.

Even the more moderate politicians, however, were under the spell (or pressure) of this concept; the result was that democracy was largely regarded as an emergency solution, an interlude pending recovery of freedom in external affairs and restoration of the Reich by revision. For Brüning, his party's expert on national economy and finance, the collapse of 1918 was an ever-present incubus; so was his conviction that the economic crisis was caused by external factors stemming primarily from Versailles and reparations. So he combined a concept of the primacy of foreign policy with one of economic austerity and tenacity; proof of German incapacity to pay as the crisis developed he regarded as the most important prerequisite for treaty revision. The implication, of course, was that active internal politics were subordinated to administrative, budgetary and technical economic measures without regard to their psychological effects. There was no place here for any thought of the outstanding importance of public opinion or its political configuration.

Such were some of the more important prior conditions, or rather encumbrances, affecting the course towards presidential authoritarian government set by Brüning at the end of March 1930 in the midst of the economic crisis. Legend has always maintained that Brüning's solution was an inexorable necessity but in fact this course had been planned by Schleicher earlier and even more precisely by Groener, Meissner, Treviranus and Hindenburg himself round about Christmas 1929, in other words long *before* the break-up of the Great Coalition, the fate of which was undoubtedly affected thereby. Brüning's memoirs make the connection quite clear. Moreover he is quite frank about the motives of those involved. Oversimplifying somewhat, it is possible to distinguish between two elements in Brüning's concept of the state; first was the long-term element based on a conservative concept of politics and democracy, memories of the monarchy and his time as a soldier, an ascetic ethos of devotion to his work and his duty; the second element was his dispassionate short-term concept of practical policy, the main features of which were the possibilities of an emergency regime standing above or even in opposition to parliament, the Hindenburg myth and the neutralization of internal political conflicts by successes in the field of foreign policy and treaty revision. Admittedly this policy did not stem solely from the ideas and capabilities of Brüning. No less important was the fact that he owed his nomination to the authoritarian plans concocted by circles centred on Hindenburg and the Reichswehr leaders. His dependence on them was equalled by the independence of democratic domestic politics which he hoped to achieve. Partly consciously and partly unconsciously, therefore, he turned from putative saviour of the republic into its first liquidator.

3

With this background we can now look at Brüning's statements and judgements in his great work. Six main themes emerge:

(i) his fixation over the Treaty of Versailles and its elimination;

(ii) his conviction that the parliamentary system should be curtailed in favour of a monarchy of Bismarckian type;

(iii) his dislike of democratic pluralism as such, of politics based on parties and associations, of parliamentarianism and his disregard of public opinion;

(iv) his ambivalent but extremely dependent position *vis-à-vis* Hindenburg and the Reichswehr leaders who were the main props of his regime;

(v) his inclination towards a future system of government for the Reich standing halfway between democracy and dictatorship. This was the background to his tendency to swing to the Right and his vacillation between feeble opposition to the Nazi Party and abortive efforts to restrain the Hitler movement;

(vi) Finally his epilogue dealing with the end of the republic and of the

Centre Party, where his critical attitude to Bishop Kaas, the Centre Party leader, and the Vatican's concordat policy is particularly emphasized.

In his review Karl Otmar von Aretin summarizes the depressing impression left by these memoirs with the words: 'There was no way of saving this state.' This was not true of the spring of 1930, though it became true as a result of the subsequent government by intrigue concealed or masquerading as realistic policy. Its legacy was the power vacuum of 1932 and the opportunity for the National-socialists to seize power. The apodictic statement is frequently made that by 1930 under no circumstances could the crisis be solved by parliamentary or democratic methods, but this is in no way confirmed by Brüning's own account. I have always maintained that parliamentary democracy's loss of authority at home was considerably accelerated by Brüning's policy and deliberately accentuated by the champions of a right-wing, presidential dictatorship; this view is supported by Brüning's surprisingly frank remarks about his own definite plans deliberately to transform parliamentary party democracy into an authoritarian monarchy with Hindenburg as regent.[9] This and Hindenburg's appeal to his sense of duty as a soldier explain the ease with which Brüning was persuaded to form an anti-parliamentary cabinet using as weapons Article 48 and the dissolution of the Reichstag. We now know from Brüning himself that this swing to authoritarianism had been prepared long beforehand and was not merely the result of an allegedly insoluble governmental crisis. There were no party negotiations, no examination of alternative solutions; the new regime stood ready immediately on the fall of Hermann Müller's majority, for which Hindenburg had explicitly refused to use Article 48. Deliberately no attempt was made to form a parliamentary government because Hindenburg's condition was a swing to the Right and the exclusion of the SPD, also because the true purpose was authoritarian, anti-parliamentary reform.

Six months later, after the fateful dissolution of the Reichstag in the summer of 1930 the parliamentary majority had already shrunk in face of the Nazi assault. But this later impasse, largely a consequence of the new policy, can now no longer be cited as the reason for the alleged inevitability of the Brüning solution. The trans-parliamentary purposes of the presidential king-makers already emerge as complete perversion, if not abuse, of the presidential prerogatives. These were originally conceived to protect democracy; now they were turned against it. This may be regarded as a disastrous consequence of the dualist structure of the Weimar state but in any case it makes nonsense of the well-known formalistic argument that

Hindenburg acted no differently from Ebert in 1923. The authority of the president was now used, not to save democracy but deliberately to plan a right-wing regime independent of parties and parliament and to eliminate the influence of the Social-democrats, for whose policy of toleration Brüning has words of praise, though apparently he never thought of including them at any level of political responsibility. Later the presidential authority was used to replace Brüning by the Papen–Schleicher oligarchy and finally (the height of illusion) to support the Hitler–Papen regime with the emergency regulations of February 1933 – which really set the stage for the fatal Enabling Law of 23 March 1933.

Looking at all this objectively, one can hardly deny that the process was continuous and 1930 was a decisive stage. Brüning's subjective conviction, of course, bore no relation to what actually happened. Arnold Brecht has aptly said that 'seldom has a government been guilty of misjudgement in better faith than the Brüning government.'[10] Brüning invariably insisted that his government, though ruling by emergency decree and merely tolerated by the democratic parties, must have a measure of parliamentary support. This was why his disillusioned partners centred on Hindenburg brought him down. It was left to the unscrupulous Papen to sail over the hurdle into anti-parliamentary, presidential dictatorship and finally career off into the Führer dictatorship. But it was Brüning's trustworthiness which made the first stage of this development possible. He was unable either to evade the consequences of his role as a useful though transient figure or to control its long-term repercussions. These particular consequences he certainly had no wish to see and later, though too late, he raised his voice against them. He was one of those numerous figures, so imposing at the time, who toyed with the idea of a middle course between democracy and dictatorship, preferably a restoration of the monarchy based on reinforcement of the presidential regime. But what relationship did this bear to reality in a country where neglect of internal politics had led to growing unrest on the part of the masses and an inability to integrate them, while the masses themselves were being mobilized by extremist movements to support alternatives entailing the destruction of the system?

Brüning is silent on this subject although it was the basic problem of his whole policy. In his eyes the masses were not a factor in politics; the internal crisis presented itself to him as a foreign policy and financial problem; finally he regarded the deep crisis of confidence in his own system exclusively as the outcome of personal threats to his relationship with Hindenburg and the camarilla. This was, as Ernst Deuerlein has put it, 'eighteenth- rather than nineteenth-century cabinet politics which did not recognize the existence of vocal citizens, only of subjects whose duty it was to obey.'[11] This policy both misappreciated and intensified the extremist dynamism of the masses in a crisis. Realization that his policy had failed produced in Brüning a mixture of illusion and resignation explicable only by his rigid, pre-democratic concept of the state; as a result he was unable either to cope with the trend towards a mass democratic society or to grasp the possibility of a totalitarian system of domination. Even in retrospect he still insists that his policy of standing firm during the crisis (which in fact intensified the crisis) was both necessary and right and that his failure by so small a margin was due simply to the intrigues of the Hindenburg circle, the attitude of certain captains of industry and the impatience of the German public. Unemployment and the bank crisis, despair and extremism were in his eyes necessary steps towards external revision and internal stabilization. His rigid timetable took no account of the catastrophic internal political repercussions of his policy which demanded too much of the German people and overestimated his own position of political power. By his own choice this position rested, not on the support of parliament and the political parties but on the fickle 'confidence' of Hindenburg and his irresponsible advisers. This confidential relationship, calculatingly exploited and then terminated by Hindenburg and his advisers, is the underlying explanation for Brüning's whole career and his failure.

Frank and detailed though these memoirs are, they do not acknowledge the inherently contradictory nature or the fragility of the government constructed in 1930. Again and again Brüning reveals irresponsible intrigues on the part of Schleicher or the President's son Oskar; Hindenburg himself, however, he treats gently and insists that their basic relationship was one of confidence and loyalty; he bemoans the political and ultimately mental incapacity of the senile President but cites it as a mitigating factor; yet he attempts to turn this into a reason for the President's re-election or even for a restoration of the monarchy – at which point he is forced to admit that the old man was only willing to see a return either of the unmentionable Wilhelm II or of the old Prussian absolutism. Brüning's concept of the state is not in itself an adequate explanation of the deep-rooted inconsistency in this loyalty complex which overrode all differences of political outlook, religion and character between Hindenburg and Brüning; it remains the irrational nucleus of an otherwise rational, dispassionate concept of practical politics. Brüning's memoirs contain much revealing material concerning the Hindenburg myth and the presidential experiment; nowhere, however, do they deal with this fragile basis of his policy which is largely rooted in his experiences of the war and the revolutionary period.

It seems to me that the tragedy of this man and the reason for his political failure lie in his unpolitical attitude of mind, not in the dubious phrase about the last couple of hundred yards. From the moment when his relationship with Hindenburg and the schemers in his entourage was severed, Brüning's perception of the actual course of events and the dangers inherent in them became sharper. The concluding section of the book stands in sharp contrast to the broad description of his period in government. It is not as close-packed. Even so it raises a number of problems particularly the question of a coalition with Hitler in the summer of 1932; for far too long Brüning regarded the Hitler movement merely as a nationalist right-wing party; similarly his opinion of Mussolini was particularly high. He says not a word about the emergency decrees following the Reichstag Fire nor about the decisive role played by Article 48 in the process of the Nazi seizure of power. Brüning places far greater emphasis than most others on the fateful implications of the manoeuvrings connected with the Enabling Law and the Reich concordat – far more emphasis, for instance, than Ludwig Kaas, whose questionable role in all this comes in for severe criticism. Brüning's bitter comments on the vexed question of the connection between the planning for the concordat and the enforcement of single-party rule merit further examination – I once described the process as a 'stab-in-the-back for the Centre Party.'[12] Brüning considers that it was also a stab-in-the-back for the emergent protestant resistance. Brüning recalls that he warned Kaas, after the latter's departure for Rome, against concluding the concordat saying that 'in itself it was valueless; it definitely meant the end of the Centre Party ... and once the Centre Party had been destroyed the government would not keep to it because the text was far too indefinite' (pp. 671 et seq.). Finally Brüning records that when Joos, a Centre Party deputy, telephoned Kaas asking him to delay conclusion of the concordat and therefore disbandment of the Centre Party, Kaas replied with a chuckle: 'Haven't you disbanded yourselves already? Better be quick about it!' (pp. 673 et seq.). Like almost all other politicians, of course, Brüning was a victim of the illusion that Hitler would quickly ruin himself economically; in his case the specific reason was that he did not believe the National-socialists to be capable of coping with the practical problems of government, particularly not with economic policy.

This shows that to the very end, even after his bitter experiences of the past and when faced with the brutal *Realpolitik* and technique of deception used by the new rulers, Brüning was unable to shake himself free of his unpolitical concept of politics as the mere art of the practical.

During the crisis he fundamentally underestimated the problems of democratic domestic politics, reducing them to mere practical questions of external and financial policy. His ethos of the state was based on tradition and practicality and so the perspectives opened up by a totalitarian regime were even more foreign to him. He held to his chosen course tenaciously and honestly through a chaos of intrigue, short-term pressures and long-term delusions. The tragedy was that, by holding to this course and relying on the Hindenburg camarilla, he himself contributed to the destruction of parliamentary democracy and dissolution of the republic since people became habituated to oligarchic and authoritarian politics.

Despite their aridity of expression these memoirs give a vivid picture of Brüning's two main characteristics – personal integrity and sincerity on the one hand, but limited vision, rigidity and political vulnerability on the other. They contain errors and omissions; the marshalling of facts leaves much to be desired; nevertheless, as a source of information, they are of far greater value than any other set of contemporary memoirs. They are worlds removed from the distorting apologia of Papen or Schacht. The immediate and abiding impression which they make, however, is disillusioning, more so than any subsequent historico-political analysis could ever be. The uncritical postscript, written by a friend who clings to the old legends, does nothing to alter this.

I have attempted to describe and explain the main lines of Bruning's policy in the paradoxical phrase 'unpolitical policy'; it is apt, for his policy was paradoxical. On the one hand he defended a bureaucratic version of the state based on the rule of law, on the other he paved the way for dictatorship. Like the present-day argument in favour of practical, above-party politics, his policy accentuated the German aversion to democratic politics; it set the seal on the desuetude of parliamentary politics and so cleared the ground for the antithesis of an above-party system – domination by a single extremist party and totalitarian politics. The belief that a state based on the rule of law could be maintained without democracy proved to be a fatal illusion. The dust-cover of his memoirs proclaims that Brüning was the last chancellor *before* dissolution of the Weimar Republic; he was in fact the first chancellor in the process of dissolution of the first German democracy.

5

Gravedigger of Democracy—Papen

Nearly twenty years ago Franz von Papen, the forerunner and minion of dictatorship, had the presumption to publish his memoirs and entitle them *Der Wahrheit eine Gasse* (An Alleyway of Truth); they gained him no greater credit from his contemporaries or from historians than had his political career. This book, written by a naïve, conceited man who had contributed so much to the destruction of the Weimar Republic, was purely self-justificatory; Rudolf Pechel called it a 'street-song of truth'. Despite all its distortions of the truth, however, it revealed the incredible frivolity with which a small clique centred on Hindenburg made possible the German catastrophe of 1933.

Now, however, Papen sets himself up as a writer of history and political pedagogue, inveighing against the 'black–and–white picture' drawn by contemporary history which, he alleges, is subject to direction; he dedicates his great thoughts as a statesman to 'German youth'.[1] Such is the pretension of his new book, entitled *Vom Scheitern einer Demokratie 1930–1933* (Failure of a Democracy 1930–1933).

The new Papen is in fact no different from the old – as a historian he is just a failure. What he gives us is an abridged re-edition of his memoirs embellished with a few private documents and excerpts from more recent literature selected at random. The findings of critical research are brushed aside with vaguely worded side-swipes at historians (usually without naming them); Papen sees no need to recant on anything. The claim to scholarship is supported by a few haphazard footnotes.

The book produces no more than an eerie echo of the illusions and blunders of an authoritarian reactionary clique which has long since forfeited any claim to be able to teach the present day or democracy anything.

Unfortunately no one can be sure that Papen's book will in fact end up where it belongs – in the waste paper basket of history. His anti-democratic ideology is in line with the persistent and continuously reviving effort of nationalist self-justification in the Federal Republic. His picture of history and his scale of political values are based on the old (and yet new) catch-words of a patriarchal ideology. As before, Papen castigates an 'egoistic group attitude of mind', the 'domination of political parties', parliamen-tarianism and readiness to compromise; his main targets are the Left as a whole and in particular the trades unions. Otherwise the blame for failure is laid at the door of foreign countries.

By contrast Papen has nothing but praise for the 'conservative' policy of the Right which he describes as national service to the state at a level above party; he raves about the 'moral strength of authoritarian leader-ship'; he is an uncritical worshipper of Hindenburg, 'the eighty-year-old giant', and of the 'old soldier' ethos; he is almost unstinting in his praise for the policy of Hugenberg and the Stahlhelm. The 'leaders of the national opposition' are presented as the true pillars of the state, however anti-democratic their actions may have been. Only the Right is regarded as standing above party – Gustav Radbruch's 'lifelong deception of the patriarchal state'.

The National-socialists escape with only minor reproof; SA and Reichsbanner are placed on a level. Papen's primary object, however, is to incriminate his personal rivals, principally Schleicher and the leaders of the Centre Party who expelled their ambitious right-winger when he annexed Brüning's position. In all this Papen poses as the honest, innocent and benevolent keeper of Germany's conscience; he has a few words of praise for Stresemann and Brüning, though naturally he leaves no doubt that he could have done better himself had it not been for the evil machina-tions of the parties. In his self-conceit he makes no secret of the criteria by which he judges matters – he had grown up in the 'soldierly school' which had taught him 'the concept of duty and of pure selfless objectivity'. Not much of this was to be seen in his unparallelled intrigues of 1932–3!

Papen's comments on the 'dissolution of the Weimar Republic' are platitudinous in the extreme. There is no analysis; the reader is merely presented once more with all the right-wing accusations against democracy – the welfare state, class warfare and 'cultural bolshevism' sap the nation's strength, the 'accumulation of special interests and party cliques' atomize the 'body politic'. An exception is made, of course, in the case of the special agrarian interest involved in 'Aid to the Eastern Territories'; to Papen it is unthinkable that any suspicion should have fallen on 'the victor of Tannenberg' when he opposed the 'bolshevistic agrarian' settlement plans put forward by the Brüning government. Much is continually made of 'the German people's struggle for existence'. The blame for the dispute about the black–red–gold flag is attributed to 'exaggerated republican emotional complexes' and that for the failure of the 'anti-Prussian' Weimar constitution to 'an exaggerated concept of the absolute sovereignty of the people' or even 'an exaggerated concept of liberty'. Left-wing criticism of the anti-republican attitude of the Reichswehr is simply dismissed as 'disparagement of the German soldier', even when such criticism was directed at the machinations associated with illegal rearmament.

What Papen offers us is an interminable anthology drawn from the history books of German-nationalist low-brows. If he draws parallels between Bonn and Weimar this is primarily to prove that a strong state is preferable to a complex democracy. In Papen's eyes this amounts to the rugged necessity of 'putting order into the party tug-of-war'. He says not a word about the share of the blame for the failure of this democracy to function carried by the Right and therefore by himself. His basic theme is that Hugenberg and the German-nationals were to be regarded as the backbone of the state.

Sources and quotations are selected solely to give support to this view. People like Hugenberg and Schacht are regarded as incontestable authorities; others are labelled as party politicians or as left-wing supporters. Such ostensibly scientific evidence as Papen and his 'assistants' have discovered is twisted accordingly. My comments on the attitude of the SPD in 1930, for instance, are abbreviated, wrongly quoted and cited out of context. Any more fundamental criticism of the Right or of Papen himself is passed over in total silence.

Papen plays equally fast and loose with his facts. He states, for instance, that the Republic would have become a 'victim of the Spartacists' had it not been for Article 48 – which did not then yet exist. The first totalitarian majority, he says, was produced by the elections which he called in July 1932. Of the refusal by the democratic parties and the government of Prussia's demands in 1931 he writes furiously that it was 'tantamount to the use of communist methods for the seizure of power in the Reich'. He does not mention that in this campaign the German-nationals and the Stahlhelm were fighting alongside the Nazis and communists against the republic.

In complete disregard of the truth he bemoans the 'discriminatory and provocative treatment of the Right' and he invariably holds the communist party responsible for all street fighting. Frick he still regards as a 'moderate man who was a sensible government leader in Thuringia' (in 1930 Frick,

Thuringian Minister of the Interior and of Education, was pursuing a purely Nazi personnel policy and engineered a professorship in Jena for H. F. K. Günther, the Nazi racial ideologist). Accordingly in 1933 Papen accepted Frick as Minister of the Interior – the result being a resounding success for the *Gleichschaltung* policy. Papen believed himself able to cope with 'any possible (!) totalitarian tendencies on the part of the NSDAP'.

Papen's knowledge of constitutional matters does not go further than to equate 'emergency regulations' with a breach of the constitution. It is therefore hardly surprising that he regards Hitler's nomination to the chancellorship as entirely constitutional. He gives no thought to the constitutional implications of placing complete governmental authority with unrestricted emergency powers in the hands of a sworn enemy of the democratic constitution. Instead he relies on the ultimate historical falsehood that even before the March 1933 elections 'a majority of the German people' had welcomed 'this government and its programme'. In fact the Nazis and German National People's Party had scored only 42 per cent of the votes; the percentage only increased as a result of the subterfuges and terrorist methods used in the seizure of power.

Papen comes closer to reality in his criticism of the proportional representation system, which he describes without further ado as 'suicidal'. Here again he makes certain mistakes; he says, for instance (wrongly) that the five-per-cent clause in the electoral law is written into the Basic Law. He omits to say that his own government considered the reactionary plan of doing away with universal suffrage altogether. He tries to give the impression that what they were considering was the majority franchise, now so fashionable (but it would have given the NSDAP a two-thirds majority in parliament in 1932).

Equally sanctimoniously he maintains that the opponents of democracy were permitted 'full use of the democratic freedoms to destroy democracy itself'. Among these opponents, however, Papen's German-national friends were prominent and during his short period of power no chancellor contributed as much to electoral inflation as did Papen. When he refers to Weimar's suicide he is only too happy to forget that there were plenty of deliberate and vocal murderers, among whom Papen occupies an eminent position, alongside 'Hugenberg and his people', for whom Papen has so much praise.

2

Papen's detailed description of developments from 1930 to 1933 merely revives old legends long since disproved.

Like our conservative historians he maintains that, when the right-wing Brüning experiment was imposed with such suspicious haste after the break-up of the Great Coalition, a presidential regime acting without or against parliament was the only possibility. (He insists that Hindenburg and Article 48 alone guaranteed the welfare of the state; otherwise he barely refers to the constitution at all.)

He makes the grotesque accusation that, particularly in Prussia, the Centre Party had moved too far to the Left (his evidence is apparently the fact that the catholic congress of 1932 took place in the industrial city of Essen). Accordingly, he says, he attempted, together with 'some of his conservative party friends' to bring the Centre Party back on to the right track; he also used his Berlin newspaper *Germania* which he had bought in order to preserve it from 'infiltration by anti-religious elements'.

His purpose was clear. Ever since 1930 Papen had been continuously demanding the final exclusion of the Left (liberals barely existed in his eyes) in favour of a 'national concentration'. Brüning had to go because he was not sufficiently resolute about this and his camouflaged dictatorship did not discard its 'parliamentary embroidery' (as Papen wrote to Schleicher in 1931). When his own openly anti-parliamentary policy failed (he barely had a 10 per cent backing), he brought the Hitler cabinet into being.

Here again his falsifications are legion. He ends by laying all blame on Schleicher's intrigues and the muddled propaganda of the *Tatkreis* led by Hans Zehrer, which undoubtedly played a fateful role. But the corporative ideology of the Papen circle was no less chaotic. He compares his anti-trade union economic policy with Schiller's 'concerted action'. Once more he tries to give some credibility to the fantastic plans for economic salvation produced by his authoritarian, half-Wilhelmian, half-fascist state, although this time he only gives a few details quoted out of context.

What finally emerges, however, is that no one other than Papen forged the essential links for the Hitler cabinet and he did so in conjunction with Meissner and Hindenburg's son Oskar who had no constitutional position. As early as December 1932, speaking to the *Herrenklub*, Papen gave a foretaste of the Third Reich's bombast which he now quotes proudly – 'Never was the principle of leader and disciple more true, more alive or more cogent than in these days.'

This required little change a few months later. Even now Papen has no conception of what democratic leadership is, for he compares the events leading up to the Hitler government with Kennedy's phrase about 'new frontiers'. Schleicher, he says, had nothing to offer the German people; Papen, of course, had – his 'national concentration' comprising industry, the *Reichslandbund* (Prussian agrarian pressure group), Hugenberg and above all Hitler. He described Schleicher and Hammerstein to Hindenburg as 'as spineless as oysters'. There could be no better description of Papen himself.

It is, of course, no accident that Papen's book ends with 30 January 1933. It follows that he does not have to tell of his total failure in his self-chosen role of controller of Hitler, or of his readiness to serve that regime of violence even after the murder of his friends, when Hugenberg and many conservatives had long since had enough. Instead he reproduces in an appendix the charitable testimonial produced by Brüning for his de-nazification proceedings in 1949 – and then has the presumption to follow it with the full bombastic government programme of 1 February 1933 which started the Hitler–Papen government on the road to destruction of Germany and of Europe. If any lesson is to be learnt from Papen's hotch-potch it is that of the bankruptcy of a conservative authoritarian nationalist ideology – as it still is today.

6

Gleichschaltung* of the Universities

Many people still believe in the theory that the National-socialist tyranny sprang into being almost overnight and quite inevitably as a result of the distress caused mainly by economic difficulties arising from Versailles, inflation and the economic crisis; it is also regarded as a totalitarian tyranny based on force, in face of whose methods of coercion and terror the only recourse was submission, conformism or withdrawal into political inactivity.

In fact, however, this is no adequate explanation either for the procedure of the Nazi seizure of power or for the character of the regime, nor for that comprehensive process which, in the barbaric technical jargon of the time, was known as *Gleichschaltung*. The fate of the German universities from 1933 onwards was no different from that of political parties or social groups, associations and institutions but it could never have happened, had it not been for the coincidence of two fateful developments: the assault of the new rulers was a brutal one but it encountered only basic weakness, wishful thinking and gullibility on the part of university leaders, considerable susceptibility in fact to the wiles and threats of the Nazi *Gleichschaltung* policy. This was the outcome of a multiple process – the true problem of the 'German catastrophe' of 1933 lies in the relationship between ostensible *Gleichschaltung*, voluntary *Gleichschaltung* and the various forms of 'non-*Gleichschaltung*' (as Rothfels put it). *Gleichschaltung* and moral weakness must therefore be considered together and here the attitude of the universities is highly illuminating, not only in the field of the intellect and political education but as a development of overall political significance.

I

At the beginning of the 1945 winter term, with the ruins of National-socialism all around him, Rudolf Smend, the well-known constitutional lawyer, started the first series of historical-political lectures at the University of Göttingen. His opening words were:

* See Note, p. 56.

'The Third Reich did not come upon us entirely by chance. It originated and asserted itself as a result of certain prior conditions stemming from the misdirection of German political thought over at least two generations; it pursued this line of development in a way inconceivable to the previous generation. This being so, if we wish to revert to a healthy political situation, we must elucidate the point at which our fathers – or grandfathers – fell victim to this aberration in the second half of the nineteenth century.'

Two decades later this challenge is no less actual. It is applicable particularly to that ambivalent attitude to things political adopted by German intellectuals and pregnantly described by Smend in 1928 as unpolitical detachment from the state and unpolitical adulation of power. Now, with the hindsight of 1945, he traces the misdirection of German political thought from the latter third of the nineteenth century back to certain misinterpreted catchwords such as Jakob Burckhardt's phrase (coined in a very different context) of 'the state as an artifice'. Smend was not thinking of those extreme nationalist, *völkisch* or anti-semitic tendencies which found their outlet in National-socialism; they were not very widely supported in the university teaching profession before 1933. He was thinking of the widespread, almost universal, attitude of mind which considered humanist education and good civic behaviour as compatible with admiration for the great tyrants; they were thought of as subject to no legal or moral obligations, important, colourful, though often criminal individuals, brought to life in the history books such as Burckhardt's *Renaissance Culture in Italy* written in 1860.

Similarly, in a spirit of self-criticism, Friedrich Meinecke has said that 'thought along power policy and machiavellian lines was certainly not confined to Germany; perhaps we talked about it more openly but we did not practise it more intensively.' Meinecke added however:

'The specifically German contribution was to think and speak of these things without restraint, in stark, harsh, deliberate terms as a matter of principle, to take pleasure in ruthless consistency and tend to turn the practical into the ideological; this is a matter of concern for the future if thoughts initially expressed merely in theoretical terms are to become weapons in the hands of men of action.

Comments such as these reveal something of the background to the attitude and the feebleness of the universities when challenged by naked power policy and brutal disregard for legality. After the failure of the 1848 revolution followed by imposition of unity from above, the educated level of society in Germany at large–particularly in the universities and students' unions – prided itself on a concept of the state as something based on 'the realities of power', strong and standing above party; politics were regarded as a process in which morality and the rule of law were not overriding, only success counted and the influence of individual great men was paramount. The old concept of 'reasons of state' became equated with big battalions and an impressive show of force; the well-behaved citizen looked back with romantic longing and a sort of comfortable shudder to the old days, comparing them with the small-time unheroic present.

The habit of submission to an authoritarian, patriarchal state which, by good administration from above, eliminated the necessity for political responsibility, coloured the political ideology of the Second Reich; to this was added a seductively persuasive nationalist philosophy of power which preached to the 'retarded nation' (Plessner's phrase) the necessity to overhaul its rivals and presented jungle law as an object of admiration provided it was politically successful. Early in the nineteenth century there had been an upsurge of liberalism among intellectuals and in the universities which had stood the test of resistance and rebellion; it reached its zenith with the liberal-democrat student movement, the 'Göttingen Seven' and the 'professors' parliament' of Frankfurt; but this gave way to the Second Reich's doctrine of success and its ideology of the necessity to make good the nation's late start in the imperialist race. Admittedly the falsity of this doctrine and ideology was proved in the First World War. There was widespread non-acceptance of the 1918 decision however; equally unaccepted was the failure in face of the western democracies of that exaggerated and specifically German ideology set out in the professorial manifestos of the war years. The stab–in–the–back legend, a manifestation of this profound self-deception, became part of the repertoire of slogans used in students' associations, academic speeches and celebrations commemorating the foundation of the Reich, all of which acted as an antidote to the new democratic republic's claim to the loyalty of its citizens. National consciousness was governed by a pre-democratic scale of values; all too many people, particularly among the educated classes, regarded the Weimar Republic merely as an unhappy interlude, simply an emergency structure, behind which 'The Reich' was waiting for a more favourable opportunity to recapture its position as a 'great power'. They did not understand the concept of freedom as implying participation in a democracy; freedom meant external liberation from Versailles, just as after 1848 the internal political freedom movement had given way to politics based on unity and power policy applied to external affairs.

The disillusionments and crises of the post-war period, therefore, upset the relationship between power and intellect, between politics and moral values, thus creating an area in which pre-war undercurrents of barbarism, particularly anti-semitism and the concept of power based on terrorism, could develop and become politically effective. Carried along by the German-national restoration movement, romanticist propaganda in favour of dictatorship gained ground among the bourgeoisie, the intelligentsia and the youth. Ernst Jünger's war books, pronouncements such as those of the sociologist Hans Freyer in his *Revolution von rechts* (Right-wing Revolution) published in 1931 or Oswald Spengler's picture of 'barbaric Caesarism' were regarded as holding out visions of a greater future for Germany. As the most extreme movement of this type, even before becoming a mass movement, National-socialism had attracted many recruits from the student body, always thirsting for action. The terror of the seizure of power period was foreshadowed in anti-semitic machinations, in the persecution or boycotting of republican, pacifist or Jewish lecturers and in the capture of the General Students' Committees.

This trend was intensified by the crisis in the educational system, which had been building up for a long time and against which Ernst Robert Curtius, for instance, had warned as early as 1932 in his article entitled 'German intellect in danger'. Curtius saw as the great dilemma, faced by the German universities as well as other people, the almost schizophrenic differentiation between classical or humanist education and *Realpolitik* based on power. Precisely this point, however, offered an opening to the Nazi pseudo-reformers; they produced the great watchword which silenced many individual scruples, that now at last the hour of synthesis between intellect and power had arrived. To an extent almost incomprehensible today all too many people either misappreciated or accepted the fact that this synthesis merely implied that intellect must give way to power and education to totalitarian direction.

This diagnosis, of course, is belied by the vast number of those expelled or disciplined; this shows the extent of the resistance which had to be overcome before the universities could be brought to accept the introduction of politics, one-sided politics, into all forms of science and teaching. All the more horrifying, however, is the alacrity with which the universities showed themselves ready to accept or co-operate with other organizations which had capitulated to Nazism, and their readiness to leave the persecuted minority of their colleagues in the lurch. A current expression was the barbaric remark attributed by Hitler to Goebbels or even Hugenberg: when you use a plane, there will be shavings. At the root of a remark like this lay the view that the state could not be judged by normal criteria, that a statesman justified by success was not subject to the moral laws of ordinary citizens and that politics and morality were different things. Faced with the tumultuous consequences of the sheer breath-taking events of spring 1933, many people felt that insistence on their personal scruples was petty even if they did not just take the line of least resistance and submit, almost as a matter of course, to an authority which seemed to have recaptured a welcome strength. Many felt that for the sake of supposedly laudable purposes – liberation from Versailles, renewal and reform – they must accept certain dubious 'side effects'.

The basic problem of any ethic of politics is whether and to what extent the end justifies the means; in the light of the neo-German concept of the state this was all too quickly decided in favour of success, of the right of the strong and of an imposing display of power. Alternatively, however, people merely found in it confirmation of the current view that 'politics is a dirty business'; this was the outlook of many non-political citizens, officials and professors; they admired power and *at one and the same time* accepted its manifestations with resignation and legalized it by conforming. The defencelessness of the German universities in face of incipient *Gleichschaltung* lay in this stifling of conscience, not in the relatively small number of active National-socialists. In this situation many may have thought that it was their heroic duty to suppress their own personality (as Himmler later inculcated into his SS thugs), that (distorting Max Weber's thesis) their own ethical convictions, their own scruples must be relegated to second place and subordinated to an 'ethic of responsibility' in order to achieve some sublime overall object; in practice this all too frequently amounted to a mere ethic of success. In certain cases such reasoning was no more than rationalization of failure, delusion, erroneous ideas or even short-term opportunism; in every case, however, the process was facilitated by the fact that schools, universities, text-books and even many works of scholarship produced a concept of the state coloured by a combination of idealistic, romanticist and machiavellian ideas. Such views stood in sharp contrast to the cosmopolitanism and dispassionate rationality of German science in the non-ideological disciplines; this led to an incongruous heyday in the racial natural sciences and in medicine. This spiritual readiness to accept *Gleichschaltung* was evidence of a decline, of a loss of moral fibre which had gravely weakened Germany's position in the world of science long before the blood-letting of the war and the post-war period.

2

Turning now to the organizational and practical side of the post-1933 *Gleichschaltung*, it clearly does not do simply to regard the problem as one concerned with the moral or political attitude of certain individuals. Social, professional and institutional conditions played their part. Quite apart from the implications for political personalities, the fact that in 1933 the universities proved themselves so fragile makes their present-day reversion to their pre-Nazi tradition problematic.

As a result of the confrontation with National-socialism three major axioms of university life were demolished: first, that education or qualification in the sciences is productive of moral education; second, that a non-political attitude is a guarantee of scientific objectivity and the best safeguard against political manipulation and ideological gullibility; third, that science, using the word in its broad sense, is a repository of the truth and will so continue irrespective of social or political change. In fact the process of professional specialization and divorce from politics largely contributed to the universities' defencelessness and inability to react. As institutions the universities failed to live up to their own norms and standards of values; they were compelled to accept nazification of entire branches of science and large-scale penetration of their administration. In our so-called 'scientific age' politics and science are necessarily becoming increasingly closely interlocked; historically, therefore, the structural significance of the 1933 political break-through should not be underestimated. It resulted in a devaluation, not only of the political responsibility of the scientist but also of his position and the weight to be attached to his utterances, particularly in as university minded a society as the German. Science was also forced to abandon its vital function of the preservation of scientific standards together with examination and criticism of apparently scientific or ostensibly intellectual ideologies. In 1933, for instance, Hans Schemm, the new Nazi Minister of Culture in Bavaria, stated flatly to the professors of Munich: 'From now on it is not your duty to establish whether something is true but simply whether it is in line with the National-socialist revolution.'

The Nazi programme left no doubt that the main target of their ideological policy would be the educational field. Direct Nazi encroachment upon the schools became possible as a result of the *Gleichschaltung* of the *Länder* in March 1933; alleviating factors, however, were the shortage of Nazi teachers, the chaos of plans and disputes about spheres of authority for which educational policy – like the entire internal policy of the regime – became an arena. In the very first weeks after 30 January the universities were forced to abandon their proud tradition of self-administration and follow the same murky path of compulsion and capitulation as did all other spheres of public life. Disturbances took place; unpopular professors were boycotted, expelled or suspended; rectors, deans and senates were prematurely dismissed. The watchword was 'revolutionization' of scientific and personnel policy; the old catchwords about 'high school reform' and 'rejuvenation of the universities' reappeared in a new guise to give some form of cover to brutal power-policy procedures and trends. Adolf Rein, the Hamburg historian who became 'official adviser on high school reform', proclaimed that National-socialism ushered in a 'great new epoch' and would create a new type of university from which 'all tendencies threatening the interests of the state and people would be eliminated'; the aim, he said, was to produce a university of '*völkisch* science' which would be 'permeated by the *völkisch* political spirit in every fibre of its being'.

In an election manifesto issued on 3 March 1933 three hundred college teachers declared themselves in favour of Hitler. Between April and May, after a violent disagreement with Eduard Spranger, the executive committee of the Colleges' Association, the equivalent of the professors' guild, completed the process of adjustment to the new regime, intrigue and human weaknesses playing a considerable role. There followed certain sensational developments such as the inaugural address by Martin Heidegger, the philosopher, on assuming the rectorship of the University of Freiburg on 27 May 1933; the fact that Heidegger had been a pupil of the philosopher Edmund Husserl, now stigmatized as 'non-Aryan', but was nevertheless prepared to place his reputation at the service of a regime still struggling for recognition, inevitably made a considerable impression. Heidegger, author of *Sein und Zeit* (Existence and Time), now joined the ranks of self-abnegators of German science – 'Your existence is no longer governed by theory and ideas. The Führer himself, and only the Führer, is the incarnation of Germany and German law for the present and the future.' Carl Schmitt, the constitutional lawyer to whom reference has already been made, went even further, singing the praises of the trinity 'State–Movement–people', the title of an article he wrote in 1933; finally he acclaimed the mass murders of 30 June 1934, stressing their legality in an article entitled 'The Führer safeguards the law'. In November 1933 there appeared, carrying over seven hundred signatures, a 'Profession of faith in Adolf Hitler and the National-socialist state' from professors in German universities and colleges. On the eve of the plebiscite of 12 November 1933, during a demonstration in Leipzig, well-known scientists such as Sauer-bruch, Pinder and Heidegger appealed to educated people all over the world to show some understanding of Hitler's policy. On the other side, however, the Nazi critics complained that 'science no longer lends its ear to the rushing stream of life' and that 'with few exceptions the victory of the revolution in higher education has been won without any assistance from the teaching profession, sometimes in face of violent opposition from it.'

It cannot be denied that fear of the Nazi threat to dissolve the universities and turn them into specialist schools played some part in this conformism and readiness to accept *Gleichschaltung*. Hitler himself authorized the planning of a 'Nazi elite university' under Alfred Rosenberg; it was to be known as the 'Senior School'. The project was overtaken by the war, however, before more than a few institutes were in operation; they bore such titles as 'Institute for Aryan History', 'Institute for Racial Doctrine', 'Institute for Investigation of the Jewish Question, "Institute for Investigation of Freemasonry' and so forth; they possessed libraries stocked with loot primarily from Jewish sources.

Semi-official propaganda highlighted the three major tasks of Nazi educational reform: 'Creation of a new type of student, creation of a new type of teacher and formation of a new concept of science.' 'Solution' of the first two tasks was pursued during the early years by severe restriction of the number of new students, by the provision that only a limited number of those matriculating would be granted a school certificate depending on their reliability from the point of view of character and national sentiment, also by a suitable personnel policy. The Nazi concept of science was governed entirely by its racial *Weltanschauung* with its claim to omniscience and so was diametrically opposed to the whole trend of modern university life; 'unprejudiced science', alleged to be a hereditary German failing, was violently opposed as an 'obsolete scientific idea'; research and teaching became no more than instruments in the service of the new regime. All this was an obvious sequence of events. Hitler himself had been quite specific in *Mein Kampf* in allotting a new order of priority to National-socialist schooling and education; science –

which he referred to as 'scientific education' – was specifically allotted third place after 'toughening' both of the body and the character.

The new rulers contrived to enforce principles such as these in all educational institutions; the principle of authoritarian, military-type regimentation was extended from the political and social sector into the universities. In many cases this accelerated the process of ideological *Gleichschaltung*. Even reputable scholars, whose sociological and philosophical seminars had hitherto included 'left-wingers' and 'Jewish intelligentsia', now, in the months of 'revolutionary change', acknowledged that the primary duty of the universities was to dispense new-style political education and to be 'the high school of the state' (Freyer's description). Nazi educational and college ideologists such as Ernst Krieck, the Frankfurt professor (and rector from 1933), had demanded *völkisch* political education in the universities even before the seizure of power; his phraseology was unmistakable – 'Faced with the task falling to the colleges the teacher has no autonomy or liberty; he simply renders service.' The universities, he considered, should be granted only a limited degree of technical self-administration – 'The community, represented by the state, should ensure that no self-administering member breaks ranks and fails to pursue the pledged aim of a *"völkisch Weltanschauung"* and the unity of the people. This puts an end to liberalistic science as an aim in itself.'

There were, of course, signs of resistance, of some capacity to retain a minimum of independent existence in certain faculties and institutions. Top-level Party agencies were continually finding it necessary to issue 'a fundamental clarification of the relationship between National-socialism and science and to . . . hand out the necessary answer to all those who think that, from the platform of a science, they can lay down the law to National-socialism as to what it should do in the scientific field.' Despite all its voluntary *Gleichschaltung* such warnings to science were issued to the very end. In general, however, using personnel and financial policy as weapons, the Nazis abolished the electoral principle for senior academic bodies, turned the nomination of deans and rectors into a matter for official decision and made the Führer principle, hopelessly unsuitable though it was, applicable to the universities – the rector became the 'Führer' of the university and the chancellor his 'chief of staff', in other words, all on semi-military lines. Ernst Anrich, the Bonn historian, for instance, wished to see the universities 'become troop units' and professors be ready to 'co-operate on military lines' (his book, published in Stuttgart

in 1936 was entitled *The Universities as Intellectual Frontier Fortifications*).
The aim of all this was to eliminate the last vestiges of self-administration;
owing to the continuing conflict of ambitions and rivalries, however, no
permanent uniform settlement was ever achieved.

The purpose of this 'college reform', therefore, was solely to promote a
single political ideology. Qualitatively its disastrous effects can hardly be
overestimated; the frequently misused phrase about 'dismantlement of
German science' is entirely apt. Intellectual Germany moved across the
frontiers and joined the exiles; it has not yet recovered from this exodus
and self-inflicted mutilation. The most extreme case was the radical
transformation of political science (which had its enemies anyway)
evidenced in the total *Gleichschaltung* of the Institute for Political Science
(*Hochschule fur Politik*) in Berlin, also in the energy with which planning
and expansion of a new 'defence science' was pursued within the universities. There were, of course, considerable differences of opinion within
the system. Nevertheless in all relevant fields, particularly German scholarship, history, jurisprudence and biology, the guiding principles were
those of the philosophy of people and race; even in totally non-political
disciplines such as the natural sciences the campaign against Jewish men of
learning (such as Einstein) was pursued, culminating in a specifically
German, racially coloured theory of physics and mathematics.

Quantitatively the structural change in the universities is a clear
illustration of the extent of the 'revolution'. According to various tentative estimates, by 1933-4 dismissals had amounted to the following:
professors-in-ordinary 313, extra-ordinary 109, unofficial extra-ordinary
284, honorary 75, freelance lecturers 322, readers and the like 42, assistants
232, staff of scientific institutes 133, academics in schools, libraries and
museums 174. A British calculation put the total of scientific personnel
dismissed at 1,684. The Nazis attempted to conceal the official figures but
it seems that by 1934 almost 15 per cent of the pre-1933 teaching profession
and 11 per cent of professors in ordinary had been removed. Moreover
these figures cover only the notorious cases and leave out of account the
innumerable marginal cases of individual demotion, intimidation or
indirect harassment. In many cases the expulsion of one or two outstanding professors entailed the transformation of an entire faculty or
abandonment of a complete line of science. It is noteworthy that the
proportion of personnel changes differed widely in individual universities.
Heading the list were the vital universities of Berlin and Frankfurt on Main
with over 32 per cent, Heidelberg with over 24 per cent, Breslau with

22 per cent, Göttingen, Freiburg, Hamburg and Cologne with 18–19 per cent; Rostock with 4 per cent and Tübingen with 1.6 per cent were the most stable. Overall the universities with 16.6 per cent dismissals suffered more severely than the technical high schools with 10.7 per cent; statistically the greatest sufferers were the medical and, not surprisingly, the juridical faculties (21.2 per cent). Approximate estimates show that at least one-third of the lecturers in these subjects was suspended on 'racial' grounds, 56 per cent on 'racial or political' grounds and some 6.5 per cent retired 'voluntarily'; the figure for juridical faculties is of special interest since here dismissals for anti-semitic reasons reached 78.5 per cent.

The extent of the personnel changes and the resulting loss to science may be judged by the fact that in the first year a whole series of Nobel Prize winners (Meyerhof, Franck, Einstein, Haber, Hertz) were removed from office; in addition through numerous compulsory postings complete scientific units were dispersed and academic activity was hampered by the continual threat of denunciation even by pupils and assistants, with the consequential suspicion and fear. In contrast to previous tradition non-Nazi teachers could never be sure how long their appointments or salaries would continue; they were under permanent threat of intervention from outside by, for instance, manipulation of the curriculum, withdrawal of the right of examination or denunciation within their own seminars; they were forced to engage in non-academic political activity; they were tormented by the thought of their persecuted colleagues; they were continually being forced to conform and submit against the dictates of their conscience. As a sop or self-deception they clung to the remnants of the old system; formally the constitution of the various faculties was maintained; deans and rectors were given a status superior to professor in ordinary; titles, decorations and symbols acted as a sedative.

A new atmosphere invaded the faculties. On 13 December 1934 fresh regulations were issued governing the licensing of academic lecturers; these made the selection of lecturers authorized to teach (in contrast to freelance lecturers who, however, equally had to produce proof of 'Aryan' origin) dependent on the regime's requirements in such matters as non-scientific political qualifications, attendance at 'community camps' and 'lecturers' academies', estimation of character by the rector and Ministry of Culture, the leader of the lecturers' association and other Party agencies. In a news sheet (*National-socialist Education 1934*) Professor Ernst Sturm, rector of the Berlin Technical High School, justified all this as follows: 'In the new Germany the Ministry of Education will not authorize as freelance lecturers gross materialists or dessicated pen-pushers ... The place for all proper lecturers is in the SA ... so that the German scholar who has no contact with the people will soon be a thing of the past.' As early as the seizure of power phase the younger generation, new lecturers who were to be 'leaders of youth', were subjected to a new procedure even more effective than the numerous dismissals in enforcing *Gleichschaltung* on the German universities and ensuring that they were reduced to mere functional instruments of a political ideology.

3

The same tendencies were in evidence inside the German higher education system. As already mentioned the number of students was deliberately restricted in parallel with the reduction of the teaching body; those refused entry were primarily Jews, foreigners and females, a particularly glaring example of the exclusion of women from the emancipation process which was one of the main principles of National-socialist policy. At first sight such measures, apparently directed against students, may seem paradoxical. The National-socialist revolution, after all, was carried out by a combination of coercion from above and a 'movement' from below; students in general were intoxicated by the regime's promises and successes and so violent, turbulent activity on the part of students suited the regime's tactics. During the spring of 1933 students had supported and frequently intensified the regime's brutal 'purges'; they boycotted unpopular professors, attacked Jews and opponents among their fellow students, made a show of wearing uniform, made inflammatory statements both inside and outside the universities and, during both lectures and seminars, insisted on exaggerated professions of political faith, expecting and demanding that their professors do the same.

Long before 1933 a nationwide organization with *völkish* and expansionist leanings had been formed, the *Deutsche Studentenschaft* (German Students' Association); this was permanently at odds with the democratic educational authorities and later fell into line with Nazi propaganda and the National-socialist Students' League promoted by Baldur von Schirach. At the 'German Students' Day' in Graz in 1931 a Nazi majority had emerged and elected as president a leading member of the Nazi Students' League; elections to students' committees in many universities also produced the same picture, support coming primarily from the nationalist corporations. University structure was still largely on a socially exclusive basis and this fact played some part. After 1918 the privilege of higher education had remained that of the bourgeoisie; the students' unions, which worked on the majority principle, were traditionalist, nationalist, conservative and anti-semitic; they were a good recruiting ground for the anti-democratic movement directed against the Weimar Republic. Their background was black–white–red and monarchist; they were basically non-political and anti-party and therefore all the more easily manoeuvrable. Accordingly in 1923 the German students' associations as a whole were emphatic supporters of the Hitler *putsch*. In summer 1932 the last 'German Students' Day' (assembled not in a university but, significantly, in a barracks in Königsberg) put forward its demands – elimination of the principle of democratic self-administration and introduction of the 'Führer principle'. Through caution, conformism or sympathy a number of professors contributed to this development, in some cases preventing disciplinary proceedings.

The early weeks of the seizure of power were characterized by student activism in many universities. In Berlin the rector was presented with 'twelve theses against the university's un-German spirit', in effect an ultimatum demanding *Gleichschaltung*; among the demands was one to the effect that Jewish professors only be allowed to publish works in Hebrew. In Kiel the students threatened to use force and demanded the dismissal of twenty-eight professors; on 22 April 'the Fighting Committee Against the Un-German Spirit' confiscated from the university library all books written by lecturers who 'neither possessed nor deserved the confidence of the student body and who were unacceptable for reconstruction of the German higher education system'. Nazi records show that in Breslau an SA detachment under a student of philosophy appeared in many of the main bookshops and declared a large number of books confiscated, including those of Arnold and Stefan Zweig, Jakob Wassermann, Erich Kästner, Lion Feuchtwanger, Kurt Tucholsky, Thomas Mann and others. Finally the culminating point was reached in May 1933 when books were publicly burned in the squares of university cities, accompanied by inflammatory speeches by Germanist professors. The fact that so philistine a procedure was accepted or sanctioned by the universities put them finally and hopelessly on the defensive.

Then, however, the short-lived 'revolutionary' role of the students was brought to an end and its place was taken by permanent absolute direction and regimentation from above. Acceptable rectors having been installed and far-reaching 'reforms' institutionalized by law, the strict 'order' of the totalitarian state became the order of the day replacing turbulent revolutionary action; from May 1933 stern ministerial instructions emphasized discipline, authority and achievement; after a short but violent blaze of activity 'spontaneous action' on the part of students ended. The tradition of academic independence was kept within strict limits and the dictatorship's ban of silence descended on the student movement. Legal regulations were accordingly issued, starting with Prussia on 12 April 1933 and progressing from the Reich law of 7 February 1934 to the new criminal code of 4 January 1935; the students' unions or 'professional unions' (in the technical schools) were made subject to a central, nation-wide organization, the 'Reich Union' (*Reichschaft*) under the 'Reich Union Leader'. This included all students and student associations with an 'Aryan' membership; following the 'Führer principle' it was subordinate to the Minister of Culture who appointed its senior leaders.

The 'new type of student' was to be educated through semi-military community service. On 1 August 1933, for instance, as a preparatory measure for the introduction of universal labour service, the entire body of fourth-year students was called up for labour service. On 16 June at a demonstration of the German Students' Union on the Opernplatz, Berlin, Rust had declaimed:

> I must emphasize one point here: the true great practical educational establishment is not over there (in other words in the universities) nor in the High Schools but in the labour camps. There pedagogy and verbiage cease and action begins . . . Anyone who proves himself a failure in the labour camp has forfeited the right to aspire to a leading academic position in Germany.

In February 1934, some time before the introduction of compulsory labour service as the 'school of the nation' on 26 June 1935, the German Students' Union announced six months' compulsory service for all those matriculating and wishing to go to college – four months in a labour camp and two months in an SA camp. The National-socialist Students' League was maintained as a Nazi *corps d'élite* and an illustration of the parallellism between Party and state; it comprised a militant minority of the general body of students now subject to *Gleichschaltung*; it was the safeguard en-suring that, not only the Minister of Culture but also the monopoly party could exert both a direct powerful influence and unceasing control, over the life of the universities. There was no mention of elections or effective initiative in the emotional pronouncements from on high which set up the German Students' Union; it had no function other than to ensure the

Gleichschaltung of university life and to support the regime; according to the official pronouncements its political duty lay in bringing together the 'high school community' and the 'popular community' (*Volksgemeinschaft*). In contrast to the provisions of even the Prussian law of April 1933, the traditions of student self-administration and participation in the running of the universities vanished almost totally with the Reich law of 1934.

So, in contrast to the pathos about freedom issuing from the students of the 'struggle period', after a few months all academic freedom was at an end – for pupils as well as teachers. In a statement issued on 31 January 1934 even the catholic students' unions paid tribute to the National-socialist revolution as the basis of their education. Stirrings of resistance from the organization known as *Allgemeine Deutsche Waffenring* soon ceased to be a subject of public discussion. There followed decisions by most of the German students' associations to disband themselves, alternatively the enthusiastic voluntary incorporation of their remnants into the Nazi Students' Union, a special occasion being the 120th anniversary of the Wartburg Festival on 18 October 1935. Almost at the same time the aristocratic Kösen Students' Society and its affiliated organizations disbanded themselves; they had already welcomed and supported the 'national revolution'. So the external seal was set on capitulation; nevertheless, although overshadowed by the general *Gleichschaltung* and finally ostensibly as part of the Nazi Students' Union, a number of traditional groupings managed to eke out some form of independent existence.

So the road ahead was charted. The entire system of higher education was to be politically controlled and functionalized through strict regulations governing selection which insisted on active membership of the Hitler Youth together with physical, 'racial' and 'character' suitability. The pay and promotion system was also geared to the selection of future academics on National-socialist principles; this was intended to form an additional safeguard for the process of *Gleichschaltung* in matters of teaching and science; in the case of some of the older students and college teachers, where the process had not been so rapid or so thorough, it was intended to ensure that, in the future, *Gleichschaltung* would be complete. Whatever could be done through technical methods of domination and a suitable personnel policy was largely achieved during the seizure of power phase. On the surface *Gleichschaltung* was complete and, sadly, it was acclaimed by many intellectual and literary fellow travellers; hundreds of books and thousands of articles provided tragic evidence. Nevertheless the attempts to produce a broad scientific basis for the racial doctrine, to rewrite convincing technical literature and to lay the foundations of new disciplines made little progress; facts were against them and scientific discussion was repeatedly exerting its effect on scholars and teachers who had ostensibly accepted *Gleichschaltung*.

Even a totalitarian regime was unable to overcome this conflict of mind and spirit – hence the regime's continuing suspicion and the abuse hurled by the Party which was simply accepted in silence; a typical example was the remark made by the notorious Gauleiter Julius Streicher in Berlin University in 1938: 'If you put the brains of all the university professors on one side of a pair of scales and the Führer's brain on the other, which side, do you think, would go down?' Alternatively, to take an example from within a university, a speech made in 1934 by a well-known Professor of Ancient History (Kahrstedt) to commemorate the founding of the Reich ended with the words: 'We say farewell to international science; we say farewell to the international republic of scholars; we say farewell to research for the sake of research. *Sieg Heil!*' That confidence and faith in the liberating function and effect of science, which had carried all before it in the western world ever since the dawn of the age of enlightenment, apparently received a cruel setback. No book has yet been written on education and intellect under the Nazi system but when it is, its balance sheet will be a sad one. Hitler himself was entitled to feel justified in his profound scorn for science, intellectuals and lawyers.

4

Nevertheless, the Nazi regime was never able to solve completely to its own liking the problem of the relationship between science and politics. Although externally subordination was complete, at heart total *Gleichschaltung* never succeeded; accordingly the new rulers harboured an increasing and lasting suspicion of everything implied by the word 'intellect' – a word of abuse to them anyway. They were forced to recognize that they could subject institutional arrangements to total control but not thought itself. As early as August 1934 a Nazi newspaper (*Der Stürmer*) was fulminating: 'There is continuous grousing and whispering in the passages of the universities. One development is very noticeable – reading of foreign newspapers. At least 60 per cent, and probably more, are against us.' In a speech in Hamburg on 23 May 1935 Kaufmann, the *Reichsstatthalter* (Reich Regent) lamented that 'not even 10 per cent of young people in college are working actively with us'. Remarkable examples of independence of thought, research and teaching, or tenacity and sacrifice in all fields are known. Under these conditions the old phrase *qui tacet consentire videtur* (silence gives consent) did not apply. Silence, in fact, often indicated resistance because conformism and lip-service were being demanded everywhere.

Conditions differed in every case; it is not possible to generalize on possibilities of resistance. The disastrous feature was, however, that this passive resistance, this non-*Gleichschaltung* inevitably led to fragmentation and isolation. Suspicion and spying meant that a true exchange of ideas could only take place in camouflaged language or conspiratorially. The continuous process of specialization and fragmentation had made both science and the universities particularly vulnerable to the assault of rapacious political and ideological forces. The missing components were a broader view of the place and importance within society of the various specialized disciplines and political education as a part of general education; had this been adequate, not merely on paper but in practice, the dilemma of specialization could have been solved and critical judgements formed. The experiences of this period showed that it is possible to be a good professional expert but a bad citizen. The saving, preventive function of political education is to counter both extremism and quietism and to alleviate the stresses and strains betwen the worlds of science and politics without subjugating the one to the other. In 1933 there was a great hiatus here and so National-socialism was able to impose its own concept of political education which was in fact a unilateral *diktat* instead of broad and varied direction in the political and social fields.

Here was posed the basic problem of science in the modern world. Specialized in its ivory tower and as far as possible divorced from day–to–day affairs, it tries to avoid contact with actuality. Consequently it often finds difficulty in assuming political responsibility or, if need be, offering resistance in the political field. The individual protest was, therefore, doubly courageous but it was isolated by suspicion and fear; the conflict, therefore, constituted no danger to the regime as should have been the case had a common stance been adopted; this was the essential, for all were threatened irrespective of their political sympathies. Had this happened, the regime would have been vulnerable since, lacking its own experts, it needed the co-operation of science. Similarly, in the administration, the regime used and misused the old corps of officials; once determined opponents had been isolated and removed, the remainder were lulled, deceived and paralysed by the ostensible separation between party and state. The great necessity was to make a beginning (as was stated in the first resistance leaflet produced by the Scholls), to break out of the vicious circle in which 'everyone was waiting for someone else to make a move' and so all were to blame. In 1942 the clear decisive tones of this courageous call from Munich finally put an end to the paralysis which had afflicted university and intellectual life in Germany ever since its declaration of bankruptcy in 1933 followed by the years of despotism.

In terms of practical achievement resistance in the Third Reich was a failure. Its failure illustrates the fact that, in a society which is not democratic and open, education and science, particularly the intellectual and social sciences in their broadest sense, are exposed to overwhelming temptations and manipulations which can turn them into mere instruments of politics and ideology. A regime such as that of National-socialism is only conceivable and practicable if the educated classes are politically passive and if, at the same time, it is met halfway by tendencies such as those which flourished in the partially non-political, partially openly anti-democratic atmosphere of the German universities. Thinking was perverted by dreams of *Realpolitik* based on power and so these tendencies had been growing in non-Nazi as well as Nazi minds ever since 1918 or even 1870 and had found their expression in professorial speeches and students' associations.

The universities were not the only aspect of life in Germany to be struck by catastrophe in 1933 and so one returns again and again to the vital question of the wider intellectual and social conditions which made that catastrophe possible. The real disaster lay not in the criminality of a minority but in the failure of the educated majority, in their sin of omission to uphold the right – Theodor Heuss's 'collective shame'. This illustrates how short is the step between unthinking fulfilment of professional duty and culpable behaviour or action; it illustrates too the end result of that simulated or actual blindness springing from a timorous closure of the mind to everything not immediately connected with one's own specialized field. In political matters the result was 'a partial eclipse of the sun', a readiness to obey authority, to hide behind the moral defence of unquestioning fulfilment of duty and of *force majeure*. So, like the civil servants and the officers, all too many leading figures in the universities, helplessly or even willingly, accepted the Nazi *Gleichschaltung*.

7

Loyalty to the State and Resistance

'The power of state to command and compel is valid only in so far as it serves the good of the community ... If the authority of the state is obviously and continuously misused, the people have a right to defend themselves.' This was written by Eugen Bolz, ex-President of the state of Württemberg, and he wrote it in spring 1934 when the National-Socialist regime was in almost total control of the state and society in Germany. The author had been forced to resign by terrorism, had been under arrest for several weeks and was still under permanent threat and surveillance; coming at such a moment, therefore, this was clearly intended as something more than a theoretical reminder of the time-honoured principles of philosophy familiar to western thought for centuries.

Bolz was a politician of conservative leanings for whom the state signified far more than a mere practical arrangement, the validity of which could be questioned; the fact that he could openly refer to a people's right of resistance to the authority of the state, therefore, meant that he was prepared to accept a high degree of risk. This was the fundamental problem faced by the loyal German citizen when, by ostensibly legal means, a dictatorial movement, promising all things to all men and camouflaged beneath a national, social and even christian ideology, had manoeuvred itself into power and now, with bewitching success, was imposing *Gleichschaltung* at home and mobilizing Germany for adventure abroad, in other words for expansion. We now know that the people of those days who allowed themselves to be impressed by these things and co-operated, were the victims of illusion; after critical examination of our more recent history we also know more about the severe problems of a political, social and intellectual nature which prevented the democratic virtues prevailing and made people susceptible to authoritarian and totalitarian ideas.

The great test and the great failure was the break-through by Nazism, the German catastrophe of 1933. It is still today the source of renewed controversy about state consciousness in Germany and about the right and duty to resist. In the Kaiser's empire of 1870 loyalty to the state was based primarily on the political and economic successes gained by an authoritarian regime with an efficiently functioning administration. In face of this situation the old demands for democratization and modernization of the constitutional system receded.

There were weighty historical reasons for this. Modern times have seen the rise of the absolute state with its thorough organization of all spheres of life on strict bureaucratic and military lines; with this has gone an overriding concept of political obedience which has displaced the older tradition of the right to resist; it is still exerting its effect today on the relationship between authority and the subject. The revolutions in Britain, America and France, of course, offered greater scope than ever before to the citizen's right of independent decision. Simultaneously, however, the principle of nationalism gained both in intensity and potency and as a result the newly won internal political freedoms gave way to increased state centralism.

This was particularly the case in Germany where, after the failure of the 1848 revolution, liberalism, once so potent a force, withdrew in face of this development and postponed its internal political claims in favour of national unity and a strong foreign policy. For the sake of these advantages the semi-absolutist structure of the Bismarckian Reich was accepted; admittedly it was no police state but nevertheless freedom of the subject was restricted to narrow limits indeed, as shown by the *Kulturkampf* and the anti-socialist law. In the minds of the citizenry the idea of freedom became applicable to external rather than internal politics, and as a result loyalty to the state became based on external successes; the capacity for constructive opposition, therefore, by which a parliamentary system based on the rule of law stands or falls, visibly withered. Little change took place when, after Bismarck's dismissal, confidence in the patriarchal state suffered its first setbacks. No more proof is required than the helplessness of the Reichstag in the years before and during the First World War and the small practical impact made by constructive political criticism prior to the revolution of 1918.

Herein lie many of the underlying reasons for the difficulties which were the hallmark of the career and the fate of the first German republic. The republic was born not of some deliberate decision by the majority of the population to revise the relationship between rulers and ruled but of an unexpected defeat; it was a compromise emergency solution, unwillingly accepted. Its continuing crises and ultimate failure left their mark upon those who might have been prepared to resist the National-socialist dictatorship.

Naturally any statement to the effect that Hitler's dictatorship was a direct consequence of mass democracy and its system of equal universal suffrage is untenable. The fact remains that even with the most intensive propaganda campaign and under pressure of the most severe economic and political crisis, the National-socialists never succeeded in mobilizing more than one-third of the German electorate. It is equally significant, however, that the two-thirds who were opposed to National-socialism (or at least, not voting for it) on 30 January 1933 were incapable of producing any effective defence against the imposition of Hitler's dictatorship. They seemed to be in a state of stupor or self-deception, of susceptibility to illusion, opportunism or readiness to accept *faits accomplis*; foreign countries reacted similarly when they accepted the Third Reich as partner in alliances or made concessions to it which they had refused to the Weimar Republic.

A major reason for this failure lay in the cloak of legality under which Hitler was nominated chancellor and was then able to progress from presidential coalition government to unrestricted dictatorship. Despite increasing loss of power by democratic and parliamentary agencies, when Hitler took the oath to the republican constitution an overwhelming number of powerful positions were still in the hands of non-Nazis. This was the case with most *Land* governments and with their police; it was so in the case of local governing bodies, the trades unions and economic interest-groups; it was even the case in the Reichswehr, although there, as the position of the Reich president was soon to show, little reliance could be placed on formal positions of power to guarantee the exertion of any actual control over the new rulers or support of any resistance against them.

The history of the Weimar Republic had shown that a constitution, however carefully contrived, was of little assistance if attitudes of mind originating from the pre-democratic, patriarchal concept of the state persisted, giving rise to increasing suspicion of the republic and of democracy together with renewed yearnings for authoritarian leadership. Large sections of the populace, even if not caught up in the impetuous rise of the NSDAP during the closing years of the Republic, were not prepared for any form of resistance to the new regime; after all it proclaimed itself as the true German state as opposed to the feeble interlude of democracy. Like the majority of constitutional lawyers people overlooked certain facts which patriotic politicians like Eugen Bolz realized only too well despite all their criticism of the Republic's weaknesses; these facts were that the National-socialist concept of the state was diametrically opposed to one based on good order and the rule of law, that for Hitler and his *apparatschiks* the state was no more than an instrument for the pursuit of their racial and expansionist aims, that the National-socialist tyranny had developed parallel to and superimposed on the state, leaving the state as an empty façade. The party became the state and the state the party, as Waldemar Besson put it. The Third Reich's 'dual state' exemplified for Ernst Fraenkel in his book written in 1941 by the parallel existence of the judiciary and the concentration camp system, inevitably developed into the SS state and the SS empire. A victorious war was then to set the seal on what, as Eberhard Jäckel has recently shown, had been Hitler's *Weltanschauung* ever since 1923. Many ideologists of the state realized only too late that the Third Reich's ostensibly so legal and efficient totalitarian state was an illusion and that the reality was chaos, deliberately created by an arbitrary tyranny raised to the status of an ideology.

The fact, therefore, that the regime's *coup d'état* was camouflaged by a process of pseudo-legal seizure of power made the conditions for resistance and its prospects decidedly more difficult. Any attempt at constitutional protest or opposition according to the previous democratic rules of the game was stifled or suppressed by the security measures or terrorist methods of the new rulers, combined with a claim to legality put forward with considerable sophistication. Only two possibilities apparently remained: for the remnants of the persecuted groups, particularly the left–wing, who escaped murder or the concentration camp and would neither resign themselves to the situation nor conform, disappearance into the 'underground', the logical step but a dangerous one; alternatively the attempt to acquire some influential position in the regime in order to organize resistance from within or at least have some possibility of exerting a restraining influence. This second course of action raised the whole problem of opposition by means of partial collaboration, a problem debated over and over again to the bitter end. Continuing loyalty to the authority of the state played its part here. People felt too that, if effective action was to be taken against the totalitarian system with its rigid controls, they must have influential contacts inside the machine. This, however, led to complicated situations covered by the ambiguous saying so frequently misused during those years for purposes of self-justification: that despite realization of the criminality of the regime one must remain in office in order to prevent something worse and exploit one's position to build up effective opposition from within.

This naturally applied with particular force to the civil servants who, though severely intimidated, were left with some freedom of action owing to the lack of qualified Nazi personnel. The situation in the Reichswehr was similar, though there only a small number of officers were able to resist the attraction exerted by the community of interest between the military and the new rulers who were so much more 'defence minded' than the republican governments. Outside the state organization and in areas not so directly exposed to persecution and oppression the view generally held was that a certain degree of co-operation was acceptable in order to assist the – supposedly – good elements in the regime and protect one's own interests. This was the case over considerable areas of industrial and cultural life; it also applied to the ambiguous and highly debatable attitude of the churches to the National-socialist tyranny. In many cases it was a long time before the final decision between collaboration and resistance was taken – in contrast to those who were persecuted and outlawed in the early days and had long since chosen the first alternative – non-co-operation and the underground. All the more significant, therefore, was the fact that scattered groups were to be found working together consisting of men who, irrespective of their political or social background, stood out against terror and deception; they bore witness to the fact that, even in Germany and in the face of inhibiting tradition, the citizen's sense of moral and political responsibility had not been entirely eradicated. They looked back for support to the traditions of socialism, liberalism and conservatism, too, to the religious and humanist view of mankind and the world. Their purpose was to break the paralysing yet intoxicating spell which the regime had cast over the whole life of Germany, but the decisive impulse for their actions came from a tortured conscience; this steeled them and gave them courage. Conscience had been aroused by the sight of fellow human beings being tortured, persecuted and terrorized and would not be lulled by fashionable remarks such as Hugenberg's appalling comment with which he tried to console his following: 'When you use a plane, there will be shavings.'

There were stirrings of resistance frequently stemming from entirely individual decisions and cutting across all the old party and ideological boundaries. This gives the lie to the accusation so frequently made that resistance sprang solely from fear of loss of the war. Its origin lay in far deeper human and moral reactions, in a revolt of conscience produced in men of the most varied background by the brutality of the Nazi tyranny. The flame of resistance activity was lit by the fundamental and urgent duty to bring aid to the persecuted and dispossessed; men of similar views came together and exchanged information on what was really happening behind the smokescreen of official propaganda issuing from a regimented press and literature: finally they sought to organize contacts and build bridges to other people and groups in order to expand the basis of their charitable but at the same time oppositionist activity and finally proceed to political action. In the light of the historical and psychological inhibitions, of the profound problem posed by any decision to resist, the fact that there was resistance at all shows that more people had the courage to refuse to conform than has been the case in much of recent German history.

All this means that the decision to resist was one taken in terrible lone-liness in the midst of a mass society. It entailed the permanent strain of suspicion, scepticism and silence, danger for family and friends, isolation from the misguided majority of one's compatriots; to counterbalance all this there was no visible heroism, no halo of political glory. Here lay the difference between the German opposition and resistance movements in the occupied countries.

Above all, however, after the long decline of the bourgeois democratic movement, the resistance could not trace its antecedents back to any political tradition, as could the political Left. The impulse to civil resis-tance sprang from the daily confrontation with the manifestations of dictatorship, from decisions of the individual conscience and from the sense of right and wrong. This was the special feature of the German situation; historically one of the great services rendered by the resistance was that it brought some fluidity to the political groupings which had solidified under the Weimar Republic; its confrontation with the totalitarian regime led to a multiplicity of contacts across the frontiers of the old anti-fascist/socialist camp and the old parties or ideologies. In-dividual resistance circuits often formed spontaneously and they frequently included the most disparate social and political characters. This fact was of major significance for their subsequent wider co-operation, particularly after 1938.

There was much debate over the question (to which Goerdeler's efforts were primarily devoted) whether and to what extent it was possible to infiltrate important key positions and win over their incumbents; a further problem was the reinforcement of contact with the military and the involvement of the army, the most important force outside the Party, in political action against the Nazi regime. A long and dangerous road had to be travelled before 20 July 1944 gave the answer to these questions. This date has come to be regarded as the ultimate great symbol of the resistance movement, although it was in fact only *one* action among the innumerable attempts to save the situation made from 30 January 1933 onwards.

In this situation the figure of Eugen Bolz is noteworthy for two major reasons: his view of the state was coloured by his Württemberg origins and he tended to support Brüning's questionable policy of practical politics placing the state above parliament and party; second, following the tradition of the Centre Party, Bolz was by no means whole-hearted in his acceptance of democracy. This aspect has been the subject of fundamental examination in the valuable books by Waldemar Besson, Max Miller and Rudolf Morsey. It is particularly significant that in the years before 1933 Bolz, like many of his colleagues including Brüning and the Centre Party leaders, was increasingly critical of the parliamentary democratic system and this he combined with a belief in the possibility of a de-politicized policy based solely on practicality and standing above party. In contrast to most others, however, he had no illusions about the much-trumpeted 'national rising' which promised, with a wealth of popular slogans, to replace the much abused multi-party system by a tightly controlled state.

Few heads of government of the *Länder* were so outspoken as Bolz after 30 January 1933; he was certain to become a special target for Hitler's wrath, for he placed obstacles in the way of the Führer's demonstrations and in Ulm on 12 February 1933 spoke plainly and courageously against Hugenberg, the spirit of Potsdam and the Nazi terror, calling for adherence to the constitution, the law and liberty. Murr and Mergenthaler, the Nazi potentates in Stuttgart, accordingly started a violent campaign of vilification against him; Bolz was the target for the tirade of hatred to which Murr, his successor, gave vent at the Nazi victory festival on the evening of 15 March 1933 – 'The new government will strike down with the utmost brutality anyone who opposes it. We do not say: an eye for an eye and a tooth for a tooth. No! If anyone tears out our eye we will knock off his head and if anyone breaks one of our teeth we will break his jaw.'

As the years went by Bolz saw his worst fears confirmed until ultimately he became a member of the inner resistance circle and was destined to participate in the planned post-Hitler government. His attitude is illuminating from two points of view: first it illustrates the questionable nature of Centre Party policy and second, it throws doubt upon the possibility of the formation of a bourgeois block with a concept of the state based solely on efficiency and the ethos of practical service combined with scepticism about any solution of the crisis by democratic means involving the inclusion of the social-democrats and all non-totalitarian forces. On the other hand, Bolz was one of those few who remained incorruptibly loyal to the constitution, who realized that unalterable limits were set to the authority of any state and the degree of co-operation which could be demanded by its rulers and, finally, who recognized the citizen's right of self-defence. He is an illustration of the fact that such an attitude could spring from a conservative, christian, liberal or socialist background.

On 21 December 1944, after months of close arrest, Eugen Bolz faced Freisler's bloody assize. The picture of the accused is still with us – emaciated, marked by suffering but still standing foursquare. On the afternoon of 23 January 1945 he was executed in Plötzensee prison, Berlin, together with nine other resisters including Graf Moltke, Theo Haubach the socialist, Nikolaus Gross the christian trade union leader, and Erwin Planck, son of the great physicist.

2

Resistance to dictatoral despotism, *coup d'état* against a state based on injustice, assassination attempt to liberate the people from the spell of a criminal leadership – these are the phrases to be heard when tribute is paid to the events of 20 July. Political murder, oath-breaking and treachery – these are catchwords still used in wide circles today to cast suspicion on these events or condemn them. The view we take of this historical controversy will determine our attitude, not only to the phenomenon of National-socialism but to more recent German history in general. Under such different political circumstances, however, is an aversion to the Hitler regime and its failure a matter of immediate practical import? We must not be deceived by festivities frequently of an artificially encouraging nature; both the historical data and their relevance to the present constitute a problem which is still with us; yet though it remains the subject of debate for some, others simply push it aside.

As always, the view taken of the anti-Hitler resistance fluctuates; it may be regarded as of relative importance only in the context of history or be the subject of uncritical adulation; it may be used by those who indulge in a non-political search for an alibi for the nation or by those who defiantly insist that there was good in National-socialism. Primarily, however, the change in thinking and attitude brought about by the end of the post-war period and the transition from the generation which lived through these things to that which was born afterwards have pushed these problems into the background so that any attempt to relate them to the present seems increasingly unrealistic. Terms such as opposition and resistance, impotence and the right to use force have undergone far-reaching change and now carry very different meanings whether applied to actual or historical, practical or theoretical problems. There is, after all, a fundamental difference between a struggle against dictatorship and a demand for greater democratization.

The concrete historical data, which must form the basis of any estimate of the resistance or lessons to be drawn from it, have only been fully brought to light in recent years as a result of a series of fundamental investigations. For twenty years solemn, often somewhat apologetic, appreciations were the order of the day as exemplified by the books of Hans Rothfels, Eberhard Zeller and Gerhard Ritter; now, however, books such as Eberhard Bethge's biography of Bonhoeffer, Gerd van Roon's specialized account of the Kreisau Circle, Harold Deutsch's and Peter Hoffmann's detailed description of the conspiracies and a recently published biography of Stauffenberg by Christian Müller have produced the basis for accurate realistic evaluation of events and motives. There is still much to come to complete the picture – on the position of the working class and political Left, for instance, as also on the controversial role of the catholic church and the attitude of officialdom and of industry.

Any discussion must start from the assumption that the decisive date of the German catastrophe is 1933 – not 1939 or 1944-5. This applies particularly to the problem of the resistance. Nazism's pseudo-legal seizure of power presented the old question of resistance to tyrannical domination in a new light. The difficulties to be overcome by an opposition to a state which, ostensibly legally, had come under control of a single party by means of emergency regulations, an enabling law and plebiscites were quite different to those faced by the classic type of resistance to a violent *coup d'état* or open usurpation. The effect of the Nazi theory of the 'legal revolution' was to confuse people's minds and weaken all opposing forces. This both influenced the character and impaired the prospects of opposition to a regime which, in so short a space of time, had managed, by ostensibly democratic manoeuvres, to impose an all-embracing tyranny upon the state and society. Moreover the intellectual and social conditions of the time were not conducive to a definite expression of public opinion or the establishment of definite criteria by which the Nazi seizure of power might have been judged. In contrast to the West, when the modern German concept of the state was forming after 1848, the old tradition of the right of resistance to arbitrary authority was pushed into the background, swamped by the bureaucratic structure of the patriarchal state. This fact was highlighted by the problem of the oath sworn to Hitler.

The traditions of the German patriarchal state also provide some explanation of the mistaken ideas which exerted a paralysing effect on potential resistance to the Nazi seizure of power. For the Weimar politicians and parties the basic problem in 1933 was the extent to which they could influence or even control the new rulers by co-operating with them and the point at which opposition, in whatever form, became unavoidable. The problem is reflected, each in its own way, by the illusions of the trade union leaders, the wait-and-see attitude of the Social-democrat leaders, the bourgeois parties' fruitless attempt to adapt themselves and the retreat of the German Communist Party. But in this way the moment was allowed to pass when action could have been taken from the old positions of power. Only as parties were disbanded and political positions lost did scattered centres of resistance form and even these were inhibited by the conviction that Hitler would quickly ruin himself economically and all that was necessary was to survive a short period of oppression.

A distinction must be made between the very different groups of opposition to Nazism or specific aspects of the Nazi regime; they emerged at different times with different methods and different aims. Initial opposition came from the old political enemies of the Left and Centre, soon joined by disillusioned conservatives: then reinforcement came from the churches; there were also lone operators from officialdom or industry; finally in 1938 and again from 1942–3 the military became the focus of opposition planning and action. Evaluation is therefore both difficult and debatable because the criteria used may be very different – is the main emphasis to be placed on motives, prospects of success or political purpose, for instance? Upon this will depend the estimate made of the left-wing, the bourgeois, the ecclesiastical, the conservative and the military opposition, their relationship to each other and their anti–regime tactics.

The debate on the political, social and ideological aspects of the resistance has so far suffered from the inhibitions resulting from the euphoria which its story produced. Hitherto there have been four main lines of argument. First, there are the two extreme views which place in a separate category (i) communist resistance, which is labelled as 'treason' or (ii) that of the conservative and military faction, regarded as mere disagreement with the regime. This purely pro- or anti–communist view of the resistance is historically unacceptable. From the point of view of the Nazi leaders with their claim to totalitarian domination both these forms of resistance represented a threat. Admittedly, once the regime was firmly in the saddle, it ultimately became evident that it could hardly be overthrown without the participation of the armed forces. This, however, is no justification for the next viewpoint (iii) namely that consideration can be confined to the military resistance; during the first half of the Third Reich's reign it barely existed and even after 1938 it can only be considered in conjunction with the political opposition.

Finally there is the view (iv) that the churches gave birth to a popular anti-Nazi movement and that the catholic church in particular was almost solid in opposition; this is as questionable as the opposing theory: that a communist, anti-Hitler mass movement existed. Opposition from the churches, highly important though it was, was a somewhat kaleidoscopic affair. Naturally it was a political factor, but only in a few cases did it rise above defence of its own positions and interests and turn into political resistance. On the other hand, criticism of the illusory ideas of the conservatives including, for instance, the Kreisau Circle's constitutional drafts, objectively justified though it may be, overlooks the fact that at no stage in the Third Reich did a popular rising seem possible, that a *coup d'état* from above was ultimately attempted on 20 July 1944 and that this postulated contact with the official machine and parts of the establishment. This is not to deny that such attempts had their moral aspects and raised both spiritual and social problems.

At no point in time under the Third Reich, therefore, was there a unified resistance movement. Naturally at certain specific moments of crisis the multiplicity of political and intellectual forces which sooner or later either evaded or resisted the Nazi *Gleichschaltung*, came closer together; their general attitude and their plans, however, remained very different and their differences emerged in highly concrete terms after the end of the regime. Nevertheless the extent of internal German opposition in the pre-war period was far greater than the standard declamations of unity issued for foreign consumption would have one believe. Tens of thousands of the Nazis' political opponents were arrested; thousands were murdered for active opposition. Even disregarding the figures for those subjected to collective persecution outside the judicial system and in the concentration camps, the number of actual acts of opposition must be put far higher than Nazi propaganda would naturally have us believe; the Gestapo's secret surveillance reports give a very different picture. For many, of course, the step from non-conformism to civil disobedience and thence to active resistance was a large one but under totalitarian conditions the fact that it was taken at all constituted a political factor. The fact remains that although opposition came subsequently from the churches, the military, the bourgeoisie and the conservatives, the first resistance was offered by those who (in Reichhardt's words) 'suffered first and most' from the Nazi regime's terror and whom the regime 'regarded as its most dangerous enemies – the organizations of the working-class movement'. It is particularly difficult to be specific on this; much is usually made of the persecution of the Left and the activities of the émigrés but sources are lacking for a comprehensive description of this widespread, faceless opposition. Under the conditions of totalitarian domination conspiratorial activity by left-wing resistance groups was confined to the darkness and anonymity of the underground; evidence is therefore meagre and far less revealing than the documents and plans produced by the bourgeois and conservative opposition. Innumerable trials prove that this 'silent revolt' (as Weisenborn called it) was widespread and continuous; they often give a distorted picture, however, since the regimented Nazi 'legal system' invariably tried to present the accused as marxist enemies; in many cases, moreover, action was confined to the concentration camp world, outside the judicial system.

The left-wing opposition was divided and too weak to initiate an active popular movement against National-socialism; this applied with even greater force, however, to all other social and political groupings. The left-wing parties, particularly the communists, had a tradition of underground cell-building and organized resistance but the others had no such foundation. As the years went by, increasing resignation became the order of the day in the socialist camp; expansion of the underground groups into a mass movement was obviously not succeeding and such opposition as there was was the work of individuals in contact with friends of similar persuasion; at the same time, however, the bourgeois camp was attempting to exploit its positions of power in state and society to capture starting points for opposition and a change of regime. Initially three developments seemed to offer such starting points: partial resistance to *Gleichschaltung* by the churches, growing qualms in liberal and conservative circles about the true nature of the Nazi tyranny and finally the criticism by disillusioned officers of Hitler's brinkmanship and gambling with war which really made its voice heard for the first time during the crisis of summer 1938.

The churches seemed most likely to provide a basis since they had been able to avoid complete *Gleichschaltung*. This was not universally the case, however. In later stages ecclesiastical opposition to the regime's claim to total domination was a political factor; it did not, however, imply *political* resistance in the strict sense of the word; its purpose was not to resist the Nazi 'authorities' as such but to preserve the churches' autonomy and educational freedom. In later years the fronts frequently became blurred; many compromises and concessions were made restricting active opposition even from the Confessional Church. The outcome was a sort of armistice; only a few travelled the whole logical road into the political resistance movement. Protestant resistance was handicapped by an inability to draw the political consequences, summarized as follows by Ernst Wolf, the theologian:

'national and conservative prejudice, failure of liberalism as a way of life, an aversion to democracy (labelled "western calvinism") which had become part of the confessional creed, support for the concept of the Reich combined with wishful thinking about a "second" Lutheran-protestant empire comprising the whole German nation against a background of the synthesis "Throne (or nation) and altar", discontent with the Weimar Republic and with republicanism in general, and anti-marxist ideology turning communism into a bogey, the trauma of Versailles and, initially at least, defence of its own "political catholicism", finally an anti-semitism which was only latent.'

Such were the main protestant prejudices and legacies from history; behind them stood the Lutheran doctrine of authority. In both churches only a minority was able to rise above 'ecclesiastical nationalism' and the myth of 'Reich, people and Fatherland' inherited from the patriarchal state. Initially the churches had supported the Nazi state in principle; their subsequent opposition has been described by Wolf as 'an unwilling resistance movement'; it was a defensive reaction forced upon the Church to counter 'encroachments' but there were many relapses. At its conference

in Stuttgart after the 1945 catastrophe the Evangelical Church acknowledged that it had been at fault – in contrast to the apologia with which
other social groupings, including the Catholic church, sought to escape
their share of the blame.

So even in the churches only individual persons and groups, not the
churches themselves, succeeded in reaching a clear-cut position in regard
to resistance. This fact was further illustrated by the equivocal attitude of
the churches to the Jewish question. Though they criticized the Aryan
paragraphs of the Nuremberg Laws, this did not prevent the continuance
of traditional anti-semitism; both protestants and catholics protested
against euthanasia but not against the Jewish policy; action was confined to
individuals or measures of assistance. Only on rare occasions did the
churches pluck up courage to issue general declarations. Major exceptions
were the Confessional church's resistance synods of 1934 and the memoranda and denouncements from the pulpit of the Council of Brothers
(the most Senior body in the confessional church) in subsequent years. In
October 1943 the Prussian Confessional Synod, meeting in Breslau, openly
disputed the government's right to proceed with its extermination policy,
stating: 'The divine order knows no such terms as "exterminate",
"liquidate" or "useless life". Extermination of men simply because they
are relatives of a criminal, are old or mentally defective or members of a
foreign race is not "a use of the sword which is the prerogative of authority".' This applied also to 'the existence of the Israelite people' and the
statement ended with the words: 'We cannot allow our responsibility
before God to be taken from us by our superiors.'

There were three problems with which even those closely involved in
the churches' resistance could never come to terms. In the debate on the
problem of the oath only a few managed to rise above the traditional
loyalty to the state. On the subject of the war the churches mostly reverted
to the 1914–18 attitude, giving patriotic duty and prayer for victory
priority over many of their earlier scruples – even during the Sudeten
crisis of 1938 the Lutheran bishops had kept their distance from the
Confessional Church. The 'fight against bolshevism' proved to be an
argument which exerted an overwhelming influence even in circles
inclined to be critical; similarly anti-communism proved to be a bridge-
builder between protestant or catholic thinking and National-socialist
policy; it neutralized much of the opposition to the regime. Only a few
followed Karl Barth in drawing the conclusion that war should be outlawed; equally only a few were found to agree with Dietrich Bonhoeffer's

alternatives for the German people: 'either to hope for the defeat of their nation in order that christian civilization might survive or to hope for victory entailing the destruction of our civilization.'

Many of the impulses and prejudices described here were common to both churches, though their manifestations may have been different. The difference lay, first, in the fact that, from the points of view both of organization and of dogma, catholicism was far more highly organized and, second, was supra-national in character. Nevertheless its relationship to National-socialism can by no means be clearly defined. Catholicism's surface unanimity did not prevent, in fact necessitated, early abandonment of its original opposition to Nazism in favour of acceptance of *faits accomplis*. Even more far-reaching tendencies to support the regime appeared. Admittedly the attempts to build an intellectual bridge between catholicism and National-socialism never reached the strength or extent of the German–christian movement. The confrontation with National-socialism did not coincide with a severe structural crisis. For a time, however, the process of voluntary *Gleichschaltung* made considerable inroads even into the Catholic Church.

The main obstacle and limitation to catholic opposition was the belief that it was both possible and essential to differentiate between loyalty to the state and criticism of the regime. Accordingly proclamations from bishops called emphatically for the return of the Saar to Germany and contributed to the Nazi victory in the plebiscite of January 1935; despite intervening experiences the process was repeated three years later with the significant declaration by Cardinal Innitzer of Vienna on the occasion of the Austrian Anschluss. A second factor was the support given to the war; this produced horrifying testimonies of a disposition to co-operate. Closely allied to this was the support and approval given to the anti-bolshevist campaign. The theory that Germany was the bastion of Europe contributed largely to that ambivalent attitude which prevented Pacelli (Pope Pius XII from 1938) from issuing a public condemnation of National-socialism during the war. In his defence it is frequently emphasized that he failed to do so only out of concern for the precarious situation of the German churches and to avoid a crisis of conscience among the soldiery – but this merely highlights the problem further. Finally anti-semitism was a traditional component of catholic thinking and this prevented any divergence of principle from Nazi Jewish policy, though individuals were outspoken in their criticism of its methods and manifestations. Only the efforts of the last Papal Council initiated a change in the basically anti-Jewish attitude of the Catholic Church; recently it has become clear that this still persists today. For these reasons it is impossible to equate the Catholic Church with resistance. In contrast to the Evangelical Church there was no acknowledgement of guilt and no critical discussion in 1945; this fact has constituted a problem ever since the controversies over the Reich concordat of 1956 and the role of the Pope during the war. The fact remains, however, that misgivings about and opposition to the regime had a wider and more effective influence in the churches than elsewhere. The churches formed obstacles to the policy of ideological *Gleichschaltung* which even Hitler himself thought he could surmount only after a victorious end to the war. Pending that the regime relied on organizational restrictions, press bans, the arrest of prominent leaders such as Niemöller (in 1937), abolition of theological faculties and intimidation of all pastors or priests who read from the pulpit the Confessional Church's declarations of opposition or pastoral letters. Underground activity and organization were the answer, particularly on the part of the divided evangelical churches.

The consolidation of the Nazi regime confined resistance both by the socialists and the churches within strict limits. There was no hope of a popular rising and neither was strong enough to bring about a change on their own; the only possibility was to gain contact with men in powerful positions in society, the state or the armed forces and so bring some influence to bear on the Third Reich's political and military decisions. It became clear that under a totalitarian regime a popular opposition movement had little prospect of starting or doing anything effective and that the masses were ill-suited to illegality and resistance. This meant that the rise of anti-totalitarian opinion among the officials and the military, neither of whom was basically democratically minded, acquired increased importance. Outstanding in this respect was the tireless activity of Carl Goerdeler – the ex-German-national and ex-Burgomaster of Leipzig – in the years that followed. He pursued three main lines of action: he attempted to influence the nation's leaders by memoranda; he established contact between the various circles of the emergent bourgeois and conservative opposition; and he brought influence to bear on the bureaucracy. Finally, as the conviction began to grow that revolution from below was out of the question and that only a *coup d'état* from above was possible, the resistance began to turn increasingly to the army.

The *Wehrmacht* was anything but prepared for this role. Contrary to the hopes of many conservatives it had accepted without protest the seizure of power, the murder of Generals Schleicher and Bredow and the oath to Hitler. Though its attitude was based on illusion it nevertheless helped the Nazi regime to establish its tyranny. At the root of this was Seeckt's ideal of the 'non-political soldier', the background to which was in fact anti-democratic – Hitler had succeeded in pacifying the old school of officers by guaranteeing them their autonomy. The generally held view, moreover, was that the military interest coincided with that of the Nazis; a policy of rearmament and removal of the Versailles restrictions were aims for the sake of which officers were prepared to accept many of the Nazi practices as mere aberrations. After its débâcle in 1934 the *Wehrmacht* was no longer in a position to act as a power group on its own. Even military resistance, therefore, could only be a partial movement, the effort of a minority which might temporarily possess itself of important positions and contacts but could never succeed in exerting adequate influence at the top level. This determined both its form and its limited possibilities.

Events proved that the German military tradition offered no adequate foundation for political resistance; military resistance remained confined to individual initiatives on the part of independent-minded officers. Its root lay, not in the traditions of the Reichswehr, but in decisions of conscience on the part of individuals. For far too many officers tradition was used as a reason or an excuse for evading the crisis of conscience on the pretext of their duty to obey and refusing to participate in resistance to the end. Nevertheless in the summer of 1938 the first military resistance group to produce definite plans formed around Beck; for the first time almost all shades of political opinion were represented. The conspirators were in contact with the Social-democrats, trade union leaders, senior civil servants and the *Wehrmacht's* semi-civilian secret service; they planned for a change of regime at the moment of the anticipated military crisis. From this time the centre of active conspiracy was to be found in a circle which formed inside the *Abwehr* (Intelligence) Division of OKW (Oberkommando der Wehrmacht – High Command of the Armed Forces). They were the most closely in touch with the true situation; the driving forces were Colonel (as he then was) Hans Oster and later Hans von Dohnanyi, a High Court attorney (*Reichsgerichtsrat*). The central feature of the plan was the arrest of Hitler the moment he issued the order for war which, it was anticipated, would be followed by declarations of war by the western powers. It was calculated that the German people would be so taken aback that the enterprise would have wide support and so the threat of civil war would be avoided. The resisters had reason to hope that, once the criminal and catastrophic nature of Hitler's policy had been made plain to all, even the disciplined bourgeoisie and the military would support them and that refusal to obey would not appear as sabotage and treachery. As a warning background to these expectations, however, stood the experience of November 1918.

These plans were designed to avoid two dangers: a civil war, the outcome of which was uncertain in view of the power of the Nazi Party, and a stab-in-the-back legend in reverse – a future new regime might have been saddled with the accusation that the army and opposition had stabbed Hitler in the back at the moment of victory. The execration of which the action of 20 July 1944 was later the target, shows how well founded these fears were, although, even had it succeeded, it would merely have brought to an end a war long since lost. Hitler's triumph at the Munich Conference, however, cut the ground from under the feet of these plans. In the next three years the regime went from victory to victory. As its prestige grew the ranks of the opposition thinned and action against the regime had practically no hope of success; a *putsch* would inevitably have brought the consequences the conspirators feared – civil war and a stab-in-the-back legend. Any future action was now dependent on military participation which was problematical and hesitant anyway; the failure of summer 1938 introduced additional complications. A further factor was the increasingly strict measures for the security of Hitler's person taken during the war.

3

At this point the moral and political problem raised its head: when and how, could and should the opposition have recourse to force. The churches were not alone in raising objections of principle and, with few exceptions, opposed the use of force, including the killing of Hitler. Many of the bourgeois and conservative opposition, from Goerdeler to the Kreisau Circle were undecided on this problem and were content to leave an attempt at assassination to the military, the majority of whom clung to their oath and their duty to obey orders. This constituted a major problem not only in the preparation of the *coup d'état* but also in obtaining agreement between the various opposition groups; in the end it decisively prejudiced the attempted *coup* itself. To the very end far too much confidence was placed in subterfuge and surprise. The basic pattern of the September 1938 plan was followed: first ensure military support for the *coup* which was, if possible, to be bloodless, then win over the populace by proclamations and dissemination of information about the criminal nature and catastrophic policy of the Hitler regime.

War both complicated and assisted the opposition's task. On the one hand it became increasingly difficult to differentiate between National-socialism and Germany – the appeal to patriotism was stronger than misgivings about the regime. Further factors were the wartime increases in regimentation and controls and the general acceleration in the tempo of life. On the other hand, war entailed a greater degree of improvisation and pragmatism; it also tended to make the hierarchical structure, both in the civilian and military fields, more fluid and accessible to outside influences and personalities; this obviously helped the resistance to organize itself and expand. Most important of all, however, war meant a sudden and violent increase in the weight carried by the *Wehrmacht* and, despite its previous feeble reaction, it had kept its distance from the Party and, above all, the SS. Moreover there were now numerous civilian opponents of the regime in military posts. Covered by Admiral Canaris, Oster had been recruiting men like Dohnanyi and Dietrich Bonhoeffer into the *Abwehr* from the outbreak of war.

In the situation of 1939–40, before the war had spread, these men maintained contact with the Allies; Oster even attempted to give one final proof of the opposition's sincerity by passing to Holland the dates for the German attacks on Scandinavia and France. Even today many critics of the opposition still decry this effort, like all foreign contacts, as 'treason'; it has even been used as a pretext for a new stab–in–the–back legend. It was in fact an expression of Oster's uncompromising opposition and his determination to do his utmost to end the war and overthrow the regime. Under a dictatorship the distinction between treason against the government and treason against the country is blurred in any case, but Oster's action was justified by his knowledge that Hitler was about to assault five neutral countries whose inviolability he had explicitly guaranteed. Both politically and morally Oster had good reasons; he was only too well informed about the unscrupulous nature of Nazi preparations for aggression. If treason against the country implies an intention to damage one's own country, then, even in the case of this exceptional step, right was on the side of a man who was striving with all the resources at his disposal against breach of treaties and violation of law. Here was a state, based on injustice and disregarding all its obligations both to its own citizens and the outside world; in such circumstances it may be thought that greater right is on the side of treason against the country and breach of an oath.

Since the outbreak of war confidence in the German opposition had been shattered and Oster's action was a determined and desperate attempt to re-establish it. His efforts were of no avail since his warnings were not taken seriously and the military efficiency of the German operations led to an unexpectedly rapid and complete victory in the West.

Hitler's new triumph changed the situation fundamentally. The German victory over France implied the most severe defeat for the opposition. The resistance movement now entered upon a period of severe trial, for it had to maintain itself in face of the enthusiasm generated by a victorious dictatorship. All previous contacts with the West had vanished, as had hopes for a quick end to the war and revolt at home. The opposition was isolated, without prospect of winning popular support; almost its sole remaining strength lay in the moral and humanist basis of its existence; there seemed to be no grounds even for thinking of any concrete external action. The degree of continuity, therefore, with which the opposition organized and expanded itself, seems all the more remarkable. The fact that it did so is the answer to those who later maintained that German resistance sprang merely from fear of defeat, from an eleventh-hour panic. This may be true of certain of its military champions. It is certainly not true of those who, at the time of the Third Reich's greatest victories continued to carry the burden of the perilous battle against Hitler and his apparently invincible regime.

Fresh plans for the overthrow of the regime could not follow the previous lines; even less than in 1940 could any help be expected from the military, now intoxicated by victory and in many cases promoted and bemedalled. Vast numbers of Hitler disciples had been accepted into the officer corps at the junior and medium levels and this inevitably affected the generals' readiness to act. Moreover, as the power of the SS grew, the regime's security measures were continually being tightened. Since the start of the Russian campaign Hitler himself had been living almost exclusively in the bunkers of his hermetically sealed headquarters in East Prussia or the Ukraine; planning for any future assassination attempt was a matter of the utmost difficulty. This was doubly serious since it became increasingly clear that, under wartime conditions and in view of the personal power of Hitler, the murder of the dictator was the *conditio sine qua non* for any change of regime.

All this brought to light the two great problems which governed the further development of the resistance. First was the fact that each German victory reduced the internal political prospects of the opposition but at the same time gave rise to external political claims of an almost presumptuous nature from the German-nationalist wing of the opposition including Goerdeler and the Foreign Ministry. The other problem was the debate about the political and moral implications of the murder of Hitler. As the crimes of the regime multiplied the intensity of discussion about the future new order in Germany grew and this brought to light the fact that the various opposition groups had very different ideas on political and social matters. After the failure of all 'normal' attempts to change the regime and the shattering of all tradition, fundamental rethinking seemed even more urgent than before the war. If the much debated ideas on the constitution and social affairs put forward by the resistance in the years 1940–3 be studied, it will be seen that all the opposition's drafts, from those of the Right to those of the Left, suffered from inhibitions, illusions and misappreciations; these drafts also show that resistance and conspiracy against Hitler did not *ipso facto* imply that their authors were opting for democracy or were abandoning all ideas of nationalist power–policy.

Particularly illustrative of this are Goerdeler's alternative proposals for the reorganization of Europe. Quite rightly they have been sharply criticized; it has even been said that they offered no genuine alternative to the Hitler regime; by contrast the Kreisau Circle's ideas on Europe have frequently been idealized and held to be entirely in line with the post-war policy of integration. They too, however, bore a somewhat questionable relationship to the National-socialist's European claims; initially the Kreisau Circle's ideas included the total renunciation of nationalism but at times, under the influence of the Goerdeler group, this gave way to a concept of synthesis between the Reich and Europe.

The ideas most clearly expressed were those of the Kreisau Circle led by Graf Moltke; they included abandonment of nationalism; progress towards internationalism in Europe which would do away, both with the French hegemony established by Versailles and German hegemonic tendencies both old and new; and finally Franco–German and Polish–German understandings instead of insistence on controversial territorial claims. These ideas were put forward primarily by the socialists (Haubach, Leber and Reichwein); Leber's requirement regarding future foreign policy had always been that relationships between states should be governed by the principles of economic co-operation and democratic politics at home. Moltke and his friends, however, deliberately abandoning the traditional political ideas of the aristocracy to which they belonged, now talked about thinking on European lines and a change in the concept of the state which should no longer be considered an end in itself. Ideas of a supra-national, federalist solution were engendered primarily by the problem of policy towards nationalities in East Germany and Eastern Europe; Moltke himself had been preoccupied with minority problems at an early stage. This formed the common ground enabling Moltke and his friends to work with the socialists whose thinking was primarily international. In certain respects Moltke went even further and developed somewhat utopian ideas about dismemberment of Germany and Europe into small, self-governing bodies. Such an extreme form of federalism, with sovereignty restricted to an overall European state, represented a revolutionary departure from nineteenth- and twentieth-century habits of thought which had always been opposed to 'particularism' and presented the unified nation–state as the ultimately desirable solution.

The plans for internal political reform produced by the resistance inevitably arouse some scepticism; looked at today they seem either pre-democratic and restorationist in character or applicable only to a utopian society. Account must be taken, however, of the circumstances at the time of their production and in some cases of the tactical reasons behind them – the effort to win over the generals, for instance; it must also be remembered that the theoretical considerations of the various groups are not necessarily indicative of the actual forces which would have taken a hand in the reshaping of Germany after the fall of Hitler. The Left and the liberals, for instance, carried much weight and the group headed by Oster was at the centre of activity but few drafts from these sources are extant; the various drafts and ideas cannot simply be categorized in terms of the well-known groups and their frequently used names obscure their character; the civilians in Dohnanyi's and Oster's office, for instance, were bourgeois liberals but are usually referred to merely as the *Abwehr* group. It would also be wrong to assume that the ideas of Goerdeler or the Kreisau Circle were representative of the whole resistance and its policy of reform for the post-Hitler period.

The real problem was that of the *coup* itself and with it the role of the Stauffenberg–Leber group; like the Dohnanyi–Oster group they had little time for theory and concentrated all their energies on the three great urgent tasks: the removal of the Hitler regime, the termination of the war, and the re-establishment of justice and freedom. Men like Dietrich Bonhoeffer were entirely consistent in their views; as early as 1942, in sharp contrast to Goerdeler and others, he had said that Nazi Germany's guilt did not permit any 'escape by foreign policy means'; resistance should be regarded more as an 'act of atonement' and should clearly be seen to be so. Like Leber and Moltke, Bonhoeffer regarded unconditional surrender as inevitable. Similarly, towards the end of 1943 Moltke went further than his fellow members of the Kreisau Circle and described 'the unquestionable military defeat and the occupation of Germany' as 'absolutely necessary on political and moral grounds'.

This was the attitude of mind behind the attempted revolt against the political passivity of the German educated classes staged by the students, headed by the Scholls and Professor Kurt Huber, who distributed the 'White Rose' (Weissen Rose) leaflets in Munich. But such resistance remained isolated and was looked upon with horror even by the centres of learning. Against the background of German tradition the minds of scholars were no more attuned than those of the generals to a conflict with conventional patriotism and obedience to the state. Fear of prosecution and the odium of being branded as a traitor scared away those who should have known better seeing that they were in daily contact with the political and military realities or with the world of intellect and morals.

The significance of the Munich protest, however, lies in the warning which the fate of the resistance in the Third Reich has left to us. Education and science were subjected to temptations and manipulations such as are only possible under a regime like Hitler's; they were possible because the political passivity of the educated allowed free play to tendencies which flourished in the partly non-political, partly anti-democratic atmosphere of the German schools and universities. The disaster lay not merely in the crimes committed by a National-socialist minority but in the failure of the 'educated' majority who can rightly be accused of the sins of omission and conformism. This is the answer to those clever people today who write off the awkward episode of the 'White Rose' as unrealistic idealism and blindness to the harsh realities of political power; similarly – from the ivory tower of *Realpolitik* – they condemn Stauffenberg's deed as dilettante or even reprehensible. On this the critics both of the extreme Right and the extreme Left are in agreement.

4

I do not propose to pursue the story. We know what happened on 20 July 1944 and we know the frightful consequences of that failure – the regime claimed more victims than ever before. This meant, of course, that National-socialism's full responsibility for the catastrophe could not be obscured by some new stab–in–the–back legend, although such legend has been pertinaciously cultivated by widespread neo-Nazi publicity of which the NPD's utterances and the *Nationalzeitung* form part. The outcome was that, in an atmosphere of spell-bound terror, the mass of the people followed the regime to the bitter end, even when that regime's leader issued from his Berlin bunker his senseless orders for resistance to the end and scorched earth. So the question with which a *coup d'état* would have confronted the German people was shelved and remained unanswered: what had the people to say concerning the crimes committed in their name? The reckoning with the Nazi criminals which Stauffenberg demanded should be conducted by Germans, never took place; in Ehler's words it remained 'frozen in the realm of the past, irrecoverable'.

The much discussed 'conquest of the past', however, was not the only failure. There is no certainty regarding the present-day significance to be attributed to an experience which most people have either pushed into the back of their minds, forgotten or consigned to ancient history. Not unnaturally, on the surface the second German democracy traces its origin back to the resistance. Reference is made to the 'other Germany' as an argument against the verdict of the victors or the equation of Germany with National-socialism. At the same time, however, it cannot be denied that this 'other Germany' was a small minority, ferociously hounded and destroyed, never acknowledged by the vast majority of the population.

The consequence is that a curious dichotomy in political thinking still exists today and it is characteristic of the Federal Republic's development. Any mention of collective guilt is met with indignation but people fail to draw the logical conclusion from this attitude – an unequivocal rejection of the Third Reich. Even today the opposition's 'treachery' is as unpopular a subject as the sentences on the Nazi criminals. This negative attitude shows that the scale of values inherited from the patriarchal state still predominates, as is also proved by the declamatory nature of the 20 July festivities. It matters little whether emphasis is placed on the faults and weaknesses of the resistance or whether a synthetic halo is placed around it. What does matter is the decision of principle whether the people have the right, indeed the duty, to refuse to accept the state as something immutable and to call it in question if it transgresses the laws of morality and the dignity of man.

The present-day significance of 20 July, however, is in fact dependent on the question whether the basic responsibility for the crimes of the Hitler regime is acknowledged as a German responsibility. When a case is made against the consequences of the German catastrophe by referring to a people's right to its homeland or when anti–Israel campaigns are launched by Right or Left, this has little to do with the justice of the case but much to do with a dishonest, unpolitical attempt to suppress memories of the past. Controversies about the Oder–Neisse Line or the problem of Israel merely show how lively the memory still remains of the policy of that regime which, in the name of Germany and with the approval or acquiescence of the majority of the German people, embarked upon the annihilation of Jews and Slavs and so took upon itself full responsibility for the problems of Eastern Europe and of Israel. Here and not in superficial legal argument lies the significance of an acknowledgement of the resistance – and it is tantamount to an acknowledgement of moral guilt and political reality. The German resistance attempted to avert the frightful consequences resulting from the existence of the Nazi state which was based on injustice; justice to the case of the resistance therefore means an end to demands for revision and recognition of the fact that Germany has little right to advance her claims. Neither the Federal Republic nor East Germany can present themselves as unprejudiced arbiters in the conflict of demands, particularly in the Middle East; both are successors to a regime which, as the prime instigator of injustices, still exerts its influence on the world conflicts of today.

Internally, however, the German problem, so starkly exemplified by National-socialism, is still with us. The role of opposition and the right of resistance are still unpopular, uncomfortable subjects even in the second Republic – to say nothing of their complete suppression in the People's Republic. Democracy, however, stands or falls by recognition of the existence and validity of opposition. Opposition is a permanent duty, not a natural state of affairs. Karl Jaspers once said that opposition was 'contrary to human nature; man wishes to live at one with his environment, to vote Yes in concert'. Nevertheless it is precisely what the logic of democracy requires. Because everyone can be involved and therefore carry a share of the responsibility, democracy needs a knowledgeable, critical public and precisely for this reason that public should not only tolerate but acknowledge, and if necessary protect, minorities which think differently. The dictatorial state, not being based on the rule of law, necessarily carries the odium of illegality and use of force; there can be no comparison between resistance to it and non-parliamentary opposition to the system as a whole in a democratic constitutional state. The argument generally used to justify such action is that political domination is tantamount to use of force and that therefore use of force against it is legitimate. This, however, bears no relation to the reason which justifies resistance to dictatorship – the demand for re-establishment of constitutional conditions and the safeguarding of human rights.

Here the fundamental distinction emerges: resistance is undertaken to safeguard the rights of man when the constitution of a state based on the rule of law has been violated; revolution designed to overthrow the state is embarked upon in the name of perfectionist utopian visions of the future and without regard to the sacrifices involved. Obviously there can be various intermediate situations; even in the case of the anti-Hitler resistance there was no question of mere reversion to the pre-dictatorial or even pre-republican conditions; this fact placed a question-mark against the alternative drafts produced by the Goerdeler group which was both constitutionally and socially conservative. The object was to re-establish a liberal social state based on the rule of law and to put an end to arbitrary misuse of the law in the service of superhuman or inhuman purposes. The argument may be adduced that a right of revolution exists and that, had it not existed, modern democracy would never have been born. On this subject, however, Germany, the country of frustrated and mistimed revolutions, has much leeway to make up.

The bankruptcy of 1933 and the failure of the resistance under the Third Reich, however, contain a lesson: it is that a civilized political democracy is dependent upon the right of opposition being established both morally and by the constitution. In contrast to the western democracies no generally accepted tradition of the right to resist continued in Germany when the patriarchal state was established by revolution from above after 1848. Neither the Weimar Republic nor our second democracy have been able to build on a solid, generally accepted, concept of the state on the part of its citizens. The Third Reich has therefore left us a dual legacy: the tendency either to take refuge in the comfortable security of the patriarchal state or to erupt into extremist movements opposed to the system as a whole; as a result we are in danger of reverting to the extreme polarizations of the Weimar Republic.

Both these trends show that we have not yet learnt the painful lesson which the failure of the Weimar Republic and the sorry history of the resistance should have taught us. The title of a recently published paperback much oversimplifies the problem; it is: *German Resistance – Progress or Reaction?*. Certain Germans refused to be seduced; they resisted the call of opportunism and unthinking intoxication with power and victory; they fought alone, accepting persecution and death. Their sacrifice is not to be judged on the basis of the fashionable capitalist-socialist alternative nor of controversial moral and theological principle. The overriding aspect of the resistance seems to me to be that it demonstrated the old conviction, long abandoned in Germany, that there must always be two sides to politics: on the one hand construction and consolidation of a social order, on the other, resistance to biased and unjust exercise of power. Under certain systems of government there is no room for a difference of opinion of this nature; their aims may be the establishment of a classless society, maintenance of order in an established, patriarchal state or the victory of a militant ideology which considers itself the sole repository of truth. Whatever its purpose, however, such a system of rule violates the basic law of any politics worthy of the human race.

The dead of the resistance are martyrs, witnesses to this conviction which has formed the basis of western politics ever since the days of Greek democracy and revolt against the power of tyrants. They were carrying on this international tradition renounced by Germany with her anti-western cult of the state. This is all the more remarkable in that they were largely men and women who had been reared as prisoners of that traditional, disastrous and specifically German concept of the state which called for obedience, devotion to duty, authority and national power. They were not naturally inclined to revolutionary views or revolutionary action but they 'put back into the German vocabulary' (in the words of W. Hennis) the words 'resistance' and 'tyrannicide'; they were able to rise above the German metaphysic of the state, the belief in the state as the be-all and end-all. The fact that they did so constitutes a milestone in the history of our political consciousness.

Those who are calling today for greater national consciousness and greater state consciousness both in politics and the Federal armed forces overlook this basic lesson of the German resistance. It is that the state, authority and the nation should no longer be regarded as absolutes, that the primary objects of the citizen's loyalty should be a standard of values transcending the state and a form of political process worthy of the dignity of man, that the overriding consideration should be, not the state or some oath or some order of society as such but an alert constitutional consciousness, a democratic consciousness. Herein lies the great justification for a resistance which has been vilified as illegal and treacherous. A critical political sense must prevent the resistance being pushed into the background and written off as historically irrelevant. At the same time, however, if the opposition in a pluralist democracy, whether on the extreme

Right or the extreme Left, carries the banner of some one-sided, per-fectionist utopia, we must resist the temptation to place a halo round its head and call it resistance.

Thomas Mann once called politics an attribute of humanity. The significance of the 1933–45 resistance, into which such loyal citizens as Eugen Bolz and Ludwig Beck found themselves forced, cannot be grasped if its political and moral aspects are considered separately and in isolation. Its significance lies in the close connection between the two – the one has often been played off against the other in Germany's more recent history and in interpretations of the anti-Hitler resistance. We are faced once again with the old question of the relationship between the law, justice and force. The answer given by the Germans of 20 July was not that force was justified, as the superficial saying goes; it was that they were prepared to accept the odium and the sacrifice entailed by the use of force in order to re-establish the rule of law and justice in face of inhuman criminal tyranny. Their legacy is that force should no longer be necessary since freedom, the rule of law and peace have become established as the main pillars and purpose of any state constitution.

Part II

Germany's Second Democracy

8

Changes in Western Europe

1 The Background

Since the Second World War both the meaning of the term 'Western Europe' and developments in that area have differed fundamentally from those associated with the period, lasting into our present century, when the world of European states was taking shape. Of course far-reaching changes began both before and after the First World War; they were, however, largely obscured by the continuance of old structures and illusions. The real trends of development only emerged when the global decisions of 1945 were taken; these introduced new factors accelerating changes long foreshadowed. From four major points of view Europe's situation has visibly and effectively changed.

(i) First and most important is the stark fact that *world politics are no longer centred round Europe*, are no longer governed by a concert of powers concentrated in Europe. Basically this was, of course, also true of the period between the two world wars, but realization of this fact on the part both of the peoples and their statesmen lagged far behind the realities. Such realities of the inter-war period were the weight carried internationally by the United States, the crises of the colonial empires, the rise of Japanese and Russian potential both in Europe and Asia. Failure to recognize these facts contributed much to the failure of post-war reconstruction and the origins of the catastrophic Hitler policy. It is significant that the League of Nations in practice limited itself to the European dimension of the policy of the powers and was never able to come to grips with the realities of a global expansion of international relationships and the interdependence of political and economic problems. The First World War and its consequences, the catastrophe of the world economic crisis and the spread of fascism were expressions of this international interpenetration, in face of which the traditional nation-state politics were totally obsolete. With 1945 the age of 'classical' politics played by sovereign nation–states came irrevocably to an end as did the period when world history and world politics were governed from Europe and determined by the antagonisms and alliances of the European powers. Instead supra-national organs appeared, wider in scope than Europe, and they rapidly divided Europe into two parts; they were dominated by two super-powers whose policy was increasingly affected by problems of the extra-European world of 'new states'. From the time that American and Russian troops met in the middle of Germany and the United Nations Organization (UNO) provided a platform for worldwide politics, Europe became the object rather than the subject of international politics. In contrast to the 1917–19 upheavals when great empires were toppled, regimes fundamentally changed and new states created, the second post-war period re-established the system of European states that had been overrun by Nazi imperialism; apart from the Soviet annexation of the Baltic States and eastern Poland the only major change was the destruction of the German Reich. But this restoration of the nation–states of Europe did not imply re-establishment of their traditional claim to sovereignty. Upon it was superimposed bipolar bloc politics dominating the scene militarily, economically and ideologically.

(ii)   This far-reaching change in the international position of Europe also had a decisive effect on the *internal structure* of the European countries. This was primarily the result of the formation of blocs governing external relations; the confrontation between East and West, between the Soviet and American hegemonies dominated the ideological and internal political scene. As early as 1946 the division of Europe between liberal parliamentary systems and communist single-party regimes was firm and, as far as internal politics were concerned, Western Europe had clearly taken a different path from Eastern Europe. Within the two systems variations between different countries may be of importance for an estimate of their value, their national character and their political weight. The division of Europe into opposing fronts, however, had its influence upon the internal structure even of those countries which had contrived to preserve a certain degree of independence between the two blocs as they solidified. It was soon to be seen that outside the area controlled by Soviet military forces, including in other words the neutrals (Sweden, Switzerland and Austria), the western non-communist form of governmental system remained predominant; on the communist side Yugoslavia constitutes a special case as does maintenance of a multi-party democracy in Finland.

During the inter-war period the feature both of international and internal politics was the plethora of states enabling various forms of state to exist and various fronts to be formed in Europe. By contrast, since 1945 the terms 'Western', 'Central' and 'Eastern' Europe have acquired a political rather than geographical significance, 'Western' Europe being taken to include countries with a non-communist form of government. The word 'western' is used in a sense broader than that of geography or the politics of alliances; it is applied to that part of Europe in which the political process and political rule is based on a pluralist method of giving expression to the popular will – in the form of multi-party systems under which opposition and a change of government are possible. Exceptions are the authoritarian systems in Spain and Portugal and, since 1967, also in Greece; these show that membership of 'the West' in so far as external affairs are concerned does not yet necessitate adoption of a western democratic' system inside a country.

(iii)   In this 'Western' Europe the apparent causes of *socio-economic and cultural change* have been the havoc of war, the change in population structure and the end of extra-European colonial domination. In the longer term, the process of reconstruction, with its increased prospects of modernization and industrialization, has overshadowed the traditional forms of nation-state politics and has made possible, even essential, new forms of supra-national co-operation. Admittedly this process was initiated as a result of the politico-military factors stemming from the Cold War and was furthered through NATO; it is not, however, confined to the area covered by the western alliance or bloc but includes also countries which are members of neither bloc. This would seem to support the theory, therefore, that these are long-term, overriding developments not to be explained solely by the primacy of external and bloc politics. The development of this wider 'Western' Europe would seem to be dependent on special conditions of an economic, social and cultural nature, initially to be found only on this side of the Iron Curtain; with the loosening of the barriers between East and West, however, gradual convergence of the two systems would seem to be within the realm of possibility.

(iv)   As a system of government *parliamentary democracy* is showing a surprising capacity to rise from its ashes. Between the wars it was rocked and in some cases destroyed by authoritarian, fascist regimes; in the post-1918 period one of the most frequently heard catchphrases was the 'crisis of parliamentarianism' and the majority of the new democracies soon fell victim to anti-parliamentary movements. Now, however, the western type of parliamentary democracy seems to be in process of stabilization to an extent not hitherto possible and hardly to be expected under the catastrophic conditions of 1945.

The lesson of the experiences of the 1920s and 1930s was that modern democracy is a complex form of government, always precarious and never complete, that under conditions governed by industrialization and technology, social regrouping and intellectual change it was subject to a continuous process of reorganization and adaptation. Two fundamental problems of modern, western-type democracy emerged. They were characterized by profound tensions and divisions – between liberty and equality, between government and self- or co-determination, between social order and individual self-expression, between the idea of sovereignty of the people and the practicalities of representation, between direct democracy and parliamentarianism without which the formation of political purpose and democratic government did not seem possible in large-size countries. The second fundamental problem of modern democracy lay in extension of the authority of the state over wider and wider areas of society and the economy – this is the internal structural crisis of the parliamentary system as a whole. The vast expansion of the administration, the shift of power from legislature to executive, the reduction of the power of parliament to determine and control policy by the trend towards bureaucracy, meritocracy or mere party domination – all this imperils the effectiveness and credibility of the democratic process.

These were the major problems faced in the construction and development of the western democracies after the Second World War as well. Most of the post-1918 European democracies had failed functionally; they had been unable to overcome the political and social tensions of the mass society age and produce a stable but adaptable order. After 1945, on the other hand, conditions for reconstruction of parliamentary democracy in Western Europe were both changed and improved from three points of view:

(i) *constitutionally* the example of previous bitter experience was available. Constitutional provisions to safeguard the parliamentary system, its ability to function and its stability could take account of these. This applied with particular force to the governmental system of the West German Federal Republic; elsewhere too, however, particularly in the Fifth French Republic, definite measures were taken to prevent political fragmentation, to regulate and stabilize parliamentary procedure;

(ii) *sociologically* the upheavals of the war and post-war periods resulted in a process of regrouping and a certain fluidity in the traditional structure of society; as a result political parties were ruled less by ideology and more by pragmatic considerations. This made coalition and co-operation between the various social and political groupings within the system easier; politically it reduced the traditional cleavage in society and finally it reinforced the tendency to adoption of a three– or two–party system which had been the object of certain constitutional and electoral provisions.

These trends were particularly visible in West Germany where the resettlement and incorporation of over ten million refugees had its effect. In other countries too, however, this social fluidity and mobility eased the democratic process and simplified the formation of parliamentary decision in that it tempered the rigidity of ideologically based fronts and engendered an attitude of democratic co-operation and practical compromise, thus removing the bitterness from political conflict.

(iii) *externally* the stabilization of Western European democracy was safeguarded from the outset by a policy of alliances and co-operation formed to counter Soviet Russian claims to domination in Eastern and Central Europe. After the First World War unrestrained nationalism had governed the policy of the countries of Europe and destroyed the very foundations of democracy at home; the United States, the arbiter of the war, sponsored the peace settlement and inaugurated the League of Nations, but then withdrew from international politics. The post-1945 situation was very different. American policy aimed at 'containment' of communism and so, through the Marshall Plan and the NATO alliance, Western Europe was integrated into a wide and vigorous system of international co-operation. Supra-national integration of the West European and Atlantic societies could be visualized and this again provided a sort of protective screen for the new parliamentary democracies. This did not mean that political fragmentation and the existence of strong communist parties, particularly in Italy and France, did not imply a permanent threat of internal political crisis. In all cases, however, repetition of the pre-war crises of system which had led to surrender to fascism, was avoided.

After 1918 the turmoil of national ambitions had opened the way to the victorious progress by nationalistic dictatorship movements; the miseries of the second post-war period, however, opened people's eyes to the necessity for some voluntary limitation of national sovereignty. The resistance movements had already produced far-reaching plans for closer European co-operation or even the political integration of Europe. The

1945–6 emergency could only be dealt with by recognizing the fact that the countries of Europe were economically, militarily and politically interdependent and could not pursue isolated policies. The continuous dismantlement of the colonial empires constituted a further factor in this process since it led the countries of Europe to devote more attention to their internal structural problems and a policy of co-operation between themselves. Faced with these problems the traditional animosities between the nation–states gradually faded; the possibility of compromise both between and within the various countries grew. The most obvious instance was the West German democracy; after the respite of the occupation period when it was shielded by the west European and Atlantic alliances, it was enabled to develop and stabilize practically undisturbed. The experience of a parliamentary democracy working efficiently both politically and economically came as a striking and welcome contrast to the inter-war period when people had become used to thinking of parliamentary politics as synonymous with crisis and failure.

2   Tendencies of the Post-war Period

However different the national traditions and political position of the individual countries of Western Europe may be, as far as internal development is concerned a number of features are common to them all. In the period immediately after the end of the war three main tendencies emerged:

(i)   almost everywhere the political Left emerged with so great an increase in strength that the expression 'general lurch to the Left' seems justified. The first and most striking evidence of this was the great victory of the British Labour Party in the elections of July 1945; it was to be seen also in the strength of the communist and socialist parties in France and Italy, in the attempts of the early post-war governments to form left-wing, anti-fascist coalitions, in the part played by social-democrat governments in Scandinavia and in the full-scale incorporation of the Left in bourgeois governmental coalitions. In contrast to developments under Soviet influence in Eastern Europe, however, in no case did this lurch to the Left lead to permanent union or fusion between socialist and communist parties;

(ii)   the other side of the coin was that, in general, the political Right was discredited and in retreat. Admittedly only in Italy was monarchy replaced by a republic, but the existing monarchies, in so far as they had not already been fully constitutionalized and made subject to the authority of parliament (as in Great Britain or Scandinavia), were modified on democratic lines and their prerogatives restricted. In some cases the right-wing parties carried the stigma of collaboration, but even where this was not the case their ambivalent attitude to authoritarian and fascist ideologies and regimes was reason enough for the post-war wave of anti-fascist feeling to be directed primarily against the conservative Right. A further factor was the bankruptcy of conservative–liberal economic policy between the wars which had contributed so largely to the crisis of the democracies. Moreover any return to capitalism was out of the question because the economic crisis measures of wartime inevitably had to continue during the post-war emergency. The general trend towards planned economy and a policy of nationalization and towards far-reaching political and social reform seemed to confirm socialism as the dominant force in western Europe; according to the current diagnoses and prognoses socialism was the inevitable sequel to the failure of capitalism and the catastrophic career of fascism;

(iii) after only a few years, however, different though the circumstances were in each individual country, there was a general swing of political opinion in the west European democracies. The main hallmarks of this development were the exclusion of communist parties from participation in government, an access of strength for the moderate Centre and in particular the rapid rise to key positions in state and society of christian-democrat parties. They constituted a new element in the party structure of Western Europe. Although they were the offspring of the older forms of christian-confessional party, they were themselves supporters of parliamentary democracy, they rallied the supporters of christian socialism and they relegated to the background the traditions of the conservative clericals; they therefore spread their net far wider than the previous ecclesiastical interest-groups and opened the way to formation of larger popular parties of the Centre; they hoped to be able to form coalitions in either direction and to bring socialism and capitalism together. Thus emancipated, the christian–democrat collective movements were able to integrate the major part of the bourgeoisie; they were supported by the churches which had emerged from the ideological breakdown of this period as the only strong authorities – in Italy and Germany in fact they were almost the only authorities of any sort to be recognized as institutions by the occupying powers; they were in touch with groups of the anti-fascist resistance and they could make play with the watchword of a fresh start in democracy after the horrifying experience of the anti-democratic experiment, the end of which had been bloody failure.

A whole series of causes were at the bottom of this rapid change in the internal political scenery in Western Europe. Signs of this major swing of opinion were to be seen from 1947 onwards and it was accelerated by economic as well as political and military factors. An intricate combination of internal and external political influences characterized this decisive development in 1947–8. The fluid, crisis–ridden situation of the post-war years with its prospects of major transformation of state and society on socialist lines led with unexpected rapidity to the consolidation of parliamentary, multi-party regimes and a reversion to liberal economic and social systems with a corresponding access in strength for the Centre and Right. In Germany the process was termed the swing towards a 'social market economy' and with its subsequent effects, known as the 'economic miracle' it gained overwhelming popularity. Thus was the stage set for the political development which has continued until the present day.

This was a historic decision but there was hardly any realistic alternative. The facts were only too plain. The economic stabilization brought about by the Marshall Plan contrasted sharply with the fiasco of communist economic policy in Eastern Europe; the confrontation between the two super-powers, the USA and the USSR, was increasingly seen as a trial of strength between two social systems, one based on free consent and the other on direction by force; the answer to the imposition of the stalinist policy of domination culminating in the Prague *coup* of February 1948 and the Berlin blockade was reinforcement of the American policy of containment by means of economic and military aid to Western Europe. All this had its effect upon the prospects for a socialist transformation in Western Europe and the end result was the exclusion of the communist parties from all political leadership.

The stabilization of Western Europe on liberal and democratic lines was not merely the outcome of some deep dark conspiracy by capitalist imperialists, as Soviet propaganda would have us believe. As a result of the Soviet policy of *Gleichschaltung* in Eastern Europe, not only communism but also ideas of socialist reform and development of a Europe independent of the super-powers were lastingly discredited. This produced governments basically anti-communist in character, including that of Great Britain after the defeat of the Labour Party in 1951; for purposes of reconstruction they looked to the United States for economic aid and military protection; economic recovery and political stabilization helped to restore the traditional structures both of state and society. The increasing co-operation both on the European and Atlantic levels tended in the same direction. So by the end of the 1940s the decision had been made and it has governed the development of Western Europe until the present day.

Such was the framework, and the limits, within which the major events of the 1950s and 1960s took place – both those affecting European politics and the internal politics of the West. The main sufferers were the democratic Left; their opposition on social and foreign policy grounds to the restorationist trend in the West remained fruitless until sooner (in France) or later (in West Germany) they were forced to recognize established facts. Under these circumstances possible alternatives to the confrontation between East and West, between liberal–conservative and socialist–communist social policy were never really put to the test of practicability. There is therefore no means of knowing whether the numerous critics were right when they spoke of the 'missed opportunities' of the post-war period or whether stern necessity imposed the decision to divide Europe (and Germany in particular); under the shadow of the threats and crises of the Cold War and in view of the incomparably greater degree of freedom and better standard of living in the West those responsible for action and a majority of the population were convinced that this was a necessity. The situation naturally differed between and within the countries of Western Europe; there were strong oppositionist tendencies and sharply defined differences. In the light of the East–West confrontation, however, the strongest and most determined support for the policy of stability came from West Germany. Here the spectacle of the Soviet policy of coercion in East Germany and the prospects of political rehabilitation and rapid recovery from the catastrophe, were particularly powerful motivations.

3 Problems in Individual Countries

Against this background of the general trends the history of the individual countries of Western Europe in the post-war period has still been governed by the special problems stemming from the circumstances of their development into nation–states and their differing socio-economic conditions. Conflicts between them had been almost the sole deciding factor for so long that this was only natural. Not only did it reflect the great weight carried by traditional customs and ideologies and the fact that they had not kept abreast of the changed circumstances, but it was the inevitable outcome of the very heterogeneous conditions and interests of the countries and peoples of Europe. In fact the tug-of-war between the policies of individual countries and a European policy has been an important factor in inter-state relationships, in the politics of economic interests and in the formation of public opinion and awareness in the societies of Western Europe. These conflicts increasingly faded as co-operative institutions were actually set up, ultimately to take concrete shape in a European Economic Community, the Common Market. This was a major step forward in the settlement of conflicts and in co-ordination, particularly of economic interests; contrary to the expectations of its supporters, however, it did not automatically lead to political integration, to the formation of a West European federal state. Qualitatively this would have been a major innovation and, despite all official pronouncements in its favour, it ran counter to very definite interests on the part of individual countries.

(i) The most obvious instance was the difference between those nation-states of Western Europe which had remained intact and West Germany which could only achieve nationhood and equality of status through a supra-national European policy. On the other side stood France. Her policy was aimed primarily at complete rehabilitation after the 1940 catastrophe and preservation of her position as an independent great power in the victors' camp. Some *rapprochement* between these two opposing points of view was the prerequisite for any European policy. Its first signs were visible after the political swing of 1948. Initially, however, despite many constitutional changes and notwithstanding the reduction of French influence both as a European and colonial power, the Fifth Republic's political system seemed to approximate closely to that of the pre-war Third Republic. There were, of course, important new elements including the role played by de Gaulle and the continuing influence of the Resistance. Their effect upon political development, however, was ambivalent.

De Gaulle was a man of imperious egocentricity, a controversial figure but not one which could be disregarded. Twice he emerged as the central figure in French history – with his call to resistance in 1940 and with his solution of the Algerian crisis which at the same time set the seal on his far-reaching reform of the tottering republic to produce the Fifth Republic's gaullist presidential regime. In 1945, however, he had failed in his attempt to use his great authority as resistance leader to insist on reform of the parliamentary party state on authoritarian lines. The combination of absolutist and traditionalist, plebiscitary and democratic ideas which was the dream of the gaullist movement in succeeding years, had no hope of acceptance until the near civil war situation of 1958 arose. Moreover, under the conditions of post-war Europe the mystical glorification of the nation, of which de Gaulle saw himself as the incarnation, proved to be no more than an anachronistic intermezzo. De Gaulle's attitude may have had a certain effect in assisting to reduce the rigidity of the relationship between the Eastern and Western blocs since in that context nationalism was still a factor; neither militarily (by development of a French nuclear force) nor economically, nor in international politics, however, could France compete with the super-powers. As far as concerned the policy of European integration and relations with Great Britain and the USA, de Gaulle's influence was a negative one and his attitude a disturbing factor.

De Gaulle's historic contribution was that in 1945 he was the embodiment of the broadest possible anti-fascist coalition extending from the Right to the Left. With this as a foundation the Resistance, which included all shades of opinion from communist to conservative, established itself as the main political prop of the Fourth Republic. The process of parliamentary compromise under this republic was complex and unstable; nevertheless it survived the crisis and divisions of the Indo-China war and in fact initiated the economic expansion the benefit of which was reaped by the Fifth Republic, enabling it to exploit, to stabilize and to pursue its ambitious policy. Equally important was the fact that the Resistance was pro-Europe and so threw its political weight behind the first tentative initiatives of the movement for a united Europe, for which the French attitude was inevitably decisive. From the tug-of-war between nationalistic gaullism, persistent communist opposition and European co-operation, the latter emerged as the dominant force.

Internally the political process was a confusing one. In January 1946 de Gaulle ostentatiously withdrew and then, after the exclusion of the communist party, came the NATO alliance and the Coal and Steel Community of the Six in 1950; in 1952 the European Defence Community (EDC) Treaty was signed but this had proved a failure by 1954; finally came the Paris Treaties in 1955 and the EEC in 1957. European policy, therefore, suffered many setbacks both before and after the return of de Gaulle in 1958; nevertheless, compared to the period following the First World War, French policy was fundamentally different both in method and purpose. All attempts to give national prestige and a great power policy precedence over a concrete policy of internal expansion and supra-national co-operation came to nothing, as did de Gaulle's own efforts. This is all the more remarkable in that the relative positions of the political parties were highly complex. In the first elections for the constituent assembly in October 1945 three blocs of almost equal strength confronted each other – communists with 26 per cent, socialists with 24 per cent and popular republicans with 26 per cent. As in Italy, the trades unions too were split three ways.

An important role in all this was played by a new christian-democrat umbrella movement, the MRP (*Mouvement Républicain Populaire*); it was based on the Resistance and so attracted support not only from bourgeois conservatives but also liberals and moderate left-wingers. In contrast to previous christian parties which had opposed the liberal and secular France of 1789, the MRP sought to combine in a single popular party, irrespective of class, the traditions of democratic republicans, christian conservatives, liberals and socialists. The socialists, who gave their support to most of the governments, profited little therefrom and were continually losing supporters; the communists were regarded as unacceptable in a coalition; the liberals degenerated into a splinter group; from 1947 the gaullists represented the intransigent Right. So under Robert Schuman the MRP was able to lead the country into a full-scale European policy and, despite the difficulties of obtaining a parliamentary majority, they were able to count on the support of a pragmatically-minded population. The new trend was helped by the fact that in Italy, the Benelux countries and the newly formed Federal Republic of Germany, governments under christian-democrat leadership were in control. This, of course, gave the European policy a conservative and bourgeois tinge and the non-communist Left hesitated for a long time before giving it their support, the first in the field being the moderate trades unions.

MRP foreign ministers continued to pursue this policy. In contrast to its European sister parties, however, the MRP was hard pressed and weakened by gaullist competition for the support of the conservative bourgeoisie. They reaped no reward for the vital part they had played in the decisions of 1948–52, as the CDU – Christian Democratic Union – in Bonn was beginning to do at this time. Finally the MRP was almost ground to pieces in the polarization between the Left (communists) and the Right (gaullists). Attempts were made to institute more decisive reforms under the left-wing liberal Pierre Mendès-France; he brought the Indo-China war to an end and may be credited with a decisive effort of modernization both in industry and social structure (the reward of which was reaped by the Fifth Republic); none of this, however, could arrest the increasing paralysis of the republic. Sceptics drew comparisons between the fate of the Centre under the Weimar Republic and de Gaulle's seizure of power. But de Gaulle was no Hindenburg and certainly no Hitler; he succeeded in pacifying the army which was disillusioned and ready to revolt. Most important of all, however, the French public at large, critical though it had been of the Fourth Republic and much though it welcomed the conservative stability of the gaullist presidential regime, was not prepared to turn its back on politics and capitulate to dictatorship. This became clear when it was seen that the counterpart to the Fifth Republic's stability was stagnation and refusal to recognize realities concealed behind a façade of modernization and a nationalist great power policy. The great crisis of 1968 and the final withdrawal of de Gaulle was primarily proof of the capacity of a democratic culture to withstand autocratic and fascist tendencies, to force a strong communist party to adopt a reformist policy and to harness almost all political forces behind the republican tradition of 1789. In contrast to Italy or Germany, French politics, with their political and ideological controversies, may give an impression of confusion and chaos but behind them lies a decisive minimum of consensus.

Industrial interests and calculations played an important part in all this; industry was finding de Gaulle's nationalistic policy of autonomy increasingly expensive and disadvantageous – a further symptom of the influence European politics can exert on the structure and development of individual countries. This was the true background to the expectation that economic interdependence would lead to political integration. By the time de Gaulle died in 1970 the gaullist system was increasingly adapting itself to the requirements of democracy and Europeanism. Even the General himself had become less anti-American; his two curt vetoes of British entry into the Common Market sprang from deep-rooted personal animosities, but they were followed by substantive negotiations; de Gaulle was also forced to change his tune when France took two historic decisions, the painful decision to abandon her colonial empire and the decision to co-operate with West Germany both on a European level and bilaterally. His concept of a *Europe des patries* under French leadership proved to be no more than a manoeuvre in retreat; the really decisive steps had been taken under the Fourth Republic.

(ii) Developments in *Italy* were far less dramatic, although innumerable governmental crises and continuing problems of economic and social structure constituted major obstacles to the country's internal modernization and the adoption of a European policy. The revival of democracy proved difficult, not only because of the legacy of fascism but also because of the country's long history of foreign occupation, the continued existence of feudal structures and the deep-rooted differences between the industrial North and the agrarian South; like Germany, Italy was a 'retarded nation' and so she had great difficulty in developing a democratic national consciousness. On the other hand, unlike Germany, she had contrived to overthrow fascism and bring the war to an early end, but this merely accentuated the internal divisions; the resistance movement which fought against Mussolini's rump republic in the north visualized far-reaching political and social reform, whereas by the end of the war, the pre-fascist 'establishment' had long since restored the old state structure and the old order of society in southern and central Italy.

Admittedly, by a referendum held in June 1946, a 54 per cent majority ultimately abolished the monarchy which had been discredited along with fascism; only in the north, however, did a majority vote for a republic. Nevertheless a new feature appeared in Italian politics, the *Democrazia Cristiana* (DC), a broad-based party with right- and left-wings; it did not, however, divorce itself from the conservative church to the same extent as other christian-democrat parties; it was centred on the underdeveloped South and became the permanent governing party, primarily by forming right-wing coalitions. This party constituted a powerful obstacle to any potential reorganization of the state and society on the lines demanded after the end of the war by the left-wing resistance, particularly in the North. Alcide de Gasperi was a capable champion of the anti-fascist Centre in the DC; he knew how to play the opposing wings off against each other and ultimately, in May 1947, outmanoeuvred both the communists and left-wing socialists.

As in France political forces were divided into three main camps with the DC as the right-of-centre party in by far the strongest position; it could muster 38–48 per cent of the votes whereas the communists never achieved more than 25 per cent and the socialists 15–20 per cent (including 6 per cent for the social-democrats). From June to December 1945 an anti-fascist, all-party government was attempted under Ferrucio Parri but it could do no more than plan for reform; when the country opted for an anti-socialist, western and European policy, the left-wing, strong though it was, was banished into permanent opposition; the result was a crisis-ridden policy of *status quo*. Not until 1962, with the *apertura a sinistra* under Amintore Fanfani of the DC, was any attempt made to institute the broader-based and long overdue social reform and modernization.

Until his death in 1954 de Gasperi did his utmost to lead the country into the christian-democrat era of European politics; the result was that Italy too achieved a (belated) economic miracle, the fruits of which, however, were very unevenly distributed. The consequence was a certain consolidation but the problems of the underdeveloped areas remained unsolved and nothing was done to reform the antiquated educational system or the bureaucracy which was partially corrupt and partially overstaffed; its continued existence accentuated the traditional anti-state feeling among large sections of the population and the deep cleavage between politics and society. The essential structural reform on federalist lines was not undertaken; fragmentation and inflexibility are still the order of the day and this is primarily the result of the weakness and disintegration of Italian socialism, once so powerful; the reason is its ambivalent relationship with the communists. The facts that a crisis of state on 1922 lines was avoided, that communists and neo-fascists have been brought under control and that, with the formation of a left-wing coalition, there is now some prospect of social and democratic reform are largely the outcome of co-operation on the Western European level.

(iii) The *smaller West European democracies* equally had their specific problems and interests. In the Benelux countries, as in Scandinavia, parliamentary monarchy on the British model was maintained. The major questions of the post-war period in the Benelux countries were collaboration with or resistance to the occupation regime, continuity or reform of the political structure, the anti-communist trend and the problems of social and economic reform; all these were closely linked with the debate about the national and international vistas held out by future policy.

This was particularly the case in *Belgium*, where wartime and post-war conditions had revived the old linguistic and cultural dispute between Flemings and Walloons. Anachronistic though this conflict may seem, it was intensified by the socio-economic differences in development between the two sections of the population. In the Walloon areas, where socialist, anti-clerical and pro-French tradition predominated, the old-established coal industry was in a state of permanent crisis; agrarian Flanders, on the other hand, which was primarily conservative and catholic, gained in importance as a result of economic and industrial modernization. Brussels, the capital, in the Flemish zone but French-speaking, constituted a special point of dispute. Flemish pretensions were regarded as a defensive reaction to French (Walloon) preponderance in cultural affairs; further factors were the prolonged conflicts concerning King Leopold III (who abdicated in 1951) and concerning collaboration on the part of certain Flemish groups. Political forces were divided between three main camps (christian-social, socialist and liberal) but the situation was complicated by the existence of extremist Flemish and Walloon parties; the major parties, who governed through a series of varying coalitions, only succeeded in holding the country together with difficulty. Belgium never wavered in her support for a European policy and she became the headquarters for most of the European institutions and (after de Gaulle's anti-American decision) for NATO as well; this did nothing, however, to solve the main problem – constitutional reform to produce efficient government.

In contrast to Belgium *The Netherlands* recovered from the severe damage suffered during the war and the loss of their colonial empire in Indonesia by embarking at once on a policy of economic modernization, particularly of agriculture; they also pursued a determined European policy visualizing a supra-national union including Great Britain. The main problem was still the traditional division of society into exclusive social and confessional bodies or 'columns'; this phenomenon of division into socio-political 'columns' still persists as a structural principle of the political system. In contrast to the remainder of Western Europe no christian-democrat umbrella party was formed in Holland. Parties were the catholic People's Party with about 30 per cent support, the moderate Labour Party with about 25 per cent and the Liberals with about 12 per cent; in addition there were two separate parties representing the pro-testant bourgeoisie, the Anti-revolutionary Party and the Christian-historical Union (each with about 10 per cent). The trades unions were similarly divided – into socialist, catholic and protestant camps. Dutch politics, therefore, featured certain historical peculiarities; society was conservative and frozen into integrated fractional organizations. There is no comparison here with the French or Italian class society or the cultural division in Belgium. As a result the people had remained remarkably solid under the German occupation regime; there was solid support too for the policy of reform which subsequently ensured that the Netherlands played a particularly important role in European politics.

4 The Bonn Democracy

In this rapid development of Western Europe the German question has played a dual role.

In the first place, the problems of overcoming the consequences of the war, organizing reconstruction and ensuring the necessary co-operation were intimately bound up with that of the control and direction of occupied

Germany. After the turning point of 1947–8 the Marshall Plan and the policy of 'containment' made the connection even clearer. Control of Germany had initially been negative and restrictive but this was now changed into a system of positive controls through co-operation and partial integration. This was the true import of the negotiations and treaties which started with Western European Union and led via the formation of the Federal Republic, the Coal and Steel Community and NATO to the Paris Treaties and the European Economic Community.

In the second place, a European policy aiming at political integration began to take shape, based upon the plans of the resistance movements during the war and a variety of European movements during the early post-war period, and this offered concrete prospects for a supra-national solution of the problem of the German state. Both economically and politically the idea of Europe exerted a powerful influence as a substitute for the German nation-state which had ended in failure. The idea filled the vacuum left in the minds of most Germans by collapse and disillusionment. From the outset Konrad Adenauer, the first German Chancellor (1949–63), made much play with this aspect of European policy; in the light of the actual power-policy situation at the end of the 1940s the arguments of the social-democrat opposition in favour of the nation–state were not regarded by the majority of the West German population as offering a realistic alternative.

The problem of the division of Germany therefore acted as a major factor in accelerating and stabilizing the integration of Western Europe. Moreover integration served the immediate interests of the West German people. This implied, of course, that the declared aim of reunification was now a distant one; ultimately it became unrealistic despite the emphasis still laid upon it by the government and the majority of the people. All concrete material interests, however, weighed in the opposite direction; as time went on it became increasingly clear that the alleged primacy of reunification was no more than an ideological postulate used to justify stabilization of the West German state and that it was this stabilization which best served the material interests and security requirements of West Germany. This was the background too to the restoration, with only minor modifications, of a liberal capitalism. *Dirigisme*, socialism and controlled economy carried the odium of dictatorship and the wartime and post-war miseries; the spectacle produced by the imposition of socialism in Eastern Europe with its consequential continuing economic crises was not very attractive.

In the event West Germany benefited more than any other European country from the decisions which, almost without exception, have governed development from 1947 until the present day. They gave rise to a number of problems peculiar to Germany as compared with other West European countries. The most noteworthy feature, however, was the country's marked stability; this was the result of the rapid economic recovery, the concentration of a disillusioned people on work and private gain and the long period of stable government produced by the availability of an experienced tactician in Konrad Adenauer and the change in the party system. The Federal Republic has avoided those constitutional weaknesses which so rapidly became fatal to the Weimar Republic. People have become habituated to a more efficiently functioning parliamentary system and so take a more positive view of democracy itself – which they did not after 1918. Helped by the chancellorship of a single great old man of authoritarian leanings, this sytem has been a bridge-builder between the German tradition of the patriarchal state and free multi-party democracy. Instead of the historic fragmentation of parties, political groupings have concentrated into two parties of almost equal size, the CDU (Christian-democrats) and SPD (Socialist-democrats), the only other party of significance being the liberal (Free-democrats – FDP) which has less than 10 per cent support. The party system, therefore, increasingly resembles that of Britain or America, under which co-operation is possible, rather than the fragmented party systems of continental Europe. Admittedly this has necessitated a prolonged process of substituting pragmatism for ideology and only after twenty years could the system stand the test of a change of government from CDU to SPD. Moreover the Bonn party system has never been subjected to a prolonged crisis of the extent experienced by the Weimar Republic. This should be remembered when electoral figures alone are assumed to indicate that we now have stability and a political culture capable of withstanding shocks.

After twenty years we are confronted with a change of generation, a change in the international situation and a crisis of the reunification concept. These developments throw the immaturity and problematical nature of the Bonn state into greater prominence than in the years when West Germany's incorporation into the western world and subsequent development as part thereof were apparently matters of course. That this should be so is, of course, the legacy of the peculiar problems which West Germany was inevitably faced with during its formative period.

The Federal Republic's starting point was the historical fact that, in terms of external politics, the state of 1871 had been destroyed; that was a state, moreover, which from the outset and more particularly after its losses of the First World War, had considered itself an incomplete nation-state. The experiences of the Weimar Republic and the Third Reich, the net result of which had been the bankruptcy of the national and imperialist ideas inherent in the Greater Germany concept, postulated a completely fresh definition of the German concept of the state. The Basic Law did not set this out with such clarity as to preclude the possibility of highly varying interpretations. This problem affected both West Germany's situation and boundaries in terms of foreign policy and the view taken of the new state in terms of internal politics.

As regards the boundaries of the country the Federal Republic looked upon itself as a provisional structure pending reunification of the two halves of Germany; although the *de facto* frontier was the Oder–Neisse Line, West Germany staked her claim to the territories as they existed under the Reich of 1937, to which she proclaimed herself the sole legal successor. This implied a refusal to recognize the realities of the foreign political situation and this inevitably became increasingly obvious. As far as internal politics were concerned the Federal Republic was definitively established as a democratic social state based on the rule of law and federalist in nature; at this point, however, opinions soon diverged concerning the actual implications of the concept of a democracy based on freedom and the rule of law. Views ranged from socialist through liberal to traditionalist theories which sought to explain or criticize the Federal Republic's democracy by the old standards of the patriarchal and administrative state. This divergence repeatedly emerged during the later arguments about all-German policy, rearmament, state security, emergency legislation, electoral reform and federalism. The Federal Republic of 1949 had not been formed as a result of revolution from below and, after the disillusionments and exertions of the Hitler period, large sections of the population adopted an attitude of aloof suspicion towards the state. A democracy requires the participation of all its citizens but Bonn was faced with this de-politicized attitude on the part of many of them.

The Adenauer era was a vital transitionary period. It succeeded in identifying the people with the system, however, primarily by excluding from discussion the basic political questions – reunification and the eastern frontier. When the scene changed in the 1960s criticism of the system as such grew. With the questionable experiment of the Great Coalition in 1966 the shadows of Weimar seemed to be looming on the horizon – extreme polarization and anti-parliamentarianism both on the Right and the Left. But Bonn is not Weimar. The profound difference was illustrated by the change of government in 1969 when, for the first time in forty-five years, social-democrats occupied the two most senior positions in the state – Willy Brandt, the frequently abused émigré, became Chancellor and Gustav Heinemann, the consistent democrat, President. The permanence of the new leadership and with it the ability of the system to function will depend on the solution to the basic problems so long by-passed – internal reform and, even more important, stabilization of an eastern policy which must finally acknowledge the consequences of 1945 as regards the all-German problem and Germany's eastern frontiers.

There can be no question here of any policy that attempts to play off East against West. The Federal Republic remains dependent on its membership of Western Europe and the progress of the integration policy to which it owes both its existence and its rapid development. Only if pan-European co-operation in more concrete form seemed a possibility would the problem of the existence of two German states, one in the West and the other in the East, become actual once more. This, however, presupposes changes in the world political situation which can hardly be visualized for a long time to come. The immediate problems lie in the field of further interdependence and co-ordination of Western Europe. Here, after the disappearance of the great obstacle, de Gaulle, two primary tasks emerge: political intensification of economic co-operation with the ultimate aim of integrating Western Europe on federal lines and the expansion of the economic community of the Six by the inclusion of Great Britain and other countries.

At present these two aims seem contradictory or even mutually exclusive. The entry of other countries, particularly Great Britain with her great tradition of parliamentary democracy and pronounced sense of sovereignty may considerably complicate the process of political integration. This process, however, stands or falls by the decision to set up a directly elected European parliament and here Britain's political experience may make a great contribution once she has jumped the hurdle of economic integration which for fifteen years she felt to be too high. The introduction of a parliamentary system for the European community as a whole necessitates a considerable degree of renunciation of sovereignty on the part of all those involved. Success or failure in this process will decide whether, with changed conditions both in East and West, the 1970s will see the continued disappearance of the divisions between the nation–states of Europe which has differentiated post-war West European development so sharply from the sorry history of the 1920s and 1930s.

9

Theodor Heuss and the Foundation of the Federal Republic

Theodor Heuss is not easy to place in any single category; he was politician, parliamentarian and statesman, historian, theorist and interpreter of democracy, a steadfast representative of the liberalism which had had so chequered a history in Germany, a patron of the arts and a 'man of letters' in the full sense of the word – the only qualification which he acknowledged.[1] As journalist and speaker Theodor Heuss had been indefatigable in his efforts to build a bridge between intellectuals and politics, between intellect and power; as lecturer at the Berlin Political Institute under the Weimar regime he had tried to instil some understanding of democracy into his pupils. Only a few months before his death he attended a meeting of the German Association for Political Science, of which he had been a co-founder after the war – he never regarded membership of such institutions as a mere formality. As a historian and biographer of an independent turn of mind he had studied and commented upon a century of fluctuating efforts to establish democracy in Germany. As politician and German Democratic Party member of parliament he had been intimately involved in the experiment of the first German republic. After 1933 he managed to maintain himself as a 'freelance' writer, though frequently threatened and forbidden to write. Finally, however, he occupied the centre of the stage when, step by step but far more quickly than anticipated, a Germany which had totally destroyed itself reintroduced democracy.[2]

I

Three great incentives determined the political role played by this man in the reconstruction of German politics: his wide-ranging view of history, his bitter experience of the failure of the first German democracy

156

and his grasp of the reciprocal relationship between the power of the state and the spirit of its citizens, of authority and freedom as constituting a single problem which Germany in her more recent past had not been able to solve. Here lay the special contribution of Theodor Heuss as politician and political pedagogue. It therefore seems necessary to examine the formative period of the Federal Republic in the light of these views in greater detail than has been done hitherto. Theodor Heuss has been known to his contemporaries for decades as historian and writer; many compliments have been paid to his oratory as the politician and Federal President – even mass meetings affectionately referred to him as 'old Heuss'; he invariably drafted his speeches himself and they were minor masterpieces – 'merely the consequence of my literary past', he would say.[3] His contribution to our most recent history, however, and the political role he played in the formation of the second German democracy are usually dismissed with general phrases producing little concrete information. The general public, which so often likes to draw comparisons between earlier and later power relationships, has hardly accorded adequate appreciation to the role played by Heuss as compared to that of Konrad Adenauer or Kurt Schumacher; in the history books he generally appears merely as the Federal President with representative rather than decision-making functions, a man allowed to make speeches but not to act.

The history of the Parliamentary Council has not yet been written. The part played in the formulation of the Basic Law by the parties, individual politicians and the three occupying powers requires more precise definition than existing commentaries and accounts have yet given us.[4] Heuss's memoirs unfortunately end at 1933.[5] Even in 1953 Heuss was lamenting that he had written too voluminously about the earlier years – 'my career was such that for a long time I was merely a journalistic observer and participator in legislation and did not appear actively and visibly on the stage until after 1945.'[6]

In the developments leading up to formation of the Federal Republic there were three important features. In the first place the constitutions of the various *Länder* had been fixed before the discussions on the Basic Law took place; these discussions did not therefore start from 'Square One' as in 1918 and rejection of the previous regime was far more unequivocal than at that time. Secondly, the Weimar constitution and its fate provided both a starting point and a warning of which all those involved took due note, each in his own way; arguments and drafts were based to a large extent upon the experiences of the first German democracy. Third, certain personalities carried far greater weight than that stemming merely from the power or authority they represented; this was shown by the role played by Theodor Heuss; he was only one of five Free-democrats in the constitutional assembly,[7] which totalled sixty-five but he was a member of the most important committees (the Main Committee and that for Fundamental Questions). He came to the fore at once with his great speech in the plenary session of the Parliamentary Council on 9 September 1948;[8] it was a counterpart to his last major speech before the Hitler period on 11 May 1932 when he had shown both spirit and courage in opposing the massed Nazi cohorts – Goebbels had shouted 'What business have you in this House? You represent no one any more' to which Heuss had replied 'I am representing my own point of view here.'[9]

Now, after unpredictably frightful experiences and all the difficulties of a fresh start, in which Heuss had been involved as Minister of Culture in Stuttgart[10] and co-founder of a liberal party, here were people assembling in Bonn, selected more or less by accident, to add up the bill and try to do better. Heuss himself produced an inimitable summary of the German situation at the conclusion of the deliberations of the Parliamentary Council on 8 May 1949, four years after the capitulation; 8 May 1945, he said, provided 'for all of us the most tragic and most puzzling paradox in history. Why? Because at one and the same time we were both delivered and destroyed.'[11] Guilt, adversity and hope were the hallmarks of the situation at the start. The Berlin blockade and the Prague *coup* formed a dark impelling historical background. Only with considerable hesitation did people comply with the urgings of the Western Allies to set up a West German state; it was bound to deepen the division of Germany.[12]

At the start of the discussions Heuss set out the problems with his habitual candour.[13] They were there, he said, 'to make a constitution which we do not altogether wish to call a constitution' – in other words they had to face the problem of its provisional nature; they must also, he continued, take a balanced view of the Weimar experiment and, though criticizing when criticism was right, must not fall victim once more to nationalist and National-socialist propaganda against the first republic; they must realize that the republic had not functioned 'because democracy had not been achieved in Germany' but had arrived 'in the wings of . . . defeat', and because the Weimar constitution had made a 'laudable error' in over-optimistically assuming that Germans possessed a sense of fairness—which they did not. Heuss regarded the real disaster as the fact that 'democracy developed in an atmosphere of nationalist romanticism, monarchist restorationism and the wretched crime of the stab–in–the–back legend. These things were of far far greater import for the non-functioning of the Weimar constitution than the technical drafting of certain paragraphs which one or other of us may today consider not to have been quite right.'

This was the basic standpoint from which Heuss approached and participated in the second attempt at democracy. This was the background too to the efforts he made to endow the position of president, weakened in terms of political power, with a wide role both at home and abroad in strengthening civic consciousness, in cleansing public life and in making democracy credible. This was more necessary than ever it had been, for he felt that 'once again democracy in Germany has not been wrested from anyone', once again it had been established in an atmosphere of 'weary resignation' or 'aimless protest'. Here Heuss conjures up a phrase of Hölderlin's; 'sacred realism', he says, is what is required since this generation has 'lost its illusions in face of reality and . . . has passed through the school of scepticism'. Here lies a chance, he says, of a fresh start. From the outset, however, Heuss insisted that this fresh start must take account of the 'historical fact' that the political cohesion of Germany had not been destroyed and for this reason he decisively opposed the particularist wishes of Bavaria. Similarly he warned against regarding the new state as 'provisional' not merely geographically but also structurally; he opposed the first constitutional draft to emerge from Chiemsee since it referred to a 'Federation of German *Länder*'. His proposal, to which he adhered, was 'Federal Republic of Germany' because, he said, this would 'exert a powerful moral attraction on the younger generation; "Federation of German *Länder*" they will merely regard as an attempt to evade the issue.'

This great speech, made at the opening of the debate, exerted a visible political effect at many stages of the wearisome, at times near-deadlocked, negotiations in the Parliamentary Council. Specifically Heuss was insistent, despite the experience of Weimar, on adherence to the parliamentary system, saying that it would constitute a 'training school in political responsibility for governments and parties in Germany'. In the early days of the Weimar Republic he had spoken against the proportional representation system,[14] but now (and here he disagreed with CDU speakers) he warned against acceptance of current slogans and of proportional representation as the panacea for all problems. In his view the British and American two-party systems had their roots in history, not in electoral technicalities; he pointed out that the frequent changes of government in France had not altered the overall parliamentary situation. In his peroration on 8 May 1949 he inveighed against 'consideration of the franchise in isolation' and the 'standard democratic interplay between Right and Left'; nowadays, he said, the two-party system spelt ruin because compromise, comprehension and toleration were lacking – 'perhaps someday . . .'[15]

At the outset Heuss campaigned for a second chamber which should not be merely a 'miniature reflection' of the Bundestag but a Federal Council independently representing the *Länder*. Looking back characteristically into the history of the German democratic concept,[16] Heuss submitted for discussion drafts produced by the *Paulskirche* parliament of 1848–9; these showed that the second chamber was to consist both of elected and governmental representatives of the *Länder*. At the same time he insisted on a provision (only recently implemented) that membership of both Houses should not be permissible: 'I advise my fellow-members to accustom themselves to a tongue-twisting word, so that they do not stumble over it. It is "incompatibility".'

Heuss was even more firmly opposed to loading the future democracy with provisions for a plebiscite. In contrast to the smaller countries with a tradition of civic sense, he said – Switzerland, for instance, which the Weimar Republic had attempted to copy – in a democracy covering a larger area the plebiscite was a 'bonus for any demagogue' and 'in an amorphous confused population placed a premium on the tub-thumper'.[17] This view was undoubtedly conditioned by his memory of the dualism between the parliamentary and presidential systems under Weimar and by his suspicion of plebiscitary arrangements which the failure of that state had induced; this aroused considerable argument. The question was repeatedly raised whether this, and indeed a 'chancellor democracy', did not imply that political mobility and capacity for expression were being sacrificed to political stability. Equally de Gaulle criticized the absence of provisions for a plebiscite in the Federal Republic. The example of the Fifth French Republic, however, remained questionable. On certain other points Heuss was unable to gain acceptance of his views. This was at least partially true of the treatment of the basic rights and cultural policy in the Basic Law. Heuss had a healthy scepticism of over-precise definition of the moral foundations for democracy or of questions of detail. In Weimar Friedrich Naumann, his great mentor, had regarded a comprehensive definition of the basic rights as the best method of integrating the new state into the consciousness of the people, but Heuss now had other views, saying: 'Then, however, the lawyers found ways round and the result was generally unfortunate.'[18] Again and again Heuss opposed over-comprehensive and detailed juridical wording on political matters in the constitution, referring disparagingly to 'playing with paragraphs'. In the event the Basic Law was not altogether immune to this danger; its excessive length – as compared, for instance, to the classic constitution of the United States – might be reminiscent of the dangerous perfectionism of the Weimar constitution. Heuss did, however, succeed in reducing not only the conflict between representative and plebiscitary elements but also the dualism between parliament and president. The basic rights were written into the constitution, thus establishing the principle of a militant democracy and contrasting with the Weimar experience when democracy found itself defenceless.[19]

The second idea which Heuss repeatedly threw into the debates on the basic rights was on similar lines. He was convinced that, after the Nazi tyranny, the rights of the individual required special protection and that the authority of the state must not be allowed to ride roughshod over them. Heuss emphasized the fundamental conditions upon which any political order should be constructed: 'Any state, including a democratic state, depends on authority to give orders and its claim to have them obeyed; the special feature of the democratic state is that that authority is granted for a defined period and can also be revoked.'[20] 'Authority for a defined period' was the argument Heuss used to both sides; to those with an exaggerated concept of the state he pointed out that power was limited in time; to those who were suspicious of the state he stressed the necessity of strong authority. This was the formula he used, not without gentle irony, after ten years of the Adenauer era when concluding a speech giving the reasons why he did not wish to be re-elected president or see the constitution changed on his account.

This was the general concept which caused him to oppose the 'sinister campaign against the much misunderstood Hegel who has now been dead for 117 years'; it was the background to the Chiemsee draft in which the basic rights of the individual were given priority over those of the state. Almost as if he was grooming himself for the political role of Federal President, Heuss took issue with an over-negative definition of the state; 'The state is not merely a piece of machinery; it has an innate dignity of its own; as the reflection of the community which has brought it into being, it is no abstract notion for man neither is man for it.' The background to such remarks is Heuss's effort to warn the constituent assembly that they must rise above the general attitude of mind of the day and must not allow their revulsion at the Nazi regime's perversion of the power of the state to be the sole criterion for their concept of the state. Finally, as a liberal politician, Heuss opposed definition in the constitutional drafts of confessional political policy in cultural and educational matters; he was concerned lest the integrating effect of education, both socially and politically, be lost by fragmentation and division and that here again the new democracy might suffer through undue emphasis being placed on the Nazi misuse of the system. Heuss expressed the fear that the German tendency to perfectionism might overload the constitution and that overemphasis on parents' rights might lead to 'miniature confessional minority schools'. As when he had been Minister of Culture, he wanted the general 'christian community school'.[21] He opposed any 'subjective right of a group', the inevitable consequence of which would be 'reduction in the standard of education in individual parishes and the alienation of children from each other'.[22]

Behind all these arguments was the realization of the severe losses – material and institutional but equally psychological and spiritual – and the differing tendencies with which reconstruction of democracy was faced. He was decided in his rejection of the nationalistic autarchy with which the Hitler period had imbued the German spirit; equally he was insistent upon the German contribution to culture to which, he considered, the nation should revert – 'Both as a nation and as individuals we have become poorer during the period when Hitler cut us off from the world, when the cry was "German, more German, most German" and Germans were supposed to be best at everything.' Against this Heuss liked to tell the story of the American commission which came to Stuttgart in 1947 to study the German educational system; its official report opened with the statement that 'apart from the Greeks and Romans the Germans have dispensed their gifts to the world with more effect than any other nation'. Two years later, however, Heuss added to this story a clear warning against renewed dangers of backsliding. In his speech 'Strength and limitations of a cultural policy', with which he opened the congress of German teachers' unions in 1951, he went on: 'Today one must once again tell this story with a certain caution. There are signs of a return to *hubris* among the Germans. We are not an easy people.'[23]

2

With these ideas as background it is not surprising that in the Fundamental Questions Committee (where he was *rapporteur* for the preamble and nomenclature) and in plenary sessions of the Parliamentary Council Heuss was particularly concerned with the preamble to the future Basic Law. The preamble was required to define democracy, to legitimize it, to demonstrate the spirit behind it but at the same time to take account of the fact that the development of the *Länder*, the requirements of the occupying powers and the effects of the Cold War had imposed strict limitations and roused many doubts about the creation of a West German republic. Although no preamble had been drafted either in 1848 or 1870, Heuss was convinced that in this case it was of major importance. It was essential, he said, in order to 'bring to notice and demonstrate the exceptional character of this Basic Law'.[24] Here again, however, he criticized the excessive length of the drafts, saying that 'in our German way we have tackled history too pedantically and systematically.'

At this time there was much discussion whether constitutional authority originated from the people or the *Länder*; behind this lay the hotly-debated question whether the German Reich had ceased to exist in 1945 and a German state had therefore to be constituted afresh or whether the Reich was still in existence and therefore merely had to be organized afresh; the latter was the majority view.[25] Heuss put forward a compromise proposal – that the state be 're-formed' and this became the accepted solution, implying as it did both continuity and a fresh start. He was indefatigable, however, in warning against overemphasis on the transitional nature of the present situation; he urged that the preamble have 'the simplicity and dignity of the permanent'. The provisional nature of the constitution – he preferred to use the word 'transitory'[26] – should only be detectable 'between the lines', he said; it should not detract from the 'integrating force' of this Basic Law in the consciousness of the German people. He was bent on producing something and on 'attempting to give it an air of solemnity ... but without succumbing to aphorisms or illusions'.[27]

This was the background to Heuss's objections to the theological overtones in the opening paragraphs of the constitution;[28] he did not wish to 'implicate God in all the inadequacies, stupidities and misunderstandings involved in something which is very much the work of man'; he opposed any attempt 'to give this work too firm a metaphysical basis, because we are then, in a sense, attempting to evade our responsibility'. But he could not gain acceptance of his views, not even of his proposal to substitute 'trust in God' for 'responsibility before God'; this, he said, was 'more accurate than the other. To try to make the good God directly responsible for all the stupidities of which we are guilty here, is theological presumption.' Here was foreshadowed a problem affecting the whole concept of politics and democracy, evidenced by the fact that the CDU styled itself a 'christian party'. In his closing speech Heuss specifically took issue with any attempt to label other parties 'non-christian'.[29]

Heuss, the liberal, however, met opposition not only from the CDU but also from the SPD when, during the later wearisome discussions of the basic rights in which he was always urging brevity and simplicity, he contested the important Article 5 which coupled freedom of teaching with loyalty to the constitution. As Ludwig Bergsträsser had done before him,[30] Carlo Schmid defended this on the grounds of the responsibility of men of letters:

'Before 1933 things took place in German lecture halls for the effects of which we are still paying today'; it should not be possible, he continued, for 'a man on the rostrum, on the pretext of making scholarly criticism, to play mere underhand politics by not only criticizing but pouring scorn on democracy and its institutions' and so 'undermining it in the guise of learning.'

To this Heuss objected that it was 'simply intolerable . . . to perpetuate an attitude of mistrust of a single profession as a part of constitutional law'. Rather the whole matter was a question of democracy, he said.[31] (In view of the general suspicion, undoubtedly not unfounded at the time, other proposals to leave the matter to be dealt with in the provisions concerning forfeiture of basic rights in the event of anti-constitutional activities (Article 18 of the Basic Law) or to restrict proceedings against teachers to the Federal administrative court[32] were rejected.)

The closeness of the voting (34 to 31) shows how contentious and difficult was the problem of combining emphasis on the basic rights with protection of democracy, transient experiences with a constitution capable of standing the test of time, matters of principle with matters of detail. The work of the Parliamentary Council and in particular the activities of Theodor Heuss, both of which still await scientific analysis, amply illustrate this dilemma and the semi-successful attempts made to solve it. The problem is still with us – in divided Germany's nebulous posture between the provisional and the definitive, in the present renewed conflict between the basic rights and the demands of the state, in the federal problem and in the debate on emergency regulations.

On 8 May 1949, at the end of the discussions which had lasted over eight months instead of the planned eight weeks, Theodor Heuss once more summarized the views that had led him to accept or reject individual sections of the constitution.[33] He hoped that the standpoint from which the Basic Law would be judged would not be that of the perfectionist – whether it was the 'best possible' but whether it was 'politically possible today'. His main criticism was that the Federal Council (Bundesrat) was too bureaucratic in nature. It was now the task of the parties, he said, to integrate the *Länder* and counter 'particularist tendencies'. Complicating factors were the occupying powers and the attitude of Munich. To the end the Bavarian Party and the CSU remained deaf to all appeals, however eloquent, and the Basic Law was passed by 53 votes to 12 over the head of the Bavarian government coalition. When he became Federal President Heuss insisted on making his first state visit to Munich – in the Bavarian view the correct procedure both historically and logically.[34]

At the conclusion as at the beginning of the Parliamentary Council Heuss was especially concerned with the political aspects of cultural and educational matters and the problems of parental rights and confessional policy closely connected therewith. He not only saw some danger to the state's claim to influence education; he even referred to a 'national political tragedy', by which he meant that in view of people's mobility in post-war Germany fresh divisions and isolated groups might form and this might prevent integration of the refugees. And this might take place at the moment when the old fronts were disappearing, when, in Heuss's words 'the Social-democrat party has become flexible or rather has abandoned the basically mechanistic and materialistic trend of its previous tradition in questions of religion.'[35]

Heuss's very definite political and social views also led him to deplore the fact that the churches and party politics were not to be kept separate – for the good of both. Whatever one's feelings on this matter may be, this was one of Heuss's firm convictions as a politician, despite his own religious grounding as a pupil of Naumann and his appreciation of men such as Kolping and Ketteler, Harnack and Wichern, Bodelschwingh and Barth.[36] It is worth quoting his views as expressed in his final speech before assuming the office of Federal President which placed him outside politics.

'Allow me to say one thing in all seriousness. Churches should not try to base themselves on parties. It is not worthy of them; they have their mission from the eternal God. But neither should parties try to base themselves on churches. God knows, parties are transitory phenomena; they use all sorts of tricks and tactics and are prone to petty thirst for power; they should not and ought not to burden the churches with these things. If I am asked whether something like this has its place in a final speech on the Basic Law of the Germans, I am forced to reply Yes, because we must have a breath of fresh air in these matters, particularly for the sake of the churches.'[37]

The keynote of this final speech, however, was a renewed call for political unity on matters affecting the state which should rise above all material differences; this had been the background to all the efforts of Heuss, the politician, to give the constitution a moral and spiritual foundation. Heuss, the future statesman and Federal President, was to be seen when, in his solicitude for the new democracy he said: 'There should be no winners or losers in this house.'[38]

3

So far hardly any reference has been made to the structure of the governmental system or the office of president which, after all, must be the main purpose of any consideration of the Basic Law. In fact, however, the question of the head of state raised comparatively little argument. The experience of Weimar had devalued the position of Reich president. The parliamentary system had failed principally because presidential government had all too often enabled parties and parliament to evade their responsibility and their duty to compromise.[39]

Some drafts even went so far as to propose that instead of a president there should be a federal presidency, a 'directorate' consisting of the federal chancellor and the presidents of the Bundestag and Bundesrat.[40] Apart from controlling the powers of the president one of the ideas behind this was that, if the state were represented by an institution rather than a person, this would underline its provisional character while the division of the country lasted. Against this the position vis-à-vis other countries would have been difficult and a president could do much at home to consolidate and revive a democratic state consciousness; this pointed to the institution of a federal president. This view quickly prevailed as did the determination to restrict him to representative functions. Certain proposals were made, particularly by Thomas Dehler but not by Heuss[41] for the introduction of a presidential democracy on the American or Swiss model but they had as little prospect of acceptance as a return to the Weimar system.

The restriction of presidential prerogatives in matters of practical politics was counter-balanced by deliberate emphasis upon a strong stable government. Efforts have been made to ascribe this emphasis upon the governmental aspect in the new structure to the aspirations of the two strong party leaders, Adenauer and Schumacher, and to the preponderance in the Parliamentary Council of ministers from the *Länder*, officials and lawyers.[42] It should not be overlooked, however, that in the event of crisis or with a weak chancellor, even the president's restricted powers of proposal, nomination or dismissal of the chancellor and dissolution of parliament could play some part.[43] Primarily, however, it was to prove that the field of activity and the functions of the representative of the state laid great tasks upon its incumbent and offered great possibilities in a democracy still unsure of itself, assailed from outside, discredited, divided internally and with little tradition. Depending entirely upon the personality and his style of operation, this office could definitely become 'political' in the broader sense of the word.

The traditional relationship between the authority of the President and that of the state, so often distorted in Germany, presented both risk and opportunity. When people say that the development of the presidency in the Federal Republic has been a stroke of good fortune, they are comparing it with Weimar, Hindenburg and Hitler. Have we not, however, at last achieved a normalization of the relationship because institutional arrangements and the personality of the incumbent are in accord? The existence of this office, standing above party, took root in the public consciousness far more quickly than expected and while uncertainty and division, arguments about the authority of the state and power conflicts were still the order of the day in the new democracy. This is the historic function and the political significance with which Theodor Heuss sought to endow his office and to pass on to his successors as the correct tradition.

During the debates in the Parliamentary Council no one had foreseen that the office would develop in this way. The general trend of discussion had been negative; the majority were determined to prevent repetition of the Weimar presidential rule. The fate of Friedrich Ebert, who was hounded to death and in whose memory Heuss made a moving speech in 1950,[44] was not an encouraging example. Reduction of the president's prerogatives was the watchword. Nevertheless his election was delegated to a Federal Convention, an expanded body including representatives of the *Länder* parliaments, and was not confined to the Bundestag (or possibly the Bundesrat). The idea of the Federal Convention was that of Heuss himself;

at the conclusion of his period in office he acknowledged that it was his 'personal invention . . . long before there was any word of it in the Parliamentary Council and without my ever imagining that the political situation, which later arose, would bring me to the position of Head of State, something which I had never sought but which equally did not fill me with horror'.[45]

On the other hand Heuss was the only Free Democrat politician to express some reserve about introduction of the 'constructive vote of no-confidence' which he described as 'an invention of Carlo Schmid' (when setting up the Württemberg constitution in 1946).[46] On this he spoke as a full-blooded parliamentarian. He felt it far more important, however, that election of the president by plebiscite, a method which he distrusted on principle, should be ruled out from the outset as had been any wider presidential prerogatives in respect of emergency legislation, government or dissolution of parliament. (Even in mid-term in 1954 he was still opposed to the plebiscite saying: 'A president elected by plebiscite should in theory feel that he has been endowed with increased authority; in the amorphous state of mind in which the German people is at present, however, this would simply place a premium on demagogy'.[47]) The Federal Convention, which Dehler in particular also supported, provided a broader, more representative and more demonstrative basis better suited to the future attributes of the highest office in the country.

During these discussions Heuss had no more idea of what the future would bring him than did the other founding fathers of the Basic Law. He differed from Dehler and Becker in opposing any direct political function for the federal president and he voted with the socialists against the CDU proposal that convention of the Bundesrat should be a presidential prerogative.[48] Nevertheless in his opening speech in the Parliamentary Council he urged that the federal president should not be 'relegated to the uncertain realms of history . . . Do not overlook the symbolic force which the office may have and let us avoid a directorate as a provisional solution; the people will at once label this as an attempt to provide places for various persons and parties'.[49] His basic concept of the presidency was of a symbolic office playing an integrating role and standing above party, much on the lines of the British constitutional monarchy whose role was summarized by Bagehot in the classic phrase 'to encourage and to warn'; its influence, he considered, should stem from its stature and the personal example of its incumbent.[50] This was the background to the two speeches made by Heuss after his election on 12 September 1949, one to the Federal Convention and the other to the public in the *Marktplatz* in Bonn; after all the 'playing with paragraphs', he said, he hoped to turn the office of president into 'something like a tradition, something like a force possessing influence and weight which can make itself felt in the play of political forces'.[51] He did not, therefore, wish his office to be regarded as totally non-political.

Undoubtedly Heuss was assisted by the fact that the problem of forming a coalition in the summer of 1949 gave added importance to his position as Chairman of the Free Democrat Party; the CDU required his party's votes in order to form a government. The part he had played in the Parliamentary Council, however, also contributed largely to his election. Wilhelm Keil, the old Social-Democrat president of the Württemberg–Baden *Landtag*, said that in Bonn Heuss had 'given proof of his gift of mediation between opposing views'.[52] There are indications that initially Heuss had no wish to be a member of the Parliamentary Council and had supported a younger candidate. Reinhold Maier, however, persuaded him to place the experience of his work on the Württemberg–Baden constitution at the disposal of the Bonn Council. To ensure that something eventually emerged, he assumed the role of mediator between the CDU and SPD and he believes that his election was due to this.[53] Though he had his own decided views, this mediatory role has earned him the title of 'father' of the new constitution but he himself would never admit to being more than 'merely its midwife'.[54] The Federal Convention elected him President at the second ballot with an absolute majority over Kurt Schumacher; it did so three days before Adenauer's election as chancellor and so Heuss's election marks the true birth of the Federal Republic.

His speeches on 12 September 1949 constituted the first action of the new democracy and they gave a foretaste of the way in which he proposed to fulfil his office and the style he would adopt. By nature he was apt to give decided expression to his views, sometimes with Swabian bluntness but also with dispassionate realism; he castigated the 'professional idealists'[55] for instance, and took violent exception to the unscrupulous conceit of a 'typical transitory figure' like Carl Schmitt, the constitutional lawyer (Heuss managed to prevent his appointment to the Political Institute – it was the same Carl Schmitt who had repaid his Jewish professors for their assistance in furthering his career by unscrupulous adulation of Hitler and his totalitarian state).[56] On 12 September 1949, however, and later Heuss strove to give his exalted office substance and influence by the personal touch both in speeches and conversation, by emphasizing the necessity for a sense of community and citizenship in the midst of the inevitable strife between groups. He was prepared to consider his position as 'neutral' or 'above party' provided that this did not imply that he was 'not entitled to have his own views . . . that you can hardly expect from a man of my type and background'.[57]

He remained the great liberal – in his inaugural speech as Chairman of the Free Democrats in December 1948 he had said that his purpose was to defend 'the position of the individual under the constitution' in the age of the mass society.[58] He talked to the man in the street, he gained his impressions at first hand; he broke down barriers by story-telling and reminiscing; he met over-solemnity with humour; his object was 'after the nationalization of the human being', at last to humanize politics in Germany, to bring the state nearer to the citizen and to give authority a foundation in democracy. After his election he said to the populace in the Bonn *Marktplatz*: 'I should be a poor thing both mentally and spiritually if I were to enter the prison of mere government.'[59] He opened his first and inaugural speech in the Federal Chamber with a personal tribute of gratitude to his father who had died young and who, he said, had 'inspired his young sons with the legends of 1848'. He also paid tribute to Friedrich Naumann who had introduced him to active politics and given him some comprehension of the liberal, social and national bases of democracy. He regarded his 'task of mediation' in the Parliamentary Council as legitimizing and giving purpose to his presidency – 'to be available as a mediatory force over and above the battles which will take place, which are essential, which constitute a part of political life.'[60]

4

Despite all the criticism to which he was to be subjected in the coming years – particularly during the disagreements over the European Defence Community (EDC) in 1952 – Heuss deliberately refused to embark on what he called 'elbowing politics'.[61] This was to be seen in his relationship, certainly not always a smooth one, with Chancellor Adenauer which amounted to a sort of division of labour between these two very different characters. It was also to be seen, however (as his correspondence with Heinrich Brüning in 1950–1 showed) in his rejection of all attempts to re-establish a Weimar-type presidency. Instead he devoted his efforts to participation in the pluralism of public life, which he fully supported; he attempted, however, to guide all the differing tendencies towards the good of the community as a whole and reduce their differences; this was the primary object of his voluminous correspondence and of his writings with

which he persisted over the years; all was devoted to the necessity of reconciliation, of consensus in the midst of essentially continuing conflict which,
under a democracy, must be conducted openly and according to rules
recognized as fair. He was also much concerned with reconciliation and
re-establishment of confidence abroad, with Germany's moral relationship
with the outside world, so profoundly upset by the crimes of the Hitler
regime.

On the subject of reunification Heuss, who had himself been a citizen of
Berlin for thirty-three years, made no secret of the fact that in his view
division was the fault of Germany, 'the most terrible legacy of Hitler's
policy' ('between Boniface's *Fulda* and Luther's *Wartburg**, geographically
so close, there is a frontier marked by barbed wire and separating two
ideologies, both of which were, or should be, foreign to the Germans
unless they are to become slaves to outdated theories').[62] Heuss, however,
was the originator of the phrase 'indivisible Germany' proposed to Jakob
Kaiser on foundation of the *Kuratorium*†. On his first visit to Berlin Heuss
summarized the dilemma simply but strikingly; 'The fate of Berlin depends
on West Germany but the fate of reunified Germany depends on Berlin.'
His friends often criticized the government's lack of energy over their
reunification policy and reproached him with co-operating in setting up a
state separate from the Soviet zone. To them he would reply, with a touch
of resignation, that this was a case of *force majeure* and that he had participated
in the formulation of the Basic Law 'in order to stop the western, in some
cases newly formed, *Länder* [he was referring particularly to the French zone]
growing away from each other'[63] when rigid unity was being enforced in
the East.

This did not prevent many people criticizing Heuss for keeping himself
aloof from day-to-day politics when he was so experienced and had proved
himself so valuable ever since Weimar. He himself once said facetiously that
he did not spend his time in writing 'simply to escape from Adenauer and
Ollenhauer'.[64] The real achievement of the Heuss era, however, lay in the
effort to revive confidence both at home and abroad and to do so not merely
by covering up the stern fact of German guilt. On assuming office he
announced his conviction that 'we have gambled away our external power
and must now acquire moral force'.[65] Here he could make good use of his
reputation both as a person and an author, of his journalistic experience and

---

* Boniface, who introduced christianity to Germany, was based in Fulda; Luther, the
symbol of the Reformation, translated the Bible in Wartburg Castle.

† An all-party organization dedicated to German reunification.

humanist education, of his directness of approach and conversation. During the arguments about the guilt question he coined the phrase 'collective shame'. In his introduction to the book *Die grossen Deutschen* (The Great Germans) he writes of our age being 'burdened with shame'.[66] The subject closest to his heart was what he called 'making amends for the shameful violation of the law'; this he regarded neither as a juridical nor economic problem but a spiritual and moral duty on the fulfilment of which the consolidation of democracy at home depended.

The fact that he could count among his friends numerous intellectuals who had been persecuted and exiled was of immeasurable assistance in these circles where suspicion was still acute and deep-rooted. This was strikingly demonstrated by his lectures and talks in Israel which, owing to the non-recognition policy he could only undertake in 1960 as *ex*-President. At that time Martin Buber hailed him in Jerusalem University as the man 'who came after Hitler' and personified the hope of a democratic Germany. Heuss spoke of the 'self-creation of democracy' and the great contribution, now so scandalously destroyed, made by Jews to German history; he had not come to Israel, he said, to teach but to learn.[67]

In his correspondence is to be found a small but highly indicative episode illustrating his attitude to the Third Reich. In 1937 Heuss had chosen a motto for Friedrich Naumann's book, not a word of which did he need to change after 1945; someone once asked him why he had not chosen Conrad Ferdinand Meyer's apt verse 'Patience! What grows slowly grows old late; when others wither we shall be a state.' Heuss replied: 'But think of that verse printed in such a book in 1937; it would have sounded like a paean to the Third Reich; Hitler, after all, thought that the German state had at last been created by him.'[68] Moreover, as Heuss wrote in his foreword to *Die grossen Deutschen*, he was especially depressed by the 'intellectual absurdities and brutalities' of National-socialism.[69]

After his election as President Heuss spoke of the boon of the ability to forget as applied both to individuals and to peoples.

'But I am anxious lest many people in Germany abuse this boon and want to forget too quickly. We must keep alive our realization of what has led us to the situation in which we are today. This should not evoke feelings of revenge or hatred. I hope that from this confusion in the souls of our people we shall contrive to create unity. But we must not complacently forget what the Hitler period has done to us.[70]'

This conviction was the reason for his speech at the dedication of the memorial in Belsen concentration camp in 1952[71], for his visit in 1957 to the Ardeatine pits near Rome where Germans had shot hostages, in 1958 to New York and at other times to Britain and France to speak with men who had been persecuted by Hitler. Reporting on German television on his visit to Israel Heuss said:

'And we must not let all that happened vanish from our minds, for that would simply be running away from the truth. We cannot allow ourselves to do that for the sake of our souls. Many people will not like what I am saying. They will say: enough, enough, enough of all this. That is not permissible – for our own sakes.'[72]

In his book *Die deutsche Katastrophe* (The German Catastrophe) published in 1946 and far too quickly forgotten, Friedrich Meinecke had said that the most urgent thing was 'to do one's own house-cleaning'; this was what Heuss tried to put into practice. For this reason Heuss invariably took every opportunity to pay tribute to the frequently misjudged or even vilified German resistance; he regarded it as a great heritage for the new democracy and made every effort to impress this fact on the public conscience. The speech on the right to resist which he delivered in the Free University of Berlin on the tenth anniversary of 20 July remains unforgettable; it included some forceful comments on the senselessness of loyalty to an oath sworn to Hitler, the oath-breaker, and concluded with the words: 'The legacy is still with us; the obligation has not yet been fulfilled.'[73] For Heuss the resistance was no convenient alibi for the failure of 1933.

All this made it clear that, despite casual utterances by Heuss himself, the office of federal president could be far more than a 'subsidiary' organ for representation abroad, to which the constitution-makers had thrown 'a few crumbs';[74] in contrast to the politically overloaded institution of the presidency under Weimar, in an untried democracy still subject to severe pressures it could be an integrating agency; it could establish a tradition and style essential even to a down-to-earth republic formed of sceptical citizens, pragmatic parties and special interest-groups – and it could do all this without too much fuss. Though Heuss's background was romanticist, he invariably warned against 'romanticism in politics' however ideologically based. He regarded the 'circle of anti-democratic men of letters' who had tried to construct a 'specifically German concept of the state' as 'involuntary pathfinders for Hitler'.[75] In a speech to the Bundeswehr Academy entitled 'The military profession in our times' he told the officers, with a wealth of background, that he would 'become frosty at once if anyone starts to talk to me in emotional or sentimental terms about tradition'.[76] North Rhine–Westphalia (this 'somewhat unhappy philological expression') he supported as a 'vast process of fusion' which actually had the advantage of possessing no tradition.[77] Nevertheless he was only too conscious of the advantages of 'roots in history' and 'formation of a political style'; these were the subjects of his address to the Association for Political Science in Berlin in 1952 and his speech to Bonn University.[78] His task, as he repeatedly said, though not in a spirit of criticism, to meetings of the older generation and army old comrades was 'to create a tradition'; in his view this was a 'far more difficult but far grander task than any attempt to resurrect the remnants and usages of outdated ideas'.[79]

It is not possible here to give details of all the obstacles and difficulties which Heuss encountered in pursuing his concept of the office of president during a decade of hectic developments and sometimes bitter dispute. Though never obsessed by thirst for power, he was an ardent politician[80] and his correspondence with émigré friends (Arnold Brecht, Erich Eyck, Moritz-Julius Bonn, for instance) shows how difficult it was for him at times to play his self-chosen role of mediator standing above party. There were pleasant interludes such as the revival of the peace award of the *Pour le Mérite* (the German Victoria Cross) in 1952, the creation of the Scientific Council for college reform or his work, involving much correspondence, as editor of the composite book *Die grossen Deutschen*; to this he devoted much time and energy outside his official business. All this was interspersed with more controversial activities such as his efforts to intercept his friends' criticism of Adenauer and to steer his chosen course even when he himself had his doubts about government policy.[81]

Clearly he acknowledged the pertinacity and tactical ability of the chancellor, from whom he differed as chalk from cheese; clearly too, at times he found his self-imposed detachment from day-to-day politics difficult. As what he called a 'patriotic necessity',[82] however, he never allowed any word to appear in public about his differences (or the resulting correspondence) with the Palais Schaumburg or even about Adenauer's candidacy for the presidency in 1959 when certain hurtful things were said (Adenauer, for instance, said that Heuss had not made full use of his office). There is an unconfirmed story that, when signing the law on 'co-determination', he advised Adenauer to give the principle a trial in the cabinet.[83] Petty reactions to his candid style of oratory often pained him; after a speech at Munich University in 1955, for instance, he was reproached for disparaging the title 'Doctor', which drew from him the comment:'This people's capacity to laugh at itself is not sufficiently developed.'[84] Finally there was his abortive attempt to give the Germans a new national anthem – in order to 'lead us out of our irredentist mood'. In 1951, for instance, he said: 'The Germans find it difficult to remain sensible once they have tasted the delights of *hubris* again.'[85] When, in May 1952, he finally gave way to the chancellor over the question of the national anthem, his comment was not without bitterness; Hoffmann von Fallersleben, he said, had been a follower of the black–red–gold flag and all those now so eager to sing his anthem would do well to acknowledge this democratic national symbol.

5

Theodor Heuss was a civilian and an intellectual through and through – in a society for which both were words of abuse. He was no authoritarian but was nevertheless in a position of authority; he never flattered but was still popular in the best sense of the word; he kept contact with the masses without demagogy.[86] Herein lies some hope for German democracy. The 150 years of German endeavour to achieve democracy have been labelled (by Karl Buchheim) the '*via dolorosa* of the civic spirit'; Theodor Heuss was a man to loosen the log-jam. This does not imply that from the outset or in principle he was in favour of universal military service; he called it the 'legitimate child of democracy';[87] what he considered fatal to democracy was the 'nothing-to-do-with-me' outlook.

He knew, however, how to overcome the traditional stiffness of the military by his overpowering humanity, attractive humour and free-and-easy spontaneity. The most striking illustration of this was his address (already mentioned) in 1959 to the Bundeswehr Staff College; his opening sentence put everyone at ease – 'He comes late but he comes all the same – I mean old Heuss to the Bundeswehr.'[88] Again, when visiting military manoeuvres he put an end to all sabre-rattling, which he placed in the same category as the German passion for the chase or for militant associations, with his famous remark 'Now let's have a fine victory.'

What he did oppose was any degree of autonomy for the military and any excessive differentiation between the criteria used in civilian democracy and in military or pseudo-military matters. Accordingly on several occasions he noted with sorrowful resignation that students' associations had never really revived.[89] As President Heuss never made any secret of his personal views or of his anxieties and disillusionments. Whenever the situation was difficult he was guided by his determination 'to save this fragile young state from violent controversy on public affairs and to keep myself in the clear; I therefore both spoke and acted according to the book, although during the negotiations in the Parliamentary Council I made many suggestions which were not accepted.'[90] In his memoirs he says quite frankly: 'I too undoubtedly made full use of the human right to be in error.'[91]

His re-election in 1954, which for the first time took place in Berlin, was supported by all the major parties. Public opinion polls showed that only 14 per cent of the population wanted a change of president.[92] In the same year, 1954, Erich Eyck, who had been exiled by Hitler, dedicated his great history of the Weimar Republic as follows: 'To two friends who have never failed me – Theodor Heuss on his 70th birthday and George Gooch [the great English historian] on his 80th birthday.'

Heuss held office for ten years and ultimately suffered the disappointment of seeing his whole work imperilled by the dispute about his successor.[93] Nevertheless the first federal president was eventually able to pass on his office intact and he did so out of profound respect for the constitution. He had invariably been at pains, even in face of wounding criticism, to keep within the limits of his office. Perhaps, in contrast to Chancellor Adenauer, he did not exhaust all its political possibilities. Yet the decision of 1959 was right. It was in accordance with all that he had striven for. His view was that 'a sense of law and order must once again be rooted in this people'[94] and so he emphasized that were he to stand for a third term, this would be 'a sign of the poverty of Germany democracy' which must be able to accept 'a change of personalities, even of types'. People abroad, he said, might well wonder whether democracy in the Federal Republic was not 'solely dependent on Adenauer and Heuss'.[95] Politicians of all parties urged that the constitution be altered to allow Heuss a third term but in his view this would have prevented the democratic constitution and its rules becoming firmly stabilized. In his farewell address on 12 September 1959 he said: 'Please look upon the change of federal president as part of the educative process for the ordinary citizen.'[96]

Herein lay the purpose and the now historic significance of the role played by Theodor Heuss in the re-establishment of democracy in Germany. For the arrogant claims of the 'Thousand Year Reich' he substituted democracy's 'short-term commission to rule'.[97] As ex-President, 'so to speak a free man again',[98] Heuss deliberately refused to enter the electoral campaign of 1961. He felt that 'quite simply he owed this much to the exalted position to which I have brought the Federal Presidency as pre-scribed in the Basic Law.'[99] He lived only four more years in his house in Stuttgart. His death was a double loss: to the second German republic which had been guided by the voice of this man; to the world of intellect and politics in that he could no longer draw a picture of his age, could not write the tumultuous early history of the new democracy and his presidency – he who could so vividly combine the historical with the personal so that history became personalized and vice versa.[100] He achieved much. He left us with many tasks still unfulfilled. His life was devoted to the humanization of politics and the state. His legacy is a living democracy – not merely an institution but a way of life.

10

Salient Features of the Adenauer Era

The thought behind western policy at the end of the Second World War was that Germany must be kept under control for a long time and that she must be prevented from acquiring any military potential which might enable the Germans to pursue a sinister policy of playing East and West off against each other. In the situation following the Second World War, though not the First, this was achieved; nevertheless the possibility of a revival of the much-exaggerated 'Rapallo policy' remained a western bogey. The split in the anti-Hitler coalition brought this alleged danger into the forefront once more. On the final collapse of the four-power regime in 1948-9 two main facets of the German question emerged and in both of them international and internal German problems were closely intertwined. On the one hand was the problem of Germany's reincorporation into the world of European states and the restoration of some freedom of manoeuvre to German policy, on the other, the fact that the country was divided into two states which, owing to the play of external forces, had begun their existence and development under totally different conditions and influences.

As the East-West conflict began and intensified an inter-allied solution of the German problem and in particular of the position to be occupied by a reunited Germany receded into the distance. The *de facto* situation, however, had the advantage that it reflected the power–policy situation. Inclusion of the Federal Republic in the West and the People's Republic in the East seemed to kill two birds with one stone: it ensured a clear delineation of the military and political spheres of interest of the two blocs in Central Europe and it put an end to the fear that a reunited Germany might embark on a two-faced policy reminiscent of Tauroggen, Bismarck, Rapallo or even the Hitler–Stalin pact. The remaining question was how this 'solution' could be firmly established, obtain a measure of genuine consent from the people and at the same time be consonant with the declared aim of ultimate reunification.

The Russians drew two conclusions: they abandoned any attempt to include West Germany in their sphere of influence and they turned their occupation policy into one of rigid *Gleichschaltung* on 'popular democracy', communist lines; politically the People's Republic quickly became a Soviet satellite. Movements for independence either remained ineffective or, as on 17 June 1953, were suppressed by Moscow more firmly than in any other satellite state. Things were very different in the West. Free parties and interest-groups, a freely elected parliament and a democratic constitution based on the rule of law allowed far wider scope to the formation of opinion and capacity for decision. Admittedly there were hardly any champions of an eastern orientation apart from the minute communist party and one or two tiny groups. Growing sympathy for western policy and the western way of life, however, did not imply unreserved acceptance of the great cleavage of 1949. After all it removed all prospect of the reunification of Germany on the basis of non-alignment or neutralization; at the very least, continuance of four-power responsibility would not have prejudged the solution of the German question.

Such ideas were no more than an undercurrent, however, and played only a secondary role even in the arguments of the Social-Democrat opposition; instead the vast majority both of the makers and the addressees of public opinion definitely championed and supported the Federal Republic's western orientation and the primary reason was the rapid progress of the western alliance and integration policy. It met three major requirements: it accelerated the recovery process in West Germany and held out the promise of rapid transition from the occupation regime to political equality of status; for the German national consciousness which, after the exaggerations and contradictions of the Hitler regime's nationalism, was in a vacuum, it offered a prospect of new supra-national principles and scales of value; finally for Germany's neighbours it offered a system of guarantees against renewal of any German policy of hegemony and revision; instead of unilateral foreign supervisory organs which would inevitably have been regarded as discriminatory and reopened old wounds, it provided an effective, reciprocal system of voluntary controls within a close-knit partnership of free peoples.

Differences of opinion arose not over the principle but over the form and method of its implementation. The Social-Democrats' concept was of the broadest possible framework including the Anglo-Saxon and Scandinavian countries and retaining elasticity in view of the problem of the division of Germany; the Council of Europe in Strasbourg was considered a suitable starting point. The Adenauer government, on the other hand, keeping in step with the actual progress of the integration policy, preferred the Little Europe solution of a community of the Six, which had already found initial expression in the Coal and Steel Community; close connections with the Anglo-Saxon powers and subsequent expansion of the community were regarded as self-evident necessities; the earlier idea of a European third force continued to exert some effect. Such was the situation governing the debate on the most difficult problem raised by the intensification of the East–West conflict and the inclusion of the Federal Republic in the West: the decision whether and how to initiate German *rearmament*.

The external political motives for this decision can be dealt with briefly. It was essential to reinforce the western potential; at the same time it was the Federal Republic's duty, as it became incorporated on an increasingly equal basis into the western reconstruction and security system, to make an appropriate contribution to its protection. In view of the rearmament of the People's Republic the United States in particular worked hard to remove the understandable suspicions still existing in the western camp, especially in France and Britain; in addition to this general suspicion a sharp reaction was to be expected from the Soviet Union, the consequences of which were unpredictable. What could be more obvious, however, than that the Federal Republic's military contribution should be fully integrated into the emergent European Community and so kept under permanent control! This, however, postulated not only the agreement of Germany's partners (which ultimately failed to materialize owing to a temporary French veto) but also German readiness to accept such a solution and at this point the internal political implications of rearmament emerged as a subject of serious debate.

Adenauer's thoughts had been moving in this direction from an early stage. He was set upon his western policy and his object was to consolidate Germany's position as an equal partner in the western community; he was entitled to expect that a military contribution would endow the Federal Republic with the attributes of full nationhood. This implied, however, a really revolutionary change in internal policy and the political views on which it was based. Many of the politicians who now lined up behind the new policy, Adenauer not excluded, had only recently spoken emphatically and with conviction in favour of the renunciation of military power by Germany as laid down in the Basic Law. There were good grounds for fearing that a precipitate change from demilitarization to remilitarization might once more imperil the democratic seedling, might hamper its growth both externally and internally, might provide food for animosities, both old and new, against Allied post-war policy in this matter and finally might vastly complicate the all-German question. These ideas were first vented in August 1950 in the Consultative Assembly of the Council of Europe on British (Churchill) and French initiative; in August 1951 Carlo Schmid, speaking for the Social-Democrats, gave eloquent expression in the same forum to these internal and external political anxieties; the SPD wished to restrict the German defence contribution to economic and political action at least until a supra-national European authority had been set up. This did not imply any opposition of principle to the European or defence policies; it was, however, a criticism of the form and tempo of German reorientation.

In the event the somewhat dubious consequences of this *tour de force* soon emerged. Adenauer pursued his new policy with energy and, when the Korean War ended, forced through Germany's adherence to the western alliance system. This increased the opposition's suspicion that he was pursuing primarily party political aims, was trying to reinforce his own position and attract additional support by perpetuating a nationalistic and militaristic outlook through the soldiers' societies which had necessarily been either rehabilitated or organized afresh; the experience of the Weimar Republic had shown that this was an ominous symptom. The EDC solution seemed to disprove these fears and speculations, but the fact remained that the future rearmament would be the work of a bourgeois government coalition and this might well strengthen its internal political position. One thing stood out clearly from the tangled confused conflict of opinion which from autumn 1950 shook the Federal Republic itself: the central dilemma of the Germany problem, the question of compatibility between a European policy and one of sovereignty, between the policies of rearmament and reunification. The dilemma was not eased by the very slow pace of both discussion and concrete progress. The government eventually forced its decision through against passionate opposition carried even as far as the constitutional court and in 1953, by its electoral victory, achieved the necessary majority to amend the Basic Law; even after this, however, opinions remained sharply divided on the subject of this 'political *tour de force*' (as Cornides put it). The conflict died down when the EDC was rejected by France and membership of NATO provided a quick alternative solution; even this, however, could not eliminate the fundamental German problem and could guarantee no more than maintenance of the *status quo*.

Instead a more violent debate opened concerning structure and democratization, size and armament of a German army; in particular, now that there was to be no integration at the European level, the question was raised of its status, its character as a semi-national, semi-integrated armed force. In the light of the internal situation in the Federal Republic and its relationship to the West this was not easy to answer; it was even more difficult in the light of the division of Germany and the conclusions which the East might draw from the fact that this division had now been consecrated militarily and that German armies and armaments were now to reappear. Admittedly, in a NATO framework, a West German army could be kept within limits by the USA's position of hegemony. But did not its mere existence imply a reinforcement of the restorationist tendencies both in state and society in the Federal Republic? Moreover the demand for reunification was now backed by a 'policy of strength' and the growing economic and political weight carried by the Federal Republic; did not, therefore, the revival of a German army in any case offer Soviet propaganda a welcome opportunity to label the reunification demand as an expression of militarist 'revisionism and revanchism' – and to do so with considerable effect on the neighbours and victims of National-socialist Germany?

In this respect too the theory that the Federal Republic was a continuation of the German Reich proved to be a double-edged weapon. The situation was aggravated by the fact that personnel policy both in state and industry had not been able to prevent an influx of ex-Nazis into influential positions; this was primarily the result of an over-generous interpretation (in Article 131 of the Basic Law) of the rights of Nazi officials – it was made in face of warnings from the Federal Constitutional Court; other reasons were the removal of all Allied economic restrictions and widespread patronage. In the event formation and pursuit of an independent foreign policy contrived to deal with these situations and problems during the years of the Federal Republic's rapid development. Its apparent turning points were the two most obvious encounters with the Soviet Union's German policy: the much debated Stalin note of 1952 and the surprising establishment of diplomatic relations between Bonn and Moscow in 1955.

2

German foreign policy in the first half of the 1950s was governed by the conclusions to be drawn from the experience of the Korean crisis and the subsequent hardening of the *status quo* in a divided world. Searching for some possibility of manoeuvre and some alternative in this rigid situation, attention turned to three complexes of problems: clarification of the German–Soviet relationship, conditions for a relaxation of tension, the estimate of the politico-military power ratio in the light of the nuclear balance and finally the development of American policy towards Germany after the transition to the Eisenhower–Dulles era.

From the outset the background to the division of Germany had been not only the imperatives of the East–West conflict but a general mistrust of the establishment of a united, independent Germany. Whatever lip-service the occupying powers might pay to reunification, even after the formation of the two separate states, their attitude was always tempered by this *Realpolitik* consideration. Further difficulty lay in the fact that, as the differences between the two halves of Germany took concrete shape in their institutions, each half insisted that any reunification must take place according its own standards; as a result the problem became even more inseparably bound up with the East–West conflict. Here the position of the Federal Republic was the stronger and, according to democratic ideas the more legitimate. In the first place it was far larger, comprising three-quarters of the population; second, its politics and government being based on free elections, it could from the outset present the demand for free, all-German elections as the correct and politically legitimate road to a democratic unified Germany; this was a basic advantage constituting a severe handicap to Soviet policy on Germany in the field of international relations and in particular in relation to recognition of the People's Republic. Nevertheless, though the non-communist world recognized the legitimacy of the German demand, memories of Nazidom's 'greater Germany' remained vivid. The reunification theme, therefore, propounded by a government claiming to be the direct successor of the German state, could not expect unreserved support even from this quarter.

The consequence was unadmitted acceptance of the fact that the Federal Republic had to accommodate itself to the new *status quo* situation, to a policy of restraint, that safeguarding its own existence took precedence over an uncertain reunification policy; this was an early and fundamental decision which continued to be violently contested. It was not in fact consistently opposed by the opposition as a matter of principle; their criticism was directed more at the form than the substance of the western orientation and the claim of the Federal Republic to be the legal successor and representative of Germany. Adenauer, who acted as his own Foreign Minister, threw himself whole-heartedly and energetically into the policy of integration into and alliance with the West and so drew his conclusions.

His theory that reunification could only come through the Western Alliance and reinforcement of the West German position could only mean that the freedom and security of West Germany took precedence over national unity. The decision was not publicized and perhaps not even realized to be a decision; this was shown by the horror and indignation evinced among the German public, including even the government camp, whenever the practical results of this evasive posture came out fully into the open. A good example was the storm provoked by the utterances of the philosopher Karl Jaspers in 1959; he had the courage to declare that in the light of the claim to freedom and continuity of the German state reunification was 'unrealistic', thus exposing the fact that the whole question had meanwhile become subject to a taboo complex.

Meanwhile there had been much discussion about alternatives to this policy. It was conducted on two closely connected levels: on the one hand an adjustment of interests and a compromise leading to relaxation of tension between the great powers, on the other development and improvement of German–Soviet relations. Pursuing her anti-western policy, the Soviet Union had meanwhile completed the *Gleichschaltung* of Eastern and South-eastern Europe, but with the defection of Tito in 1948 and the failure of the Korean experiment, this policy had clearly reached its limits. Basically the firmness of West German policy represented a set-back for Moscow, particularly seeing that it meant an acceleration of west European integration and was already enabling the Federal Republic to join the alliance militarily. In 1949 Moscow had answered the Marshall Plan with her own organization, COMECON, thus institutionalizing both politically and economically the integration of the communist countries into a rigidly controlled eastern bloc. Against this background the Soviet Union stepped up her propaganda for the neutralization of Germany; this, it was said, would solve the security and reunification problems, prevent the opposing fronts solidifying and subject German rearmament to adequate control. The catchword of 'co-existence' began to have its effect; it applied with special force to the German question in addition to the 'new countries' of Asia and Africa which were becoming the focus of world political rivalry. The death of Stalin and the change of President in Washington seemed to herald a new stage in East–West politics with negotiations for a *détente* and disarmament; even before this, however, in March 1952 the Soviet Union had come forward with a proposal that, like the Austrian, the German question be cleared up.

The timing of the Soviet initiative inevitably and immediately raised the suspicion that this was no constructive suggestion for a solution but a mere, though major, wrecking action. On 10 March 1952 the Soviet Union put forward fresh proposals for a peace treaty with Germany; this took place two months before the solemn signature on 26 May 1952 of the Bonn Treaties which revised the rights of the occupying powers and laid down the EDC policy, the failure of which could not then be foreseen. During 1951 West Germany had made rapid progress in establishing herself as an equal member of the European Community from the foreign policy point of view; from April 1951 legal expression had been given to this process by the establishment of diplomatic relations with numerous countries, while the Soviet Union had been unable to obtain comparable recognition for the People's Republic. Further dismantling of the occupation regime in West Germany followed; only in Berlin was incorporation of Germany into the western bloc delayed or deliberately refused. So, when Stalin's note arrived, Germany stood at the cross-roads between commitment and freedom of action; the inexorable alternatives of the German problem were highlighted once more. In 1950 Russian propaganda had still been presenting as the only solution formation of a central government manned on a basis of parity by representatives of the Federal Republic and the People's Republic; now, however, Stalin laid his main emphasis on the withdrawal of armed forces and freedom of alliance for a reunited Germany. It was therefore more important to him to keep Germany out of the West and neutralize her than to impose a communist solution. It was not easy to see through this change of front and the proposal inevitably became a subject of debate in Germany (and rightly still is so today).

The Soviet proposal must, of course, be viewed in the world-wide political context of a disarmament campaign which, after the failure of Soviet policy in Korea, was designed to offset the access in strength to the West of their system of alliances and strategic bases; in this system Germany was the most important and *still* the weakest point. Feeling that their own bloc system was secure, the Soviets were entitled to expect that such a neutralization of central Europe might have far-reaching effects on the attitudes of France and Britain; an American withdrawal from Europe, a return to the fluid pre-war situation and perhaps too a Franco–Russian security agreement might bring about a reorientation of the Federal Republic and this could not fail to have its effect upon the internal power relationships inside Germany. These considerations make it seem probable that this was the first and only occasion on which there was a possibility of submitting to serious test the genuineness of the German and Soviet-German commitment to reunification. On 14 March 1952 Otto Grotewohl, Minister-President of the People's Republic, supplemented the Soviet note by proposing free, all-German elections for a National Assembly on the basis of the Weimar Republic's electoral law and this seemed to offer an astoundingly realistic starting point; nevertheless the demand for the exclusion of what in Soviet terminology were called 'undemocratic and anti-peace-loving organizations' seemed to offer possibilities to the well-known and well-tried methods of interference.

The surprising fact was that, with this proposal, Moscow was apparently accepting not only the existence but also the rearmament of West Germany. Admittedly, for the Federal Republic, the national armed forces allowed to a neutralized Germany did not provide security equal to that of the Western Alliance. Nevertheless it remained an open question whether, despite all these objections, the delay in West German reconstruction and entry into the Western Alliance (inevitable in any case with the collapse of the EDC) implicit in an attempt to negotiate, was not justified – always provided that reunification remained the overriding aim. The risks and sacrifices involved in any serious examination of the Soviet proposal were obvious. Equally clear, however, were the inevitable implications of a total refusal to discuss the status of a reunified Germany or the Oder-Neisse Line, to subject the peace treaty proposals to hard-headed examination at a moment when far-reaching plans had been made but no irrevocable decisions taken. Germany was, after all, still occupied, under the control and at the same time the protection of the occupying powers; the question of their withdrawal could only become actual when the future status of Germany had been clarified.

Much discussion was evoked by the example of Austria; the wearisome process culminating in the treaty of 1955 seemed like a rehearsal. Austria was of course a smaller country and agreement was far simpler than it would have been in the case of a major industrial country like Germany. The fact remains, however, that Germany did not take the Soviet Union at its word; instead of engaging in some political activity or making some contribution of its own, the Federal Government showed relief at the caution of the West; it seemed to be afraid of anything which might delay a German return to self-satisfied sovereignty, of any tendency to give precedence to relaxation of tension over equality of status and full membership of the Western Alliance, of any slackening in the pace of the national European policy. Serious negotiations for reunification would undoubtedly have raised equally grave problems for the Soviet Union, particularly in relation to the communist zone of Germany with its satellite regime. The result, however, was, that without undertaking any commitments, Moscow was continually able to impress and disturb the world in general, and the German public and intelligentsia in particular, with plans for Germany and 'peace movements' – with the weapon of neutralization propaganda, as the socialist leader, Kurt Schumacher, lamented. The German answer was a firm, rigidly defensive policy, an inflexible insistence on a single reunification strategy based on legal and institutional arguments, when in fact a strong positive policy, some initiative and some effort to free the oppressed peoples by political means were required. Here was the unsolved dilemma; it became the hallmark of the Eisenhower–Dulles period, policy fluctuating between ideas of the 'roll back' and liberation or mere maintenance of the *status quo* and reaction to the other side's moves. Meanwhile the field and the initiative were left open to Russian propaganda.

Here was the real core of the problem; on the West German side it could all too easily be brushed aside by pointing to the semi-utopian, semi-nationalistic outlook of the neutralistic groups. What mattered was not the particularist sense of mission of these sectional groups but whether the purposes and weaknesses of the other side should have been probed in terms of *Realpolitik*; this rather than a negative defence pursued through an exchange of notes was the duty of any true foreign policy; this was the conviction not only of the opposition but of Pfleiderer, the Free Democrat politician who died before his time, and Gustav Heinemann, the CDU Minister who resigned over the rearmament question. The result, however, was that West Germany made no contribution to the formation of the western viewpoint; on 25 March 1952 the Western Powers gave a prompt reply to the Soviet proposal, reiterating the demand already rejected by the Eastern bloc, that a UNO commission should first ensure that political freedom was guaranteed throughout Germany. The ultimate object, of course, was the incorporation of the whole of Germany into the West; it was hardly to be expected that the Soviets would reply if the Federal Republic itself had no more to say on the reunification question. This abnegation on Germany's part has been seen on several subsequent occasions; her partners in the Western Alliance have sometimes regarded it as evidence of a comforting reliability, although latterly, however, as a hindrance and a factor in restriction of the western freedom of manoeuvre. Nevertheless the motives were understandable enough. Desire for consolidation and security, mistrust and fear of Soviet domination, already experienced and still to be seen in Berlin, were more potent factors than the aversion to rearmament and the continuing protest against division of the country. In the eyes of public opinion they legitimized the Federal Government's policy and made it appear inevitable; they gave it the stamp of necessity.

Despite all the bitter debates, the credit for avoidance of deep divisions in the Federal Republic must go to the basically loyal democratic attitude of the opposition; they were primarily anxious lest Adenauer's rigid western policy, pursued at the expense of an active reunification policy, might provoke a fresh upsurge of nationalism among the masses. Even more important was the fact that reduction in the intensity of the East–West conflict might lead to a reduction in the tempo of the German western policy and that at the same time European economic expansion might be given preference, if not complete precedence, over that of the Federal Republic. The death of Stalin gave fresh impetus to speculations about an international *détente*, to which Eisenhower, the new American president, lent his support once the explosion of the first Russian hydrogen bomb had proved that the 'balance of terror' was now fact. The place of the EDC solution was taken by that of the more leisurely but more elastic NATO solution, the defensive character of which corresponded more closely to the military and strategic situation. Here too, however, there was a conflict of views, governed primarily by technical military considerations: being inferior in conventional armaments, western defence relied upon the deterrent and retaliatory threat of nuclear weapons and their use in a future conflict had to be made credible; the result was that conventional attack became the trip-wire for a nuclear offensive. Both politically and from the propaganda viewpoint, therefore, NATO strategy entered a twilight period and this cast doubt upon the foreign and military policy of the Federal Republic – in so far as pursuit of its eastern and all-German aims was still officially its basis.

3

Hopes of breaking this vicious circle of threat and parry were concentrated on two levels; a global change in the world political situation might help to loosen the log-jam of the German problem; a more restricted field for improvement of German–Soviet relationships would at least provide a starting point for a partial *détente*. The foreign policy debates which characterized the middle period of the Adenauer era (1953–8) centred primarily around these two levels. All negotiations started from the assumption that both sides would insist on retaining their present power-policy position and spheres of influence. This meant that, as in the case of the artificial partition compromises in Asia (Korea and Indo-China) the problem of Germany remained in suspense; the field was left open to propagandistic, psychological and juridical arguments. There were ludicrous proposals for a solution such as the Soviet Union's offer to join NATO herself in order to avert her nightmare, inclusion of the Federal Republic. The offer was made at the Foreign Minister's Conference of the four great powers in Berlin in January and February 1954; the mere fact that these renewed contacts took place, however, seemed to show that in the post-Stalin era *détente* was the order of the day and that this applied to the German problem too.

Though Berlin symbolized both the problem and the hope of its solution, in the event expectations did not materialize – neither did German fears that the Four might reach agreement at Germany's expense. The German problem was far too closely bound up with the overall world political position of the two blocs. From the Soviet point of view, reunification by means of free elections implied, as a first step, abandonment of the corner-stone of their whole policy, with far-reaching repercussions on the entire eastern bloc. The West, however, regarded any real *quid pro quo* such as the exclusion of all West Germany from the military front, as equally intolerable. Here the Federal Government brought its influence to bear, supporting the American view which was that a Germany reunited through free elections should be at liberty to decide on its future status. In the eyes of the Soviet Union, of course, this was only a simulated concession; there could be no doubt of the side for which a free, all-German government would opt.

The Berlin conference, therefore, ended without result. Moscow was only interested in progress on the German question if it set limits to the Federal Republic's rearmament and integration into the West, if, in fact, it implied Germany's total exclusion. On their side the Western Powers, in view of the changed conditions of the nuclear balance, showed no inclination to risk their newly consolidated basis in Western Europe. Western European Union was formed to replace the vanished EDC; the occupation regime was replaced by a treaty with Germany (the Paris Treaties of October 1954), thus formally converting the Five-Power Alliance under the Brussels Pact of 1948, the aim of which was the control of Germany, into an alliance with Germany (and Italy); a little later, in May 1955, it was absorbed into NATO. This also implied that the Atlantic Powers (USA and Canada) together with Britain had confirmed their commitment to Europe, thus dispelling the French fears on which the EDC had foundered. As a result Paris accepted self-determination for the population of the Saar and relinquished the territory – a sign of the rapid improvement in Franco–German relations. It was a generous gesture, setting an example for reunification. Conditions of course were quite different; the Saar fell into the Federal Government's lap without any action on its part – Adenauer himself had supported europeanization of the Saar.

As a result, however, the efforts to bring Europe closer together had received a further setback. The emphasis now was on the military alliance with all the consequences this implied for the sovereignty of the Federal Republic as an equal partner; this destroyed all hopes of a west European solution of the German problem and its prospects of a supra-national organization taking priority over the national interests of a divided Germany; this might have been some compensation for abandonment of reunification or at least taken the heat out of the problem. Germany was in an even more ambivalent position; as before, West German sovereignty was dependent on the strength of the Western Alliance; even more than in the occupation period, however, and even juridically, this postulated insistence on the Federal Republic's right to represent all Germany and to be the successor to the German state. This was how it had been presented in the first instance and West Germany had been explicitly supported in this claim by the Western Powers.

In fact, quite apart from all earlier and later assurances, the German treaty of October 1954 established the incorporation of the Federal Republic into the West and its independence. Nevertheless its preamble included the statement that the reunification of Germany 'remained a fundamental common aim of the signatory states'. Further the three Western Powers explicitly reserved 'their previous rights in relation to Germany as a whole including the reunification of Germany' (Article 2). Article 7 laid down reunification as a primary objective of the Western Alliance and of co-operation between the Federal Republic and the three Western Powers; finally Article 10, the so-called revision clause, stated that the powers were ready to adjust the treaty to the requirements of reunification. This basic position was reiterated and confirmed in subsequent declarations; in July 1957, for instance, the Federal Foreign Minister together with the Ambassadors of the three powers signed a solemn declaration in Berlin that 'reunification remains a common responsibility of the four powers' – in other words, including the Soviet Union. The only question was what validity these legal statements had so long as and in so far as they were not agreed with and did not accord with the interests of the fourth great power. The Soviet Union protested violently against the western decisions of 1954–5. It was not enough (as the Western Powers did) simply to write these protests off as meaningless, counter-propaganda. To opposition remonstrances that, as a result, the Soviet Union would lose all further interest in German reunification the Federal Government could point to the fact that they were still working for relaxation of tension and negotiations and had so far succeeded in mollifying all the threats from Moscow. Naturally the Russians now reinforced the Warsaw Pact and within it accelerated and legalized the rearmament of the People's Republic, long since begun; to this extent the build-up of NATO and the conclusion of the German treaty assisted the Soviet bloc policy and offered it certain propaganda advantages in the international field. At about the same time, however, (in May 1955), the Austrian problem was solved on the basis of a four-power agreement guaranteeing the country's neutrality. This seemed to show that post-Stalin policy still held out certain possibilities for a solution of the German question, always provided that no irrevocable developments took place and that sovereignty and rearmament were not given preference over reunification and a peace treaty. Hopes were raised and there was much discussion visualizing an analogous solution of the German problem based on the creation of demilitarized and neutralized zones in Central Europe instead of further involvement of Germany in East–West bloc politics.

Neutralization would, of course, have entailed considerable sacrifices in prosperity, security and strength – greater than in Austria's case. Neither the Western Powers, who were only too well aware of the difference in terms of power policy between a solution of the Austrian question and that of Germany, nor the West German government, responsible for the vast majority of Germany's population, could be expected to take the initiative, But neither did the alternative, shelving the German problem and substituting political integration into Western Europe for unity, hold out convincing prospects. Economic progress, particularly the *rapprochement* of the six Coal and Steel Community countries and the formation of Euratom and the EEC, altered the picture little. The decisive political development did not materialize – a supra-national solution of the German problem; this would have had good prospects of acceptance by internal German opinion. The Adenauer government admittedly accepted limitations on its rearmament; subsequently, however, it insisted on equality of status and the consequential re-equipment; technically 'tactical' nuclear weapons became a necessity. Adenauer's explicit renunciation of nuclear weapons for the Bundeswehr (and of manufacture of such weapons) did not, therefore, sound very convincing to his critics either inside or outside Germany. The results were further violent conflicts of opinion and an anti-nuclear weapons campaign, plunging the rearmament problem and the whole German question into the labyrinth of emotional argument. In fact the decision had been taken; the process of 'conversion' from conventional to nuclear strategy was under way and the Federal Government could do nothing to stop it, although the time required to build up the Bundeswehr allowed it a certain breathing space.

4

Such was the situation when, in the mid-1950s, the process which had been in gestation since 1947, seemed to reach a definite conclusion; West Germany had finally become a sovereign state, a member of the Western Alliance and rearmed. From the Soviet point of view this seemed to be the moment, not to create any serious disturbance but at least to set the seal on the process by formally recognizing the division of Germany; moreover this accorded with the stand and phrases about co-existence and relaxation of tension to which Stalin's successors, who were still feeling their way, had initially subscribed, The rejection of their offers of 1952 and even more, the shattering experience of the revolt of 17 June 1953 had shown the Soviet Union that no all-German solution favourable to them could be expected. The attitude of the West during the popular rising in the People's Republic, however, had also shown that the 'policy of liberation', to which Dulles was committed, did no more than raise hopes incapable of fulfilment either now or later (Hungary in 1956); the real object behind this policy was to consolidate the western position within its own sphere of influence and power – as far as German politics were concerned this was Adenauer's object too.

The result, however, was a whole series of fresh initiatives on the German question from the Soviet side; their object was to institutionalize, both juridically and diplomatically, the existence of two German states. These efforts culminated in the partial success of Adenauer's visit to Moscow and the establishment, not altogether expected, of diplomatic relations between Bonn and Moscow in September 1955. Opinion was, and still is, divided as to whether this initiative was merely another wrecking manoeuvre or offered a real chance of progress on the Germany question. On this occasion the Federal Republic had met the Soviet wishes. The question merely was whether, at this time and in this form, this development served the interests of the West in general and Germany in particular. A glance at its consequences and subsequent events makes this seem questionable.

The first development was the revival of the disarmament and security plans already put forward both by East and West, culminating in the Geneva Summit Conference of the four great powers in July 1955. The atmosphere was relaxed, even optimistic – the result of the flexibility shown by the West, particularly over the German question. At the Berlin Conference of 1954 Eden, the British Foreign Secretary, had put forward a plan linking disarmament and security policy with free, all-German elections; the idea was revived as a subject of discussion and became known as the 'expanded Eden plan'. It soon proved, however, that his prerequisite, creation of a 'thinned out military zone', was barely compatible with the fact that, for good reasons, the Western Powers felt that they must maintain their West European defence system; without it and so long as effective controls and security guarantees did not exist, disarmament negotiations carried too great a risk.

Once again, therefore, people were faced with the fundamental contradiction inherent in the problem of Germany ever since 1945 and even more since 1949. Clearly the Soviet Union had made efforts to solve the problem on the basis of recognition of the *status quo*, of the division of Germany and the existence of two German states even before they produced their counter to the Eden plan, or rather caused the Poles to produce it in the form of the Rapacki Plan. The impulse came from the ratification of the Paris treaties which incorporated the Federal Republic fully into the western system and brought the occupation statute to an end. The Soviet Union replied with annulment of the state of war with Germany in January 1955 and an invitation to establish normal relations between Bonn and Moscow. Adenauer was thereby placed in a difficult position. He could not simply ignore the Soviet initiative without abandoning the theory of four-power responsibility for the Germany question and the claim of the Federal Republic to represent Germany as a whole. At the same time, however, in Moscow he was confronted with the pregnant consequence of Soviet recognition of the Federal Republic – simultaneous recognition of the People's Republic. If the main German negotiating object was to make the all-German problem and reunification the central theme of the discussions, this aspect of the 'normalization' process was bound to emerge.

A further question was whether, if Soviet dealings with West Germany were in future to be on a sovereign state to sovereign state basis, the Soviet

Union was not released from her responsibility as an occupying power in so far as Germany as a whole was concerned. It was no accident that Grotewohl, Minister-President of the People's Republic, should simultaneously be present in Moscow to set the seal on the twin-state solution. This left only the Berlin question which was now exposed to the full pressure stemming from these developments. Soviet pressure, backed by the moral weight of the injured but victorious party, could not simply be evaded; however hesitant they might be, neither the West German nor the western publics could shut their eyes to it. True 'normalization', however, was inseparably bound up with the conclusion of a peace treaty; this was the field in which the initiative should have been taken; this was the western, and even more West German, counter to the Russian request; this would have compelled discussion of the whole question of Germany.

The opportunity was doubly inviting. After all, the Soviet Union itself had stressed the necessity for a treaty over and over again and had made use of the argument in its propaganda both on the German and worldwide political problems. Moreover the Berlin problem still unsolved and merely shelved in 1949, was a test case, by which the *bona fides* of the Soviet desire for *détente* and 'normalization' could have been *proved*. The two weapons of the future which would be guaranteed to exert an effect on world public opinion and in the West itself were a Berlin crisis and the subject of the peace treaty; these could at least have been defused or even turned against the Soviet Union. It did not happen and as a result the effect upon development of the Germany question of Adenauer's temporary deflection on to a policy of improvement in German–Soviet relationships was a negative one. A 'normalization' which made no attempt to clear up the most important problems was inevitably a questionable quantity, as was shown by the exchange of letters setting out the views of the two sides at the end. Adenauer insisted that resumption of diplomatic relations did not imply either pre-treaty acceptance of Germany's territorial boundaries or renunciation of the Federal Republic's claim to represent all Germany; the Soviet government stated flatly that for them the Federal Republic constituted one part of Germany and the People's Republic the other.

The result was a new chapter in the series of actions with which the Soviet Union had parallelled any step forward by the Federal Republic, starting with currency reform and leading via the formation of the People's Republic to its integration into the eastern bloc. That very month, with ostentatious rapidity, the Soviets concluded a treaty with the People's Republic modelled on the treaties of Paris; its purpose was to underline the equality of the two German states under international law. Initially its international effect was small and was in fact confined to the eastern bloc; nevertheless it constituted a first step in invalidating the West German claim to represent all Germany, a claim given legal expression in the 'Hallstein doctrine'. This contained an explicit threat by Bonn to break off diplomatic relations with all countries recognizing the People's Republic and initially this had logic on its side in terms both of power-policy and economics. Once more, however, it was a purely defensive reaction, the antithesis of an attempt at a solution; neither resumption of relations with West Germany's eastern neighbours nor entry into UNO were compatible with this legalistic standpoint; in any case its whole basis was now illogical since full-scale diplomatic relations existed with Moscow, the protecting power of the People's Republic. As before, moreover, the Soviet Union possessed another lever which it could use for the furtherance of its policy. This was the Berlin question or, in more precise terms, the unsolved contradiction between the juridical pronouncements on the subject and the actual situation of divided Berlin in the midst of the People's Republic, one of two German states declared sovereign though controlled by the Soviet Union.

The reasons for the resulting dilemma were to be found not only in West German ideas and policies but in those of the Americans as well. The formation (and the recovery) of the Federal Republic had been closely bound up with American policy, were dependent upon it in fact; Eisenhower and Dulles clearly favoured the Adenauer government. These facts discouraged or even silenced all internal German criticism of the Federal Government's rigid defensive tactics, all efforts to develop some German initiative or make some German contribution to the problems of *détente*, security or reunification. The social-democrat opposition in particular was exposed to this pressure whenever it attempted to oppose the rigidity of the rearmament policy. It was hardly ever taken into serious consultation and its efforts to participate in government were ultimately described by the chancellor (in the electoral campaign of 1957) as a recipe for the 'ruin of Germany'. Their warnings and their pleas that the western position be rescued from stagnation by an approach to the Soviet Union on the German question were regarded with suspicion by the American leaders as endangering and dislocating the western front. The Americans accepted Adenauer's conviction that only he could guarantee that Germany would remain democratic and affiliated to the West; he made use of this both internally and electorally, pointing out that only his policy could ensure the confidence and support of the West and particularly of the USA. At the time this self-assertive summary of the position was not entirely a figment of his imagination and in the light of the Federal Republic's early history it appeared not unfounded. It was not unconnected, however, with another aspect of the rise of the Federal Republic – and the somewhat doubtful result was that the Germany problem was handled in the belief that the Soviet Union would give way in face of the strength and superiority of the West German demand for reunification, made with western support; there would, therefore, be no need for a compromise which would have entailed substantial sacrifices in matters such as frontiers, security or the status and control of a future, reunited Germany.

All lip-service paid to freedom and self-determination on the part of the population of the People's Republic was meaningless so long as it did not take into account considerations such as these. By contrast a purely legalistic and diplomatic agreement such as the resumption of official relations between Bonn and Moscow proved to be barely relevant despite the astonishment it aroused when compared with previous policy. In relation to the primary questions of the next few years – development of the so-called Hallstein doctrine, nuclear arms, the Oder–Neisse Line, the peace treaty, the Berlin crisis or recognition of the People's Republic – this passing excursion into a German eastern policy was of negative significance because it produced nothing pointing the way forward. Even a decade later the German question was still regarded merely as one of the main ingredients of the 1949–55 decisions. It will be essential for us to subject it to far more critical examination than hitherto. The change of government of 1969 may be a turning point.

5

During the first five years of the Adenauer government, when the Federal Republic was forming and growing, German politics, both internal and external, stabilized and took shape more quickly than expected. After the division of the country had become established fact through the decisions of 1949–55 German politics faced fresh crises which found visible expression in the Berlin dilemma from 1958 onwards. One might have expected that the conflict between the various interests and ideas would assume a new intensity although, or perhaps because, the official line of West German foreign policy was still anchored to the premisses of 1949. That this did not occur was due primarily to the peculiar way in which internal stabilization of the Federal Republic took place.

The Adenauer government laid claim to the ability to guide and, from the political viewpoint, to form internal German currents of opinion; in the mid-1950s this was increasingly possible as a result of the outstanding position reached by Adenauer as head of the 'chancellor democracy', legitimized for the first time in the history of German democracy by the achievement of an absolute majority by his party in the elections of 1957. Admittedly the Social-Democrat opposition made certain gains and maintained their position; with one-third of the seats in parliament they were at least a minority capable of exercising some control. Meanwhile, however, almost all the smaller parties had been sucked into the wake of the government party which was being so successful economically; they had either succumbed to the trend towards a two-party system, had fallen victim to the five-per-cent clause or had been semi-annihilated by Adenauer's divisive tactics.

The reasons were primarily internal-political in nature. There were the effects of the 'economic miracle' but in addition the traditional division into 'bourgeois' and 'socialist' camps persisted and, despite the wartime and post-war shifts in West German society, this largely still governed political opinion and the voting at elections. The result was that, both in internal and external politics, the fronts remained immobile. Undoubtedly, however, a considerable part was played by Adenauer's continuous references to the advantages and guarantees obtained by membership of the Western Alliance; not without reason he claimed the sole credit for his policy, which, he also declared, offered the only prospect of solving the all-German problem. Even more important, however, were his successful tactics vis-à-vis the various associations and interest-groups. He guaranteed their representatives direct access to the federal chancellery, largely pushed his government, his party and parliament into the background and so made his position unassailable. The current phrase about 'government by association' was not inapt; at the same time, however, it was descriptive of the more dubious aspects of this method of government – dubious not only from the point of view of the infant German democracy's future development, but also from that of its ideas and self-imposed difficulties in matters of foreign policy.

In fact, contrary to the eulogies of his admirers and equally contrary to the accusations of the opposition, Adenauer's real strength lay in the internal political field; he was an experienced Burgomaster and he ruled the state. The basic decision to side with the West had been a convincing one; the sequel, however, was nothing less than obstinate adherence to the arrangements of 1948-50. The over-worked comparison with Bismarck is not valid since German foreign policy did not concern itself with the all-German question, Berlin or the eastern problem. Instead, Adenauer's undeniable contribution to the consolidation of the Federal Republic lay in the skill with which he picked his way through the initial confusions and subsequent contentions of the plethora of political and social interests, the bewildering multiplicity of groups, aims, traditions and animosities, contriving to direct them all into the channel of his successful policy.

There was another side, however, to these basic tactics, and it was a serious one. Adenauer had greater authority and more solid support than any other statesman in the history of German democracy; this very fact clearly made it impossible for him to stake his position of strength on a policy which had contributed so largely to the Federal Republic's self-deception and basic inconsistency over the all-German problem, the Oder-Neisse Line and the Berlin question. It was not surprising that the refugee associations, the ex-nationalists and Nazis, the captains of industry and the rehabilitated military showed no inclination to help in solving the dilemma inherent in the uncompromising juxtaposition of integration into the West and demands on the East. Foreign criticism of the activities of these 'revisionists' is understandable, but it misses the point. The unhappy fact was that, to consolidate and maintain his internal political position, Adenauer felt himself compelled to take account of all the various circles and tendencies and this precluded any foreign policy initiative on the part of the Federal Republic; lacking this incentive, the western Allies, who were not vitally affected and were preoccupied with the Suez and East Asia crises, saw no need to embark on any great activity. Internally the 'conquest of the past', about which there was so much talk, was pursued at considerable cost and with some success by means of education and consolidation of democracy in the Federal Republic; in the foreign policy field there was no counterpart. As the declared successor to the Hitler regime the Federal Republic redeemed its mortgage to the West but not to the East.

Particularly serious was the fact that, apart from one statement (quickly denied) by von Brentano, the Foreign Minister, made to a British audience in May 1956, the Federal Government never made clear the fundamental difference between the problems of the Oder-Neisse Line and reunification; it never used this as a starting point for a German-Polish *rapprochement*, although at the moment of the Polish 'thaw' this might have had some effect upon the reunification and security problems, of which it formed part. Further, from the moral point of view, it was unfortunate that no adequately clear distinction was made between the burden carried by the Germans beyond the Elbe on behalf of the nation as a whole and the academic revisionist desires of the former refugees who were meanwhile enjoying the security and good living of the Federal Republic. In addition to an All-German Ministry a Ministry for Refugees still existed and it was run by a politician previously prominent as a Nazi. The children of refugees from the East, who had grown up or even been born in the West, were given special status and so swelled the host of refugees. Their desire to return to their former home was highly doubtful but officially the principle remained inviolable.

As a result the self-chosen area for manoeuvre became even smaller than the circumstances necessitated – and the 'circumstances' included a taboo on all discussion of the eastern frontiers, those who thought otherwise being pilloried as 'give-away politicians'. Naturally good reasons were given why the German claims should not simply be renounced.

In the meanwhile, however, assimilation of the refugees had made such progress and political extremism had been so far controlled that the stability of the Federal Republic was no longer dependent on the goodwill of these groups, if indeed it had ever been so; the BHE, the refugees' party, had long since shrunk almost to nothing. Yet mass meetings of East Germans continued – attended out of sentimentalism or to meet old friends but organized by men holding posts in the government. Responsible ministers conjured up rosy pictures of a return to the East German homeland, naturally disclaiming all use of force but promising an overall European solution. But was that not further away than ever? It was contradicted by Germany's own policy and the settlement of the Poles who had suffered so much – they had as good a 'right to a homeland', the resounding catchword of the 'back-to-the-East' ideology. The claims of the Sudeten Germans inevitably seemed even more dubious; they implied no more than a return to Hitler's 'Greater Germany' revisionist policy, could count on no support of any sort from Bonn's allies, and were in fact calculated to arouse suspicion. Nevertheless ministers such as Seebohm attended mass demonstrations, supporting the Sudeten German demands for a homeland with promises and appeals, and raising fresh hopes of revision by vague, emotional statements.

It is difficult to estimate how much damage was done by this taboo imposed by the Federal Republic on a possible eastern policy (which was not even attempted); West Germany still seemed, not only to her eastern neighbours but also to her western partners, to be a country bent on revision, which had not totally abandoned, or did not dare abandon, the heritage of the Hitler regime. Worse still, the question of reunification became tainted with a flavour of 'revisionism', although the problem was in fact on an entirely different level. Reunification was no mere territorial problem; it concerned the fate of 17 million people who were denied the right of self-determination or freedom of choice of their government or way of life. Reunification was a legitimate demand, justified both politically and morally; the eastern frontier was an unsolved dispute which had been turned into a territorial problem by refugees, deportations and Germany's debt to her neighbours. By linking the two reunification became in Germany and even more in the eyes of the West a theoretical idea which, as time went on, would fade before the 'reality of two German states', as would the unrealistic demand for re-establishment of the 1937 frontiers. So two problems and sets of motives which were in fact unconnected, became linked and the result was disastrous from two points of view: the Oder–Neisse question lost what value it might have had, if used at the correct moment by the West as a subject for negotiation – having not been so used, it has hardly any value at all today; secondly, it isolated the problem of the western position in Berlin which now became divorced from the German problem and a matter for separate solution. The result was a threat both to the potential function of Berlin as the capital of a reunited Germany and to its present function as a shop-window and beacon of hope for the people of East Germany.

One of the results of Adenauer's brilliant governmental tactics, combining authoritative leadership with flexible and successful pragmatism, was that the German people, satisfied with the present and full of hope in western strength and assurances as regards the all-German question, stumbled almost unsuspectingly into the great crises of 1958 and 1961. The sputniks and a series of ultimata had given it clearly to be understood that this was no time for delaying tactics, for mere rigidity or for blind confidence in an automatic reconciliation between the western policy and reunification. Nevertheless, the Soviet Union had already given warning by its reaction to the integration of the Federal Republic into the West; in 1952 and 1955 she had first come forward with offers and then recognized and confirmed the division of the country. More important still, however, and in contrast to western, and particularly West German, policy, she had kept matters moving by drafts and proposals. These fluctuating offers and plans may be criticized, their content and the risk entailed debated. The outcome of the western wait–and–see policy, however, is hardly less deserving of criticism.

6

While the world in general was preoccupied with the major international crises of 1956 in Eastern Europe and the Middle East, the problem of Germany remained frozen in the position in which it had been left by the 1955 decisions. The Federal Republic completed its rapid rise in status; it did not shift from its initial position and used its growing weight *vis-à-vis* its western partners, the new countries of the ex-colonial areas and the Third World to underline the basic requirements of West German policy – non-recognition of the *status quo* in respect of a divided Germany and its development into two states, non-recognition of the People's Republic, great power responsibility for reunification, the treaty obligations of the three Western Powers. Against this efforts were being made and plans produced for wider-scale solutions of the disarmament and security problems and they did not exclude a *détente* at the expense of the Federal Republic; they also held out hopes of some relaxation in the rigidity of the fronts and of further talks on the Germany question, now at a standstill. It was therefore understandable that argument should revive in West Germany on the question whether and how to participate in this movement and whether any modification should be made to the purely defensive Hallstein doctrine over and above mere moralistic and juridical declamatory statements. Facts such as the position of Berlin in the middle of the People's Republic, the development of inter-zonal trade and relations with the Soviet Union forced the Federal Government in practice to modify its stand of ignoring the existence of two German states. While the government looked with suspicion on all indications of 'deviation' from Bonn's legalistic standpoint, Adenauer's policy still faced the contradiction inherent in the formation, growth and pretensions of the Federal Republic.

The first actual development to attract attention was the great re-equipment debate of 1956–7. The main subject since Franz–Josef Strauss had moved into the Defence Ministry in October 1956 had been the re-equipment of the new Bundeswehr with tactical nuclear weapons. In July 1956 universal military service had been introduced in face of violent opposition from the Social-Democrats and Free Democrats; now tactical nuclear weapons provided a further reason for an internal German conflict of opinion and also for further misgivings about the reunification policy. Once the basic decision had been taken there was much to be said for it on security grounds. The position in the Federal Republic, however, did not make matters easier; in particular the army was forming slowly and its small practical value bore little relation to the psychological effect it produced both internally and externally. The first (volunteer) West German soldiers were not called up until April 1957. A whole year earlier the People's Republic had completed transformation of the 'barrack police' into a 'People's National Army' and had been able to make good propaganda use of the fact that it had not had to resort to military service – totalitarianism's means of compulsion guaranteed an adequate number of 'volunteers'.

The situation was not improved by Adenauer's repeated demands in March/April 1957 that the Bundeswehr be accorded equality of status with the allied armies; its requirement for nuclear equipment was still not clear. Slogans about West German revisionism, revanchism and militarism made a great impact on the eastern bloc and were not without their effect in the rest of the world. Signs of restorationism multiplied in the Federal Republic; ultra–right–wing publications such as the *Deutsche National und Soldatenzeitung* (German National and Military Newspaper) for a time enjoyed official support; assemblies of refugees and soldiers were the order of the day; the delay in the integration of Europe meant that the insoluble dilemma of the Federal Republic's hybrid position impinged increasingly on day-to-day affairs. People began to wonder whether the vacuum might not be filled by nationalism with an anti-communist twist which would ultimately sweep away all supra-national safeguards or alternatively drag its partners in the alliance into some adventure. If there could be no compromise with the East, people said, might not a dangerous automatism be inherent in the combination of rearmament and demands for revision?

The effect of these complications and apprehensions was all the greater when it was found that Adenauer was fixedly opposed to all ideas of neutralization or controlled military zones in Central Europe, now presented in the form of an atom-free zone. Admittedly, while Germany was re-equipping, such an attempt at a solution entailed considerable risk; in view of the impasse in which western policy towards Germany was caught, however, an ostentatious refusal by Germany was even more risky, at least before the idea had been submitted to thorough examination and discussion as Britain in particular wanted. One of the results of the policy which had culminated in the resumption of diplomatic relations between Bonn and Moscow, was that the Soviet Union now insisted that reunification was henceforth an internal German matter between the Federal Republic and the People's Republic. There were good reasons for West Germany to reject this view; in the first place it forced Bonn on to the same level as a totalitarian, satellite regime which clearly existed against the will of its people and which was legitimized solely by the presence and protection of the Soviet Union; second, it contained the seeds of the threat which Adenauer feared above all else – great power agreement on *détente* over the head and at the expense of Germany.

In the light of the Soviet campaign urging some flexibility Paris and London did in fact show some inclination to abandon the tiresome priority hitherto accorded to the German question, now at dead centre; once rid of this, they felt, the questions of European security, disarmament and *détente* in the East–West conflict could be dealt with. Such tendencies were clearly visible during the disarmament negotiations in London in March/April 1956. The Soviet Union met them adroitly. In addition she contrived to spread suspicion that Washington itself was inclined towards a global settlement between the 'Big Two' before solution of the German and European questions. In this situation Soviet policy towards Germany made great play with the People's Republic. If the security problem were now to take priority over that of Germany and if plans for 'disengagement' now took precedence over Adenauer's policy for Germany, there seemed to be some prospect that the catchword 'co-existence' might really apply to Germany. On 30 December 1956 Ulbricht openly referred for the first time to 'co-operation between the two German states' and launched a plan for an all-German confederation. There could be no doubt that the primary purpose of this plan was general recognition and legitimization for the People's Republic; this would be followed by 'democratization' of such a 'confederation' on communist lines. The confederation plan was then pertinaciously pursued in further international discussion, being presented as 'the only true road to reunification' fitted to the new circumstances; its effect was not inconsiderable. It had, of course, not the smallest prospect of acceptance either in Germany or the West; Ulbricht proclaimed that eventually the superior 'popular democratic order', 'progressive forces' and the communist social system would prevail – his meaning was only too transparent. In February 1957 Ulbricht and Grotewohl listed as prerequisites for the confederation demilitarization, abandonment of fascism and socialization in West Germany; in August 1957 they added equality of status between the two countries.

Apparently, however, Ulbricht was able to exploit the eastern bloc's difficulties, which were slow of solution, to assert the ostensible sovereignty of the People's Republic more effectively and to give the confederation plan greater precision than Moscow had originally intended. The seal was set on this development by Khruschev's visit to East Berlin in August 1957.

This could be ominous, particularly if coupled with an attempt to take the Berlin question out of the context of four-power responsibility and make it the starting point of a general settlement of the German problem as in fact happened from autumn 1958 onwards.

Meanwhile the disarray of the West had hardly grown less. During the confused debate on 'disengagement' plans the problem of Germany became the subject of all kinds of experimental theories. Admittedly readiness to discuss, as demanded by the opposition both in Germany and Britain, by no means implied acceptance of the plans for confederation. By the summer of 1957, moreover, the situation on either side of the Iron Curtain had become so rigid that comprehensive solutions had little hope of success. Helped by Moscow's continuing disarmament campaign during 1956–7, however, Soviet proposals on Germany wore an air of constructive initiative. Temporarily Adenauer was in a difficult position, almost tantamount to isolation. Although his own policy had not altered, he had apparently turned from the West's model pupil into the mischief-maker of world politics. In this situation *attentisme* was a doubly dubious policy which the German opposition did not fail to censure; it could do no more than proclaim rearmament and the old theories that without a reunited Germany there could be no free, integrated Europe and therefore no security for the free world. For the first time the great weakness of Adenauer's policy was exposed – as it was to be later at the height of the Berlin crisis and even more whenever there was any tendency towards an East–West *détente*; it was incapable of adapting itself to changed circumstances, particularly when they touched the assumptions and exposed the dilemma which lay at the root of the Federal Republic's existence and its claims. It was realized with a sense of shock that the position of strength, thought to have rehabilitated both the Federal Republic and Germany, was a fragile one. More and more influential voices were to be heard in western countries disputing the West's obligation to support Bonn's all-German policy at the expense of a relaxation of tension.

The crisis continued under the shadow of the Suez débâcle which also entailed a NATO crisis; the repercussions of the Hungarian tragedy were, to say the least, ambiguous, particularly in the light of the co-operation between the USA and the Soviet Union in the Security Council. Fresh approaches to Moscow for negotiations on the Germany question were met by the reply that this was now an internal German matter between the Federal Republic and the People's Republic, a theory unacceptable to all West German parties. Nevertheless Adenauer stubbornly refused to consider a change of emphasis in foreign policy, as was passionately demanded by the opposition during these weeks. Both the strength and weakness of his policy emerged with even greater clarity in these months; he clung to his western policy and refused to take any substantive experimental initiative on the subjects of Germany or policy towards the East. The opposition could do no more than advance untried ideas and issue warnings, throw doubt upon the usefulness of the Atlantic alliance and deplore Adenauer's aversion to bipartisan discussion and planning. They were continuously defeated, as they were also electorally, and gradually lost the will to put forward alternative solutions; the SPD's 'Germany Plan' of 1959 was no more than a final convulsion.

Several reasons, both internal and external, contributed to this development. Most important was the fact that by 1957 the threatened isolation of the Federal Republic was past. France had been weakened by the Suez adventure and, by meeting her more than halfway, Adenauer succeeded in reducing her opposition to a Europe policy and reactivating European politics which had been stagnant since early 1957. Efforts revolved around Euratom and the EEC, the object clearly being to re-establish Bonn's battered position as far as the question of Germany was concerned. This took priority over the well-founded reservations voiced even inside the Federal government, primarily by Erhard, the Economics Minister, against an exclusive economic policy on the part of the six Coal and Steel Community states *vis-à-vis* the rest of Europe and the NATO allies; there were signs of damaging rivalry between the two European economic blocs, the EEC and the European Free Trade Association (EFTA). In July 1957, however, even the Social-Democrats agreed the treaties setting up the two communities; the overriding consideration was that the low point in western policy on Germany had now been passed, as evidenced by the formal inclusion of West Berlin in the two communities.

On the other hand, internal opposition to nuclear weapons for the Bundeswehr remained as strong as ever. Adenauer hoped that this step would stop any disarmament agreement being reached at the expense of his German policy and make Moscow more ready to negotiate; the opposition, on the other hand, could invariably point to the unhappy experiences resulting from such a German policy in 1956. In appeals, declarations and debates in parliament the Social-Democrats, the Free Democrats, the trades unions, protestant theologians and leading atomic scientists all demanded that the Federal Republic unequivocally renounce nuclear weapons; instead they proposed that all-German policy be more closely linked to the efforts being made towards disarmament and *détente*. The attitude of the Federal Government remained ambivalent and so presented the Soviet Union with the opportunity to issue further savage threats. The debate on the actual issue of nuclear weapons was not assisted by an almost universal ignorance of the technical aspects. Deep rifts were exposed by the opinions expressed on the political, psychological and moral aspects. In its reply to the Soviet note of protest on 23 March 1957 the Federal Government insisted on its right of decision as a sovereign state and in this it was formally correct. As a result, however, as it had already done by establishing diplomatic relations with Moscow, it provided confirmation of the Soviet thesis on Germany and laid itself open to all the implications of the two-state theory. The problem remained more acute than ever: after its previous experiences how was Bonn to extricate itself from its all-German predicament if its claim to sovereignty was confirmed by the possession of nuclear weapons and if inertia prevailed in so far as any constructive eastern policy was concerned?

7

Contrary to the general expectations and apprehensions both at home and abroad Adenauer had almost totally refused to exploit the new relationship between Bonn and Moscow established in 1955. In view of the potential Rapallo complex in the West and the juridical arguments on which the reunification theory was based the Federal Government confined its efforts to the return from the Soviet Union of condemned German prisoners of war; suggestions for commercial or cultural relationships were met with hesitation. Adenauer seemed to have no thought in his mind of extending his foreign policy to cover the eastern bloc. German relations with Poland were a case in point and they were of special importance in the light, not only of past debts but also of plans for a *détente*. The reform and relaxation of the communist system after the events of autumn 1956 offered opportunities; Warsaw repeatedly expressed the wish to normalize its relations with Bonn. Both West German and western critics have deplored the fact that these efforts failed in face of the obstacles of the revision thesis and the theory that the Federal Republic alone represented Germany. Even taking full account of the Hallstein doctrine, there were possibilities; Poland had already and compulsorily recognized East Germany and the establishment of relations between Bonn and Moscow could be regarded as constituting a precedent. Quite apart from the legal problems the political and moral aspects of the establishment of German–Polish relations carried a weight which more than justified the risk entailed in the resumption of diplomatic contacts; such a step might be of considerable significance for the all-German question, for Poland's position between East and West and for her relationship to the People's Republic. Was it sound to leave Germany to be represented in Warsaw by the People's Republic, particularly when relations between Ulbricht, still a stalinist, and the Poles, eager for reform, were already strained? Such aspects merited the utmost attention; Bonn could have played an important part in Poland's efforts to achieve greater independence from the Soviet Union.

Disillusionment was all the greater, therefore, when Adenauer refused to move from his regressive policy and cold-shouldered all initiatives either from the West or inside Germany. It may be argued that the pressure of the refugee associations played some part in this; in May 1956, for instance, von Brentano, the Foreign Minister, was hauled over the coals because he had said in London that 'one day we shall have to choose between reunification with 17 million Germans in the Soviet zone and insistence on territory beyond the Oder–Neisse Line'; refugee functionaries replied with an assault on the chancellor, who reacted with his usual tactical skill. Equally in 1956 Carlo Schmid, speaking for the opposition, had vainly implored the Bundestag and the Federal Government, saying: 'The taboo on the Oder–Neisse question must be lifted, otherwise one day it will become our master. It will bewitch us.' Sieveking, the CDU Burgomaster of Hamburg and reigning President of the Bundesrat, also demanded in vain that German–Polish relationships be normalized.

The taboo on the Oder–Neisse Line had a paralysing effect; it forced the Federal Government into an incredibly revisionist posture and closed the door to any constructive eastern policy. As was soon to be seen, it carried with it a threat of isolation for the Federal Republic; the Allies gave vent to displeasure and finally de Gaulle said quite openly that he recognized the Oder–Neisse Line. In November 1956 the Soviet Union reiterated its guarantee of the Polish western frontier; China and Yugoslavia issued similar declarations. Nevertheless Poland continued to express the wish 'to normalize its relations with the Federal Republic on the basis of mutual recognition and in the interest of relaxation of tension in Europe' (Gomulka on 22 September 1957). Bonn, on the other hand, insisted on the following order of events: (i) the formation of an all-German government (ii) a peace treaty and (iii) the settlement of frontiers, without itself taking any real action on these matters. The proximity of Federal elections even led the government to support the cry of the 'right to a homeland'; all suggestions for Polish–German talks were rejected; immobility continued.

The same was to be seen in October 1957 when the Federal government replied to Belgrade's recognition of the Oder–Neisse frontier and the People's Republic by breaking off relations with Yugoslavia. Not only the opposition but also the government parties and the Western Powers raised considerable objection. Once more, however, the legalistic dogma of the Hallstein doctrine was enforced against a country which had not only suffered much from the Hitler regime but also was in a position to play the role of mediator. With this in mind economic relations were maintained and this made the decision more tolerable but hardly more comprehensible. This breach of relations was not without its effect upon the new countries; the world in general, however, was gradually becoming habituated to the division of Germany and (in the absence of any western proposals) to the Soviet theory of two German states, and so it had little practical effect. It may well be asked whether it was not German policy which was constricted and placed in a difficult position rather than that of other countries; all they stood to lose, after all, were their relations with Bonn, not contact with the realities of world politics. The Hallstein doctrine could only have offered some prospect of solving the Germany question in the event of loss of power by the Soviet Union, as might have been hoped a few years earlier. Now, however, this was less probable than ever. So the formalistic logic of this doctrine continued as the main plank of Adenauer's foreign policy; under the changed circumstances, with the Soviet Union taking the initiative, however, its political and psychological effects were more than dubious. Any approach to reunification and a peace treaty necessitated thinking based on *Realpolitik* and psychology, not legalism; but the way was blocked by the doctrine that the Federal Republic alone represented Germany.

Once more the opposition attempted to draw up a balance sheet of a foreign policy which economically was increasingly successful, but as far as the Germany question was concerned, stagnant; they tried to put forward alternatives. This was the background to the Social-Democrats' 'Germany Plan' of 1959. In the SPD's view the division of Germany was a by-product of the East-West conflict; German policy, therefore, must be directed against the formation of blocs and an arms race; its interest lay in regional security arrangements, in meeting the security requirements of the Soviet Union and Germany's neighbours and in the simultaneous withdrawal of the Federal Republic and the People's Republic from their respective military blocs. Even so the process of reunification would be difficult and wearisome; it should take place through arms limitation in various phases and simultaneous decision on the future status of a reunited Germany. Most important – the SPD also refused to consider settlement between the two Germanies alone, any release of the great powers from their responsibility, any abandonment of the demand for free elections or any 'confederation' on communist lines between the two very different German states. The SPD did, however, believe that, if disbandment of the opposing military alliances and creation of a security system covering the whole of Europe were put forward as subjects for discussion, the Soviet Union would, in the light of her own interests, be ready for constructive negotiations and a possible settlement of the German problem; if guaranteed by Washington and Moscow, such a security system could include Germany and make the questionable idea of neutralizing central Europe unnecessary. Above all, however, such a proposal would at last give the West back the initiative; it would be more likely to solve the problem of German rearmament and reactivate Bonn's foreign policy than mere insistence on a policy of strength which had become unworkable and had failed to achieve its aims as regards either Germany as a whole or Europe as a whole. Admittedly this 'Germany Plan' entailed considerable risks; security guarantees in the various phases were inadequate; it presupposed a readiness to negotiate on the part of those involved hardly likely to be forthcoming in view of their differing systems of government and differing ideologies. As a proposal, however, it did offer certain possibilities of starting negotiations and testing the other side which could have provided German policy with a way out of its impasse; whether it was practicable without considerable risk remains to be seen. It was not pursued and was finally overtaken by events and pigeonholed; even the opposition ultimately swung round to Adenauer's apparently impregnable policy. Not until ten years later, when the Social-Democrats and Free Democrats came to power, was there an opportunity for a fresh start.

At the time the Social-Democrats could count on support from their sister-parties in Europe. But their ideas met violent opposition from the German government parties. So did the somewhat vaguer alternative proposals put forward from early 1956 by the Free Democrats, another opposition party; they laid greater emphasis on the national-political aspect; they appealed for a postponement of integration and even supported direct negotiations and contacts with the People's Republic. Adenauer made it clear that he had no intention of taking these projects into consideration in his policy. His victory at the September 1957 elections was won with the slogan 'No experiments' and this had shown that the German people's desire for security was stronger than any urge to try new solutions of the Germany problem. This was so despite the fact that Adenauer's foreign policy had been the cause of considerable crises and setbacks and had been responsible for the waning international interest in the problem of Germany with corresponding boredom and disenchantment in Germany itself; the end result was something very different from the permanent optimism of Bonn's reunification propaganda. However heated the foreign policy debate, internal political and economic considerations had been the deciding factors in the elections. It was not surprising that henceforth the Germans' existential interest in reunification became a subject of increasing doubt. Equally it was not surprising that the Germans stumbled in astonishment and helplessness into the Berlin crises of 1958–61 and the subsequent efforts at *détente* of the Kennedy era. The end of the Adenauer era, which came in 1963, was foreshadowed in the decisions and lack of decision of the 'middle years' ending in 1961. Its salient feature was that all-German policy moved from stabilization to stagnation.

II

The Bonn Party System

I

Any comparative examination of the second German democracy will show that nowhere does its dissimilarity from the Weimar Republic emerge more clearly than in the altered structure of the party system. A feature of internal German politics ever since modern parties were formed in the nineteenth century up to the present day has been the strong continuity of political groupings. Under the 1871 empire four great political camps confronted each other – liberals, socialists, catholics and conservatives. Even after the semi-revolution of 1918 they dominated the republican scene, although with changed party labels. Cracks in the system appeared with the advance of racial *völkisch* groups, further fragmentation of the middle class and the divisions of the socialists. Nevertheless this was still the general alignment against which the destructive forces of the extremist movements advanced both from Right (the Nazi Party) and Left (the Communist Party); with the crises of 1923 and even more that of 1930 the fringe zones of nationalist and communist persuasion expanded enormously. No one party, however, not even the Nazi Party in 1932, had any prospect of a parliamentary majority.

This historic pattern was not only interrupted but profoundly modified by the National-socialist dictatorship. In contrast to 1918 a greatly changed party system emerged from the collapse of 1945; its main features were increasing concentration into a smaller number of parties and a changing concept of the structure and functions of the party system as such. These were the most striking and the really new features of the second German democracy. Two basic factors were especially prominent. Besides the resurrection of social democracy a great inter-confessional umbrella party was formed combining the traditions of the catholic, conservative and to some extent liberal camps; its aim was to prevent fragmentation of the bourgeois forces. No less significant was the recognition as a matter of principle that democracy implied the 'party state' entailing institution-alization of parties as the main agents in formation of political will and implementation of the political process.

As the Federal Republic developed through its various stages the idea of party democracy became embedded both in constitutional theory and political practice, a deliberate antithesis to the previous constitutional tradition and public attitude in Germany when political parties were unrecognized and outlawed. Even under the first republic they were largely regarded as 'extra-constitutional' elements and the Weimar con-stitution only mentioned them in a negative sense; emphasis was placed on the 'non-party' or 'above party' aspects, the traditional foundations of the 'state standing above party'. The failure of the Weimar Republic and the experience of the Nazi single-party state led to rejection of the 'above party' theory, Gustav Radbruch's 'life-long deception of the patriarchal state'. The alternative now was not party state or no party state but single-party state or multi-party state.

Connected with this has been the increasing tendency towards a three- or two–party system characteristic of the Bonn governmental system in the 1950s and, even more important, reflected in the popular vote at elections. Under the Weimar Republic something like thirty different parties entered the lists and of these, over twenty obtained seats in the Reichstag. The post-1945 trend, however, has been exactly the opposite; in 1949 ten parties obtained seats in the Bundestag; by 1953 the figure had sunk to six and by 1957 to four. Since 1961 only three parties have been represented in parliament in Bonn. The trend is even clearer if one looks at the votes cast for the two major parties. In 1949 60 per cent of the population voted for the CDU or SPD. Since then the proportional increase in votes for the two parties combined has been almost uninterrupted – 74 per cent in 1953, 82 per cent in 1957 and 1961, 87 per cent in 1965 and 89 per cent in 1969. The picture is even clearer if all three main parties are considered – 72 per cent in 1949, 83 per cent in 1953, 89 per cent in 1957, 91 per cent in 1961, 96 per cent in 1965, 95 per cent in 1969. The provisions of the electoral law and the institution of a five-per-cent barrier have, no doubt, contributed to this process of concentration into two or three parties, but they do not explain it. As before, the German electoral system is based on proportional representation and this, despite certain modifications (the dual-vote system and the minimum percentage clause) guarantees all parties representation in parliament according to the votes cast for them; this is basically different from a straight majority vote which directly encourages, if it does actually enjoin, a two-party system. This novel development in the party system was more than a matter of electoral statistics or electoral technicalities; it reflected a far-reaching change in the whole attitude to political parties.

The pre-1933 parties had been based on ideology or social class; they had proved incapable of survival or of functioning as the main agents of parliamentary democracy. Their reconstitution after 1945 faced a changed society characterized by increasing mobility, the removal of traditional barriers and a loosening of ideologically fixed positions. This 'anti-ideology' mood was not mere reaction to the super-charged atmosphere of the Hitler period. Disillusionment and mistrust, resignation and disinterest in politics offered an opportunity for a wholesome descent to earth in political thinking after three-quarters of a century of abortive great power politics which had so largely contributed to the ineffectiveness of political parties. Late in the day and after a period of deliberate divorce from the democratic West, that pragmatic concept of an efficient party system characteristic primarily of the British and American democracies began to permeate the German body politic. Its prerequisites were: a readiness to co-operate and to find a solution to conflicts through the parliamentary system; a form of polarization between governmental majority and opposition superseding all other shades of difference and presenting the voters with a choice between alternatives clearer than those obtainable in a multi-party state.

As already mentioned, this was a process, not a sudden revolution in the nature of parties. The stage was set by the development of the CDU which in a bare ten years managed to absorb all the bourgeois groups with the exception of the Free Democrats. The corollary unfortunately was a loss of conceptual vitality by the parties; they adopted a middle line and tended to become 'all things to all men'. So they inevitably became 'people's parties', sacrificing not only revered political traditions but also the composition of their body of support, their assured reservoir of party electors. This was as true of the SPD's 'socialism' as it was of the changing picture of themselves presented by the Christian-democrats and Liberals.

Nevertheless this brought about that basic consensus of the political élite and the voters which is the prerequisite if a free pluralist democracy is to be able to function. This had been the decisive defect of the first republic. This was the primary reason why of the second post-war period's smaller parties only the FDP survived the trend towards a two-party system. All other groupings were particularist organizations serving regional or social ends, mostly thrown up to deal with outstanding, but limited, problems of adaptation but unable to accommodate themselves to a nationwide integration party. Apart from a few small remnants they – the Centre Party, the BHE (Refugees' Party), the DP (*Deutsche Partei* – German Party) and the Bavarian Party, for instance – were generally absorbed by the CDU which was the umbrella party *par excellence*. Here again the electoral laws and the constitution helped, particularly the provision in the Basic Law which, based on the experiences of Weimar, permitted anti-democratic and anti-constitutional parties to be banned. This prevented the development of extremist movements; the threat was a real one, for this clause was used against the Right (the SRP (Socialist Reich Party)) in 1952 and against the Left (the KPD (German Communist Party)) in 1956; the legal and political objections to the principle of banning parties in a democracy remain valid nevertheless.

At first glance, therefore, there are three main general features of change in the Bonn party system:

(i) The concentration of political groupings which has facilitated majority and opposition politics in parliament and led to greater stability in the political system;

(ii) the integrating effect of the two major parties, the CDU and SPD; for the first time in German history they have used democracy to curb the centrifugal forces generated by divergent ideologies, social groupings and interest-groups; they therefore more nearly fulfil the intermediary function between the state and society than did the Weimar parties which were entrenched between social particularism and an authoritarian concept of the state and so succumbed to National-socialism's anaesthetizing propaganda in favour of integration;

(iii) fluidity and change in the relationship between parties, the electorate and interest-groups leading to greater structural mobility and permeability over the years (and as the system continued crisis-free this led to a greater degree of interrelationship and interdependence between the party élites); thus both through collaboration and confrontation they learnt and practised habits of behaviour compatible with the system.

2

On closer examination, however, this positive picture of the Bonn party system is subject to a whole series of reservations. Its background is a painful process interspersed with many setbacks. The Federal Republic had been in existence for twenty years before it was subjected to a real test in the form of a change of government from one major party to another. A purely historical estimate runs the risk of overestimating the consistency of the development and of assuming to be definitive that which was in fact only an intermediate stage or a starting point for further changes in precisely the opposite direction. There is a continuous conflict between continuity and change. Neither the process of concentration of the Bonn party system nor the idea of stability inherent therein are immutably established factors. They have not yet had to face external or economic crisis in any way comparable with the permanent crises of the Weimar Republic. This must be remembered when the conclusion is drawn from electoral statistics that people are now accustomed to an efficiently functioning system of parliamentary democracy and that this has led to a more deep-seated identification with the political system itself, so conspicuously lacking after 1918.

Against this empirical surveys have shown how defective electoral results and external stability are as a guide to the state of political consciousness, the 'political culture' of a state. Since the end of the Adenauer era the restlessness and extremist trends both to right and left of the established party system have highlighted the fact that it is still tentative and insecure. The change of generations and the alteration in political loyalties reflect the change in the international situation and the crisis of the reunification idea. In contrast to the years when incorporation into the West was apparently a matter of course the basic problems and contradictions inherent in the formation of the Federal Republic are coming to the fore. An outstanding feature has been the existence of a constitutional order, institutionally firmly established and regarded as a 'militant democracy' contrasting with a passive attitude on the part of the people, whose minds have been primarily fixed on economic recovery and safeguards against Soviet power–policy. Adenauer's successful chancellor democracy met the demand for good order and security and so bridged the gulf between the tradition of the patriarchal state and the dynamism of democracy – which was where Weimar failed. But this was only possible by disregarding or pigeonholing the basic problems of the Bonn democracy. The tug–of–war remains: between deliberate definition of the system as provisional and the desire for stability; between national consciousnesss and state consciousness in the light of increasing consolidation of two German states; between the hardening of the Cold War fronts and the trend towards international *détente*; between a pragmatic *status quo* policy and the demand for a change in the *status quo*, the former redounding to the credit of the Bonn system as the guarantor of economic advance and the latter providing the only method whereby German democracy could be made complete by means of free self-determination for all Germans.

Naturally these differences were aired with much eloquence in the arguments between government and opposition parties during the 1950s. It is significant, however, that Adenauer won his greatest electoral victory (in 1957) with the slogan 'No experiments'. The Social-democrat opposition never stood a chance of upsetting the government's majority by arguing the questions of Germany or democracy. On the contrary the CDU's lead over the SPD increased with every election until eventually (in 1959–60) the SPD swung round to the *status quo* policy. Starting from a position of near equality (1.8 per cent difference) in 1949 the gap between the two parties increased to 16.4 per cent in 1953 and even reached 28.4 per cent in 1957; only after the great debate on Germany had ended was the trend reversed (9.2 per cent in 1961, 8.3 per cent in 1965, 3.4 per cent in 1969). It was quite clear that the growing support for the Bonn governmental and party system was based primarily on economic and not on political considerations, as was also the decline in preference for the imperial period (45 per cent in 1951, 16 per cent in 1963) and the Hitler period (42 per cent in 1951, 10 per cent in 1963). The fact that reunification and eastern policy were lying dormant hardly carried weight; the demands and threats of the powerful refugee associations clearly bore little relation to reality – and this was the view of a population consisting of one quarter of refugees.

The view taken of democracy and the growing support for the Bonn system depend primarily on two sets of conditions, neither of which obtained under the first republic: continuous economic growth as compared to the total failure of a non-democratic system; length and stability of governments which, by guaranteeing peace and full employment at home and external security through the Western Alliance and European integration, have become identified with this progress. The trials to which the Federal Republic has been subjected since the early 1960s – the end of the Adenauer era, governmental crisis under Erhard, American–Soviet *rapprochement*, stagnation of European policy – have shown how fragile and sensitive the system is. Symptoms of fresh unrest have revealed both the old and new weaknesses of German democracy. The rapid rise of the neo-Nazi, reactionary and nationalistic NPD and the equally rapid trend to extremism on the part of an admittedly small student movement call in question the pragmatic self-assurance of the 'established' party system and open up vistas of latent crisis which should not be underestimated.

Factors tending to stability, however, were fears of economic recession, aversion to weak governments and governmental crises (1966) and dislike of distortion of the democratic process by experiments such as the Great Coalition.

Compared to the democracies with great traditions, in the Federal Republic allegiance to the existing political system is not a strong factor and positive support for the political arrangements has remained small. The attitude is largely one of formal passive acquiescence; the high polling figures do not contradict but rather support this statement – voting is regarded as fulfilment of a duty rendering further participation in politics unnecessary. Private affairs and the personal virtues stand far higher in peoples' estimation. Economic success is a source of pride; the causes of popular self-esteem are the national character, the countryside and German cultural achievements rather than the political system. The non-political, almost disinterested attitude to their own communal arrangements stands in sharp contrast both to the exaggerated identification with the state characteristic of the imperial and Hitler periods and also to the emphatic aversion to the Weimar democracy. Support for the present state and party system is in general no more than support for an efficient system which guarantees and promotes prosperity. The threat of a political vacuum can only be countered by more consistent democratization in every sphere so that the citizen, in actual fact and day by day, is brought face to face with the problems of orderly government.

As recent experiences have shown, such 'democratization at the grass roots' may lead Germans from one extreme to another. The subject of much of the extreme criticisms and proposals for reform, both in the social sphere and in that of political parties and parliament, is that a traditionally abstract concept of government and the state as something standing above society may be replaced by a no less abstract ideological concept of a superhuman democracy. Absolute or total democracy is death to efficient democracy; perfectionist utopianism is as non-political as that violent fluctuation between indifference to the state and worship of the state which was so long the traditional bugbear of the Germans. As before the main danger lies in the tendency to extend the competence of the state until the state becomes a matter of ideology, allegedly above party and in practice non-political. Patriarchal and technocratic tendencies combine to present as the ideal the 'efficiency state' which would use, or alternatively neutralize, state-financed parties together with a more technically efficient parliament as organs of the modernized, administrative state.

3

A glance at these present-day problems throws a different light on the actual development of the Bonn party system. It has undoubtedly led a disorientated disillusioned people, bent on reconstruction, to adopt a non-negative attitude on the surface. In the eyes of the post-war generation, however, the origins and determinant factors of the second republic – Weimar, the Third Reich and the outbreak of the Cold War – are unknown or abstract historical facts, less and less suited to provide criteria for judgement. The 1945-9 system was clearly based on three sets of experiences: the failure of the first republic, the glitter and the misery of totalitarian dictatorship and its war, and fear of Soviet might and anti-communism born of the division of Germany and of Europe. This applied particularly to that party which not only constituted a new factor in the party system of the second republic but with unexpected ease and permanency ruled it and personified it. Historically the CDU (and its Bavarian branch the CSU) sprang from the idea of an inter-confessional, christian umbrella party; the idea had first been mooted in Centre Party circles and by the christian trades unions after the First World War but had been unable to make headway against the weight of the confessional parties; taught by their errors and by the resistance to the Third Reich, both churches now resurrected it. Some part in this was played by the steadfast attitude adopted by the churches during the 1945 vacuum and by the effort to prevent that fragmentation of the bourgeois vote which had been so prejudical to the working of the Weimar Republic. Formation of the CDU, moreover, was in line with the general trend towards establishment of christian centre parties which had emerged with such force from the European resistance movements; only in Germany, however, did it produce a major inter-confessional party.

The groups from which the CDU originated, though formed about the same time, were extremely heterogeneous and dispersed; initially there was no definite headquarters and the party was no more than a loose association; from the outset this was characteristic of the party structure. Political tradition, social background and regional organization differed as much as did the conditions and prospects in occupied Germany where strict controls, poor communications and deep suspicion of all political parties were the order of the day after the exaggerations and exertions of the Hitler period. Three basic types of party member emerged: ex-Centre Party leaders who, with few exceptions and with the agreement of the churches, joined the new party instead of the re-formed Centre Party; protagonists of the former christian workers movement who, from similar motives and to prevent division of the trade union movement, joined the united Trade Union League (DGB – *Deutsche Gewerkschaftsbund*); finally various protestant groups of christian-social, conservative or liberal origin, mostly connected with the resistance movement.

All the non-socialist parties of the Weimar period were represented in this 'Union'. Both by its title and in the initial outline of its programme it called for a fresh start in German political life; after the failures and perversions of the traditional ideologies this could only happen, it maintained, on the basis of a christian and human outlook on the world. On the more practical side the churches, which alone had preserved their authority and organizational strength, proved effective allies in the battle against the ubiquitous occupation policy. The first groups to form (in the summer of 1945) were those in Cologne and Berlin; their programme demanded determination to make a fresh start, social reform and a broad political basis; initially Konrad Adenauer regarded them with scepticism and held aloof from them until it was clear that they were making headway. Until 1947 (the Ahlen programme) efforts were devoted to far-reaching reform – 'the overlooked reform' in the phrase of O. H. von der Gablentz, one of the party's co-founders; it did not visualize restoration of the old socio-economic structures. The left (trades union) wing led by Karl Arnold, later Minister-President of North Rhine–Westphalia, who operated in the British zone (Britain had a Labour government) tried to prevent a return to a monopolistic, capitalistic economy by nationalizing the steel industry. Barely two years later, however, with the party growing rapidly, the liberal–capitalist wing had gained the upper hand. The main theme of the Düsseldorf programme of July 1949 was the idea of *soziale Marktwirtschaft** propounded by Ludwig Erhard (in alliance with the liberal Free Democrats); this steered first the economic administration of the Bi-zone and then the economic policy of the first Bonn government in the direction of capitalism.

The success of this policy was the result of the rapid change in conditions following the currency reform and the end of dismantling, both of which were the consequences of the rapid intensification of the Cold War, not of long-term planning or studied decision. This unexpected success, however, was the governing factor both in the development of the CDU and the policy of the Federal Government. Both in its structure and its aims the CDU took on the character of a bourgeois conservative party; its strong

* Lit.: 'social market economy'; Richard Hiscocks suggests that it is best translated 'free enterprise tempered by social conscience' (Translator).

industrial and agrarian sections called the tune and the social and trades union wing took a back seat, although the claim to be a christian people's party still guaranteed the party a broad appeal. Further support came from the Catholic Church which, throughout the 1950s, recommended the election of christian candidates; the protestant wing of the party did not receive comparable support from their church and so remained the weaker; the organization of a CDU 'Evangelical Workers' Circle' had little effect.

The main area of rivalry between the CDU and the second major party, the SPD, was the ability to deal with the concrete political situation. Though they co-operated on the level of the *Länder*, both parties were determined not to form a major coalition but to draw a clear distinction between responsible government and constructive opposition, thus producing an efficient parliamentary democracy; here the spectre of Weimar had its effect – there far too much license for destructive opposition had been allowed to extremist parties. The struggle for governmental power, however, necessitated coalition with the bourgeois-liberal Free Democrats and so they were able to exert considerable influence on CDU policy. A further factor was the bitter personal rivalry between the party leaders, Adenauer and Schumacher. Contrary to initial expectations the CDU entered the national political scene as the government party at the head of a decidedly anti-socialist, middle-class, capitalist bourgeois bloc. Adroitly and unscrupulously Adenauer contrived to harness to his successful policy all discordant tendencies within the party; the CDU became both the people's party and the chancellor's party and so gained an absolute majority; the Federal Republic wore the air of a CDU state.

The party structure was governed by its rapid development; it reflected the party's loose association of differing elements. In catholic areas the tradition of the Centre Party predominated, in protestant areas, the tradition of middle-class conservatism; in North Germany the national-liberal element was strong; then there was the particularist tradition of Bavaria which set up its own party organization and emphasized its independence by its rejection of the Basic Law. A high degree of decentralization was the hallmark of the party's organization; the first party congress (in Goslar) was not held until October 1950, five years after the formation of the party and over a year after it had formed a government.

Moreover the CDU, although it ultimately won greater electoral support than any other party in German history, was a party of prominent personalities rather than of members; members (some 250,000) provided only 2 per cent of the electoral support (as against the SPD's 7 per cent).

The confessional structure was far from ideal for that of a christian people's party. Among its electors the catholic element predominated in the proportion 3:2; in the parliamentary party the disproportion was even greater (3:1); governmental positions were ostentatiously allotted in accordance with this strength ratio. Though electoral support was broadly based the social structure of the membership was definitely primarily middle class (only fifteen workers as against forty-five in the SPD); the self-employed and landowners were much over-represented. Though the party claimed to be a true people's party and to stand for confessional and social equality, it was in fact tied to industrial, middle-class and agrarian interests; all these were much over-represented both in the parliamentary party and in government offices. So the CDU gave the impression of being a great *ad hoc* agglomeration of interests comparable to the American platform parties whose primary object is to place in office candidates from the various interest-groups.

The structure of the party leadership presented a similar picture. In contrast to the SPD's rigid organization the CDU suffered from continuous shifts of power and responsibilities; personalities were more important in this than regional considerations. While Adenauer held undisputed authority as permanent Chairman (and Federal Chancellor) this state of flux was to some extent an advantage, though it hardly furthered the cause of democracy within the party. Throughout his fourteen years as chancellor and even into the Erhard era, Adenauer managed to play off the various groups against each other and, using the superior resources of the chancellor democracy, to control both his party and the state. CDU party congresses became little more than occasions for acclamation; reforms put forward by various *rapporteurs* were generally pigeonholed. The crises of the Erhard period brought the CDU face to face with a situation in which the pragmatic and personal structure of the party's leadership under Adenauer was no longer adequate.

Since then the CDU has been torn between the necessity to streamline and modernize its structure and the aversion of its leading group, centred on Kiesinger, to abandonment of its squirearchical style, so successful in the past and also cosier. Its period in opposition will cause it to think and decide whether to live on the irrecoverable memory of the 1950s and the resulting prestige of the Adenauer party or whether to recapture some of its original flexibility and adapt itself to the changed situation – it has, after all, existed for far too long purely as a governing party.

The CDU's future depends on decisions to be taken both in the internal and external political fields. By reform of the party organization, shelved until the end of the Kiesinger era, it must cope with its unaccustomed task of opposition politics; it must also take account of the change in voting habits on the part of sections of the population hitherto loyal to the CDU, of the loosening in its ties with the churches and the reduction in their support and of the danger of falling behind in cities in process of transition to a modern industrial society; these are the objects of the efforts of the younger generation of members (the Youth Union and the RCDS (*Ring christlich-demokratischer Studenten* – Christian-democrat Students' Association)). In the field of foreign policy the party must bid farewell to the traditional recipe for success, the policy of strength under which anti-communism and integration into the West were supposed to pave the way for reunification and eastern policy was either not a subject for discussion or was considered in purely defensive terms. Since the construction of the Berlin Wall, the worst crisis of the Adenauer policy, this has long since lost its appeal to the electorate. Capacity for adaptation to the changed situation regarding East–West relationships and the all-German question will constitute a test case for the ability to develop of a party whose politics are still based on the problems of the 1950s and the clear, simple confrontation of the Cold War.

In dealing with these problems the CDU has certain advantages and qualities which should not be underestimated. It has a strong tradition of government; it has inherited the pragmatic ability of the Centre Party, which throughout its history has always known how to combine firm convictions with the capacity to compromise and cope with changing situations; it has admittedly variegated but massive support in all classes – as the 'people's party' in German history it can still be assured of almost half the total popular vote, more than the Nazi Party itself achieved in the 1933 elections despite all its terrorist methods.

4

The development of the SPD (the socialist party) in the second republic was fundamentally different. It was considerably influenced by two unfavourable circumstances. The division of Germany cut the party off from the old socialist strongholds of Saxony and Prussia. The development of the CDU into a bourgeois umbrella party and its decision against a coalition in 1949 forced it into opposition, only by a small margin, but there it was to remain for a long time. Adenauer's election as first Federal Chancellor – by a single vote (his own) – foreshadowed a wearisome period of exclusion from government. All this contrasted sharply with the optimistic expectations of a party which had once been the largest democratic force and which had projected itself as anti-Nazi with much greater emphasis than the bourgeois parties. It seemed to be driven back into the dilemma of the Weimar Republic when it had been outmanoeuvred and outvoted by bourgeois bloc governments.

In contrast to the CDU the SPD at once resumed the party tradition interrupted in 1933. It was the oldest, and for years had been the largest, German party; it could even point to some continuity of leadership in exile spanning the period between the ban on its existence and its rebirth. Severe self-criticism and far-reaching proposals for reform had been its answer to the 1933 catastrophe. After the heated debates in the resistance and among the émigrés the SPD found itself confronted by two questions: first, could it and should it continue as a workers' party with a marxist basis or should it follow the general trend towards broader-based, popular parties with a pragmatic outlook? Second, should it adhere to its internationalist orientation or should it place greater emphasis on its role as a national umbrella party of the democratic Left? The decision against becoming a class-based party was finally taken with the Godesberg programme of 1959; this gave priority to practical reformism over the traditional ideological programme, to which the democratic and revisionist policy of the SPD had in fact never been attuned. Its attitude to the national problem was largely influenced by its unhappy experiences of the Weimar period – had not its disregard of the patriotic emotions and its old label as the party of 'stateless fellows' been the cause of its failure? Had it not missed the opportunity to emphasize its services to the nation and so form an adequate counterweight to the surge of nationalism?

Kurt Schumacher's conclusion was to oppose Adenauer's policy of integration with the West on the grounds that the division of Germany necessitated a policy based on German national interests; the new emphasis in Social-democrat policy was summarized in Schumacher's criticism of Adenauer in October 1949 as 'the Allies' Chancellor', which also, of course, implied sharp criticism of the occupying powers. This was a determined attempt on the part of the SPD to project itself as a national party after its bitter experiences of being labelled nationally unreliable. It was unsuccessful in face of Adenauer's propaganda leading to the electoral victory of 1957 when the chancellor delivered himself of the pronouncement that victory for the SPD would mean the ruin of Germany. Nevertheless the Social-democrats had good grounds for their criticism – would not a policy of alliance and integration with the West further complicate and finally seal the division of Germany?

The re-born SPD, therefore, was a party based on more than mere old tradition. Its differing elements were reflected in the personalities of its leaders. Schumacher was a West Prussian, wounded in the First World War and bearing the marks of his struggle against Nazism and 'life' in a concentration camp; with almost fanatical faith and conviction he did his best to overcome the deep disillusionment of 1949 and lead the West German SPD into battle on two fronts, against communism and the bourgeois parties. Erich Ollenhauer represented the exiles; he was irreproachable but lacking in force of personality; he presided over the difficult transition from the Schumacher to the Brandt era during a decade of apparently interminable opposition. At the head of the East German SPD was Otto Grotewohl, a somewhat colourless functionary, whose policy visualized formation of a socialist unity front, a disastrous failure prior to 1933; a wealth of illusion but even more the pressure of the Soviet occupying power led him to complete the process by amalgamating his party with the communists in April 1946 to form the communist-run monopoly party, the SED (Socialist Unity Party). The SPD was therefore thrown back upon the West and had to abandon all hope either of forming an all-German socialist party or acquiring a leading position in the new Germany. A further major vexation was the fact that during the critical years of the Cold War, when the SPD was brought face to face with the communist claim to domination – during the Berlin blockade under Ernst Reuter, for instance – the CDU contrived to use the general anti-communist sentiment as an anti-socialist weapon. In the hubbub of the anti-Left campaign Schumacher's pronouncement that Germany would either be socialist or not exist at all passed unnoticed.

The fact remains, however, that the party organization was rebuilt with astounding rapidity and that by 1947 a membership of 900,000 had been achieved. In this respect too the tug–of–war between old and new elements provided further material for conflict, a conflict reflecting the advantages and disadvantages of rigid party organization and strict party discipline– greater solidity and capacity to withstand renewed setbacks on the one hand, bureaucratic inflexibility and immobility on the other. More than ever before, however, the SPD was bent on winning the support of new classes of the electorate – it had no need to fear competition from the communist party which was nearing extinction long before it was banned. Movements of population during the wartime and post-war periods helped to break down the traditional class structure and this, combined with the greater flexibility resulting from the introduction of younger people and a more elastic attitude towards the Right, helped the party develop into a progressive popular party. Results were slow in coming; ten years after the end of the war the SPD had only just topped its electoral figures of the initial period. Then, however, for the first time since 1919 they passed the 30 per cent mark and at each election thereafter the CDU's lead was reduced. When the Berlin crisis of 1961 showed that there were cracks in the Adenauer myth, personalities began to play a part in the Bundestag elections similar to that of the elections for the Chancellorship in 1953 and 1957 and this was something which the party could never have achieved under Ollenhauer.

The turning point of 1959–60 bade fair to imperil the traditional strength of the SPD as a class party with a large membership. There was much ideological disagreement; the party had dissociated itself from the nuclear disarmament movement and expelled the left-wing students' association, the SDS, together with its sponsors. The long-term consequence of this was the development of extra-parliamentary, anti-system movements directed against the SPD as well as the government, and reminiscent of the extreme polarizations of the Weimar Republic. All this, however, appeared as the lesser of two evils; all the efforts of the left-wing failed in face of the pragmatic party policy pertinaciously pursued by the reformist group led by Willy Brandt, who had made his name in the Berlin crisis, Herbert Wehner, the experienced party strategist, and Fritz Erler, the cool-headed expert in external politics. They steered the party into becoming a progressive people's party. The tight-knit organization was maintained. In the programmes as revised in Berlin in 1954 and Bad Godesberg in 1959, however, 'socialism' was no longer treated as a semi-religion; instead emphasis was laid on the universal values of a democratic emancipation movement, humanism, classical philosophy and christianity.

This was a process of adaptation, the results of which were particularly noticeable in the party's refurbished relationship with the churches. This 'kiss–and–make–friends' policy on the part of the SPD was much criticized; it led to acceptance of the papal encyclical *Mater et Magistra* and an intensive campaign to persuade wide sections of the bourgeoisie to join a 'positive opposition'; the latter even entailed support of an Erhard–Schröder faction against Adenauer and Strauss; it culminated in Wehner's efforts (starting with the 'Spiegel' crisis at the end of 1962) to achieve SPD participation in government by means of a great coalition. These were tactical matters but the policy as a whole was based on a realistic appreciation of the social and intellectual changes taking place in an increasingly mobile society, reflections of a more pragmatic approach to politics, increasing disinterest in ideology and the change in class structure. Empirical observation of the attitudes of the electorate replaced socialist theories on society; new methods of politico-psychological analysis and lobbying were based on the modern practices of market research and opinion polls.

The 30 per cent mark was passed primarily because, with the abandonment of the socialist class doctrine, increasing inroads were made into the catholic working-class population, the progressive bourgeoisie, the intelligentsia and finally even into the underdeveloped agricultural areas; meanwhile the expanding urban agglomerations became strongholds holding out prospects of increasing success at the polls. The SPD was bent on becoming the party of positive progress equal to all modern requirements and this was shown in its non-political canvassing among all sections of the population and in the change of its colours from the red of battle to the blue of propaganda. If non-socialist voters were to be recruited, the party had first to exorcise the deep-seated animosities and fears which the words 'red spectre' had aroused among the liberal bourgeoisie ever since the SPD had existed. So it presented itself as a party with a great history whose 'marxist' past had now given way to growing understanding of the changes and requirements of the second industrial revolution.

Basically this development presented a delay parallel to the rise of the CDU – emergence from a social ghetto in one case, from a catholic ghetto in the other. It was a slow process with many setbacks and the price paid in both cases was loss of intellectual and emotional appeal. It resulted, however, in increasing moderation of the classic confrontation between the solid citizenry and the revolutionary 'reds'; it helped to alleviate the ordinary man's fear complex. The rise of Willy Brandt as a candidate for the chancellorship was compared to the progressivism of the Kennedy party; the SPD now regarded itself as a flexible platform party in a two-party system in which government and opposition parties presented alternative methods of political operation but were no longer solely representative of a certain class or ideology. At the same time this cast doubt upon the CDU's ideological claim to be regarded as the only 'christian party'. It also meant, however, that the SPD had to abandon the search for a socialist alternative to the practical economic policy of *soziale Marktwirtschaft*; it might be given more pronounced social overtones and subjected to greater political control but the principle was no longer called in question.

After its failure at the 'Ollenhauer elections' of 1957 the party concentrated upon grooming more attractive candidates. Initially this took the form of advertising well-known SPD leaders in the *Länder* where the party had been far more successful in gaining political prestige and influence; the names of Zinn, Kaisen, Brauer, Kopf, Reuter and Brandt became well known. This showed up the compensating effect of the Federal Republic's federalist structure. Against considerable resistance from the party machine 'party intellectuals' such as Carlo Schmid (and Erler) were accepted into the headquarters team, at the head of which after the death of Ollenhauer in 1963 was Willy Brandt; Wehner and Erler respectively ensured that the machine and the parliamentary party followed the reformist policy line. This division of authority was not without its problems but Brandt's retention of his position in Berlin until 1965 proved of great advantage to him. When the fall of Erhard finally presented the SPD for the first time with a prospect of a 'change of power', however, it proved that after its long years of disappointment the new SPD was still not free of its old inhibitions.

The decision to form a great coalition had much to be said for it on paper. The deciding factor was the thought that only coalition with the CDU would prove to the public that at last the SPD was reliable and capable of governing. This entailed further concessions, the most obvious being on the matter of the debatable emergency legislation; moreover the absence of a major opposition party was not good for the democratic system as such. In the regional elections the party suffered further losses; the protest vote even went to the NPD. Continuation of the artificial coalition would have placed a severe strain on the reformist policy; so the SPD once more presented itself as the alternative to the CDU and laid claim to a full-scale change of power, so being in a position to contest the vital elections of autumn 1969; they ended twenty years of CDU rule and proved that not only the SPD but also the second German republic had graduated to the stage of full democracy.

5

The change of government in autumn 1969 was historic. The CDU still held a slight advantage over the SPD; the background, however, was not the attempt to force through a fundamental change in the electoral law, much publicized though that was to the point almost of becoming a fetish; both statistically and politically its results would have been highly doubtful though undoubtedly it would have helped to keep the CDU in power for years to come. The change was due instead to independent decision by the one party which had contrived to avoid being sucked into the wake of the two major parties but which would almost inevitably have been eliminated had the law of straight majority voting been introduced. Thus emerged with greater clarity than even before the pros and cons of a third party, of its much debated role as the balancing factor; in this particular case it both facilitated and accelerated the development of a party system which functioned correctly because it was capable of change.

The years of the FDP may be numbered but in the history of the Federal Republic it has played a vital role both as a bourgeois-liberal alternative to the 'christian' and 'socialist' parties and as a factor of fluidity in internal politics and in the streamlining of overrigid party structures. This will be true at least as long as social and ideological barriers still exist and so long as a bourgeois minority still feels that its pronounced liberal, anti-clerical and anti-socialist views are not adequately represented by the two major parties. This is neither so questionable and illogical nor disastrous as it may seem to the ideologists of the strict two-party system. Even under the British system, which they quote as an example and where tradition is strong, a liberal party has contrived to maintain itself despite the handicaps of the British electoral system. Even in America third parties do in fact exist if true account is taken of the very distinct wings in each of the major parties. Similarly the CSU laid claim to independence in the event of introduction of a majority voting system. More important than all, however, the pressure for liberalization exerted by a third party in a central position is in itself adequate justification for the existence of the FDP alongside the major parties.

Like the others the FDP regarded itself as a re-formed party. After 1945 German liberalism, traditionally divided, was partially absorbed into the CDU (Lemmer, for instance) or the SPD (A. Arndt and L. Bergsträsser, for instance). Even had it managed to heal the old divisions, a liberal party would have been condemned to a minority role from the outset. It reflected, moreover, the great regional and social differences of traditional liberalism. The old strains and stresses between progressive liberals (in the south) and national liberals (in the west and north) re-emerged at once.

It is almost impossible to disentangle the dramatic conflicts and crises characterizing the FDP's political career over the years whether in government or opposition. Headstrong groups and personalities played a disproportionately large part; organization was weaker than in any other party. South German dignitaries of the old liberal school such as Reinhold Maier, Dehler and Heuss took their cue from 1848 and the Weimar DDP (German Democratic Party); in North Rhine–Westphalia 'young Turks' such as Döring, Weyer, Scheel and Mende pressed for a more active, though more ambivalent, policy; right-wing liberals such as Blücher, who brought Erhard into politics though not into the FDP, went over to Adenauer altogether. Provision of the federal president for the republic's first decade was the sacrifice made by the party for its decisive role in formation of the first federal government; it placed the party's most respected leader in a position above party, thereby neutralizing him.

Being left-wing culturally but right-wing economically, the FDP claimed a large share of the credit for the acceptance of *soziale Marktwirtschaft*; in the minds of the electorate, however, the 'economic miracle' was ascribed to Adenauer and Erhard's CDU. The persistent conflicts with Adenauer culminated in a temporary split in the party. Adenauer used the methods which had proved so successful with other small parties (the BHE and DP) but in this case without result; finally in 1961 the FDP scored an astonishing success at the polls with its demand for the removal of the eighty-five-year-old chancellor (its percentage rose from 7.7 per cent to 12.8 per cent). After five years in opposition, however, the party rejoined the new Adenauer–Erhard coalition under the National-Liberal Mende. Not until the fall of Erhard could the party extract itself from its position as a mere appendage of the CDU; when Mende gave way to Scheel early in 1967 the party engaged in a costly struggle against the Great Coalition until ultimately, in 1969, it was able to initiate the decisive movement leading to 'change of power'. Despite its divergent personalities and groups and to the astonishment of the sceptics, under its new leadership the party managed to survive the severe tests of the elections for the presidency and chancellorship.

The old divergence between the wings of the party remains. Whether the FDP can avert the threat of the five-per-cent clause will depend on a complex compromise between progressive and conservative forces, on a streamlining of the organization and also on the success of the Brandt government. Its continued existence between the two major parties depends on the number of voters unable to accept either the social progressivism of the SPD or the cultural conservatism of the CDU and upon the estimate of the value of a liberal corrective in both directions. The party has not much elbow-room; nevertheless growing recognition of the attraction of a socialist-liberal coalition and the CDU's crises in its unaccustomed role as opposition may open up new vistas for the FDP.

All other parties have vanished from the parliamentary scene. The process was completed with the collapse of the DP (German Party) and BHE (Refugee's Party) in 1961 which may be ascribed primarily to the CDU's absorptive capacity and Adenauer's tactical ability. This also illustrated the change in concept of political parties under the second democracy, to which reference has already been made: the claim to be an integrating force made by the 'people's parties' has spelt the doom of parties too closely tied to regional and special interests or particular ideologies. The same applies to the radical groups both of the Right and Left, which were mostly short-lived. Even the KPD (Communist Party) had long been reduced to a small splinter party before it was (quite superfluously) banned in 1956; it has re-formed as the DKP but seems to have few prospects so long as it is identified with the East German SED. After the SRP (Socialist Reich Party) was banned in 1952 right-wing extremism took refuge in the tiny DRP (German Right Party); with the fusion in 1964–5 between ex- and neo–Nazis, hitherto divided and sheltering in other small parties, right-wing extremism could provide a receptacle for a wider protest vote. In 1969 with a total 4 per cent vote it just failed to meet the requirements of the five-per-cent clause but, under the special conditions of past German history, the potential of right-wing extremism remains a problem *sui generis*.

6

Compared to fragmentation and coalition-forming problems characteristic of other parliamentary democracies the Federal Republic's party system seems to have attained an astounding degree of stability and efficiency. The prospect of four or more parties is becoming slimmer and even the third party is engaged in a struggle for existence. To the present-day observer the Bonn party system seems more concentrated and unassailable than ever before. Obvious though this may seem, the fundamental problems of the modern party system as practised in Germany have not in fact entirely vanished. Safeguards for a stable party system are very far-reaching. If further extended they may become counter-productive and lead to certain dangers – primarily that of over-institutionalization and over-stabilization which could affect the very substance of the parties as such. There are pronounced trends in this direction. From the outset certain CDU circles have been campaigning for further modification of the voting arrangements including dual voting with a five-per-cent clause. At the height of the quarrel with the FDP in 1956 Adenauer took everyone aback with a proposal for a 'trench system' which would have practically destroyed the FDP.

Two major dangers are inherent in the subtle manipulations of the franchise still under discussion, ultimately with some support even from the SPD. In the first place, if measures generally considered to be inequitable and undemocratic are taken to entrench the *status quo* in favour of one or two parties, the political system itself may lose credibility and, in a democracy still so young, this may lead to violent reactions against the 'establishment'; second, if parties are institutionalized and officialized (particularly if they are state-financed), their whole nature and function as flexible, open, free associations standing between the state and society would be affected and the traditional anti-party sentiment might revive. Implicit in both these trends is an unwelcome desire to suppress political dynamism in society and state or to promote the traditional non-participation in politics.

The privileged position accorded to the existing party system has been reinforced by the fact that the parties have voted themselves grants from the state, at first disgracefully camouflaged as 'for political education work'. There were sound reasons for improving the financing arrangements; the much quoted article in the constitution dealing with political parties (Article 21) required that the structure and aims of parties be democratic and in addition that they publish their accounts. The proposed party law was rejected over and over again through the action of various interest groups – the bourgeois parties existed largely on under-cover contributions from industry. Public financing might remove the dilemma. For good reasons, however, the Federal Constitutional Court restricted public financing to electoral expenditure, making the smaller parties eligible also. The compromise of the 1967 party law leaves open the problems thrown up by the trend towards official party financing, an inevitable step in the end. In a country where the traditions of the patriarchal state still persist, further officialization of the parties might imperil the capacity of the existing party system to function in crisis situations and reinforce the trend towards the administrative state which threatens the parliamentary system itself.

Twenty years still seem too short to form a final judgement. The Bonn party system has benefited from advantageous economic development and from political protection, neither of which were available to the first German republic. At the same time, however, it has drawn the lessons from earlier distressful historical experiences and has created conditions for further development of a modified but efficient democracy in Germany better than has ever existed before. The smooth change of power in 1969 was perhaps the most vital step in this development since the foundation of the Federal Republic. Much will depend upon whether the economic foundations and the political conditions which have given rise to this development can be adapted to the changed circumstances of the new decade. If this is to happen, however, the internal structures of the parties must be made more democratic, they must become more accessible to the citizen and the party system must be able to absorb, to integrate and to harness to a forward looking policy the new generation with its changed aspirations and expectations. For this purpose the stimulus produced by extra-parliamentary movements must be taken seriously, although violent or anti-democratic tendencies must be firmly suppressed. Pluralist democracy's capacity to survive stands or falls by the ability to solve differences peacefully, without the use of force. Independent parties capable of co-operating and of acceptance of an effective opposition are the *conditio sine qua non*, the indispensable element in the survival of a free democracy.

The state of the party system is more indicative of the state of the political system than any formal distinction between democracy and dictatorship. However severely the shortcomings of the Bonn system may be criticized, it cannot be denied that in no sphere does the difference between the Weimar Republic and the Bonn system emerge more clearly than in the nature of the parties, now mature and assured.

Part III
Political Criteria

12

Democracy and Political Parties—
Theory and Practice

I

Among current political terms that of democracy is as much used and misused as any other. It has become part of the vocabulary of all parties and systems but as a result its true meaning has become more uncertain and controversial than ever. Its practical manifestations are to be seen in the wide spectrum of antagonistic forms of state and society ranging from conservative and liberal monarchies and republics to authoritarian, communist, single-party systems. The same applies to the catchword of 'democratization'; it is used, manipulated or called in question as is required to serve anything from particular interest policies to wide-ranging demands for reform or revolutionary change.

Obviously it has become more difficult than ever to agree upon a scientifically accurate definition of the term democracy. One questions whether, under such circumstances, it is objectively employable at all; historical and political terminology has become so distorted that we should perhaps resign ourselves to using such words as mere instruments to be applied to subjective conflicts of interest or power, as mere catchwords in the battle of ideas and opinions associated with political systems. Should democracy as an ideology be avoided or even eliminated by serious historians and social scientists and replaced by a more clear-cut, empirical body of ideas? This, however, would mean one of two things: either a return to the traditional doctrine on forms of state which took as its criterion the external forms of political institutions or abandonment of present terminology in favour of a doctrine of political processes and functions which either did not categorize states at all or at any rate took no account of the concepts upon which they were based.

The concept of democracy and the meaning of the term differ widely in the West, in the East and in the Third World; to clarify it, therefore, a historical stock-taking is first required. Admittedly democracies, both ancient and modern, have been set up under political conditions which differ so fundamentally that historical deductions and comparisons are apt to be misleading. Moreover in the original form in which democracy came into existence and was implemented, there were so many deficiencies and limitations that it has been accorded only a lowly place in the history of political ideas; from Plato until the present day far more has been heard of those doctrines of state and society which were critical of democracy or actually anti-democratic. In view of the deficiencies in existing political arrangements continually brought to light by criticism, political theory has been primarily concerned to draw a picture of the perfect state in which conflict would be a thing of the past. This implies, however, that fundamentally this state is authoritarian, even though it may proclaim that its object is the perfect democracy; the central notion is the rule of the people, the *consensus omnium*, the prevalence of a *volonté générale*, the popular community or popular democracy free of conflict. Ever since Plato put forward the idea of government by philosophers this concept has amounted to a demand that the realities of life as they actually exist in all their multiplicity be moulded according to some preconceived 'idea'; this inevitably means that anything different or divergent will be suppressed, eliminated or brought into line by authoritarian methods.

In fact, however, the empirical theory of democracy deliberately rejects perfectionism. This fundamental difference emerged long ago in the contrast between Plato and Aristotle, between the speculative idealist theorists and the empirical realists. Aristotle was critical of any system of rule based on perfectionism because it was monolithic, oversimplified and would sweep away or suppress anything which differed from it. Since then the antithesis has come to the fore over and over again both in theory and in practice. In modern times the debate on democracy has furnished major examples in the confrontations between Montesquieu and Rousseau, between the American and French revolutionary doctrines, between British reformist socialism on the one hand and marxist continental socialism on the other; since the First World War the antithesis is to be seen in the difference between social-democrat and communist policies, also in the fact that democratic nationalism was overtaken by nationalistic, fascist, tyrannical ideologies; they equally invoked the idea of the perfect state, the true democracy as justification for oppression and *Gleichschaltung*. Even present-day arguments about democracy, ranging from those of the extreme Right to the radical Left, reflect the fundamental confrontation between the perfectionist and realist concepts of the state and of society.

Of course this is a much oversimplified picture. More detailed historical differentiation is necessary. The experience of history, however, shows that in practice democracy stands or falls by its ability to liberate the greatest multiplicity of individual and social forces and permit the freest possible interplay between them. This implies, not the imposition of some rigid, though ideal, structure but as flexible and mobile a governmental system as possible under which an open, mobile society – the antithesis of the perfect order – can develop. For this there must be certain defined historical and socio-economic conditions and a habit of social behaviour, without which no democracy is possible. To this extent, therefore, if democracy is to function, it must be regarded as a historical phenomenon, not the result of the philosopher's or constitutional lawyer's logic, however brilliant. It must be conceived as a process, never concluded but always developing, in order to overcome existing limitations and the ever recurring problems of a free and therefore incomplete society; in contrast to a dictatorship conflicts must not be suppressed but solved peacefully.

This rudimentary definition of democracy provides some insight into the differences existing between democracy in its ancient, uncomplicated form and that required in a modern industrial state. The fundamental characteristics (and the political terminology) had already been developed by the Greek city-states, particularly Athens, in the fifth and fourth centuries BC. The concept of democracy as the rule of the people originated as a battle-cry and a counterweight to autocracy and arbitrary rule. The overriding criterion was that power emanated from the people who were sovereign; from this followed the demand for effective distribution of political power making possible both the participation of the people and control over the wielders of authority. The rules by which this distribution and control of political authority were guaranteed, were ultimately established and institutionalized in constitutions. The fundamental difference between this and all previous forms in which sanction to political rule had been given was that the foundation upon which political authority and order rested was a rational one, and not religious or mythological. The Greek discovery of man as a free individual and citizen led to the secularization of social relationships and obligations; the doubt cast upon the mythological legitimization of a system of rule produced the requirement for democracy. Initially, therefore, democracy was no consciously theoretical concept; instead it was a practical effort towards limitation, de-mystification and accountability of authority; it was the vital step from blind subservience to the actual existing authority towards an authority founded on and justified by intellectual, moral, 'civic', social, in short 'political', considerations. Ever since then this has been the real purpose and meaning of any democratic constitution.

The eminently practical and empirical background to Greek democracy is reflected in the fact that, despite the wealth of philosophical literature, no theory of democracy was developed. The major drafts and such published material as we have are anti-democratic – a fact which has governed and warped the judgement of German historians, more so than others, up to the present day.[1] The same applies also to that central feature of democratic politics, the political parties. Even their rudimentary beginnings in the Greek city-states and the Roman republic were the object of severe criticism on the part of the constitutionalists; even today the words 'party politics' carry a negative connotation. In fact almost throughout history criticism of democracy has been based on deep-rooted, anti-party sentiment which is as old as democracy and the parties themselves.

2

The divergence between theory and practice emerges with even greater clarity in more recent developments in different countries. Political parties are the *sine qua non* both of modern parliamentary practice and modern democracy. They are (in R. Thoma's phrase) 'the life-blood of democracy'; their rise has coincided with the evolution of the political systems which have taken the place of absolutist forms of government from the eighteenth century onwards. James Bryce, the pioneer of the comparative history of democracy early in the present century, describes them as indispensable. E. E. Schnattschneider opens his great book on *Party Government* (New York 1942) with the thesis that 'the political parties created democracy and that modern democracy is unthinkable save in terms of the parties.' More can be learnt about the state of a political system from the state of the parties and party system than from all the formal treatises about constitutions and institutions with which lawyers or philosophers try to define and categorize the various countries. To this extent research into political parties has become a central feature of political science in its capacity as a science of democracy.

It is frequently impossible to distinguish between democratic and dictatorial systems from the text of their constitutions or the lay-out of their institutions. Often enough an ostensibly perfect constitution has served to conceal the reality behind a pseudo-democratic façade – for example, almost half mankind is dominated by the single-party regimes of communist countries and other authoritarian and fascist systems. The difference between these and a democracy is best seen if the structure and function of the political parties in any political system is analysed, for however different in form they may be, political parties 'have conquered almost the entire world as a modern instrument or principle of organization for the formation of the political will and the recruitment of political personnel'.[2]

Political parties, therefore, occupy a central position but research and theory on the subject has by no means kept pace. Even today, when historians, lawyers, economists or philosophers concern themselves with the state, they take far too little notice of the political parties. They deal with the working and organization of parties only grudgingly and often with some contempt. Parties are regarded as extra-constitutional agencies which the constitution either does not mention at all or does so in a negative sense. In contrast to 'state' or 'national' politics 'party politics' are consigned to the dirty morass of human and social corruption. The story of political parties' graduation from a position of outlawry to one of at least partial toleration and recognition is a long and tortuous one. Naturally it is not the same everywhere. For historical reasons parties in Britain and America have been far more closely involved in the development of the modern state than they have on the continent; there pre-democratic structures and habits have persisted even after the constitutional introduction of a democratic parliamentary system.

So, particularly in Germany over the last hundred years, there has developed a deep cleavage and discrepancy between the economic and social sub-structure which has been changing rapidly as a result of the industrial revolution and modernization, and the superstructure of the state which has remained outdated and traditionalist; in many respects the patriarchal state is still in existence even today, in other words the pre-democratic ideals of good order and authority remain, though the outward forms are democratic. It is in the nature of modern democracy that social and political conflicts should be neither concealed nor suppressed; under democracy they can be brought out freely into the open, opposition and minorities are protected, their vital role in the political process is recognized and institutionalized. Political parties and associations are both protagonists and intermediaries in this continuous process of argument and in the political field it is the duty of political science – as it is that of sociology in the social field – to enquire into the protagonists in the argument and the forms which the argument takes. Instead of the traditional normative science of the state this postulates a science of reality based on empiricism.

The history of the modern social sciences, however, is a short one. At the time of Aristotle politics as a science was regarded as an aspect of philosophy; later, from the seventeenth century onwards, it developed as a science of administration. So when, with the break-through of modern democracy and the emancipation of the bourgeoisie and working class, political parties originated, there was no adequate science capable of dealing with them. This is the explanation of the ludicrous fact that until a few years ago no recognized modern research into political parties had been instituted even in the universities. From early in this century one or two great pioneers did devote themselves to the subject but they were voices crying in the wilderness and far too little notice was taken of their work.

To quote only a few names: it is generally known that M. I. Ostrogorski's two-volume work published in 1901 is entitled *La démocratie et l'organisation des partis politiques* (Democracy and the Organisation of Political Parties).[3] This was followed in 1912 by Robert Michels's critical study *Zur Soziologie des Parteiwesens* (On the Sociology of Parties),[4] a second and fuller edition of which appeared in 1925; Michels's sub-title – 'Investigation of Oligarchic Tendencies in Group Life' – shows that he was highly sceptical about the internal organization of parties. Penetrating and rich in material though these studies were, they hardly touched the real problem of modern party research, the position and function of political parties in the democratic state. More important still, the influence of these books on the traditional theory of the state and the constitution was either very small or counter-productive. Michels's criticism of the party élites (he later turned to fascism) was calculated to intensify the widespread anti-party sentiment, particularly in Germany; there, after all, the first republic collapsed in 1933 primarily under the pressure of the traditional doctrine of state which was anti-party and of the Nazi 'movement' which definitely proclaimed itself as anti-party. Inadequate appreciation of the position and function of parties undoubtedly contributed materially to the victory of authoritarian single-party regimes between the wars.

Historical accounts then began to be written in Europe and even more in America; some literature appeared about programmes and elections (in Germany the best was Ludwig Bergsträsser's history of parties which remains a valuable book today). None of these works, however, dealt with the comparative and systematic aspects and so they are of little value for a general theory on the nature of political parties. We owe the first really balanced study on the subject in Germany to the German–American scholar Sigmund Neumann. In 1932, one year before the end of the German republic and the annihilation of democratic parties, Neumann, then still a young lecturer at the German Political Institute in Berlin, published his book *Die deutschen Parteien* (The German Parties) – a new edition appeared in 1965.[5] On the eve of the Nazi single-party regime this was too late to arrest the disease in German minds. The book, however, provided a good example of the combination of historical examination with structural analysis as applied to the party system, a method resumed after the dictatorship ended in 1945. In 1956 Neumann was the editor of the composite work *Modern Political Parties*[6] which provided an international survey of political parties in the various continents. At the same time, in his great summary, Neumann laid down criteria and set out the results of comparative analysis of the various parties within existing political systems. A year earlier, in 1955, he had written a deep-thinking foreword to the first general work on parties in the second German republic published by the Institute for Political Science in Berlin under the title *Parteien in der Bundesrepublik* (Parties in the Federal Republic).

This was the real beginning in Germany of the new phase of more intensive and systematic research into political parties. Its starting point was Neumann's attempt to typify the various parties. In the Weimar Republic, for instance, he distinguished between the following types: absolutist integration parties both of the Left and the Right (the communist and Nazi parties), integration parties based on confessional or class ideologies (the Centre and Socialist parties), and upper class and representational parties (the Liberals). The rationale of his classification, written in 1932, is remarkable and is still applicable today:

'All previous attempts to systematize parties are unsatisfactory and unrelated to the opposing party fronts – if indeed they are related to reality. This applies particularly to the popular distinction between parties based on ideology and those based on interest. In fact all genuine parties ... display a mixture of ideology and interest; it is, however, invariably more difficult to relate the ideological content of a party's thinking to the usual division into conservative, liberal or socialist ideas; the interests on which affiliations are based are by no means solely economic... On the other hand, in the development of the modern type of party it is possible to detect the formation of fronts which are partly the consequence and partly the cause of fundamental change ... In general it may be said that at present the pure *representational party* is increasingly giving way to the typical *integration party.'*

This diagnostic method of typifying parties has the advantage that it is closely related to reality; in fact, four decades after the event, it uncovered the essential point in the development, not confined to Germany, which led from liberal upper-class democracy to egalitarian party democracy. Among theorists on this subject the German author deserving of special mention is Gerhard Leibholz;[7] he places the permanently organized parties squarely in the centre of the political process in a democracy. Naturally there is considerable opposition to this realistic viewpoint among political scientists, quite apart from the numerous constitutional lawyers with conservative learnings. The Basic Law, however (in Article 21) gave constitutional recognition to political parties; in the judgement of the Federal Constitutional Court, the Federal Republic is a party state and the state financing of parties, though rightly a debatable question, is now under discussion. Research and interpretation are therefore becoming directed more and more towards party democracy.

3

We must not, of course, fall victim to the error, once so common, of thinking Germany to be the most important country in the world. We have, nevertheless, our own experiences, our own party histories and traditions. In the Federal Republic, moreover, interest in discussion and investigation has been concentrated much more (too much in my view) upon questions of electoral systems and electoral sociology – primarily at the expense of investigation into the parties themselves. In this field the whole matter is still almost in its infancy. Strongly urged by the Americans, electoral sociology really made a start in Germany in the 1950s with a major work published by the Berlin Institute for Political Science in 1957, *Wähler und Gewählte* (Electors and Elected); it was followed in 1965 by a comprehensive exercise in international comparison, *Empirische Wahlforschung* (Empirical Electoral Research) by Niels Diederich.[8] While on this subject just one comment: democracy is impaired if the parties, which are its central element, are manipulated by manoeuvring the electoral law for political purposes, as a group of dogmatic protagonists of the simple majority franchise led by F. A. Hermens of Cologne is trying to do at present.

Meanwhile a flood of American literature on the subject has appeared. Far more influential than this, however, and far better known than its German counterpart is the French contribution to research into the party system; the outstanding names are those of André Siegfried, Maurice Duverger and George E. Lavau. Siegfried was the pioneer of political science in France; even before the First World War he had founded the French tradition of electoral geography, *Géographie électorale*, representing the first beginnings of research into the parties. Duverger's book, *Les Partis politiques* (Political Parties) has been published in numerous editions and translations since 1951[9] and is internationally by far the best known book on party research. It is a 'broad-brush', comparative analysis with an attractively simple categorization of parties by type; the worldwide recognition accorded to it is understandable when it is considered how little competition the book had at the time. Rightly, however, an immediate and violent debate began about the methods and content of Duverger. In this a considerable role was played by George Lavau's investigation which carried the illuminating title (indicating Duverger's deficiencies) *Partis politiques et réalités sociales* (Political Parties and Social Realities).[10] Further discriminating analyses on electoral sociology have since been published, particularly by Matthei Dogan. In general, however, Duverger was accepted as the bible or at least he was regarded as the sole guide through the perplexing multiplicity of forms and systems of party.

Although this book might appear to invite further studies on the subject, there were considerable risks involved. It is no accident that no other book of this type has so far appeared despite the enormous increase in volume of specialist literature on political parties. Duverger's strength was at the same time his weakness – his highly simplified characterization and categorization and his idealization of the two-party system as the prerequisite for any efficient democracy. The inevitable consequences were numerous factual errors and deductions which flew in the face of social and political reality. This was fundamentally different from the sober empirical stock-taking without regard for ideology characteristic of the vastly increased research into political parties emanating at the same time from Britain and America (though not from elsewhere); standard works were Robert MacKenzie's *British Political Parties* published in 1955, V. O. Key's *Politics, Parties and Pressure Groups*[11] and Schnattschneider's and Neumann's books already mentioned.

Duverger's method was one of systematic comparison centred on the question of parties' structure and functions as intermediaries between society and the state, between social and political life in the modern 'mass democracy'. In his typology he included all forms of government, even authoritarian or totalitarian single-party states, and this produces the first question-mark. Democratic and dictatorial parties can only be compared to a limited degree both as regards function (in a single-party regime) and background ideas. It is in the nature of a party that it is only part of a whole, *pars* but not *pars pro toto* as totalitarian parties claim to be. In the first instance democratic parties resemble associations based on common interest; both parties and associations try to promote their particular interests by reference to an imaginary 'good of the community' (*bonum commune*) which can in fact only be achieved by co-operation and argument. The point is, however, that parties (in contrast to mere groups of electors) are organized combinations of various groups with concrete political aims; their purpose is to be represented in the decision-making agencies, to acquire and exercise power, in short to engage in full political activity. In the multi-party state 'parties' are only conceivable and effective as freely competing groups; by combining in an organization the individual, who by himself is weak, becomes a political power factor.

There are therefore two aspects to any democratic party; a party has a dual task which is both difficult and productive of stresses and strains. On the one hand it must have its sights set on parliamentary activity, on legislation, education, support and control of the government. On the other hand it must have the support of public opinion and electoral associations among the population. This highlights the fact that a party's character stems from definite historical traditions and habits of social behaviour to an extent not detectable from its institutions or internal organization. On this point Duverger seems to me to have failed; he certainly did so in his picture of the German party system as of many others also. A further question arises to which no convincing answer has yet been given: is it possible to produce a general theory on parties which is not either purely formalistic or empirically erroneous in its details? In contrast to Duverger, Lavau says that it is not possible.

Duverger himself was well aware of this problem; in his introduction he emphasized that it was 'still impossible today to give a basic comparative description of the mechanisms of political parties' so long as empirical research remained so uneven; this in turn, however, postulated formulation of wide-ranging questions, in other words a 'general theory on parties' (op. cit., p. ix). He attempts to break the vicious circle which is the bane of every science by collating and examining the various practical and methodological theses; the result is an effort to produce a theory on the subject and this he continuously tests and checks in the light of historical and sociological analysis. To this extent, therefore, he was practising political science in its capacity as an integrating science; political science, after all, seeks to concentrate on the special problem of the structure of power taking account of juridical, historical, sociological, economic and philosophical considerations; at the same time in its capacity as a discipline of its own, it seeks to support and complement the other social sciences. Unfortunately, however, almost all the apparently up to date hypotheses upon which was based this attempt to classify political parties and arrange them by models and types, were disproved rather than confirmed by subsequent investigations. Duverger did not concentrate his attention upon the links between ideas, programmes and party formation, on which liberal theory laid stress, or upon the connection between social structure and party as emphasized by marxism; he considered that modern parties were primarily characterized by their organizational structure. Rules and regulations, however, are only the external manifestations of organizational practice and of tradition; only the initiated are admitted into the inmost circles and they have all the greater difficulty in drawing objective comparisons.

The same applies to the problem of the electoral system; here Duverger argues far too forcibly in favour of an allegedly perfect solution. Throughout his book the simple majority system is presented as the political panacea, the main foundation of an efficient two-party system (pp. 232 et seq.); this cannot be accepted, however, as an overriding law; it is not supported either by the much misinterpreted British experience or by the German. It springs from a belief and a hope that introduction of the 'right' electoral system can solve the basic problem of directing political development by statute and that democracy based on the two-party system can be assured by institutional methods; this underestimates the multiplicity of historical, social and intellectual factors.[12] It has been necessary to draw attention to the limitations of this book because it is still regarded as *the* standard work and still exerts some influence on research. Compared to Ostrogorski and Michels it has the advantage that it is less rigid and its political appreciations are therefore more correct; Ostrogorski's and Michels's criticisms are so severe that they practically write off political parties as undemocratic and so assist the growth of prejudice and of attacks not only on the parties but on democracy itself. Duverger's theory, however, stands or falls by his main, though unproven, thesis that there is a direct relationship between parties and electoral systems, also by his statements that a two-party system is under all circumstances the best and that such a system will automatically be produced by a relative majority electoral system with single-member constituencies. Lavau rightly objected that such theories could just as well be turned the other way round and result in *reductio ad absurdum*. The implication is that investigation into political parties should be confined to electoral systems, which constitute only half the problem. Neither Neumann in his *Modern Political Parties* nor the numerous other studies on political parties in recent years have adopted Duverger's methods of formalizing and typifying political parties – nor could they, for the reality is far more complicated than the bold theories emanating from Paris.

4

Basically this showed that a classification based on party organization or the electoral system was inadequate; historical, sociological, regional and ideological criteria had also to be applied; a broader basis than that of Neumann was required. This necessitated much detailed work in monographs and studies of particular aspects. In West Germany an increasing amount of material has been produced in recent years and set out in some cases historically, and in others, systematically; this is the result of collaboration between political science, sociology and contemporary history. This was all the more significant since, compared to the older democracies, Germany, with its long tradition of an authoritarian state, had to be regarded as a developing country. In addition to one or two major surveys[13] particular mention should be made here of the studies by Thomas Nipperdey, *Die Organisation der deutschen Parteien vor 1918* (Pre-1918 German Party Organisation),[14] Wolf-Dieter Narr, *CDU-SPD, Programme und Praxis seit 1945* (The CDU and SPD, Programmes and Practices since 1945),[15] Heinz-Josef Varain, *Parteien und Verbände* (Parties and Associations),[16] Ossip K. Flechtheim, *Dokumente zur partei-politischen Entwicklung in Deutschland nach 1945* (Documents on the Development of Political Parties in Germany since 1945),[17] together with Hans-Gerd Schumann's comprehensive and systematic bibliography in *Die politischen Parteien in Deutschland nach 1945* (Political Parties in Germany after 1945).[18] At the same time, political parties having been given a place under the constitution, lawyers, political scientists and sociologists produced a whole series of studies dealing with the qualifications demanded of parties by the constitution from the institutional and empirical points of view – democracy within a party, for instance, publication of accounts, state financing, democratic objectives.[19] Admittedly legalistic and formalistic views still predominated. As we know, on the basis of these regulations the Federal Constitutional Court banned two parties – the ultra-right SRP in 1952 and the Communist Party in 1956. This led to further analysis of the available material.

Similar problems coloured the long process which ultimately ended in the rejection of a party law. Here the interaction of political theory and political practice was particularly visible. In the mid-1950s the Federal Government appointed commissions composed of scholars in public law, history, sociology and political science to assemble material and elaborate views on a comprehensive party law (the memoranda of 1955). Owing to the conflicts of interest of individual parties this was a failure and in fact formal regulation of the party system to some extent runs counter to the nature of political parties as free, flexible associations. The requirements of the Basic Law of 1949, however, like so many other points in the constitution, stem from the experience of the failure of the first republic; political parties had then been stamped as extra-constitutional phenomena and this had led most interpreters of the constitution, who were conservative and authoritarian, to regard political parties and indeed democracy itself as of little value. This was one of the main reasons for the triumph of National-socialism and Italian fascism. Accordingly, after the horrifying experiment of a totalitarian single-party regime, first the Italian constitution in 1946 and then the West German in 1949 explicitly recognized the importance of political parties as a channel for the expression of the popular will in a democracy. Once political parties and the multi-party state had been accepted as the foundation of any free democratic state based on the rule of law and as the main agencies for political organization of a mass society, more precise definition of the concept and nature of political parties seemed indispensable.

Critical discussion of this question shows that so far-reaching an institutionalization of the party system raises considerable problems not only for the parties themselves but also for democracy. The parties approximate to official organizations; their development, both sociologically and politically, is restricted; in particular state financing (which at present takes the form of financing electoral campaigns) threatens to change their character and to immobilize the party system in the existing *status quo* at the expense of any political dynamic; the tendency to bureaucratize and officialize parties will be reinforced as a result. Against this it cannot be denied that the previous dependence of the bourgeois parties on liberal contributions from industry constitutes a danger, as was shown by the rise of Nazism before 1933 with all its consequences. Once political parties have been formally recognized and given a place under the constitution, it seems hardly possible to avoid some canalization, institutionalization and control of their functions, as also of the various associations. Whether this is a suitable arrangement for other countries, where conditions are different, remains an open question. Germans tend to try to prescribe and codify everything, not to work by the broad rules of the game as do the British. This may well be unavoidable so long as a political culture does not accept democracy as a matter of course.

In scholarly circles doubts are now being voiced whether the earlier theory that party democracy was essential is universally valid. Its basis is empirical, not logical and it rests on the limited experience of western democracy. This empiricism looks somewhat different when one considers the emancipation of the new countries of Africa and Asia; the experience of Latin America has been different too.[20] The great question, however, is whether parties do not lose their pristine function if they are so closely linked to the state which recognizes them or if public opinion so openly welcomes a great coalition, in other words government by two parties holding 90 per cent of the seats in parliament as happened in the Federal Republic in 1966. Are we not tending towards an efficient administrative state organized on a decentralized basis and so dispensing with the expensive luxury of party pluralism? Certain perspicacious analytical thinkers (E. Krippendorf, for instance) have already announced the 'end of the party state'; others pose the question whether 'party government' is really indispensable, even in a democracy.[21]

5

Such prognoses, however, postulate the utopian assumption that unity rather than conflict is in the nature of politics, and moreover unity without coercion. Single-party regimes are not conceivable, either in logic or empiricism, unless based on coercion. All that can be conceived is a single party wide enough to include strong wings or sections; an example of this for a time was the Indian Congress Party but this is now no longer the case. Of course there is a crisis of the party system but it is today primarily a crisis of adaptation to the continuously increasing requirements of official and public authority, to the complexity of the actual tasks on hand; all this makes it difficult to formulate political opinion and political will, to carry on the political process and to take political decisions. Single-party regimes are no less prone to similar crises but they have proved to be a spurious solution, a dead end.[22] This much is proved by the studies on the East German Socialist Unity Party produced by the Berlin Institute for Political Science.[23]

Moreover the crisis of the party state, about which we hear so much, is more a crisis of the parliamentary system than of the parties. As the parties contrive continuously to extend their grip the first sufferer is the member of parliament. Constitutional theory still clings to the notion of the independent member responsible only to his conscience; in practice, however, the individual member finds himself entangled in a whole nexus of social and political obligations which become more compelling as modern industrial society grows more complex and as the parties and interest-groups become more solidly organized and carry greater weight. The result has been that, contrary to the intentions of the constitution, the member of parliament has, consciously or unconsciously, found himself subjected to directives from his party or interest-group and restricted by an 'imperative mandate'. The member does not, therefore, fulfil his role as representative of the people as a whole. The classic liberal form of parliamentarian representative of the citizenry as a whole is replaced by a parliamentary democracy based on plebiscitary methods and officialized parties; this fundamentally changes the whole process of political opinion forming and the function of parliament as the agency of decision and control.

The connection between this 'structural change in democracy' (Leibholz's phrase) and the history of modern parties has meanwhile been the subject of exhaustive investigation. The old postulate of representative democracy has, of course, been preserved in the constitution as set out in the Basic Law. Members of parliament are 'representatives of the people as a whole, in no sense tied to orders or directives and subject only to the dictates of their conscience' (Article 38). In theory, therefore, they are not subject to the 'imperative mandate' to which in practice they are so largely bound by the procedure for nomination of candidates, the electoral process, parliamentary practice and party discipline.

The whole divergence between theory and practice can be reduced to these controversial points. Moreover, the situation in other European countries seems hardly to differ at all. Constitutions perpetuate the fiction of the 'party-less' parliamentary system and the free-thinking member of parliament, but in practice, with their laconic, generally anodyne references to political parties, they merely perpetuate the 'conspiracy of silence'.[24] Worse still, the expansion of the state overtaxes the capabilities of members of parliament; their position and the importance of their work is thereby lowered in the eyes of the public. In the nature of things an elected member of parliament cannot cope with the multifarious and detailed tasks with which he is loaded by society and the bureaucracy. The fact that he is supposed to speak, to decide and to exercise control on all these matters as if he were an expert contributes to a lowering of parliament's prestige in the eyes of the public and makes the individual member vulnerable, unsure of himself or resigned when faced with the real or ostensible specialists both inside and outside the political machine. This is not calculated to make membership of parliament any more attractive to men really suited to the task. At the same time actual and political authority is concentrated in the hands of a minority in the parliamentary party; the member becomes dependent on a machine staffed by desk officers and experts; parliamentary debates turn into mock battles conducted for the record, while in the background faceless and almost uncontrollable machines are at work, to which in all practical matters the member of parliament is largely subordinate.

The result is that parliamentary debates become less acrimonious but at the same time they lose both substance and interest and this has become characteristic of much of parliamentary activity apart from a few fundamental debates; this applies particularly to parliament's primordial field – for example, budgetary policy, now so complex a subject. The number of members present in the House is often small; the parliamentary parties function as mere voting machines; to a critical public their activity seems to be an expensive luxury and a complication. Disparaging remarks about the activity of parliament, whether from the government and the bureaucracy or from the associations, gain a ready hearing; ultimately the institution itself is no longer taken seriously because either its strength is over-taxed or it is misled. Presented with tasks which it cannot master, parliament then confines itself to subjects which have some influence on elections and leaves the really important decisions to the bureaucracy which in practice becomes the planning and implementing authority. Parliament and the executive, therefore, in effect frequently exchange functions; legislation becomes the prerogative of the government machine and parliament loses authority to a semi-dictatorship by the executive. The parliamentary art consists of subjecting officialdom's decisions to political decision and control but ultimately the will of the experts triumphs – the decisions have been taken beforehand.

This problem has only become the more acute with the change in structure to that of the party state. Decisions are outlined beforehand by the party caucus; party members, whose existence is dependent upon party approval, are bound by them even when the party whip is not applied; a member's freedom of action in parliament is therefore severely limited. This is so, as the case of Britain shows, even under a two-party system with a majority franchise; since the time when parties replaced the squirearchy in parliamentary democracy, elections have no longer been centred on personalities. One has only to think of examples such as the defeat on two occasions in 1965 of the prominent Labour politician Patrick Gordon Walker; the deciding factor here was the party, not the man. Discussion, the basic component of democracy, no longer takes place mainly on the parliamentary level but in the pre-parliamentary, party political sphere and frequently without publicity. The decision of parliament has therefore been prejudged and becomes a mere matter of form since the votes can be counted beforehand; the minority, or alternatively the opposition, can do nothing but resign themselves – until the next election – or take refuge in futile rage which may eventually turn into enmity against the regime itself, into an anti-system or revolutionary attitude of mind.

Wolfgang Abendroth and Otto Kirchheimer[25] have drawn attention to a further consequence of all this – 'the withering away of democracy inside the parties'. In fact any democratic party must keep its eye and base its calculations on two points: the ultimate outcome of internal party discussion and alignment with the estimated desires of its electors. However great the degree of internal party democracy may be, it is unavoidable that distribution of functions within the parliamentary party be made with an eye to improvement of the party's prospects at the next election. This may 'ultimately result in party members becoming mere lay figures or appendages'. In Kirchheimer's words the party becomes no more than an 'organ for the legitimatization and co-ordination of interests'.

All attempts, both recently and in the past, to counter this development – by a ban on the 'imperative mandate', for instance – have been doomed to failure. Its repercussions can be reduced, however, by two things: first, the relaxation of party discipline resulting from decentralization and federalism; and second, greater elasticity on the part of the parties themselves. Parties may well become less strictly tied to certain definite classes of society and programmes; there is already a tendency towards greater flexibility and pragmatism and this has been characteristic of post-war development, particularly in Germany but during the last few years even in communist eastern Europe as well. Daniel Bell underlined this trend by calling his book, published in 1960, *The End of Ideology*.[26] Since then there has been a strong reaction from the 'New Left'. Behind this return to ideology lies the view that with the abandonment of ideology the old parties have lost much that was great and valuable, their creative, social and moral ethos in fact. After the disappearance of the representation party the integration party based on class or way of life (*Weltanschauung*) is now dissolving into the new type called by Otto Kirchheimer the 'all–things–to–all–men' party.[27] This is a development which could lead to the disappearance of opposition and there is considerable argument as to whether it should be welcomed or not – does not the abandonment of ideology and the 'popular party' imply the disappearance of politics? In this loss of substance by the parties lies a threat to the vitality of democracy itself. One of the main roles of political science in the future is to conduct a realistic investigation into political parties; if this is to be possible, however, research must deal, not merely with programmes, organization and elections but with the functional *and* social aspects of the parties based on their social history; then it will be possible to grasp their role in the changing political process.[28] One aspect of this investigation must be the study of opposition which has hitherto been neglected, particularly in Germany, and has become the 'cinderella' of research; on the other hand, during the 1960s research into opposition in Britain and America produced a flood of forward-looking contributions to research into political parties. Only in this way, not by superficial involvement in politics, can political science fulfil its true task which is to contribute to the promotion and consolidation of democracy. Political science can only exist and flourish under a democracy because democracy, which stands or falls by the right of opposition, is the only form of regime to permit and encourage free criticism of its own component elements.

13
Nationalism and Internationalism

I

Nationalism is tantamount to a political ideology which has been in continuous, though fluctuating, conflict with internationalism. In the old days the word 'nation' was taken to mean an ethnological group originating from the same area; more recently it has come to mean a people conscious of their political heritage, united by history, culture and common purpose. The basic idea of present-day nationalism is formation and perpetuation of a nation-state with an autonomous policy in face of the claims of other nation–states.

The above is no more than an initial definition. In fact the concept of nationalism ranges from mere self-assertion by a solid and generally accepted community to an aggressive ideology stemming from unsatisfied, irredentist expansionism, with demands expressed in absolute terms and seeking to impose them at the expense of opposing groups, supra-national values and the requirements of other states. Accordingly national consciousness, presented as something 'natural', has acquired an explosive force culminating in the totalitarian claims of 'integral nationalism'; from the outset this has exerted so powerful an influence upon the development of modern nationalism that, next to racism, it must be counted as one of the most dangerous disruptive forces threatening peaceful co-existence between the various nations and the formation of international organizational structures. In the light of historical experience this applies also to the renewed call to be heard in present-day Germany for a 'sound national consciousness', taking its cue from the resurgent nationalism of gaullist France and the new states.

In Britain and France the nation–state had become a reality as early as the sixteenth century; nationalism, on the other hand, was primarily a product of the socio-political emancipation movements which came to fruition in the nineteenth century. From this point national sentiment was acclaimed as the very foundation of the modern state, as something naturally inherent in the formation of any human community; it was regarded as the supreme virtue of any political entity. In Germany, Italy and eastern Europe all the more emphasis was placed on this idea in that the attempt to equate language, people and race with nation and state did not correspond to reality. German history in particular has been plagued and distorted by the exertions and perversions stemming from this frantic attempt to identify the state with the nation. The ultimate and logical consequence of artificial, supercharged nationalism was Hitler's mobilization of the entire people behind the 'Greater Germany' idea, making any supra-national relationships impossible and itself anything other than 'natural'.

One result of strategic theory and imperialist ideology was the insistence upon 'natural frontiers'; this was initially the mainspring of French nationalism and it led to the development of the plebiscite as an instrument and to domination imposed by collaboration. Claims were based on history and geo-politics; linguistic and racio-biological arguments were used to support them; all this culminated in the compulsory resettlements and mass deportations of the Second World War. In Sulzbach's words the process may be summarized as follows: 'The idea of national sovereignty first originated in the brains of a few men only. Then it gained support among the masses. Finally, by education and propaganda, it became a generally accepted notion . . . Nations were created.'

In some cases the growth of nationalism served to set the seal on a state already in existence (Britain or France, for instance); alternatively it was used to prise peoples loose from other states and to unite them. Naturally there are examples to prove the contrary – Switzerland contradicts the theory of the linguistic nation and Israel, that of the territorial. Only a small minority of the nation-states are co-terminous with the linguistic frontiers; equally politics can form linguistic entities if it is politically important to do so; in parts of Europe language and nation coincide but this can hardly be said to be the case either in Latin America, Africa or Asia. Fictions and ideologies, however, are the real stuff of which politics are made. This is shown by the continuing influence and relevance of the nationalist argument and also by its effects upon the formation and self-assurance of the new states of Africa and Asia. The feverish nationalism of the 'Third World' contributes to the creation and integration of states composed of highly divergent groups and tribes – in other words, the process of 'nation-building'. It seems to indicate an attempt to imitate and catch up with Europe; it is the main force for europeanization and modernization in the world. The transition from colonialism to 'national' independence, however, widens the field for international tensions; it turns the internal conflicts of the ex-empires into foreign policy conflicts, now pursued in the name of nationalism. At the same time these conflicts repercuss upon the old states; the trend towards supra-nationalism, which was beginning to gain ground even before Europe was exhausted by two world wars, is now countered by neo-nationalist tendencies.

On the other hand the revival of a sense of distinct nationhood is of growing importance in reducing the rigidity of the blocs and fronts which are tending to move away from a worldwide ideological polarization. The idea is gaining ground that East–West relationships might be normalized and 'polycentrism' replace the hegemony of the two super-powers; de Gaulle summarized the concept in his phrase 'European Europe' and the revival of claims to national sovereignty on the part of the smaller states has much to do with it. The limits set to this process are, of course, demonstrated by events within the eastern bloc; only Yugoslavia has managed to pursue a neutral, national-communist policy; similar attempts in Poland and Hungary (in 1956) and Czechoslovakia (in 1968) were failures; progress has been limited in Albania and Rumania and has only been possible at all because of the Soviet–Chinese schism.

In general the modern form of nationalism must be considered as ambivalent a development as gaullism which was only enabled to pursue its pronounced policy of national sovereignty thanks to the protection of NATO; after all, nationalism only won its victory against the universally established but particularist powers of the pre-industrial era a bare two centuries ago. The forms in which nationalism has manifested itself have been governed primarily by its relationship, still problematical, to the modern development of the state and of society; it has been the main agent in introducing all classes of a population to a sense of politics and instilling the idea of democratic self-determination both within and between states; it has also, however, served as an ideology to camouflage and gain popular support for authoritarian and imperialistic regimes. Nationalism's potential as an instrument either of modernization or reaction emerges with particular clarity in the overall nationalist movements which transcend national boundaries; slogans about 'Arab nationalism', for instance, are used to ensure the support of their masses by monarchical or national-socialist, single-party dictatorships which are in bitter competition with each other; they serve to divert attention from social and political problems to the battle against Israel.

The relationship between nationalism and the supra-national ideologies has also undergone manifold changes. Marx condemned nationalism as the bourgeoisie's instrument for disruption of the international solidarity of the proletariat; marxists such as Otto Bauer, on the other hand, and even more so Lenin, attempted to link it to the internationalist class-warfare theory. The dynamic force of nationalist movements in Europe (Austria, Hungary) and Asia (China) lent support to the communist theory of 'national wars of liberation', interpreted as the first stage in international revolution. Even the Soviet Union set itself up as a federation of nationalities and in its struggle against Hitler emphasized the patriotic angle; this proved to be of decisive significance for the nation-wide mobilization of the masses and partisans. The same was to be seen even more clearly in the role played by communists in the national European resistance movements in 1941-5 and then in the nationalistic guerrilla movements in Asia (Vietnam) and Latin America (Cuba).

On the other hand, to obtain some economic or strategic advantage in the struggle for spheres of influence, imperialist and capitalist forces have frequently sought to mobilize radical nationalism and even promote revolution (an example was that of the Arabs versus the Turkish Empire); in this they have disowned the theory of western liberal democracy and have been in apparent contradiction to their own supra-national aims. Instances such as the American support of communist Yugoslavia or Soviet support for Egypt (where the communists are an oppressed minority) demonstrate the part played by nationalism in the calculations of the Western Powers even when it cuts across the ideological fronts. In all these cases nationalism has been looked upon as being still *the* prime factor governing political emotions and the formation of political will both internally and externally. This is confirmed not only by the increase in the number of 'nations' and the worldwide expansion of the nation–state principle since 1918 and 1945; it is also to be seen in the transition from nineteenth-century nationalism which was primarily bourgeois and anti-socialist to nationalism as a mass movement presenting itself at the same time as state socialism.

Even UNO, despite all the insistence on its international character, is in fact organized on the basis of national sovereignty; irrespective of size every state claims equality of membership and voting rights, although it is true that the five permanent members of the Security Council have a certain special position. National inviolability heads the list in the scale of values and is defended with suspicion and sensitivity. Nevertheless the various forms of nationalism are now so extensive and variegated that the fundamental postulates upon which nationalism is founded have become obscured; today, for instance, in the case of many 'nations' neither language nor race, nor common culture are valid as criteria – which does little to prevent them providing explosive material for disputes. One has only to think of the linguistic quarrels in Belgium or India and the continuing minority conflicts in most other countries.

In present-day Europe emphasis is increasingly being laid once more on 'healthy nationalism' as both the basis and the expression of realistic policy based on national interest; the main arguments used in its favour are the setbacks in the efforts to achieve European or Atlantic unity, the Russian hegemony in eastern Europe and the ineffectiveness of UNO. Experience seems to confirm once more the old theory, always advanced by the national sceptics and opponents of international politics – that as a political entity only the nation is viable; for instance, they say, the new states which have grown up on the territories of the former colonial empires have all developed, apparently inevitably, as nation–states, some being actually formed as such. Naturally, as before, these new states have a constructive, almost indispensable, function as protagonists of the democratic idea of self-determination. Nevertheless, just as the projects and hopes of enlightenment embracing all mankind once gave way in face of radical nationalism, so now disillusionment with the failure or stagnation of supra-national institutions is leading to a nationalist pluralism, justified as *Realpolitik* but in the nationalistic chaos only too liable to offer a temptation to an imperialist policy of hegemony.

Military dictatorships and civil war situations in Africa, Asia and Latin America, racialism and the oppression of minorities are evidence of the undiminished strength of nationalism today, cutting straight through international 'systems' and ideologies. In divided Germany a resurgence of nationalism carries with it the special danger of a relapse into the pretensions and dreams of the German nation–state, never fully achieved and difficult to delimit territorially, This is true of the agitation of the neo-Nazi party, the NPD; it is also true, however, of speeches by luminaries of the democratic parties such as F. J. Strauss, bemoaning the disappearance of a national ideology, criticizing as a 'negative phase' the efforts to expunge by means of a supra-national solution the memory of National-socialism, that most terrible hypertrophy of racist nationalism, and calling for more national consciousness and greater pride in their own achievements from the Germans. Had not 1933 already provided fearful confirmation of the futility of such attempts to initiate a competition of ideas with intractable nationalists and to 'divert the nationalist flood into the pro-government channels of the parties which were so-called pillars of the state'? Understandably, the reward from the extremist right-wing newspapers (the NPD's paper *Deutsche Nachrichten* on 17 February 1967, for instance) was patronizing scorn.

The truth is that those who regard national entities as the only permanencies in history are (in R. Aron's words) 'setting the seal of perpetuity on the historical philosophy of the nineteenth century'. Nationalism which visualizes a free-for-all struggle but in fact has always found its limits in the power and expansionist policy of the great powers is the very antithesis of that in which the humanist and democratic pioneers of the idea of nationhood placed their hopes; it can provide no pattern for international coexistence and the peaceful solution of conflicts; it lays emphasis on the aspects which divide the nations and so, under modern conditions, when economic and technical development is leading to world wide interdependence even in the matter of social and political structures, it is highly anachronistic. Nationality is no innate, immutable characteristic; it is the result of processes of social education and adaptation; it has a function as a means of modernization but, compared to the worldwide process of intercommunication and democratization, its importance is now relative.

Nationalism, if it implies an exaggerated, supercharged loyalty to the detriment of all other loyalties, is no longer compatible with the plurality of political relationships and factors of interdependence; it is no longer compatible with the requirements of supra-national planning and control, upon which the co-existence and survival of the peoples depend. It has long since been proved scientifically that all the characteristics upon which the idea of the nation is based – language, geography, history, culture, race – are of limited validity only and have been generally unscrupulously manipulated; this fact should be made known and acted upon so that it may form a counterweight to the emotional potential of nationalism in international politics.

2

Ever since the nineteenth century external political relationships have been thought of primarily in terms of an order of nation–states and their power in relation to each other; at the same time, however, forces have been at work, the purposes and fields of activity of which have been supra-national. They have been generally referred to by the term internationalism but this should not blind us to the fact that these tendencies are of very varied origin, purpose and importance. On the one hand were the pre-national endeavours to reach inter-state agreement or reach a state of supra-national humanitarian universalism based on the law of nature, the christian faith or enlightened motives. On the other hand, dialectically opposed to the modernizing but also centrifugal tendencies of nationalism, there appeared political movements and ideologies laying claim to overall validity; their watchwords were economic liberalism, democratic pacificism and finally, socialist revolution, and with these they fought against the narrow limits imposed on social and political emancipation by the nation–state which was primarily bourgeois and conservative in character.

In this new form internationalism sought to adjust the cosmopolitan ideas and proposals of the age of enlightenment to the changed social and intellectual conditions and at the same time to find fresh solutions for the problem of inter-state relationships. It did not take as its guiding principle the ancient or medieval ideal of universal world monarchy but took as its pattern the democratic method of formation of public purpose and resolution of conflicts. Here was a good illustration of the close interconnection between internal and external politics; the internal political notions of freedom and good order carried over into external politics and so provided a method by which the effects of the principle of nation–state self-determination, internationally so problematical, could be overcome. Institutionally, however, development lagged far behind. The first efforts came from the socialis ts with the organization of the various 'socialist internationals' (from 1864); then came liberal–democrat attempts in the field of international law such as the Hague Peace Agreements of 1899 and 1907; finally the League of Nations was set up in 1920. The most universal organization, however, finally set up in the form of UNO in 1945, left the principle of nation–state sovereignty intact. It can do no more than exert an indirect moral and psychological influence; it serves to habituate people to permanent international contacts and discussions which may assist to promote the tendency towards internationalism but at the same time may have a disillusioning effect.

In very general terms there are three main fields of internationalism:

(i)   the old ideas of a universal order as advanced by the philosophers of the Stoa in the Hellenistic period, by ideologists of the Roman empire and under the concept of a christian empire; for almost two thousand years such ideas were regarded as representing the highest form of political organization and offering a guarantee of universal peace,

(ii)   the modern demand for supra-national means of co-operation and settlement of conflicts; this is visualized as something transcending the conventional system of treaties and alliances; international law having lost its force and supra-national states having disintegrated, this is seen as an increasingly urgent requirement in answer to the claim to absolute sovereignty by nation–states;

(iii)   ideologies born of the great revolutions and visualizing an international order, elimination of the sovereignty of individual states, abolition of the state in fact, and world revolution (marxism); socio-political aims are regarded as constituting a structural element in international relations binding people together horizontally and existing either alongside or above normal diplomatic relationships. For the present this has given rise to a modified form of internationalism within the power blocs controlled by the super-powers and expressed in 'communities' with limited economic or political aims (the EEC and COMECON); it acts as a stimulus to further efforts in Europe, Africa and Latin America.

No mention has been made of the broad field of strategic military collaboration. Since the end of the Second World War social and ideological differences have led to a bloc policy which in turn has led to the formation of military coalitions visualizing a higher degree of organization than the traditional military alliance and promoting or even necessitating supra-national institutions. Like the Warsaw Pact, however, the NATO organization (and even more so the regional *ad hoc* pacts in the Middle and Far East) is clearly governed by the attitude of the two super-powers with their nuclear supremacy; from the supra-national point of view, therefore, they are of little greater significance than the previous systems of single-state hegemony.

Any appreciation of modern internationalism depends mainly upon the question whether it is considered from the sociological and cultural or the political angle. Whatever the starting point taken, however, and whatever the conclusion reached, it will be agreed that it is the vast and continuous progress in methods and efficiency of international communications which has both initiated and determined the scope of twentieth-century supra-national trends. Sociologically the result has been assimilation between the forms and values of differing civilizations whether the process is labelled europeanization, americanization or simply modernization. In political terms the process is expressed in the growing interdependence between states and the reduction in importance of purely national relationships in favour of overriding interests and ideologies. Admittedly the political process is lagging considerably behind the sociological. In contrast to the internationalist dreams of the Second World War the theory of 'national interest' has survived or even been revived – by the 'realists' led by Hans Morgenthau, for instance. Even in this case, however, the concept is rather one of pluralist interest implying the possibility of international compromise on the lines of democratic internal politics.

In fact, of course, antagonisms still exist between different states and different power-policy or ideological systems. This does not belie the fact, however, that increasing communication on social, economic and political matters is having its effect upon the various power structures, highly different though their institutions may be; they are being downgraded or reduced to the status of sub-systems. There is increasing 'convergence' between the systems reducing the antagonism between the super-powers, as was shown by the admitted or tacit understanding between Washington and Moscow to maintain the international *status quo* in crises such as those of Suez, Hungary, Cuba, Berlin, Vietnam and Czechoslovakia. One of the aspects of the apparently irresistible expansion and globalization of the nation–state principle is that increased communication, which once enabled a people to be integrated into a nation–state, now applies to political society; the result is 'political socialization' (G. Almond's phrase) followed by 'political nationalization' (K. Deutsch's phrase), opening the door to larger-size communities organized in regional systems.

This does not mean, of course, that all the old dangers inherent in large-scale supra-national organization, the counter to which was the nation–state principle, have vanished. International communications have not done away with dependencies or oppression by imperialist hegemonies; abuse and manipulation show that international communication is not synonymous with political internationalism. But the road can now be seen which leads from external politics based on states and systems to internal politics on a worldwide scale; as technical development proceeds the sociological conditions pointing in this direction become increasingly prevalent. Though East and West are still in opposition, it is possible that, with an overriding consensus in favour of peaceful competition, a process of economic and socio-political *rapprochement* will slowly be initiated.

There are two major problems: on the one hand, the strategic confrontation between the super-powers with their material and demographic preponderance; on the other, the threat of an increasing cleavage between the industrial and the underdeveloped countries. There is an increasing discrepancy between the development of social intercommunication (with the resulting raised hopes) and economic development together with distribution of economic benefits; in the field of international politics this manifests itself in the contrast between rich and poor nations and this threatens to reproduce the conflict situation resulting from poverty and class-warfare which had so explosive an effect upon internal politics in the early days of capitalism. Even at that time the incompatibility between the idea of egalitarian emancipation and the growing economic and social inequalities led to an intensification both of nationalism and imperialism, bogeys though both had become. Reversion to such a situation on the international level would be tantamount to a revolution of rising expectations; it shows, nevertheless, the extent to which politics based on national interest have progressed towards a form of world internal politics; national conflicts are becoming social conflicts; external political struggles are turning into world civil wars; economic aid is becoming one of the most important weapons of international politics in the settlement of disputes; international politics are being thought of as social politics on an international scale.

These are admittedly prospects for the future; they contrast with the actual present-day power position, the bipolar divide in internationalism, the undiminished validity of the nation–state principle and the hypertrophy of dramatized nineteenth-century ideologies. The chain reaction of the student revolts, which showed such an astonishing similarity despite all the differing social and political factors, was a reflection of the length to which the intercommunication process had progressed; its continuance is due to realization of the inconsistencies in both national and international politics. This 'movement' was a vigorous sign of the existence of internationalism, of the realization of social and political interdependence; at the same time, however, it was handicapped by remnants of outdated ideologies whose internationalist content had largely been absorbed by imperialist or nationalistic power policy. This students' international, therefore, barely amounted to more than battle-cries condemning parliamentary democracy, capitalism and political domination or acclaiming an obsolete soviet system and a utopian system of direct democracy.

To summarize, it cannot be denied that the development of institutions and ideas has not kept pace with the true impetus and potential of internationalism resulting from the continuous growth of worldwide means of political communication and of interdependence. There is a wide divergence between the economic and technical tendencies towards a world society and the persistence with which people cling to political and ideological practices, the end result of which is the nationalist state based on power or alternatively ideological imperialism. Here lies the central problem for present and future international politics; it must be prepared for a large-scale infusion of internationalism but so far only possesses inadequate structures to give political reality to such tendencies. So long as the first beginnings and the opportunities of supra-national development and international integration are not balanced by corresponding progress in the fields of international law, international legislation, organization and methods of resolving conflicts, this rudimentary and all too easily discredited internationalism is in permanent danger of being met by disillusioned resignation or cynical reaction. The consequences of reversion to anti-internationalist sentiment and practice could only benefit the imperialistic and nationalistic ideologies.

Between the two extremes of world revolution and nationalist policy a modified form of internationalism seems to be practicable even under present-day conditions; it would be based on supra-national forces now actually in existence such as the workers' movement, economic interests, humanitarian or ecclesiastical or religious organizations (the ecumenical movement). Its starting point would be that nation–states exist; as pre-requisites for further development of a world system of peaceful co-opera-tion and resolution of conflicts, however, democratization and internal self-determination are essential. Vital stages in the process would be the formation of regional federations together with attempts to 'integrate' the smaller countries on a basis of equality into viable entities for purposes of economic or external relations. The ultimate aim should still be the for-mation of a world government under an internationally binding 'world rule of law'. All this seems a long way from realization; if, however, these ideas are regarded as a practicable utopia, as Ernst Bloch has put it, they may help to remove the ideological element from political differences and lead to a more profound understanding of the problems of international politics and their possible solution.

14
Racialism and Politics

I

Since the mid-nineteenth century, when nationalism and naturalism increasingly took over from the enlightened humanist theories, the concept of race has played both a significant and a questionable role in international politics. Taking as its starting point the fact that differences exist in the appearance and behaviour of human groupings, racial theory deduced from the doctrine of heredity that inherited qualities and physical conformation were immutable and decisive factors in determining the intellectual, spiritual and social capabilities of the various peoples. In the eighteenth century the liberal humanitarian theory of environment had seen as its aim the improvement of the human race as a whole and it had considered external influences to be primarily responsible for individual and social development. This was now largely replaced by the notion of race.

Throughout history, of course, ethnical and national differences between politico-social groupings have played a considerable role as the reason or pretext for conflict. Only since the rise of modern nationalism and the natural sciences, however, has racial theory laid claim to define human 'races' in systematic scientific terms and so provide an overriding criterion by which to explain politico-social developments. This idea was turned into a political ideology in the form of racialism; in contrast to the optimistically inclined liberal and democratic movements with their internationalist and egalitarian trends it laid stress on the pessimist, nationalist and chauvinistic theory of human disparity, presenting it as an established, unalterable and fundamental fact.

The pioneering works were those of Count Gobineau (1853–55) and Houston Stewart Chamberlain which evoked a considerable response, particularly in Germany; finally the pattern was completed by Alfred Rosenberg, the Nazi ideologist. Two things were specially characteristic of the widespread and rapidly increasing flood of racialist literature: first, its affinity with conservative and reactionary ideologies and second, its pseudo-scientific amalgam of subjective impressions and prejudices with allegedly generally accepted biological laws and data. As part of this process the darwinist interpretation of nature was applied to the sociological field; 'social darwinism' gave rise to the catchwords about the right of the strong, superior and inferior races, breeding and extermination, giving them a pseudo-scientific validity. The 'struggle for existence' became a 'racial struggle' (L. Gumplowitz, 1883) and was turned into a fundamental principle of public and social life. It meant nothing less than this: as in nature's battle of selectivity, between the various peoples the questions of survival and victory would be decided by racial quality and 'racial hygiene'.

Domestically racialism became an instrument for the oppression of minorities; it also served to divert political and socio-economic discontents on to an enemy pictured as absolute. In foreign policy it served to mobilize the dynamic of racial nationalism; at the same time it was used to justify and reconcile with christian principles the process of capitalistic, colonial and imperialistic expansion, postulating a natural, God-given mission for the 'superior' races; examples of the resulting conflicts were those of white versus black, 'Aryan' versus semite and Teuton versus Slav. This process of blend and fusion between socio-political and biological arguments (the so-called 'social-to-biological feedback') has not prevented the idea of race remaining an extremely hazy one, but this has in fact contributed to its popularity – all the multifarious and perplexing conditions governing socio-cultural development could be reduced to a simple formula, the superior worth (as a race) of one's own people.

Two facets of the Nazi ideology of domination were anti-semitism and the cult of the nordic, germanic, Aryan 'race'; both in domestic and foreign politics these notions were carried to their most extreme conclusion and theory was turned into most definite practice. Racialism combined with the theory of *lebensraum* formed the basis of Hitler's expansionist policy; at the same time this provided a semi-rational foundation for German imperialism which, up to the First World War, had relied mainly on the traditional national, cultural, economic and politico-military arguments. The racial argument, moreover, in addition to its domestic function as an instrument of oppression and mobilization of the people in the name of a cause represented the most extreme and highly coloured version of those ideologies, used as justification for an aggressive, nationalist and imperialist policy.

2

Even after the end of colonial rule and the Nazi plans for world domination, racialism and the notion of racial struggle have continued to exert their effect as a motivating force and structural principle in the political relationships between governments all over the world. Admittedly the background now is social and cultural rather than biological, but nevertheless, with the emancipation of the 'coloured' world, conflicts within heterogeneous populations (the USA, South Africa, Rhodesia) and between old and new states have intensified. These conflicts are either openly or potentially coloured by racialism; sometimes they have taken the form of counter-racialism on the part of groups or peoples hitherto subject to discrimination (the 'Black Power' movement in the USA, for instance); they cut across the ideological fronts formed by the capitalist and communist systems. They constitute a major factor in the international political power game; its effect is to be seen in the efforts to organize a 'third force' in face of the bloc policy of the great powers and its attempts to obtain a majority in UNO.

Even in the new countries, however, problems of racialism persist. After the disappearance of 'white' colonialism a considerable role is still played by the animosities between Arab and negroid peoples (in the Sudan) or between various developed African tribes (in the Congo and Nigeria) together with anti-Japanese, anti-Chinese or anti-Indian phobia in Africa and Asia. Although the background to these seems to be primarily socio-economic or cultural and religious, the irrational forces aroused by racial convictions and prejudices act as an emotional spur in mobilizing hatred of the foreigner, intolerance and ultra-nationalism.

On the other hand it must be admitted that, even today, there is no scientifically adequate concept of race, just as there is no rational basis for racial policy. It is rooted in the emotional sphere of prejudice, fear psychosis and aggressive instinct. A biological explanation of actual differences between human groupings cannot do justice to the manifold factors in socio-cultural development. Outstanding specialists such as Franz Boas have long since disproved the theory that there is a causal connection between race, language and culture; he has also drawn attention to the great differences in forms of culture within certain racial groupings. As a criterion for the formation of political communities, therefore, the racial theory fails, since the applicability of the term 'race' to nation or tribe, linguistic family or skin colouration is extremely varied.

Any attempt to draw distinctions between physiological types is invariably confronted by the fact that throughout history peoples and states have generally been built on half-breeds and cross-breeds, not on 'pure' races. Whatever the value placed on attempts to differentiate in terms of natural science, application of this method to the political sphere tends to result in its abuse as an ideological means of inflaming social conflicts and as evidence that 'natural' differences exist between slave races and master races. In South Africa and to some extent in the USA the principle of segregation has been followed but its results have been political domination and discrimination; it is no solution of the problem; it merely institutionalizes racialism.

It is right to emphasize the fundamental difference between the biological and social concepts of race and draw attention to the subjective significance of racialism in the attitude of peoples and states. The fact remains, however, that 'biologically' similar groups of people such as negroes may remain 'racially' distinct in one case (the USA) and apparently be integrated in others (Brazil for instance); this shows that in the political and social field categorization by race is of relative and questionable value only. This aspect of the matter is put very clearly in the UNESCO declaration of 1951, in which well-known scientists were involved:

'National, religious, geographical, linguistic and cultural groups do not necessarily coincide with racial groups and the cultural characteristics of such groups have no circumstantial connection with their racial characteristics. The Americans are not a race any more than are the French or the Germans or any other national group. Mohammedans and Jews are no more races than Roman Catholics and Protestants; people who live in Iceland, Great Britain or India or who speak English or some other language or who are culturally Turkish, Chinese or some such cannot for this reason be described as races. It is a great mistake to use the term "race" when such groups are meant, a mistake often made out of habit.'

It is an even greater mistake to refer to 'social' instead of biological 'races'; in each case physical characteristics can only be regarded as subjective supporting factors, not as determinants.

This applies particularly to the situation and the fate of the Jews after their expulsion from Palestine in the first century AD. Their long, sorry history is characterized by adherence to a special religious tradition, persecution, confinement to ghettos and compulsory restriction to specific callings and functions; these were the conditions under which the 'special role' of the

Jews was transposed from the religious and social to the biological level and connection with race disputed. From this transposition the extreme conclusion was drawn based on a spurious natural science: whenever this foreign race attempted to assert, whether domestically or on a world wide scale, a claim to dominate other 'races' and nations, it was labelled a 'subversive' element to be removed from the body politic like weeds or vermin and ultimately to be destroyed altogether. In fact the Jews were a minority subject to discrimination and persecution but National-socialism invented the theory of an international conspiracy and turned this into the basis for its policy of tyranny and annihilation. So it provided a particular illustration of the way in which racialism, socio-psychologically motivated but biologically based, can be manipulated and assume the character of a mania. According to this theory membership of a race, unlike all other labels applied to a group (nation, people, stratum, class) is declared to be unalterably fixed by birth and physical characteristics; disregarding all individual or social differences, the Jew, the negro and so forth become stereotyped figures. This form of racialism regards a certain social or political attitude as the inevitable attribute of a certain race and, if the 'racially determined' barriers are not respected, this is regarded as infringement of the social and official rules of the community (the Nuremberg Laws of 1935, apartheid from 1948 onwards). This type of racialism declares that the natural community is that based on a common bloodstock; it disowns and opposes the democratic concept of man's freedom of decision and his ability to discard natural and social ties and so arrive at self-determination. In its fixation on 'blood' and lineal descent it stands in complete contrast to the modern concept of the open society and pluralist democracy which is based on free consent and the right to differ.

On this point two ideologies, very different both in origin and purpose come together – biological and socio-economic determinism; for them world history and world politics are governed either by the 'racial struggle' or by 'class-warfare'; both demand unconditional commitment from their followers; both aim to expel, remove or destroy those who differ from them. Naturalism and economic theory therefore appear as the two major factors standing in the way of assured peaceful co-existence and international politics geared and pledged to compromise and co-operation. Both in the internal and social political field, therefore, and in inter-state relationships racialism destroys the very foundations of political culture in that it gives rise to irrational and emotional group fanaticisms. Ultimately, therefore, it must be to the detriment of all groups, peoples or states whose existence depends upon rational, calculable settlement of their mutual relationships.

Racialism, therefore, proves to be no more than a political fabrication but it is pregnant with consequences. Its pseudo-scientific pretensions are based on an arbitrary synthesis of heterogeneous components from which is deduced a mono-causal, structural principle. As always and despite all its frightful manifestations, the notion of race serves to arouse those reactionary, archaic, mouldering emotions which lie at the root of anti-modernism, which under a cloak of science oppose the liberal and humanist concept of mankind, which glorify war and the right of the strong as *Realpolitik*, which regard international relations aiming at the peaceful solution of conflicts as illusory or even unnatural. Whatever the biological, anthropological or socio-cultural facts which may be unearthed in support of the racial theory by research into the limited fields of race and culture, when presented in the form of an all-embracing ideology racialism has shown itself to be an atavistic force, a reversion to barbarism. Its doctrines suffice neither to explain historical developments nor to organize social and inter-state relationships. Both on the national and the international levels it must be counted as one of the most dangerous forces standing in the way of rational politics.

15

On Imperialism

I

The term 'imperialism' was first used early in the nineteenth century by French and British critics of Napoleon's tyrannical policy. Subsequently journalists and politicians and then, even more frequently, historians and social scientists have applied it broadly to all states or movements bent on an expansion designed to extend the area which they controlled politically and/or economically. In this sense, first the Roman empire and other great empires of antiquity, then the medieval and more recent power structures have been described as imperialist if their purpose was to add to their original territory dependencies acquired by conquest, colonization, marriage policy or influence. From the outset, therefore, the word 'imperialism' carried a primarily critical, polemical connotation. This was disputed by the defenders of imperial policy, primarily those in Britain at the turn of the century (Seeley, Kipling), but also in the German Reich of 1871; like the ideologists of the *Imperium Romanum*, they stressed the positive functions of a great empire, the assurance of law and order, civilization and technical progress; imperialism was raised to the status of an ideology. As in Rome the idea of federation played some part in all this, though it was, of course, visualized as being under the domination of the mother country.

The very broad and usually polemical sense in which the word 'imperialism' was used until it became a catchword, naturally reduces its usefulness for any scientific analysis in the field of international relations. In general, however, the term 'imperialism' has been employed to cover three major differing sets of political and ideological circumstances:

(i)   from the point of view of the nation–state system and the liberal democratic movement imperialism violated the fundamental principle of the formation of autonomous states based on self-determination;

(ii)   for marxism, particularly that of the later Leninist school, imperialism was regarded as the final stage and ultimate result of capitalism;

270

(iii)   the anti-colonial movement in the new states regards imperialism in an even more general sense as the cause of all oppression, subordination and underdevelopment suffered by non-European peoples.

All these three meanings and uses of the word 'imperialism' (in the critical sense) can be explained, though admittedly in very differing degrees, in terms of politics, economics and ideology. It is significant that they made their appearance only after the acceleration in the process of expansion and modernization brought about by European colonial policy, industrialization and socio-political emancipation. In contrast to the historic process of subjugation by war followed by the formation of political empire, the variegated forms in which modern imperialism appears stem from the novel conditions of the nineteenth and twentieth centuries when politics aimed at spheres of influence and domination. This produced an irreconcilable antithesis between the idea of universal empire on the pattern of Rome and that of the colonial empires which were necessarily restricted in area and in violent competition with each other.

An important stage was the Napoleonic policy of hegemony which exploited the ideological and modernizing potential of the French Revolution in order to subject other European states. Napoleon created an 'empire' in the space of a few years using modern methods of warlike and administrative techniques; by means of repeated annexations, dictated alliances, protectorates and military regimes it was extended over an area far wider than that associated with a normal expansionist policy; at the same time it imposed upon its subject peoples its concept of its supra-national mission. The second major attempt at imperialist expansion was to be seen in Hitler's expansionist policy based upon the power of a single nation–state; this also laid claim to autarchy within an enclosed political and economic system. In this case, however, a far larger part was played by ideological dogma; the Nazi claim to racial domination turned imperialism into an ideology, the ultimate consequences of which were conquest, subjection and annihilation. Russian imperialism too, however, has sought to raise to the status of an ideology its impelling desire for expansion and protection of its spheres of influence; Moscow has presented itself in turn as the 'Third Rome', the champion of pan-slavism and the leader of communist world revolution.

Colonialism, which was an imperialist struggle for overseas territories conducted on a worldwide scale, must be distinguished from the continental imperialism of France, Germany and Russia. After the demise of the old colonial empires of the sixteenth to eithteenth centuries, completed with the liberation of North and South America, European colonial imperialism reached its height with the partition of Africa and East Asia around 1900. Germany and Italy arrived late in the day and attempted to play their part alongside Britain and France; the proclamation of the fascist 'Impero' in 1936 and the vast German colonial plans of the First and Second World Wars must be seen in this context. A considerable part was played in this by the conviction that, as great or world powers, the European countries must control wider areas providing raw materials, labour and markets if they were to maintain themselves. The concept of the British Empire was characteristic of this universal urge for expansion to which even the USA, anti-colonial though it originally was, could not remain immune. Brutal insistence on economic interests but also an irrational thirst for power played their part in this; in many cases advantages achieved by no means justified the effort involved, as was to be seen in the cases of Germany and Italy in particular. No single reason can be given as explanation of this process. Economic, racial and pseudo-religious motives all played their part, as did internal political and strategic considerations.

Like the old colonialism, more recent European imperialism has foundered owing to its own internal conflicts; internal European rivalries, culminating in two 'world wars', have destroyed the very foundation of European hegemony outside Europe; political emancipation, following in the wake of the europeanization and nationalization of the world, has been instrumental in bringing to the fore the ideas of democracy and socialism. Of course the dissolution of the colonial empires has not put an end to imperialism. It persists in the conflict between the bi-polar and nation–state structures, in the confrontation between East and West, in the strategic interests, inherent in great power politics, of the Soviet Union and the USA and finally in the polarization of the world on social and ideological lines. Moreover the rise of the 'Third World' of new states and polycentric tendencies both in East and West (China, Yugoslavia, Rumania, France) are still largely influenced by considerations of imperialist power-policy and spheres of influence, as is shown by the Soviet occupation of Czechoslovakia, the American war in Vietnam and the Middle East conflict. Attempts have been made to substitute a development policy for that of colonial imperialism and to divorce its economic and civilizing functions from the externals of government; the accent is therefore now more on the economic and technological aspects than on the political. This has, however, by no means eliminated the problem of imperialism.

2

Broad-based, scientific discussion began with the work by John A. Hobson published in 1902; this was written from the liberal–radical standpoint that imperialism stemmed from the problems and corruptions of European capitalism. Based on this idea, marxist authors such as Otto Bauer, Rosa Luxemburg, Rudolf Hilferding and finally, of course, Lenin attempted to construct a systematic theory of imperialism; left-wing liberal economists and historians in Britain and America were also considerably influenced. Lenin's essay on 'Imperialism as the ultimate stage of capitalism', published in 1917, also exerted a direct effect on political thinking. In Soviet ideology as interpreted by Stalin, Lenin's theory was used to justify the expectation (contrary to the teaching of Marx) that the proletarian revolution could succeed in a backward, semi-colonial, agrarian country like Czarist Russia. Primarily, however, it provided anti-capitalist and anti-colonialist propaganda with a platform from which more precise and more severe criticism of imperialist policy could be made than was possible on humanitarian or liberal–democratic grounds.

Like all mono-causal explanations marxist–leninist theory is misleading in that it attributes everything that happens in the world, and particularly imperialism, to some form of conspiracy. It therefore provided fascists and National-Socialists, who were critical of capitalism and opposed to communism, with good arguments against the 'Jew-ridden plutocracies'; for a time (1939–41) a pact was even concluded on this basis with fascist neo-imperialism. Here was proof already that the term 'imperialism' could not be applied solely to the capitalist Western Powers; this became even clearer with the expansion and stabilization of the Soviet Union after 1945, with the Russo–Chinese conflict over leadership of the communist world and with the suppression of national–communist tendencies in Eastern Europe by military force and economic pressure. So imperialism became a catchword in the worldwide propaganda war; it is used against any tendency to dominate or expand on the part of state monopolies as well as private capital, against both the 'new' and old forms of imperialism, against neo-colonialism as well as the classical form of colonalism.

The resulting disillusionment, however, does not imply that critical scientific analysis of imperialism has become useless; such analysis has been made by democratic and socialist theorists with the object of de-mystifying and moderating the power-policy aspect of external politics. Imperialism as one of the mainsprings of great power policy has remained a phenomenon of international politics, even though its external manifestations and ideological trappings may have changed; nevertheless the attempt to provide a theoretical systematic interpretation of its historical, political and economic components remains of undiminished importance. The data to be mastered, however, have become far more complex, the problems of producing a viable theory far more delicate than in the age of rapid colonial expansion by the capitalist powers.

Efforts have been made to adapt the theory of imperialism to the changed world situation; instead of the old confrontation between capitalism and socialism people referred to the clash between modern industrial countries and developing countries, between white and coloured peoples, between old and new states. Obviously, in view of the loose way in which the term is used and misused, it would be easier if the word applied only to the limited period of European expansion between 1870 and 1940. Apart from the fact, however, that this would lead to misappreciation of subsequent historical repercussions, the continuance of the process into the post-colonial period, together with the increased use and general validity of the term, do not allow the issue to be evaded in this way.

To this day the marxist theory of imperialism has remained the clearest and most influential. Even here, however, the basic premiss of the close connection between capitalism and imperialism has been presented in very different lights. In some cases it was given a determinist basis, economics being said to produce a cause–and–effect relationship; in other cases deliberate action on the part of powerful capitalist groups was held to be responsible; imperialism has also been considered to be a deliberately manipulated method used by the ruling class to divert the internal dynamic to external affairs, social imperialism in other words; this was especially characteristic of German development both before and after 1914 when external expansion became a substitute for internal reform. In the eyes of Rosa Luxemburg and Lenin wars were the inevitable result in a capitalist world.

The realization that there existed economic and internal political reasons for external expansion contributed greatly to scientific analysis of international politics deeper than that provided by the traditional history of diplomatic relations. The multiplicity of factors emerges. The war situation of 1914 cannot be ascribed solely to the failure of international socialism with words of abuse for the social-democrats as 'lackeys of imperialism'. In addition to the influence of social imperialism, nationalism and (in the German case) anti-Czarism played a considerable part, acclaimed even by

Marx. Even today one of the attractions, but equally limitations, of the marxist theory of imperialism is its claim to provide a single definite criterion for all forms of imperialism, as also for the distinction between 'just' and 'unjust' wars. This is to be seen with particular clarity in the profound conflict between the Chinese theory of the inevitability of a final war with capitalist imperialism and the Soviet theory of the possibility of co-existence in an age when the nuclear weapon is capable of destroying everything.

3

Any interpretation of imperialism as dependent solely on economic factors is disproved by the Soviet Union's policy of hegemony and intervention; it is equally disproved by the long history of pre-capitalist imperialism but also by the ambivalent effects of imperialism which, as a force, may promote liberalism and democracy. Many economic historians today doubt whether it was really useful. Non-imperialist countries with a capitalist economy (Scandinavia and Switzerland for instance) have achieved a higher standard of living than imperialist countries with an underdeveloped infrastructure (Russia or Italy). In 1919 Joseph Schumpeter emphasized that expansion generally in no way advantaged the population of the imperialist country; in his view any advantages were reaped by an upper class such as the aristocracy of the senate in Rome which contrived to keep the people under the dominance of a certain class and mobilize them for their own purposes – social imperialism in other words. This, however, is a socio-psychological state of affairs, not confined to specific social or economic structures. In place of the 'capitalists' a military caste may be 'professionally' interested in expansion and may justify imperialism on the grounds of strategic security; an example of this was the debate on German war aims in the First World War. Further incentives to political expansion may be a hypertrophy of the concept of government and state in the political tradition of a country whose structure is absolutist and patriarchal (such as Russia or Germany), national imperialism based on history (the claim of the Italian fascists to revive the Roman empire surrounding a *mare nostro*) or finally the deification of some tyrant ruler.

At this point irrational, almost incalculable, motives for and manifestations of imperialist activity come into play. Recognition that such reactions are possible does not imply that imperialism must be consigned to the realm of the devilish or the atavistic as Gerhard Ritter, for instance, does in his efforts to expunge Hitler and Nazism from German history. Gugliemo

Ferrero, for instance, produced a psychological interpretation of imperialism, believing that Napoleon's main motive was fear. Such theories, however, must invariably go hand in hand with critical socio-economic, political and ideological analysis. Only in this way can justice be done to the very varied starting points, forms and manifestations of imperialism. Imperialism as a basic historical phenomenon is not to be overcome by the polemics of marxism which prescribe only one remedy (the elimination of capitalism) nor by over-emphasizing the psychological angle and so underestimating the concrete material causes. Arnold Toynbee, the historian-philosopher, visualized the establishment of a universal world state to put an end to imperialist rivalries but this ultimately leads to a pessimist outlook and in any case provides no answer to the problems of a bi-polar, and in future probably multi-polar, structure of international politics.

The theory of monolithic capitalism may be a biased one but the instrumental role played by captains of industry, either in combination or in the service of imperialist aims, should not be minimized. In this connection much light has been shed on Nazi imperialism by the analyses of socialist theorists such as Franz L. Neumann (in his book *Behemoth* published in 1944), where imperialism is not attributed simply to 'totalitarian monopoly capitalism'. An anti-marxist apologia is all too apt to disregard the role played by industry in the consolidation, mobilization and exploitation of the Nazi expansionist dictatorship. It is true, however, that Hitler was far more than a mere tool of the capitalists as the Left believed or postulated in 1933, thereby showing a disastrous misappreciation of the motives and power relationships governing Nazi Germany.

More recent research tends to attach greater weight to the political and strategic factors in imperialism; moreover it emphasizes the considerable differences existing in the motivations leading to different forms of imperialism. This is so particularly if neither the use of the term nor the analysis are restricted to the comparatively short period of European colonial imperialism between 1870 and about 1940. In addition to conflict between rival powers the development of imperialist policy today is governed by ideological groupings and fronts. The number of individual factors, each varying in importance, is as great as in the field of domestic politics; they include thirst for power, diplomatic tactics, military and geo-political calculations, sense of cultural or other mission, national and racial ideologies, social, economic and technological considerations; all these come together in a barely definable mixture. In differing degrees the following may also exert an influence: purpose and chance, planning and improvisation, finally the role of certain individuals or social groups (dictators, dynasties, castes, parties and 'movements').

Finally the vast growth of means of international communication has enormously increased the dimensions of potential imperialist rule and at the same time has given fresh impetus to the idea of a world state. So long as there appears to be no possibility of regulating international politics on the lines of 'world domestic politics' and establishing rules and habits of behaviour associated with a society based on the peaceful democratic solution of conflicts, imperialist tendencies will persist as an offshoot of international power relationships and foreign policy conducted by sovereign states. As the experience of recent decades has shown, neither a balance-of-power system nor the apparently stable *status quo* produced by a bi-polar great power structure is enough to neutralize such tendencies. If the term imperialism is to have any scientifically useful meaning, is to be more than a vague catchword, its definition and its use will depend entirely upon the concept of power and of government which the ruling theory of international politics may evolve to clarify and solve the problem of inter-state conflicts.

16

Democracy and Emergency Legislation

I

In May 1968, after prolonged debate, the Great Coalition decided on far-reaching changes in the Basic Law to cater for a so-called state of emergency; the action was severely criticized and largely contributed to the embitterment of the political atmosphere in the Federal Republic. This was the most profound constitutional change since the defence legislation of 1954; it was justified primarily by the statement that no sovereign state could afford to be without regulations 'for emergency' (the previous term, both more honest and more apt, had been 'for an exceptional situation'). What view should be taken of this idea as a whole in the light of political theory and historical experience?

The general background is the widespread view that crisis situations necessitate suspension of the constitutional and democratic principle of limitation and separation of powers and its replacement by a concentration of power in the hands of the executive or even of the military. In fact hardly any other aspect of political theory and constitutional practice is as hotly debated today as the question of establishment and extension, interpretation and political justification of an emergency regime, and its relationship to democracy and the constitution. It is mere dissimulation if the impression is given that emergency arrangements and emergency legislation are natural and generally accepted components and postulates of any democracy. There are many examples in history to show that any emergency legislation carries with it, and is in fact likely to induce, the concrete danger of intensifying, if not actually provoking, the very crisis which it is designed to prevent. If applied too soon it constitutes an obstacle to further efforts to overcome problems by normal parliamentary means. If kept in force for a prolonged period, emergency regulations can all too easily turn into an instrument for a pseudo-legal *coup d'état* and dictatorial rule.

For this reason the problem of the state of emergency has always played an important part, even in ancient times. The classical historical example is that of the emergency provisions of the Roman Republic prescribing instalment of a temporary dictator; this was the much revered 'constitutional dictatorship' in contrast to tyranny which was unconstitutional and uncontrolled. Even in this case, however, the potential danger of extension, of transformation into permanent dictatorship was present; the generals of the revolutionary period in the first century AD exploited the state of emergency to overthrow the Roman Republic. The more modern history of constitutional states starting from the French Revolution and Napoleon reveals an equally equivocal state of affairs. Particularly during the inter-war period most of the new democracies fell victim to the dangerous, almost irresistible, tendency to produce emergency regulations and then exploit them to set up pseudo-legal dictatorial regimes. Crisis situations of an economic or internal political nature led in many cases, and frequently on the pretext of safeguarding democracy and the constitution, to the establishment of 'protective dictatorships', as they were euphemistically called; they did much to pave the way for Hitler's career of destruction. Examples were to be seen in Italy and Poland, in the Balkans, in Spain and Portugal, in Germany and also in Austria under Dollfuss and Schuschnigg, to say nothing of those outside Europe, particularly in Latin America.

Of this process Germany offers the most striking example. Hitler's seizure of power was made possible primarily by the use and abuse of emergency powers under Article 48 of the Weimar constitution. These gave the president the right, in the interests of 'public security and good order', to substitute emergency decrees for parliamentary legislation, to intervene in the *Länder*, 'if necessary with armed force', and also 'temporarily' to abrogate the basic rights. Quite clearly these powers were a continuation of the Prussian and imperial tradition of legislation for a state of siege or war emergency. Perpetuation of monarchical and patriarchal elements even through the period of democratic revolution, however, was characteristic of the Weimar structure as a whole; its attempt to synthesize the old and the new was not always a happy one. The position of the president was coloured primarily by his function as 'substitute Kaiser' in a society flabbergasted by the fall of the monarchy. The only restriction upon him lay in the Reichstag's right to demand, by simple majority, the cancellation of 'measures' taken under Article 48. This presupposed, however, that parliament was still capable of functioning without let or hindrance. Since, however, in addition to his wide emergency powers, the president had an unrestricted right repeatedly to dissolve the Reichstag provided that he merely had a chancellor willing to countersign and since he also had a free hand in the appointment of the chancellor, he could in practice govern by emergency decree without parliamentary control; he could thwart any reaction from the *Länder* by a threat to use the Reich's executive powers. In fact he could annul the parliamentary and federalist structure of the republic and the principle of the separation of powers.

In origin the Weimar emergency provisions were dictated by the situation; their purpose, however, was democratic, as shown by the fact that they were tailored entirely to suit the role played by Friedrich Ebert. Even in the stormy year of 1923 they seemed to function. To avert internal political crises and attempted *putschs* the first President of the Reich had recourse to his dictatorial powers on numerous occasions; he did so, however, entirely in accordance with the idea of 'constitutional dictatorship'; measures decreed had a time limit; guarantees that the rule of law would be maintained were preserved; the whole procedure was aimed at the protection and re-establishment of democracy. When, however, power was placed in the hands of a man like Hindenburg and his non-democratic or anti-democratic entourage, the questionable aspects of such a concentration of authority were to be seen; without a decision of parliament, even by qualified majority, he could in practice eliminate the parliamentary governmental system. Then it became clear that the President's emergency powers, combined if necessary with his right to dissolve parliament and appoint the chancellor, gave him a handle to suspend the constitution using pseudo-constitutional means, and to destroy democracy by pseudo-democratic methods. The potential danger inherent in any emergency legislation became actual.

Admittedly various other circumstances played an important part in the erosion and dissolution of the Weimar democracy. They could only do so, however, because the constitution failed to provide effective controls; in fact it was full of weak spots and loopholes. The traditional patriarchal attitude of mind persisted in public opinion, in the publicity media and in constitutional doctrine; this availed itself of the sweeping possibilities offered by an emergency regime in the hands of anti-democratic persons or groups. Under Ebert their chances had been limited; now, however, they deliberately adopted ideas, the purpose of which was to reform and then overthrow the parliamentary republic by means of an authoritarian, presidential and emergency regime. The elimination of the Reichstag and *Gleichschaltung* of Prussia, the republican stronghold, were stages in this process, a process which led directly to the seizure of power (using terrorist methods) by a presidential minority government under Hitler.

The starting point was the fall of the last major coalition during the worsening economic crisis of spring 1930. There can be no doubt that the political parties were to blame and that the difficulties of forming a parliamentary government were great. This fact and its consequences, however, were not to be explained (as authoritarian critics of parliamentary democracy still do) solely by an alleged 'crisis of the party state'. The overriding fact was that plans for a non-parliamentary regime, 'above party' and bypassing the Reichstag, had been prepared long beforehand. Brüning was appointed Reich Chancellor at Hindenburg's behest; there was no attempt at regular negotiations to form a government; the appointment was made with astounding rapidity and with a clear reference to the possible use of Article 48. The obligation to form a responsible political government and to co-operate constructively was thereby removed both from the Reichstag and the parties; the long-heralded crisis of the party state had become fact.

The President's right to rule by emergency decree was then increasingly used to transform the governmental system itself on the pretext of guaranteeing 'public security and good order'. It quickly became apparent that use of dictatorial-type methods to surmount a crisis was a more questionable procedure than dealing with it by the formation of a broad political consensus and by widening the basis of government through parliamentary compromise. The fateful premature dissolution of the Reichstag in the summer of 1930, which led to the rise of National-socialism as a mass movement, the paralysation of parliament and the rapid turn of the population to extremism, were directly connected with the installation of an emergency regime subject to no controls; it governed, not politically but bureaucratically, relying solely on the dictatorial provisions of Article 48; the Reichstag could do no more than take note of measures placed before it. The summary dismissal of Brüning and installation of the Papen cabinet meant that the process was now directed against the republic itself. Parliament was now completely eliminated; abuse of Article 48 led to Papen's *coup d'état* in Prussia; though critical of his action the Constitutional Court accepted the *fait accompli*; Papen's far-reaching plans to remodel the state and constitution on authoritarian lines were based entirely on use of the President's dictatorial powers.

Contrary to one general view the Nazi seizure of power itself did not take place by the legal methods of victory at an election and formation of a parliamentary majority, but through an emergency regime under Article 48. Hitler was never even near possessing a Nazi majority in the Reichstag until 1933; in all his negotiations he invariably demanded that emergency powers be made available to him. The final decision was taken when, in January 1933, Hindenburg was persuaded to grant these powers by the intrigues of and pressure from his immediate entourage, particularly Papen. Without massive use of Article 48 the Nazi seizure of power, cynically termed the 'legal revolution', could never have taken place in the confusingly pseudo-legal form in which it did. Dissolution of the Reichstag, the final *Gleichschaltung* of Prussia, terrorization of public opinion, abrogation of basic rights and finally the *Gleichschaltung* of all *Länder* with non-Nazi governments and of the Reichsrat were all achieved, not by parliamentary majority but by manipulation of the emergency powers. The Enabling Law, which made further use of Article 48 superfluous, was passed under the pressure of a permanent state of emergency; by abuse of the presidential dictatorial authority in the 'Reichstag Fire Decree' of 28 February 1933, the state of emergency was in fact perpetuated for the whole duration of the Third Reich.

The experience of Germany seems to point the moral clearly. Overemphasis on constitutional dictatorship led to permanent totalitarian dictatorship, an extreme illustration of the dangers necessarily inherent in emergency provisions under a democratic constitution. Whenever, in order to surmount some crisis, constitutional arrangements are suspended, there exists a danger that, ostensibly legally, controlled dictatorship will become uncontrolled. The Weimar situation was characterized by the incredible elasticity of its emergency provisions and the fact that they were linked to the presidential prerogatives. There was no precise delimitation of emergency authority with the result that it could be used to bypass and change the constitutional system instead of safeguarding it. The safeguards should have carried with them the establishment of controlling agencies of a parliamentary, judicial and federalist nature with the widest possible powers. At the same time, however, the experience of Weimar shows the limitations of mere institutional safeguards.

One conclusion which emerges from this – and it should be borne in mind in all further discussion of the subject – is that a clear distinction must be drawn between the extreme emergency of a war situation and actual or supposed internal crises. Difficulties in the exercise of parliamentary government will only be increased by use of emergency provisions, particularly if emergency powers are always available because they are enshrined (beckoningly) in the constitution. It is not accidental that the classic proven democracies such as those of the USA, Great Britain or Switzerland, have no explicit constitutional provisions for emergency; in a crisis all forces are bent towards a democratic solution and no constitutional change takes place. In these countries an emergency is dealt with either by parliamentary methods, parliament formally delegating plenary power as in the last war, or through the established prerogatives of the president as in the USA, where, however, Congress and the courts always retain full power of control.

Significantly the contrasting example is that of the Fifth French Republic which, with its dualist presidential structure, is reminiscent of the Weimar Republic; in Article 16 its constitution provides for similarly comprehensive and undefined emergency powers for the president (though naturally de Gaulle cannot be compared with Hindenburg). This can hardly be taken as a model, neither can the emergency provisions in countries like Greece or Turkey. In Italy, Norway, Luxemburg, Denmark, Belgium and Canada, on the other hand, there are no emergency provisions at all. Holland and Sweden are to a certain extent exceptions; there emergency provisions exist but they are of an extremely restricted nature.

2

So a great question-mark stands against all attempts to institutionalize provisions for a state of emergency. Neither history nor the established democracies provide a simple guide. On the contrary, much has been made of the fact that emergency provisions run counter to the intentions behind the Basic Law, resurrect the errors of Weimar and invite the establishment of a dangerous parallel constitution capable of threatening and eroding the basic rights including even the governmental, federal and constitutional structure of the second German republic. For this very reason, instead of including provisions for emergency or exceptional situations, the Basic Law laid down very strict regulations against anti-democratic tendencies and included precautions intended to stabilize the structure of government and parliament. The intention was to make the subterfuge of emergency politics both unnecessary and impossible. All agencies were placed under obligation to safeguard the basic rights and the democratic federalist structure of the state.

Even if it is agreed, however, that emergency legislation is essential, four fundamental questions still remain to be answered. First, who establishes and announces the existence of an emergency? In no case can this be the executive, since it acquires vastly increased powers as a result. The risk is still great even if a parliamentary committee is interposed in the chain of decision, as is now the case in the Federal Republic. Both government and executive will always be able to claim that they are better informed and technically more efficient and this is all in line with the general trend towards the bureaucratic, technological, and administrative state. We should therefore insist upon approval by a qualified parliamentary majority and it must be more than the mere governmental majority; properly it should be a two-thirds majority since the substance of the constitution is affected.

The second question – when does an emergency exist? – is equally a question of definition. If confined to a state of war, this must be regarded as the least of all evils and this is the procedure in the established democracies. Any attempt to define it with terms such as 'imminent threat', 'period of tension' or 'increased defence preparedness' as used in the Federal Republic, or to make it applicable to internal political problems as has now been done by allowing the Bundeswehr to be used internally – all this can only lead to a jungle of differing interpretations, the end result of which is likely to be abuse of power and a *coup d'état*.

The third question – what should an emergency regime imply and what should it not? – is still largely the subject of debate and still remains unclarified. The democratic view is that it implies merely concentration and simplification of the process of government and remains strictly confined by parliamentary responsibility; against this there is the concept of a dictatorship limited in time, under which democracy itself is largely placed in suspense. With this is connected the contentious question of the controls to be retained or alternatively introduced in order to guard against the dangers inherent in any emergency solution, particularly the danger that responsible government may be replaced by a bureaucratic dictatorial interregnum. If the purpose of the emergency regime is really to save democracy, then it can only be based on the broadest possible multi-party government along the lines of the British and American wartime governments; the constitutional and democratic controls will then continue in operation. If, however, there is a considerable transfer of power from legislature to executive, then additional controls become necessary to check the tendency to prolong, extend and consolidate this abnormal distribution of powers. The basic essentials are complete continuity of parliament and the constitutional courts, freedom of the press and of expression. The question remains, however, whether the principle of voluntary co-operation and voluntary restriction of powers, upon which the democracies without codified emergency provisions rely, is not far better and more effective than a system of elaborate emergency provisions which can never fully anticipate the measures actually required in some future crisis.

Finally, however (and this is the fourth question) the central problem remains: how can an emergency regime be brought to an end?; how can it be prevented from perpetuating itself or turning into permanent dictatorship? This danger is inherent in all democracies in which the government is not fully responsible to parliament. Government and the executive will not willingly relinquish their emergency powers unless parliament is effectively in a position to demand that they do so and this necessitates the fullest possible continuance of parliamentary politics even during the period of restriction. It is questionable whether a small exclusive parliamentary committee (as in Bonn) is sufficient; its mere existence may have the disastrous effect that parliament may renounce its responsibilities in favour of a few 'emergency experts' even before a crisis has actually developed.

There must therefore still be doubt whether emergency provisions are in any way compatible with democracy. Their protagonists have often enough proved to be devotees of authoritarian regimes. Carl Schmitt, for instance, the notorious constitutional lawyer, began by requiring perfectionism from the Weimar democracy; then, in his decisionist doctrine he placed political decision above the constitution and declared the capacity to deal with an emergency situation as central to the state; finally and logically he became a champion of the totalitarian Führer dictatorship of 1933. The arguments advanced today by right-wing journalists like Winfried Martini are little different; their complaint is that the Weimar Republic had inadequate emergency powers and they acclaim Portugal's authoritarian regime; similar views are to be heard from the neo-fascists and the military dictators or from the panegyrists of left-wing revolutionary regimes and the stalinist system. The anti-party sentiments of a great man like de Gaulle, however, or the perfectionism of a bureaucracy imbued with patriarchal or military and technological ideas are also calculated to perpetuate the influence and the impact of such tendencies and to institutionalize emergency regimes. This is so whether their ideological justification is fear of some military menace or undiscriminating anti-communism or fear of socio-economic crisis or exasperation with the complications and imperfections of parliamentary democracy.

Political history shows that crises are best dealt with by the involvement of all forces from parliament to the trades unions and a free press, not by their exclusion from the political process. We misjudge the very nature of democracy if we regard it merely as a form of game to be played only when times are good; equally the popular but elementary and dangerous viewpoint that the stronger the state has to be, the less democratic can it be and the less interference the government has to fear from parliament, the better will it be able to cope with an emergency, should not be allowed to spread. The answer to the perfectionists who advocate emergency provisions is this: if, under the constitution, technical possibilities exist of riding roughshod over that constitution, then the appetite to make use of these possibilities will grow; this is a psychological phenomenon of which there are many examples. The responsible agencies – the parties, parliament, the trades unions, the courts and even the press – may be misled into evading difficult and unpopular situations, leaving the field open to emergency regulations which allow them to feel that they are rid of their uncomfortable responsibility. This is what happened in Germany in 1930–3.

All components of a democratic state and democratic society must be fully involved in an emergency regime. A crisis can only be overcome by democratic co-operation, by control and responsibility; it will be overcome by a sense of the ultimate superiority of a free society with responsible government, not by continuous alterations of the constitution and suspension of the fundamental rules of democracy. The perfectionists may be well-intentioned but, once the trend towards non-parliamentary government has been started and the way to dictatorship opened thereby, return to full-scale democracy from a fully developed emergency regime is a highly difficult process.

These considerations are entirely applicable to our emergency provisions of 1968. Admittedly the earlier and much more far-reaching proposals have been modified and there has been no return to Article 48. The basic problems inherent in any emergency regulations, however, remain unsolved. There are openings here for authoritarian, bureaucratic and even military intervention into the democratic structure of the Federal Republic. At a time when extremist movements are on the increase and the call for law and order is to be heard more loudly this demands the critical vigilance of the citizen lest the power of the state grow unduly. This is the prerequisite for any free, crisis-proof democracy.

17

Peace and War

I

The science of war has been the subject of study since the earliest times; more recently, however, it has been paralleled by and contrasted with a systematic empirical 'study of peace'. Peace and war have been regarded as nature's two fundamental categories of social and political behaviour bearing a reciprocal dialectic relationship to each other. This formal, fatalistic outlook, however, has now been overtaken by realization of the hard fact that, under the conditions of modern weapons development and world political interdependence, war carries with it the risk of global self-destruction; it can therefore no longer be regarded as Clausewitz's traditional 'continuation of politics by other means'. There is a further factor: worldwide communications and the impact of ideologies have led to phenomena such as the Cold War and a situation of latent 'world civil war' (Sigmund Neumann's phrase), a prolonged twilight situation between peace and war.

With the diversification and increasing technicality of military methods the distinction between peace and war has become more and more blurred and in many cases has been completely erased. Since the start of the era of great political and industrial revolutions armies have become mass armies, whole populations have been armed, partisan and guerrilla warfare has made its appearance, technology has dictated that war preparations must be economic and organizational as well as military, the scale of war has risen until it embraces and uses entire peoples as its instrument. The result has been that periods of peace have been largely transformed into periods of rearmament and war preparation.

The formal traditional criteria by which a distinction was made between a state of peace and a state of war were such things as peace treaties, declarations of war or diplomatic relations; with the disappearance of this distinction it is no longer possible to apply the term 'peace' indiscriminately to all periods when there is no war. Hitherto the philosophical or theological concept of peace has been an ingredient of political thought; now, however, an attempt is being made to apply socio-scientific analysis to the conditions and forms of peace and its potential for transition into a state of non-peace. The international legal terms hitherto used are now inadequate to describe the internal mechanisms and problems of the complex relationships between modern states; similarly, in present-day international politics, the old criteria governing the thinking of the international lawyers and the military are no longer adequate for the purposes of solving conflicts and assuring peace.

Politically the terms peace and war are the expression of social rather than legal organization. Their form is dependent on the existing level of social relationships. Depending upon their use to describe relationships between social groupings, between peoples and nations within some supra-national system or world organization, the problem of peace appears in a different light, the interplay and solution of conflicts will vary. The 'classical' military science of war was largely isolated from its political and social context; realistic research into peace, however, is closely bound up with research into conflict. Its starting point is an examination of the relationships between men; the peaceful solution of conflicts on the lowest level, in other words between individuals, seems to be the prerequisite and also the model for the solution of conflicts on the higher levels of social and political organization. The family, the school, the profession, the group, form the starting points; the ultimate aim of this exercise in the settlement of conflicts and preservation of peace is the application of its principles in the international or supra-national field.

So far systematic scientific analysis of peace has lagged far behind that of war; the science of peace has been in danger of being written off as a utopian process of speculative, subjective extrapolation applicable only to the future; it has taken second place to the 'realism' of empirical enquiry into conflict and war. From the outset theories of peace have suffered from the multiplicity and breadth of the definitions used; peace can be defined, for instance, in a negative sense, as the absence or prevention of violent conflict between states or (in the case of civil war) between associations or groups seeking internal power; it can also, however, be conceived in a positive sense, as the requirement for ordered collaboration and progressive integration of such groups and entities. The word peace can be used to cover such situations as that of cold war between states and power blocs, in other words, co-existence without positive co-operation, but in this case it implies no more than a state of 'non-war'. Only the second – the positive – meaning of the word peace is of any real significance for theoretical clarification or practical solution of the peace–and–war problem.

The history of international politics shows that conditions of conflict, or alternatively their absence, within a state or a society can exert considerable influence on inter-state relationships. It has not, however proved possible to discover any clear correlation between social and governmental systems on the one hand and their international role in the politics of peace or war on the other. The phenomenon of militarism is not, in the first instance, a manifestation of aggressive tendencies towards other states (as Gerhard Ritter, for example, has maintained in his attempt to exonerate Prussian–German militarism); it signifies that a certain society is permeated by the ideals of military order and is organized accordingly; temporarily this is compatible with a non-warlike policy (if the negative definition of peace be accepted). Conversely the sense of mission of a democratically mobilized revolutionary society which feels itself threatened by the old regimes can lead to a warlike attitude towards other countries, as happened in the aftermath of the French Revolution. Naturally there are reasons why a democratically organized society has less inclination towards war in that it will tend to apply to inter-state relationships the principle of the peaceful solution of conflicts used in internal politics. On the other hand Quincy Wright's researches have shown that the more highly organized societies are more inclined than the primitive to try to assert their claims by warlike means (*A Study of War*, 1942 and 1965).

There is, in fact, little to prove the validity of the assumption that a general rise in the standard of living and a more equitable distribution of goods would automatically solve the problem of war and lead to a general peace. Solution of internal conflicts may well divert the thirst for power and aggressive tendencies with even greater force towards the outside world. Even with democratization and industrialization, with socialism and the welfare society, thoughts of war persist for historical and psychological reasons. Modern regimes and ideologies do no more than alter the forms in which disputes take place; often enough, in fact, they contribute to their intensification and extension. This has been strikingly proved by the epoch of the two world wars. The efforts, therefore, to develop systematic peace plans and peace systems at the various levels of potential conflict are of all the greater importance. They are based partially on the earlier attempts by philosophers and international lawyers but their unparalleled importance and urgency spring from the fact that, in our century, wars may lead to global suicide. In this situation even pacificism, the rejection in principle of any warlike action, may gather strength as a political and social movement.

2

Basic to any theory of peace is the question – analogous to peace at home – of how political power can best be distributed between states, canalized and controlled; extremely varied models spring to the mind: peace guaranteed by a predominant imperial or ideological power (the *Imperium Romanum*, the universal church, the British empire, the USA or Soviet Union as representing the principle of a universal, democratic or socialist world); the 'balance of power', in other words prevention of war by the mutual deterrent or immobilizing effect of systems of equal strength which may be bi-polar or multi-polar in form; limitation of armaments by binding agreements on disarmament or arms control. Repeated attempts to use the latter method have been made ever since the Hague Peace Conference of 1899. In contrast to the theories of single–state predominance or balance of power this does provide a concrete method of preventing the preparation and conduct of war; it can be rationally set out and properly planned. Assurance of peace by means of arms controls is therefore a modern method, suited to the present day and preferable to the older models because it is related to the technique of war which is continuously growing in complexity and scope; moreover it operates in the transitional periods between peace and war.

This, of course, does not prevent the same problems and obstacles emerging; on the one hand, the concept of peace may be obscured by ideology and manipulated; on the other hand, *Realpolitik*, which sees only the nation's interests, is averse to self-imposed supra-national restrictions over which it has no control. In addition there are the almost insuperable difficulties of effective control and the problems thrown up by the increasingly direct interreaction of arms policy with economic and scientific development. The use of certain weapons of mass destruction and the spread of 'small wars' may be made more difficult, but arms control by itself can neither prevent war nor introduce nor assure a full-scale peace system. Worse still, restriction of the problem to one of weapons means that it can only be a surrogate solution; indeed it may divert attention from the overall aspects of the solution of international conflicts and assurance of peace; it may induce a false sense of security when the urgent requirement may be a sense of anxiety and the effort to find overall political solutions. The pacifist demand for general and complete disarmament and the belief that this can be achieved by a unilateral example set by one side are obviously utopian. Disarmament must apply to all without exception if it is not to lead to total domination by those who have failed to disarm. The theory of of renunciation of the use of force and of passive resistance seems to be applicable only to certain situations (India in 1947, for instance, but not Czechoslovakia in 1968). Total disarmament presupposes the possibility of a world government, of a binding world constitution and an active world conscience; this in turn presupposes that democratic procedure has become the rule in international politics.

From the beginning of our century, therefore, pacifist convictions have invariably failed to make headway in face of the realities of policy based solely on the pursuit of certain socio-political interests or of claims to ideological hegemony; when faced with actual political responsibility even the declared internationalist, anti-war movements such as liberalism, socialism and communism have proved as realistic as the rest. Possibilities for the future include a growing social and economic convergence between the industrial states of East and West; the following obstacles are still present, however: the almost uninterrupted persistence of claims to national power and sovereignty, the problems of 'north' versus 'south' and the increasing economic gap between developed and underdeveloped national societies.

The traditional methods of guaranteeing the peace, however, do not provide any adequate solution either. International order maintained by some predominant power on the model of the *Pax Romana* or perhaps a *Pax Americana* or *Pax Sovietica* would not be tolerable; in addition to mere maintenance of the peace it would inevitably imply a hegemony involving interference with the systems, interests and ideas of subordinate nations and societies. It would necessitate a generally accepted scale of values and a whole series of special safeguards, imposing a considerable degree of restraint upon the predominating state in the use of its power; this would be the purpose of a federal world state, which presupposes above all else general acceptance of democratic principles. In our century of dictatorships, however, this is a distant dream and, this being so, a threat to the existing democracies (one has only to think of Germany united under an authoritarian Prussia with the consequential reversion to the patriarchal state).

So far the balance of power system has remained the most effective method of preventing war. Its main weakness lies in the instability of the system of equilibrium. It carries with it a permanent temptation to change or upset the balance by power-policy methods and this implies a danger of the reciprocal escalation of armaments and threats of war, a danger increased by misappreciation of the opposing side and the resulting reactions. The balance of power is closely linked to certain defined power relationships and ratios of strength with the result that its effectiveness is questionable and, as a solution, it is inevitably uncertain and short-term. If based largely on a bi-polar system (as it has been since 1945) it has a greater degree of stability than had the multi-polar concert of great powers in the periods preceding the First and Second World Wars.

Nevertheless the problems posed by the permanent threat of alteration in the balance of power and a ruinous arms race have not become less. Moreover it is clear that in a world of nation–states rigid bi-polarity is not possible. The more distant or newer states will contrive to extricate themselves from the system by insisting upon neutrality or even independence and constituting a 'Third Force'; traditional ideas of sovereignty (gaullism) or the cross-pressures of differing interests can neutralize various conflicts; a vacuum may develop between the super-powers and their sub-systems. In such zones there can be no question of an assured peace. They are still in the stage where traditional foreign and military policies predominate. A bi-polar system may well be able to limit local or regional conflicts but they will continue to smoulder (as in the Middle East or Vietnam). They offer a permanent temptation to change the balance of power. Above all, however, the balance itself is necessarily fluid since, to protect and control its own allies and to keep pace with the rapid development of weapons technique, each side will be compelled to make continuous efforts to prepare for a future major war; in the light of nuclear rocket strike which must be anticipated, even if strategy is declared to be defensive, the resources for an immediate counter strike must be available. A further factor is the interraction of war preparations with scientific, technical and economic development.

Against this, by empirical analysis, research into peace has shown that expansion and acceleration of arms production is of no economic advantage; it is not even of importance for scientific and technical development, neither is it essential to the functioning of a capitalist society, as bourgeois and marxist theorists have tried to prove with remarkable unanimity though for opposite purposes. This is the outcome of a misappreciation similar to the view taken of colonial imperialism; there are still believers in the old idea that war lies at the root of all things which culminated in the philosophy of the social-darwinists and the fascist ideology – 'war's bath of steel' as history's test of worth and the training ground for the best peoples and races. In fact arming for war and war itself amount to a gigantic waste of life and resources which can advantage only a few interested persons and can in no case benefit industry, science or society; it is highly damaging to peaceful development and leads into blind alleys. Scholars such as Quincy Wright, the 'grand old man' of research into peace and war, have demonstrated convincingly that economic factors have neither direct nor indirect influence upon the origin or outbreak of war or in any way promoted it. Of far greater importance are subjective political ambitions, ideological convictions, technological development, claims to certain rights, irrational psychological complexes, ignorance and inadequate readiness to preserve and improve the conditions for peace in a changing world. The enormous tasks facing space travel, originally initiated for military purposes, are no exception. It may be true to say that, in the long term, space travel may divert the dynamic of military expansion to peaceful scientific purposes. But the problems of inter-state development and inter-state relationships upon earth remain and vital energies and resources may not be available for their solution as a result; new problems of the delimitation of political, economic and military interests in space will emerge. There can be no doubt that these will be closely affected by arms policy and the increasingly horrifying picture presented by war.

3

Arms control has proved incapable of arresting the arms race; similarly the political concept of positive peace as visualized by the researchers into peace has been obscured by anticipation of war; few people have a clear idea of the actual effectiveness of supra-national solutions. A concrete starting point is available, however, in the dilution of nation–state loyalties as lateral contacts increase. As the ordinary citizen comes in contact with supra-national organizations, as he comes to feel himself identified with a number of bodies and gains contact with the people and culture of other nations, he may become more resistant to the regimentation of mobilization for war, which itself is a fearful limiting factor on human thought and action. Admittedly, for the individual, this conflict of loyalties will pose difficult problems of conduct and it may often lead to a fanatical, emotional, friend-foe attitude of mind, as was shown by the large number of overseas or 'racial' Germans among the Nazi leaders. Results capable of reducing the risk of war and increasing the prospects of peace are not to be expected until supra-national contacts have been further expanded, divergencies between peoples and cultures further reduced and communications considerably extended. This will also reduce the risk of misunderstandings, so frequently the cause of serious disturbances of the peace. This process of dilution of national identification, however, and its replacement by supra-national, plural links is countered by the claims of national interest and exclusive ideology, by censorship and propaganda manoeuvres, particularly in countries with dictatorial governments.

In the light of historical experience attempts to use as criteria for prospects of stable peace between states the degree of similarity between them and their societies or the level of their economic and cultural relationships are unlikely to produce a sound answer. Family quarrels and civil war, the best examples of conflict between closely related human groupings, can lead to particularly violent disturbances of the peace. On the other hand, when peoples know nothing of each other, are complete strangers to each other, this is liable to remove all inhibitions against making war or even exterminating the other side, as colonial wars and racialism have proved. Quincy Wright's researches have also shown that statistically wars are more frequent between countries with highly developed mutual relationships; such relationships do not therefore necessarily contribute to the maintenance of peace. The reason is obvious, however: wars between neighbouring states are more likely and more directly motivated. This may change as international communications expand and supra-national organizations are developed.

An increasing number of theories centred on the idea of an 'international system' are now appearing; they seek to draw the conclusions from the growing interdependence which an international framework has imposed on the foreign policies of the various nations. Basically they foresee the world developing in such a way that the conduct of all countries will have its effect upon the fate of other countries; peace and war will ultimately become indivisible. This is the starting point for efforts to develop a global peace system; the eternal peace visualized by philosophers from the Stoa to Kant is still beyond their reach; ideas go further, however, than those of a mere assemblage of sovereign states as in the League of Nations or, even now, in UNO. The central idea is that the principle of peaceful settlement of conflicts as observed internally should become applicable to the field of inter-state relationships and that this should be done in a semi-institutionalized form by means of a comprehensive international system. Whether this can be done and whether the system would function depends, of course, upon the establishment of a recognized decision-making centre analogous to a democratically legitimized government.

Everything else – in particular the question of the structure of such a world state – is dependent upon this fundamental precondition. Inclusion of the various nations on a federal basis seems to be the only realistic method and the one best calculated to achieve the desirable object of preserving the diversity and individuality of the various peoples and cultures. This does not mean, however, that the persistence or revival of conflicts is impossible. The same may be said of the efforts already made to establish supra-national organizations on a regional basis; as might be expected, it has proved that organizations such as the EDC which are confined to a restricted area (but exclusive) offer greater prospects of supra-national development than widespread and therefore looser associations with limited aims such as the Council of Europe, NATO, EFTA, COMECON or UNO. Their significance as steps on the road to a world system for the assurance of peace and avoidance of war is still a matter of debate. Most of them were formed under the pressure of the East–West confrontation and may well collapse with it; if they do, they would have to be regarded merely as manifestations of the traditional balance of power system. Whether they can be regarded as preliminary steps in the formation of a more comprehensive system of supra-national co-operation for the maintenance of peace, as is so often said, depends upon the possibility of divorcing them from the situation in which they originated (the Cold War) and transforming them from communities or alliances born of economic or military necessity into political entities capable of further expansion. One essential prerequisite is that counter-ideologies such as gaullism, based on tradition and *Realpoltik*, should be confined to their sole useful function, reduction of the rigidity of the military blocs.

Compared to war the establishment and assurance of peace is a complex problem demanding an incomparably greater degree of intellectual and political effort. Despite all the advances made in development of its instruments, war and its preparation remain, technically and organizationally, the outcome and the manifestation of an archaic primitive pattern of behaviour in which politics are conceived as a display of force and counter-force. Efforts designed to prevent war demand a high level of political acumen and of planning, far superior to that required for the acquisition of armaments. This illustrates the superior worth of peace as the product of and condition for human civilization, also as the supreme object of the thought and conduct of *homo sapiens*. That he should initiate and suffer the consequences of conflict remains inevitable but whether and how he contrives to settle and solve his problems peacefully demonstrates the stage of development he has reached. This applies also to the conduct of nation–states where collective egoism is still to be seen in its most uncontrolled form.

By contrast the role played by pacificism, the peace movement and peace research is still a very limited one. Since its inception in the first half of the nineteenth century (the first Peace Conference in London of 1843) the modern peace movement has sponsored certain far-reaching initiatives and spawned a whole series of organizations but it has remained a fringe phenomenon, ridiculed and labelled as evangelistic, unpolitical and moralistic; during the major wars it has been almost entirely ineffectual. The christian churches too have largely adhered to their attitude of acceptance or even approval of war. The peace movement, despite its moral and religious background, has been regarded as an enterprise conducted by amateurs who were demonstrably failures when confronted with the realities of politics and who in fact allowed themselves to be misused by one side or the other as ideological or propagandist camouflage for their power–policy purposes. The world wide prestige of individual pacifists such as Albert Schweitzer or Bertrand Russell was never a reflection of the weight or influence of organized pacificism. The trial of strength between the aims of pacificism and the claims to power of the various countries invariably ended in the defeat of pacificism despite the numerous examples of devotion and sacrifice during and after the two world wars. Under National-socialism pacifists were brutally persecuted; since then conscientious objectors have been hounded and pacifist activity has been outlawed both in East and West (the Jehovah's Witnesses, for instance). All this shows how far we still are from real condemnation or outlawry of war in spite of all the treaties and tributes paid to the idea – by the League of Nations in 1920, the Kellogg Pact in 1928 and now the UNO Charter.

These very setbacks should be enough to show that the prime necessity is the enlightenment of a society still in the grip of archaic habits of thought. As men become more educated the politics of peace must be introduced as part of social existence. Under the conditions of the democratic age and mass communications it must no longer remain the preserve of individual groups and élites. The conditions and consequences of the states of peace and war must become a generally accepted field of knowledge instead of an occult science known only to experts. As a result of their experience of historic aberrations and political catastrophes politics and science in Germany are confronted with these problems as part of their very existence. Their contribution may also bring nearer a democratic supra-national solution of the German dilemma which is the subject of this book.

Notes

Part 1

Chapter 1   Concept of the State and Democracy in Germany

1 Alfred Weber and Eugen Kogon, 'Feststellungen der Arbeitstagung der Deutschen Hochschule für Politik' in *Die Wissenschaft im Rahmen politischen Bildung*, Weiss Brothers, Berlin 1950, p. 27.

2 A. R. L. Gurland, 'Politische Wirklichkeit und Politische Wissenschaft' in *Faktoren der Machtbildung*, Dunker & Humblot, Berlin 1952, p. 36. O. H. von der Gablentz attempts to bring the two together in 'Macht, Gestaltung und Recht – Die drei Wurzeln politischen Denkens', ibid., pp. 139 et seq. Various of the contributions in Dieter Oberndörfer (ed.), *Wissenschaftliche Politik*, Verlag Rombach, Freiburg 1962, lay particular emphasis on the 'established order' aspect.

3 See K. D. Bracher, 'Wissenschafts- und zeitgeschichtliche Probleme der Politischen Wissenschaft in Deutschland' in *Kölner Zeitschrift für Soziologie und Sozialpsychologie*, 17 (1965), pp. 448 et seq.; Giovanni Sartori, 'Der Begriff der "Wertfreiheit" in der Politischen Wissenschaft' in *Politische Vierteliahrsschrift* (PVS), 1 (1960), pp. 12 et seq. For a fundamental examination of the 'scale of values' problem see Arnold Brecht, *Politische Theorie*, Mohr, Tübingen 1961, pp. 404 et seq.

4 Gabriel Almond and Sidney Verba, *The Civic Culture. Political Attitudes and Democracy in Five Nations*, Princeton University Press, 1963.

5 Helmuth Plessner, *Die verspätete Nation*, Kohlhammer, Stuttgart 1959.

6 Basic to this subject – Ernst Fraenkel, *Deutschland und die westlichen Demokratien*, Kohlhammer, Stuttgart 1964, pp. 11 et seq.

7 See in particular two books by Hans Maier: *Die ältere deutsche Staats-und Verwaltungslehre*, Luchterhand, Neuwied 1966, and *Ältere deutsche Staatslehre und westliche politische Tradition*, Mohr, Tübingen 1966.

8 On the old concept of the state see A. O. Meyer, 'Zur Geschichte des Wortes Staat' in *Die Welt als Geschichte*, 10 (1950), pp. 229 et seq.; for greater detail see Paul L. Weinacht, 'Staat. Studien zur Bedeutungsgeschichte des Wortes von den Anfängen bis ins 19 Jahrhundert', dissertation, Munich 1967. On the general problem see Horst Ehmke, ' "Staat" und "Gesellschaft" als verfassungstheoretisches Problem' in *Staatsverfassung und Kirchenordnung* (dedicated to Rudolf Smend), Mohr, Tübingen 1962, pp. 23 et seq.

9 Hans Maier, 'Probleme einer demokratischen Tradition in Deutschland' in *Geschichte in Wissenschaft und Unterricht*, 18 (1967), p. 403. See also Rudolf Stadelmann, *Deutschland und Westeuropa*, Steiner, Laupheim 1948, pp. 11 et seq.; Heinrich Heffter, *Die deutsche Selbstverwaltung im 19 Jahrhundert*, Koehler, Stuttgart 1950, pp. 63 et seq.

10 Ehmke, op. cit., p. 33.

11 Konrad Hesse, 'Der Rechtsstaat im Verfassungssystem des Grundgesetzes' in Ehmke, *Staatsverfassung und Kirchenordnung*, op. cit., p. 71; Franz Neumann, 'The concept of political freedom' in *Columbia Law Review* (1953), pp. 901 et seq.

12 O. H. von der Gablentz, *Die versäumte Reform*, Westdeutscher Verlag, Cologne and Opladen 1960, p. 9; see also the comprehensive discussion by Ernst Maste, 'Die Unterscheidung von Staat und Gesellschaft und ihre Beziehung zum Stattsbegriff' in Supplement to *Das Parlament* (26 January 1966).

13 Hans Ulrich Scupin, 'Uber den Wandel der Wesensbestimmung der Demokratie in Deutschland während des letzten Jahrhunderts' in *Festschrift für Herbert Kraus*, Holznes, Würzburg 1964, p. 323.

14 On its bureaucratic and military character see Wolfgang Sauer, 'Das Problem des deutschen Nationalstaats' in PVS, 3 (1962), p. 166 et seq.

15 See K. D. Bracher, *Deutschland zwischen Demokratie und Diktatur*, Scherz, Berne and Munich 1964, pp. 153 et seq.

16 Helmut Ridder, article entitled 'Staat' in *Staatslexikon*, vol. VII, Freiburg 1962, col. 542.

17 Suzanne Miller, *Das Problem der Freiheit im Sozialismus*, Europäische Verlagsanstalt, Frankfurt 1964, pp. 80 et seq.

18 On this subject see Hermann Lübbe, *Politische Philosophie in Deutschland, Studien zu ihrer Geschichte*, Schwabe, Basle and Stuttgart 1963, pp. 173 et seq.

19 See criticism by Wolfgang Abendroth, 'Das Unpolitische als Wesensmerkmal der deutschen Universität' in *Nationalsozialismus und die deutsche Universität*, de Gruyter, Berlin 1966, pp. 194 et seq.

20 Max Scheler, *Die Stellung des Menschen im Kosmos*, Nymphenburger Verlag, Munich 1947, p. 51.

21 On the problem of the concept of 'nation', instead of the traditional apologetic approach typified in Eugen Lemberg's investigations, see the critical political and democratic approach in the following works: Hans Kohn, *The Idea of Nationalism*, Macmillan, New York 1945; Walter Sulzbach, *Imperialismus und Nationalbewusstsein*, Europäische Verlagsanstalt, Frankfurt 1959; Manfred Hättich, *Nationalbewusstsein und Staatsbewusstsein in der pluralistischen Gesellschaft*, Hase & Koehler, Mainz 1966; Hannah Vogt, *Nationalismus gestern und heute*, Leske, Opladen 1967; Carlton Hayes, *The Historical Evolution of Modern Nationalism*, Macmillan, New York 1959; Elie Kadurie, *Nationalism,*

Hutchinson, Praeger, London and New York 1961; Christian Graf von Krockow, 'Nationalbewusstsein und Gesellschaftsbewusstsein' in PVS, 3 (1962), pp. 141 et seq.

22 Lübbe, op. cit., p. 25.

23 Plessner, op. cit., p. 13.

24 M. Rainer Lepsius, 'Parteiensystem und Sozialstruktur: Zum Problem der Demokratisierung der deutschen Gesellschaft' in *Festschrift für Friedrich Lütge*, Stuttgart 1966, p. 393.

25 See K. D. Bracher, *Deutschland zwischen Demokratie une Diktatur*, op. cit., p. 324 (the American 'democracy as the secularization of the sense of mission').

26 Typical of this is the comprehensive but biased *völkisch* ideological book by Max Hildebert Böhm; *Das eigenständige Volk*, Vandenhoek & Ruprecht, Göttingen 1932 (new edition (!) 1967).

27 Georg Jellinek is critical on this subject in his *Staatslehre*, Julius Springer, Berlin 1929, pp. 129 et seq.; see also Otto Brunner, *Land und Herrschaft* Rohre, Vienna and Wiesbaden 1959, pp. 11 et seq., 146 et seq.; Rudolf Smend, article entitled 'Staat' in *Evangelische Kirchenlexikon*, vol. 3, col. 1107.

28 Article entitled 'Staat' in *Brockhaus*, vol. 11, Wiesbaden 1957, p. 140; Herbert Krüger, *Allgemeine Staatslehre*, Kohlhammer, Stuttgart 1964, pp. 196, 629, 988; O. H. von der Gablentz, 'Der Staat als Mythos und Wirklichkeit' in PVS, 7 (1966), pp. 138 et seq.

29 H. Maier particularly emphasizes this in 'Probleme einer demokratischen Tradition in Deutschland', op. cit., pp. 395 et seq. (with sources).

30 Scupin, op. cit., pp. 326 et seq.; see also Erich Angermann, *Robert von Mohl*, Luchterhand, Neuwied 1962, pp. 107 et seq.; Gottfried Dietze, 'Rechtsstaat und Staatsrecht' in *Die moderne Demokratie und ihr Recht* (dedicated to Gerhard Leibholz), vol. 2, Mohr, Tübingen 1966, pp. 22 et seq.

31 Martin Drath, 'Uber eine kohärente soziokulturelle Theorie des Staats und des Rechts' in *Die moderne Demokratie und ihr Recht*, op. cit., vol. 1, p. 36.

32 Ibid.

33 Ulrich Scheuner, 'Das Wesen des Staates und der Begriff des Politischen in der neueren Staatslehre' in Ehmke, *Stattsverfassung und Kirchenordnung*, op. cit., pp. 249 et seq.

34 Drath, op. cit,, p. 39.

35 Fundamental to this subject – Dieter Grosser, *Grundlagen und Struktur der Staatslehre Friedrich Julius Stahls*, Westdeutscher Verlag, Cologne and Opladen 1963, pp. 62 et seq.

36 Carl Schmitt, 'Soziologie des Souveränitätsbegriffes und politische Theorie' in *Hauptprobleme der Soziologie* (dedicated to Max Weber), vol. 2, Munich-and Leipzig 1923, p. 35.

37 Kurt Sontheimer, *Antidemokratisches Denken in der Weimarer Republik*, Nymphenburger Verlag, Munich 1962, pp. 79 et seq., 240 et seq. and *Politische*

Wissenschaft und Staatslehre, Rombach, Freiburg 1963, pp. 20 et seq. See also Felix Gilbert, 'Political power and academic responsibility' in *The Responsibility of Power. Historical Essays in Honor of Hajo Holborn*, edited by I. Krieger and F. Stern, Doubleday, New York 1967, pp. 402 et seq.

38 For summary see K. D. Bracher, *Die Auflösung der Weimarer Republik*, Ring Verlag, Villingen 1964, pp. 15 et seq.

39 For fundamental examinations of this subject see: Eberhard Kolb, *Die Arbeiterräte in der deutschen Innenpolitik 1918–1919*, Droste, Düsseldorf 1962; Peter von Oertzen, *Betriebsräte in der Novemberrevolution*, Droste, Düsseldorf 1963; Wolfgang Sauer, 'Das Bündnis Groener – Ebert', dissertation, Berlin 1956; Wolfgang Elben, *Das Problem der Kontinuität in der deutschen Revolution*, Droste, Düsseldorf 1965; Wolfgang Ruge, *Politik und Beamtentum in Parteienstaat*, Ernst Kleff, Stuttgart 1965. See also Udo Bermbach's critical summary: 'Das Scheitern des Rätesystems und der Demokratisierung der Bürokratie 1918/19' in PVS, 8 (1967), pp. 445 et seq.

40 Karl Loewenstein's apt phrase or 'Der Staatspräsident' in *Beiträge zur Staatssoziologie*, Mohr, Tübingen 1961, p. 388; see also K. D. Bracher, *Deutschland Zwischen Demokratie und Diktatur*, op. cit., pp. 35 et seq.

41 Rudolf Morsey, *Die deutsche Zentrumspartei 1917–1923*, Droste, Düsseldorf 1966, pp. 607 et seq.

42 Scupin, op. cit., p. 326.

43 *Preussen contra Reich*, Berlin 1933, p. 470. Heller died a year later, aged only forty-two, after having emigrated to Spain; shortly before his death he sent his opponent Carl Schmitt, who had meanwhile been promoted *Staatsrat* (Privy Councillor) in Prussia, a bitterly sarcastic post-card: 'Hermann Heller congratulates you on the very well-earned honour bestowed on you by Minister Göring.' See also Klaus Meyer in PVS, 8 (1967), pp. 293 et seq.

44 Richard Thoma, 'Der Begriff der modernen Demokratie in seinem Verhältnis zum Staatsbegriff' in Carl Schmitt, *Hauptprobleme der Soziologie*, op. cit., p. 567.

45 Ibid., pp. 58 et seq.

46 Max Weber, *Politische Schriften*, Drei Masken Verlag, Munich 1920, p. 139.

47 References in G. Dietze, op. cit., pp. 37 et seq.; see also K. D. Bracher, W. Sauer and G. Schulz, *Die nationalsozialistische Machtergreifung*, Westdeutscher Verlag, Cologne and Opladen 1962, pp. 174 et seq., 516 et seq.

48 Thoma, op. cit., p. 61.

49 See, for instance, remarks by F. J. Strauss and other leading politicians in *Der Stern*, 1 (1967).

50 Ernst Forsthoff, *Rechtsstaat im Wandel*, Kohlhammer, Stuttgart 1964, pp. 61–77.

51 As always on this subject see Karl Jaspers, *Freiheit und Wiedervereinigung*, Piper Verlag, Stuttgart 1959.

52 O. H. von der Gablentz is pertinent in 'Der Staat als Mythos und Wirklichkeit', op. cit.; see also Karl Schultes, 'German politics and political theory' in *The Political Quarterly*, 28 (1957), pp. 40 et seq.

53 Werner Weber, *Das Berufsbeamtentum im demokratischen Rechtsstaat*, Deutsche Industrieverlag, Stuttgart 1952, p. 11.

54 Konrad Hesse in 'Der Rechtsstaat im Verfassungssystem des Grundgesetzes' op. cit., p. 93.

55 This is the basis (with a reference to E. Fraenkel) of, for instance, Wilhelm Hennis's attack on Gerhard Leibholz in 'Amtsgedanke und Demokratiebegriff' in Ehmke, *Staatsverfassung und Kirchenordnung*, op. cit., pp. 66 et seq.

56 Gerhard Lehmbruch, *Proporzdemokratie. Politisches System und politische Kultur in der Schweiz und in Österreich*, Mohr, Tübingen 1967, p. 58.

57 Rightly stressed by Konrad Hesse, op. cit., pp. 90 et seq.

58 Gotthard Jasper, *Der Schutz der Republik*, Mohr, Tübingen 1963, p. 271.

59 Helmut Ridder, article entitled 'Staat', op. cit., p. 543.

60 Erwin Stein, 'Rechtliche Sicherung der freiheitlichen Demokratie in der Bundesrepublik Deutschland' in *Gesellschaft, Staat, Erziehung*, 7 (1962), pp. 78 et seq.; see also K. D. Bracher, *Deutschland, zwischen Demokratie und Diktatur*, op. cit., pp. 113 et seq.; H. Maier, 'Probleme einer demokratischer Tradition in Deutschland', op. cit., pp., 408 et seq. ('a democracy capable of defending itself') with a reference to Hans Peters and Hermann Jahrreiss, *Mensch und Staat*, 1957, pp. 110 et seq.

61 H. Maier, op. cit., p. 414; see also W. Hennis, 'Aufgaben einer modernen Regierungslehre' in PVS, 6 (1965), pp. 422 et seq.

62 London 1965, et seq.; see also the fundamental studies in Robert A. Dahl (ed.), *Political Oppositions in Western Democracies*, Yale University Press, New Haven 1966; Otto Kirchheimer, 'Der Wandel des westeuropäischen Parteiensystems' in PVS, 6 (1965), pp. 25 et seq.

63 *Der Staat*, (1963), foreword, pp. 1 et seq.

64 Christian Graf von Krockow, 'Staatsideologie oder demokratisches Bewusstsein. Die deutsche Alternative' in PVS, 6 (1965), pp. 118 et seq.

65 E. Forsthoff, *Rechtsstaat im Wandel*, op. cit., p. 66.

66 Speech on 3 October 1966 published in *Frankfurter Allgemeine Zeitung* on 11 October 1967, pp. 13 et seq.; see also the apt comment by Karl J. Newmann in *Frankfurter Allgemeine* (21 October 1967).

67 See references in von Krockow, op. cit., pp. 119 et seq.

68 Ernst Rudolf Huber, *Nationalstaat und Verfassungsstaat*, Kohlhammer, Stuttgart 1965; Udo Bermbach in PVS, 8 (1967), p. 508.

69 Carl Schmitt, *Der Leviathan in der Staatslehre des Thomas Hobbes*, Hanseatische Verlagsanstalt, Hamburg 1938, p. 69.

70 Bernard Willms in *Der Staat*, 2 (1963), pp. 502 et seq. Referring to Thomas

Hobbes (and Carl Schmitt) he pleads for 'a reaffirmation of the theory of the "protecting classes" ' as '*the* task of political theory'!

71 In his book *Kritik und Krise*, Alber, Freiburg and Munich 1959.

72 Kurt Fackiner, 'Nationalismus als pädagogisches Problem in Deutschland' in Supplement to *Das Parlament* (13 September 1967), p. 23.

73 Ernst-Otto Czempiel, 'Interdependenz und Gemeinwohl' in *Frankfurter Hefte*, 18 (1963), pp. 101 et seq.

74 Georg Picht, 'Grundlagen eines neuen deutschen Nationalbewusstsein' in *Merkur*, 21 (1967), p. 12; this article is open to much criticism, particularly for its over-simplified solution of replacing an obsolete national consciousness by a new state-consciousness.

75 Gerhard Leibholz, *Volk, Nation und Staat im 20 Jahrhundert*, Schriftenreihe Niedersächsistche Landeszentrale für politische Bildung, Hannover 1967, p.33.

76 *Staat und Recht*, 11 (1962), p. 53.

77 Hesse, op. cit., p. 9.

78 This is contrary to Hans Maier's conclusions in 'Probleme einer demokratischen Tradition in Deutschland', op. cit., p. 415; in his efforts to show historical continuity and demonstrate pre-revolutionary antecedents he injects far too great an element of patriarchal tradition into the German democratic tradition.

79 Ulrich Scheuner in 'Das Wesen des Staates und der Begriff des Politischen in der neueren Staatslehre', op. cit., pp. 253-9 seems to me to over-emphasize the 'essential' interplay between politics and the state.

80 As Horst Ehmke says in ' "Staat" und "Gesellschaft" als verfassungstheoretisches Problem', op. cit., p. 49.

81 C. J. Friedrich, *Demokratie als Herrschafts – und Lebensform*, Quelle and Meyer, Heidelberg 1959, p. 22.

82 W. Hennis, ' Aufgaben einer modernen Regierungslehre', op. cit., p. 425; reference to remarks on this subject (those of Mohl for instance) made in another context runs the risk of presenting the nineteenth-century problems in an unhistorical light.

83 Hesse, op. cit., p. 79.

84 K. Sontheimer, 'Staatsidee und staatliche Wirklichkeit heute' in Supplement to *Das Parlament* (15 April 1964), p. 7.

85 Theodor Heuss, *Formkräfte einer politischen Stilbildung*, Schriftenreihe der Deutschen Hochschule für Politik, Berlin and Bonn 1952; on this subject see also Arnd Morkel, 'Uber den politischen Stil' and Klaus Eckhard Jordan, 'Zur Verwendung des Stilarguments in der BRD' in PVS, 7 (1966), pp. 119 et seq., 97 et seq.; W. Hennis, 'Zum Begriff und Problem des politischen Stils' in *Gesellschaft, Staat, Erziehung*, 9 (1964), pp. 225 et seq. On the constitutional angle see Karl Josef Partsch, *Von der Würde des Staates*, Mohr, Tübingen 1967, pp. 7 et seq.

86 Ernst Fraenkel, 'Die Wissenschaft von der Politik und die Gesellschaft' in *Gesellschaft, Staat, Erziehung*, 8 (1963), p. 284.

87 See Wolfgang Mommsen, *Max Weber und die deutsche Politik*, Mohr, Tübingen 1959, p. 273; Dolf Sternberger, 'Max Weber's Lehre von der Legitimität' in *Macht und Ohnmacht des Politischen* (dedicated to Michael Freund), Kiepenheuer & Witsch, Cologne 1967, pp. 111 et seq.

88 K. D. Bracher, 'Parlamentarische Demokratie und Notstand' in *Frankfurter Hefte*, 20 (1965), pp. 699 et seq.

Chapter 2   The Old School of Liberalism—Dahlmann on Politics and History

1 F. C. Dahlmann, *Die Politik auf den Grund und des Mass der gegebenen Verhältnisse zurückgeführt*, Göttingen 1835, Leipzig 1847; reprint with introduction by O. Westphal, Hobbing, Berlin 1920 (*Klassiker der Politik*, vol. 12), para. 266.

2 Personal files of Faculty of Philosophy, Bonn. See also Friedrich von Bezold, *Geschichte der Rheinischen Friedrich-Wilhelms-Universität von der Gründung bis zum Jahr 1870*, Marcus & Webel, Bonn 1920, pp. 351 et seq., 413 et seq.; this book is based on detailed research into the University's files.

3 In addition to A. Springer, *F. C. Dahlmann*, two vols, Leipzig 1870-2 there are the following more recent accounts: H. Christern, *F. C. Dahlmanns politische Entwicklung bis 1848. Ein Beitrag zur Geschichte des deutschen Liberalismus*, Haessel Verlag, Leipzig 1921; O. Scheel, 'Der junge Dahlmann' in *Veröffentlichungen der Schleswig-Holstein Universitäts-Gesellschaft*, III. (1925); E. R. Huber, *F. C. Dahlmann und die deutsche Verfassungsbewegung*, Hanseatische Verlagsanstalt, Hamburg 1937; E. Angermann in *Neue Deutsche Biographie*, vol. 3, Duncker & Humblot, Berlin 1957; G. P. Gooch, *Studies in German History*, Longmans, London, New York, Toronto 1948.

4 Christern, op. cit., pp. 23 et seq.

5 F. Meinecke, *Weltbürgertum und Nationalstaat*, Oldenbourg, Munich 1928, in particular pp. 206 et seq.

6 Reproduced by C. Varrentrap in *Zeitschrift für schleswig-holsteinische Geschichte*, 17 (1887), p. 52.

7 See detailed account in Springer, op. cit., vol. I, pp. 418 et seq.

8 F. C. Dahlmann, *Politik* - foreword to 2nd edition.

9 Ibid. para. 19.

10 Ibid. paras 7 et seq., 67 et seq.

11 Ever since his time in Kiel Dahlmann had relied on William Blackstone, *Commentaries on the Laws of England*, four vols, Clarendon Press, London 1765, of which an abbreviated version had appeared in German; he was critical of the French presentation by J. L. Lolme, *Die Verfassung von England* (German edition - Altona 1819), to which Dahlmann himself wrote the foreword.

12 Christern, op. cit., paras 100 et seq. with detailed references.

13 F. C. Dahlmann, *Politik*, para. 12.

14 Ibid. para. 198.

15 On these developments in general see Friedrich C. Sell, *Die Tragödie des deutschen Liberalismus*, Deutsche Verlagsanstalt, Stuttgart 1953, pp. 151 et seq.; Leonard Krieger, *The German Idea of Freedom*, Beacon Press, Boston 1957. See also Walther Bussmann's differing and critical comments in 'Zur Geschichte des deutschen Liberalismus im 19 Jahrhundert' in *Historische Zeitschrift*, 186 (1958), pp. 527 et seq.

16 Now available on this subject W. Bussmann, *Treitschke. Sein Welt und Geschichtsbild*, Musterschmidt Verlag, Göttingen 1952; Andreas Dorpalen, *Heinrich von Treitschke*, Yale University Press, New Haven 1957, pp. 55 et seq.

17 See pp. 44, et seq.

18 Dahlmann, *Politik*, para. 84.

19 Ibid., para. 133.

20 Ibid., para. 103.

21 Ibid., para. 137.

22 Ibid., para. 203.

23 See my article 'Widerstandrecht' in E. Fraenkel and K. D. Bracher, *Staat und Politik*, Westdeutscher Verlag, Cologne and Opladen (new edition 1964), pp. 371 et seq. (with sources).

24 Dahlmann, *Politik*, para. 199.

25 Ibid., paras 202 et seq.

26 Ibid., para. 207.

27 In this connection there exist two very full accounts of political science during this period, both generally (and wrongly) forgotten – Robert von Mohl, *Geschichte und Literatur der Staatswissenschaften*, three vols, Erlangen 1855–8 (reprinted by Akademische Druck & Verlagsanstalt Graz 1960), and J. C. Bluntschli, *Geschichte des Allgemeinen Staatsrechts und der Politik*, privately published, Munich 1864. On Dahlmann see Mohl, vol. 3, p. 391 and Bluntschli pp. 578 et seq.

28 For details see K. D. Bracher, W. Sauer and G. Schulz, *Die nationalsozialistische Machtergreifung*, Westdeutscher Verlag, Cologne 1960, pp. 263 et seq. and elsewhere.

29 Dahlmann, *Politik*, paras 23, 139 et seq.

30 L. von Ranke, *Werke*, vol. 24, Duncker & Humblot, Berlin, pp. 280 et seq.

31 C. Varrentrap (ed.), *F. C. Dahlmanns kleine Schriften und Reden*, Cotta, Stuttgart 1886, p. 314.

32 Ibid.

33 H. von Treitschke, *Deutsche Geschichte im 19 Jahrhundert*, part V, Hirzel, Leipzig 1879 et seq. new edition 1927, p. 401.

34 E. Angermann, op. cit., p. 480,

35 Bluntschli, op. cit., p. 583.

36 R. Stadelmann, *Soziale und politische Geschichte der Revolution 1848*, Münchener Verlag, Munich 1948.

37 H. von Treitschke, *Historische und politische Aufsätze*, Vol. 1, Hirzel, Leipzig 1886, p. 397.

38 See also O. H. von der Gablentz, *Die politischen Theorien seit der Französischen Revolution*, Westdeutscher Verlag, Cologne 1957, p. 36.

39 'Votum für Zulassung der Juden zum akademischen Lehramt, 24 Okt. 1847' in Varrentrap, op. cit., pp. 372 et seq.; here and in Springer, op. cit., pp. 357 et seq. are references to further remarks by Dahlmann.

40 Varrentrap, op. cit., pp. 370 et seq.

41 Dahlmann, *Politik*, para. 8, Christern, op. cit., pp. 138 et seq.

42 K. Buchheim, *Leidensgeschichte des zivilen Geistes – oder die Demokratie in Deutschland*, Kösel Verlag, Munich 1951.

43 Dahlmann, *Politik*, paras 283–9.

44 It is not therefore merely accidental that Dahlmann never wrote the second volume of his *Politik* which was intended to deal with the state's existence within the community of states.

45 Dahlmann, *Politik*, para. 281.

46 Varrentrap, op. cit. p. 313.

47 Bluntschli, op. cit., 2nd edition (1867), pp. 579 et seq.

48 Varrentrap, op. cit., pp. 261 et seq.

Chapter 4   Unpolitical Policy – Brüning

1 Gottfried Treviranus, *Das Ende von Weimar. Heinrich Brüning und seine Zeit*, Econ Verlag, Düsseldorf and Vienna 1968.

2 F. A. Hermens and Th. Scheider (eds), *Festschrift für Heinrich Brüning*, Duncker & Humblot, Berlin 1967.

3 Werner Conze, 'Die Krise des Parteienstaates in Deutschland' in *Historische Zeitschrift (HZ)*, 178 (1954), pp. 47 et seq., also in *Festschrift für Heinrich Brüning*, op. cit. ('Die Regierung Brüning', pp. 233 et seq.). See also new edition of my *Die Auflösung der Weimarer Republik*, Ring Verlag, Villingen 1971.

4 Karl Otmar Freiherr von Aretin, 'Ein Reichskanzler im Wettlauf mit der Zeit' in *Süddeutsche Zeitung*, (9, 10 January 1971), p. 86; Rudolf Morsey, 'Mehr Monarchist als Zentrumsmann' in *Frankfurter Allgemeine Zeitung* (5 November 1970), p. 19; Bernd-Jürgen Wendt in *Das Parlament* (19 December 1971), p. 14; Ludwig Volk; 'Brüning in eigener Sache' in *Stimmen zur Zeit*, 187 (1971), pp. 123 et seq.

5 K. D. Bracher, 'Staatsbegriff und Demokratie in Deutschland' in *Politische Vierteljahresschrift (PVS)*, 9 (1968), pp. 2 et seq.

6 On this subject see Rudolf Morsey, *Die deutsche Zentrumspartei 1917–1923*, Droste, Düsseldorf 1966, pp. 196 et seq., 607 et seq.

7 Heinrich Brüning, *Memoiren*, Westdeutscher Verlagsanstalt, Stuttgart, 1970, p. 34.

8 Rüdiger Robert Beer, *Brüning*, Politische Wissenschaftsverlag, Berlin 1931, p. 54.

9 In spring 1931 he told Hindenburg that 'the most important' of his five main duties was 'while adhering to the constitution, gradually to reinforce the authority of the Head of State *vis-à-vis* parliament so that, apart from a vote of no-confidence which was of limited application, the Head of State could basically decide upon the composition of the government.' In autumn 1931 Brüning told the President:

> 'After eighteen months, without violating the constitution, I have reached the position today when, except for the continuing abuse of the threat of withdrawal of confidence, the powers of parliament are restricted to those of the Bismarckian period; at the same time, however, I have created for the Head of State an actual range of power greater than the Kaiser ever possessed'.

(*Memoiren*, op. cit., p. 274, 387).

10 Arnold Brecht, *Prelude to Silence*, Oxford University Press, London 1944.

11 Ernst Deuerlein, 'Heinrich Brüning und seine Memoiren', West German Radio programme of 11 January 1971, manuscript pp. 30 et seq.

12 K.D. Bracher, 'Nationalsozialistische Machtergreifung und Reichskondordat' Hessische Landesregierung, Wiesbaden 1956, p. 60.

Chapter 5 Gravedigger of Democracy—Papen

1 Franz von Papen, *Vom Scheitern einer Demokratie 1930–1933*, Hase & Koehler, Mainz 1968.

Chapter 9 Theodor Heuss and the Foundation of the Federal Republic

1 Theodor Heuss, *Zur Kunst dieser Gegenwart*, Wunderlich, Tübingen 1956, pp. 13 et seq. and *Geist der Politik*, Fischer Bücherei, Frankfurt 1964, pp. 107 et seq.

2 For biography see Hans-Heinrich Welchert, *Theodor Heuss: Ein Lebensbild* (expanded edition), Athenäum Verlag, Bonn 1959; Margret Boveri and Walter Prinzing, *Theodor Heuss*, Vorwerk, Stuttgart 1954.

3 Theodor Heuss archives, Stuttgart, 'Bemerkungen zur Bundespräsidenten-Frage' (December 1958), p. 8. The archives allowed me to use extracts from their material, for which I am indebted to the custodian, Dr Eberhard Pikart. Page references are to the original text.

4 The most detailed account is that of Peter Merkl, *The Origin of the West*

German Republic, Oxford University Press, New York 1963, pp. 58 et seq.; see also Alfred Grosser, *La Démocratie de Bonn*, Colin, Paris 1958, pp. 35 et seq., 59 et seq.; Richard Hiscocks, *Democracy in Western Germany*, Oxford University Press, London, New York, Toronto 1957, pp. 44 et seq.; John F. Golay, *The Founding of the Federal Republic of Germany*, University of Chicago Press, 1958, pp. 18 et seq. (with special reference to the role of the occupying powers). Also of importance are: Thomas Ellwein, *Das Regierungssystem der Bundesrepublik Deutschland*, Westdeutscher Verlag, Cologne and Opladen 1963; Friedrich Karl Fromme, *Von der Weimarer Verfassung zum Bonner Grundgesetz*, Mohr, Tübingen 1960. Basic and comprehensive documentation is to be found in 'Entstehungsgeschichte der Artikel des Grundgesetzes' in *Jahrbuch des Öffentlichen Rechts der Gegenwart*, N.F.1 (1951).

5 Theodor Heuss, *Erinnerungen 1905–1933*, Wunderlich, Tübingen 1963, foreword p. 12 (he clearly hoped to be able to write the sequel).

6 Theodor Heuss archives: letter dated 30 October 1953, to Erich Eyck.

7 Composition was: CDU 27, SPD 27, FDP 5, German Party, Centre Party, and Communist Party 2 each and 5 representatives from Berlin.

8 Parliamentary Council, shorthand record, vol. 1 pp. 40–6 (3rd session).

9 Proceedings of German Reichstag, shorthand record, vol. 446, pp. 2587–93 (63rd session of 5th electoral period). Also in Heuss, *Erinnerungen 1905–1933*, op. cit., pp. 419 et seq.

10 Reinhold Maier in his recently published memoirs (*Ein Grundstein wird gelegt – Die Jahre 1945–1947*, Wunderlich, Tübingen 1964, p. 117) tells the story that Heuss was called the Minister of Culture 'minus the -ure' (these memoirs give a vivid picture of politics in Stuttgart at the time). In fact the title *Kultminister* instead of *Kultusminister* was an old Württemberg tradition.

11 Parliamentary Council, op. cit., p. 210 (10th session, 8 May 1949). Also in Theodor Heuss, *Die grossen Reden – Der Staatsmann*, Wunderlich, Tübingen 1965, p. 86.

12 Hiscocks, op. cit., pp. 44 et seq.

13 Parliamentary Council, op. cit., p. 40 (3rd session, 9 September 1948).

14 Theodor Heuss, 'Verhältniswahl und Parlamentarismus' in *Zeitschrift für Politik*, 20 (1931), pp. 312 et seq.

15 Parliamentary Council, op. cit., p. 231 (10th session, 8 May 1949). Also in Theodor Heuss, *Die grossen Reden*, op. cit., vol. 1, p. 86. See also his impassioned appeal (opposing Heinrich von Brentano) at the 8th session on 24 February 1949 (pp. 132 et seq.), the general sense of which was: a dogmatic attitude on the subject of the franchise is a sort of 'substitute religion'; today the majority voting rule hampers the election of the right personalities, particularly women.

16 For discussion of the federalist structure see Merkl, op. cit., pp. 28 et seq.

17 Heuss, *Erinnerungen 1905–1933*, op. cit., p. 248.

18 Parliamentary Council, op. cit., p. 44 (3rd session, 9 September 1948).

19 On this point and below see K. D. Bracher, 'Die zweite Demokratie in Deutschland, Strukturen und Probleme' in *Die Demokratie im Wandel der Gesellschaft*, Seherz, Berlin 1963, pp. 114 et seq. (now available in K. D. Bracher, *Deutschland zwischen Demokratie und Diktatur*, Scherz, Berne and Munich 1964, pp. 110 et seq.).

20 Parliamentary Council, op. cit., p. 44 (3rd session, 9 September 1948).

21 Maier, op. cit., pp. 287 et seq.

22 Quoted from Welchert, op. cit., p. 167. Here Heuss is entirely consistent with the views he put forward when analysing his own position in front of the DDP (German Democratic Party) during the Weimar period (see Bernhard Harms (ed.), *Volk und Reich der Deutschen*, vol. II, Hobbing, Berlin 1929, p. 118):

> 'Democracy cannot afford to disregard the importance of religious forces in the people's make-up; it will therefore not merely "tolerate" incorporation of religious instruction into the educational system but will regard it as natural; it will never, however, permit the nation-wide unitary character of the educational system to be shattered by acceptance of some division of schools on basically confessional lines. There may be some minor educational advantages in a divided school system but democracy must ensure that the imperative nation-wide sense of community among the people is not impaired.'

23 Heuss, *Die grossen Reden*, op. cit., p. 153.

24 Parliamentary Council, op. cit., pp. 74 et seq. (6th session, 10 October 1948).

25 On this debate see also 'Entstehungsgeschichte der Artikel des Grundgesetzes', op. cit., p. 21.

26 See *Bulletin of the Federal Government's Press and Information Office*, 169 (15 September 1959), p. 1694. Also in Heuss, *Die grossen Reden*, op. cit., p. 306.

27 Parliamentary Council, op. cit., p. 75 (6th session, 20 October 1948).

28 Ibid., p. 76.

29 Ibid., p, 42 (10th session, 8 May 1948).

30 Parliamentary Council – proceedings of main committee, shorthand record, p. 7 (session of 5 October 1948).

31 Parliamentary Council, op. cit., p. 176 (9th session, 6 May 1949).

32 'Entstehungsgeschichte der Artikel des Grundgesetzes', op. cit., pp. 89 et seq.

33 Parliamentary Council, op. cit., p. 209 (10th session, 8 May 1949). Also in Heuss, *Die grossen Reden*, op. cit., pp. 72–87.

34 Welchert op. cit., p. 194.

35 Parliamentary Council, op. cit., p. 209 (10th session, 8 May 1949). Also in Heuss, *Die Grossen Reden* op. cit., p. 83.

36 Ibid. See also his speech when awarded a Doctorate of Theology in Tübingen, 'Grenzfragen des Religiösen und Politischen' in *Universitas*, 8 (1953), pp. 897 et seq. including discussion of the problem of 'secularization'.

37 Parliamentary Council, op. cit., p. 209 (10th session, 8 May 1949). Also in Heuss, *Die grossen Reden*, op. cit., p. 185.

38 Ibid., pp. 210–87.

39 See Fromme, op. cit.; also Bracher, *Deutschland zwischen Demokratie und Diktatur*, op. cit., pp. 36 et seq. and *Auflösung der Weimarer Republik*, Ring Verlag, Villingen 1964, pp. 303 et seq.

40 'Entstehungsgeschichte der Artikel des Grundgesetzes', op. cit., p. 397; see also Heuss's discussion of the plan for a 'directorate of three' under the admittedly very different conditions of 1848–9 in Heuss, *Ein Vermächtnis – Werk und Erbe von 1848*, Wunderlich, Tübingen 1963, p. 122.

41 'Entstehungsgeschichte der Artikel des Grundgesetzes', op. cit., pp. 422 et seq.

42 Hiscocks, op. cit. p. 63.

43 See Heidenheimer, *The Governments of Germany*, Methuen, London and New York 1961, p. 94. The fact that members of the President's Office can be present at Cabinet committees – in the case of the Federal Defence Council, for instance, the President's office is represented by the State Secretary – may play some part here. On the importance of these committees see Wilhelm Hennis, *Richtlinienkompetenz und Regierungstechnik*, Mohr, Tübingen 1964, p. 23.

44 Heuss, *Die grossen Reden*, op. cit., pp. 109–19.

45 *Bulletin of the Federal Government's Press and Information Office*, op. cit., 161.

46 Theodor Heuss archives, Heuss in a letter dated 18 January 1955 to Moritz Julius Bonn.

47 Ibid., Heuss in a letter dated 10 June 1954 to Fritz Ernst.

48 Parliamentary Council, proceedings of main committee, shorthand record, p. 132 (11th session, 30 November 1948).

49 Parliamentary Council, op. cit., p. 42 (3rd session, 9 September 1948).

50 Heidenheimer, op. cit., p. 92; Hiscocks, op. cit., p. 120.

51 'Bonn – 12 September 1949'. Two addresses by Theodor Heuss, Bonn 1949, p. 4. Also in Heuss, *Die grossen Reden*, op. cit., p. 89.

52 Welchert, op. cit., p. 149. In the opinion of Alfred Grosser (op. cit., p. 82) he played a greater part than anyone except Adenauer (the Chairman) and Carlo Schmid.

53 Theodor Heuss archives: Heuss to Rudolph Woche through the secretariat, (13 September 1961).

54 Welchert, op. cit., p. 178.

55 Thilo Ramm, *Theodor Heuss. Ein Gedenkvortrag*, W. Schmitz, Giessen 1964, p. 9.

56 Heuss, *Erinnerungen 1905–1933*, op. cit., pp. 302 et seq., where he gives a short but brilliant character sketch of Schmitt: 'By confining politics to a "friend–foe" relationship he gave the coming generation a battle-cry and the Hitler regime a form of logistic justification for any act of violence.' Schmitt, Heuss continued, was 'the most striking example . . . of a clever self-assured man who throughout his career had contrived to rid himself of the tiresome burden of a conscience' – it should be added that well-known supporters are still singing Schmitt's praises today in a work dedicated to him. See also Eduard Spranger, 'Theodor Heuss' in *Universitas*, 14 (1959), pp. 1121 et seq.; in his view Heuss's most important contribution was the removal from politics of the friend–foe pattern of relationships.

57 Welchert, op. cit., p. 254.

58 Ibid., p. 147.

59 'Bonn – 12 September 1949', op. cit., p. 12–98.

60 Ibid., p. 3f.–89.

61 These controversial problems particularly the events culminating in the withdrawal of the expression of opinion demanded by Heuss from the Federal Constitutional Court, require further clarification. Heuss set out his viewpoint in an address over the radio on 10 December 1952 and a letter to Alfred Grosser dated 8 July 1960 referring to the latter's criticism in his book (op. cit., p. 81). Both are in the Heuss archives.

62 *Information Bulletin*, op. cit., 169; also in Heuss, *Die grossen Reden*, op. cit., pp. 302 et seq.

63 Heuss archives, Heuss in a letter dated 30 October 1953 to Margret Boveri.

64 Ibid., letter dated 13 December 1953 to Thomas Dehler.

65 Ramm, op. cit., p. 13.

66 Theodor Heuss, 'Über Massstäbe geschichtlicher Würdigung' in H. Heimpel, T. Heuss and B. Reifenberg (ed.), *Die grossen Deutschen*, vol. 1, Propyläen Verlag, Berlin 1956, p. 17.

67 Theodor Heuss, *Staat und Volk im Werden. Reden in und über Israel*, Ner Tamid Verlag, Munich 1960, pp. 9–27 et seq.

68 Heuss archives, letter dated 20 October 1951 to H. Callies.

69 *Die grossen Deutschen*, op. cit., vol. 1, p. 10.

70 'Bonn – 12 September 1949', op. cit., pp. 7–92 et seq.

71 Heuss, *Die grossen Reden*, op. cit., pp. 224 et seq.

72 Heuss, *Staat und Volk im Werden*, op. cit., p. 90.

73 Heuss, *Die grossen Reden*, op. cit., p. 262.

74 Grosser, op. cit., p. 80; Heuss himself also occasionally used the term 'subsidiary'.

75 Heuss, *Erinnerungen 1905–1933*, op. cit., p. 225.

76 Heuss, *Die grossen Reden*, op. cit., p. 289 and *Geist der Politik*, op. cit., p. 62.

77 Welchert, op. cit., pp. 196 et seq.

78 'Formkräfte einer politischen Stilbildung' in Theodor Heuss, *Die grossen Reden*, op. cit., pp. 184–223; also in *Schriftenreihe der Deutschen Hochschule für Politik*, Colloquium Verlag, Berlin 1952.

79 Heuss, *Die grossen Reden*, op. cit., p. 294 and *Geist der Politik*, op. cit., p. 65.

80 He was an even greater stranger to anything irrational, diabolical or intemperate in politics and this may explain the criticism of his attitude in 1933 and perhaps in 1952 – see Ramm, op. cit., pp. 10 et seq.

81 Heuss archives, Heuss in a letter dated 18 February 1958 to M. J. Bonn.

82 Ibid., letter dated 8 July 1960 to Alfred Grosser.

83 Hiscocks, op. cit., p. 120.

84 Heuss archives: letter dated 10 August 1955 to M. J. Bonn.

85 Ibid., letter dated 21 September 1955 to Albrecht Goes. On this problem see also Klaus Bölling, *Die zweite Republik*, Kiepenheuer & Witsch, Cologne 1963, pp. 315 et seq.

86 In his commemorative address (given at the 15th Congress of German sociologists in Heidelberg in April 1964) Theodor W. Adorno gave a highly important character sketch of Theodor Heuss. The following extract is taken from *Die Welt*, 17, 9 May 1964:

'It would be wrong to pay tribute to his memory without laying emphasis upon that whereby he left his mark on history and ensured that his name would remain immortal wherever the concept of German democracy is taken seriously. Allow me to try and describe briefly the significance of Heuss as a sociological figure, as a social character, what he, as an individual, represented in this society and its political constitution.

In the first place Heuss, as the first German Head of State since anyone can remember, was a civilian through and through. His famous remark when on manoeuvres "Now let's have a fine victory" removed from military training its connotation of violence and substituted that of humanity; this was typical of the man; all sabre-rattling, whether in the literal or metaphorical sense of the word, was foreign to him, not merely contrary to his beliefs. There was nothing in his nature of that respect for organized force which has been the bane of the German State. As Hegel or the Old Pythagoreans would have said, to him it was second nature to try to be a good citizen of a good state; he would probably have had great difficulty in conceiving the Head of State as the bronze statue of some imperious figure. By his manner of life alone, not primarily by what he said, he has constructed a picture of the Representative of the state and so of the state itself, unpretentious, sober, clean, disassociated from the use of force, such as has not been seen in Germany before. No effort on his part would be required to remain true to this picture.

Secondly: he was an intellectual. Ever since Goebbels coined the phrase "intellectual beast" the intellectual has been an object of suspicion in Germany as a type divorced from society because he labours with his mind; the form of his work, however, allows of no naïveté either as regards his own self-preservation or in his thinking; Heuss has removed this slur on the intellectual. As Head of State he was not afraid to use his pen instead of the sword. At the same time, however, as an intellectual, he showed certain paradoxical traits of naïveté calculated to propitiate those who retained their hatred of the intellectual even after the fall of Hitler. He possessed one of the rarest and best virtues of the intellectual, the capacity to broaden his outlook . . .

From the sociological point of view, however, the astonishing fact, which I would emphasize, is that, although he carried the stigma of the civilian and the intellectual, Heuss became popular – in the true sense of the word, not by ingratiating himself or using shirt-sleeve diplomacy methods. He restored to the term popularity, which despite all the differences is allied to the term democracy in more than the etymological sense, something of the unvarnished truth of which the Nazi "popular community" had robbed it. The know-alls are always assuring us that anyone who does not appear with an air of authority and does not at the same time flatter the people – both are given as the recipe for success in "Mein Kampf" – has no prospect of becoming a model for society or, more simply, of imposing his views on the masses. This Heuss disproved, as if by an unintentional sociological experiment. Between him and the allegedly faceless and antagonised masses there existed something scarcely conceivable – contact without demagogy. Successful demagogues resemble their adherents, differing from them only in that they allow the repressed instincts and desires of those adherents to permeate their own consciousness; Heuss, on the other hand, mirrored the millions who clung to him, not for any political power he possessed but because for them he personified an idea more deep-rooted than their collective Nazism, that of being citizen of a world in which fear no longer had any place. This idea and its German tradition, far more wide-spread than the ideas of nationalism, cannot be dislodged. Its strength lies in the fact that it promises men what they really yearn for, something which has been pushed into the background by their evil dreams of power and glory. Nevertheless Heuss was by no means soft; he was no humanitarian preacher; he was wilful, to some extent jealous of his right of freedom and this accorded very well with that which his office demanded of him. He had a certain incalculability – even the most familiar personalities possess some strange streak – which must have infinitely endeared him to men. He was typical of the type of personality which can only flourish when freedom has been universally assured. For him dialect was man's true means of self-expression and so, as seldom before in the field of German politics, Heuss turned humanity into a force which awoke an echo in the breasts of the masses.

After all this it is no mere verbiage to say that he will remain unforgettable. What he was must not be forgotten if German society is ever to rise to the height which has always been denied it but which, for a short time, was plain for all to see in the person of Theodor Heuss.'

87 Parliamentary Council, proceedings of main committee, op. cit., p. 45 (session of 18 January 1949).
88 Heuss, *Die grossen Reden*, op. cit., p. 281 and *Geist der Politik*, op. cit., p. 57.
89 Ibid., pp. 65, 284.
90 Heuss archives, Heuss in a letter dated 8 July 1960 to Alfred Grosser.
91 Heuss, *Erinnerungen 1905–1933*, op. cit., p. 12.
92 Welchert, op. cit., pp. 246 et seq.
93 Arnold Heidenheimer, *Adenauer and the CDU*, Nijhoff, The Hague 1960, pp. 221 et seq.; Grosser, op. cit., pp. 351 et seq.; Heuss archives, Arnold Brecht in a letter to Heuss dated 8 June 1959 (expressing doubts about Adenauer's candidature on constitutional and political grounds).
94 Heuss archives: Heuss to R. Woche through the secretariat on 13 September 1961.
95 Ibid., comments on the question of the federal presidency.
96 *Information Bulletin*, op. cit., 169.
97 Ibid., see p. 1693.
98 Heuss, *Staat und Volk im Werden*, op. cit., p. 89.
99 Heuss archives, Heuss to R. Woche through the secretariat on 13 January 1961.
100 See review of Heuss's *Erinnerungen 1905–1933*, op. cit. in *Der Politologe*, 5, 15 (1964), pp. 15 et seq.

Chapter 12   Democracy and Political Parties – Theory and Practice

1 See now the comprehensive work by Eleonore Sterling, *Der unvollkommene Staat*, Europäische Verlagsanstalt, Frankfurt 1965, pp. 15 et seq.
2 Erwin Faul, 'Verfemung, Duldung und Anerkennung des Parteiwesens in der Geschichte des politischen Denkens' in *Politische Vierteljahresschrift* (PVS), 5 (1964), p. 61.
3 M. I. Ostrogorski, *La démocratie et l'organisation des partis politiques*, Calmann Lévy, Paris 1901.
4 Robert Michels, *Zur Soziologie des Parteiwesens*, Kröne, Leipzig 1925.
5 Sigmund Neumann, *Die deutschen Parteien*, Kohlhammer, Stuttgart 1965.
6 Sigmund Neumann, *Modern Political Parties*, University of Chicago Press, 1956.

7 Gerhard Leibholz, *Strukturprobleme der modernen Demokratie*, C. F. Müller, Karlsruhe 1958.

8 Niels Diederich, *Empirische Wahlforschung*, Westdeutscher Verlag, Cologne and Opladen, 1965.

9 Maurice Duverger, *Political Parties: Their Organisation and Activity in the Modern State*, translated Barbara and Robert North, Methuen, London, John Wiley, New York 1954.

10 George Lavau, *Partis politiques et réalités sociales*, Cahiers de la Fondation Nationale des Sciences Politiques, Paris 1953.

11 Robert MacKenzie, *British Political Parties*, Heinemann, London 1955; V. O. Key, *Politics, Parties and Pressure Groups*, Thomas Y. Cowell, New York 1948.

12 See criticism in *Political Studies*, VIII, 2 (1959); *Journal of Politics*, 21 (1959), pp. 303 et seq. and 19 (1957), pp. 423 et seq.

13 Ludwig Bergsträsser, *Geschichte der politischen Parteien in Deutschland*, Olzog, Munich 1965; Walter Tormin, *Geschichte der deutschen Parteien seit 1848*, Kohlhammer, Stuttgart 1966.

14 Thomas Nipperdey, *Die Organisation der deutschen Parteien vor 1918*, Droste, Düsseldorf 1961.

15 Wolf-Dieter Narr, *CDU-SPD, Programme und Praxis seit 1945*, Kohlhammer, Stuttgart 1966.

16 Heinz-Josef Varain, *Parteien und Verbände*, Westdeutscher Verlag, Cologne 1965.

17 Ossip K. Flechtheim, *Dokumente zur partei-politischen Entwicklung in Deutschland seit 1945*, seven vols, Dokumenten Verlag Wendler, Berlin 1962 et seq.

18 Hans-Gerd Schumann, *Die politischen Parteien in Deutschland nach 1945*, Bernard & Graefe, Frankfurt 1967.

19 For instance Ulrich Dübber, *Parteifinanzierung in Deutschland*, Westdeutscher Verlag. Cologne and Opladen 1962; Ulrich Lohmar, *Innerparteiliche Demokratie*, Enke, Stuttgart 1969.

20 R. F. Gray, 'Political parties in new African nations' in *Comparative Studies in Society and History*, 5 (1962–3), pp. 449 et seq. – discussion and criticism; also Alan Angell, 'Party systems in Latin America' in *Political Quarterly*, 37 (1966), pp. 309 et seq.

21 Harvey C. Mansfield, 'Whether party government is inevitable' in *Political Science Quarterly*, 80 (1965), pp. 517 et seq.

22 See discussion, 'The dead end of the monolithic parties' in *Government and Opposition*, 2 (1967), pp. 165 et seq.; K. D. Bracher, *Die deutsche Diktatur*, Kiepenheuer & Witsch, Cologne 1969, pp. 6 et seq., 247 et seq.

23 Of particular value now, after the works by Ernst Richert and Carola Stern is Peter Ludz, *Parteielite im Wandel*, Westdeutscher Verlag, Cologne and Opladen 1967.

24 Karl Loewenstein, *Political Power and the Governmental Process*, Cambridge University Press, London, University of Chicago Press, 1959; see also K. D. Bracher, *Deutschland zwischen Demokratie und Diktatur*, Scherz, Berne and Munich 1964.

25 *Politische Vierteljarhresschrift*, 4 (1964), pp. 307 et seq. and 6 (1965), pp. 41 et seq.

26 Daniel Bell, *The End of Ideology*, Free Press, New York, Macmillan, London 1965.

27 'Der Wandel des westeuropäischen Parteiensystems' in *Politische Vierteljahres-schrift*, 6 (1965), pp. 25 et seq.

28 Th. Low, 'Towards Functionalism in Political Science' in *American Political Science Review*, 57 (1963), pp. 570 et seq.

Publication Register

Part I   The Problem of the German State

Chapter 1   Concept of the State and Democracy in Germany
Opening Address at Conference of German Association for Political Science in Munich 1967, published in *Politische Vierteljahresschrift*, 9th year, Westdeutscher Verlag, Cologne and Opladen 1968, folio 1, pp. 2–27.

Chapter 2   The Old School of Liberalism – Dahlmann on Politics and History
Sections 1, 3 and 4: 'Über das Verhältnis von Politik und Geschichte', speech given on 5 December 1960 in memory of Friedrich Christoph Dahlmann on the hundreth anniversary of his death (1961), Peter Hanstein Verlag, Bonn.
Section 2: 'Friedrich Christoph Dahlmann' in *Bonner Gelehrte. Beiträge zur Geschichte der Wissenschaften in Bonn. 150 Jahre Rheinische Friedrich Wilhelms Universität Bonn*, H. Bouvier Verlag & Ludwig Röhrscheid Verlag, Bonn 1966.

Chapter 3   Weimar in Retrospect
Unpublished.

Chapter 4   Unpolitical Policy – Brüning
'Die unpolitische Politik: Brüning und die Auflösung der Weimarer Republik' in *Vierteljahrshefte für Zeitgeschichte* (1971).

Chapter 5   Gravedigger of Democracy – Papen
'Vom Mörder einer Demokratie. Über Franz von Papen: *Vom Scheitern einer Demokratie*' in *Der Spiegel*, 16 (1968), pp. 160–4.

Chapter 6   Gleichschaltung of the Universities
'Die Gleichschaltung der deutschen Universität' in *Nationalsozialismus und die deutsche Universität*, de Gruyter, Berlin 1966, pp. 126–42.

Chapter 7   Loyalty to the State and Resistance
Section 1: 'Staatsgesinnung und Widerstand' in *Stuttgarter Zeitung* (26 February 1970), pp. 14 et seq.
Sections 2, 3 and 4: 'Der 20 Juli – Vergangenheit und Gegenwart' in *Recht, Gerechtigkeit und Gewalt*, lectures at 14th German Evangelical Church Assembly, Stuttgart 1969, Kreuz Verlag, Stuttgart, pp. 34–52.

Part II   Germany's Second Democracy

Chapter 8   Changes in Western Europe
Unpublished.

Chapter 9   Theodor Heuss and the Foundation of the Federal Republic
'*Theodor Heuss und die Wiederbegründung der Demokratie in Deutschland*, published by Theodor Heuss archives, Rainer Wunderlich Verlag, Tübingen 1965, pp. 9–57.

Chapter 10   Salient Features of the Adenauer Era
Sections 1–4: 'Weichenstellungen deutscher Politik in den Anfängen der Bundesrepublik' in *Die moderne Demokratie und ihr Recht* (dedicated to Gerhard Leibholz), J. C. B. Mohr (Paul Siebeck) Verlag, Tübingen 1966, pp. 15–34.
Sections 5–7: 'Zwischen Stabilisierung und Stagnation: Die mittleren Jahre der Ära Adenauer' in *Gesellschaft, Recht und Politik*, (dedicated to Wolfgang Abendroth for his sixtieth birthday), Luchterhand Verlag, Neuwied 1968, pp. 45–61.

Chapter 11   The Bonn Party System
In *Nach 25 Jahren*, Kindler Verlag, Munich 1970, pp. 254–76.

Part III   Political Criteria

Chapter 12   Democracy and Political Parties – Theory and Practice
In *Saeculum*, Verlag Karl Albert, Freiburg & Munich 1970, folios 2–3, pp. 274–86.

Chapter 13   Nationalism and Internationalism
Article 'Nationalismus und Internationalismus' in *Fischer Lexikon*, 7 (Frankfurt 1969).

Chapter 14   Racialism and Politics
Article 'Rassismus' in *Fischer Lexikon* 7, (Frankfurt 1969).

Chapter 15   On Imperialism
Article 'Imperialismus' in *Fischer Lexikon* 7, (Frankfurt 1969).

Chapter 16   Democracy and Emergency Legislation
Section entitled 'Notstand' in 'Politik für Nichtpolitiker' in Hans-Jürgen Schulz (ed.), *Ein ABC zur aktuellen Diskussion*, Kreuz Verlag, Stuttgart 1970, pp. 15–24.

Chapter 17   Peace and War
In *Fischer Lexikon* 7 (Frankfurt 1969).

Index

Name Index

Abendroth, Wolfgang, 251
Adenauer, Konrad, 151–3, 157, 167, 169, 170, 171, 174, 176, 180–1, 183, 188, 190, 192–8, 200–10, 215, 216, 219, 220, 222, 223, 225, 229, 230
Alleman, Fritz René, 50
Almond, Gabriel, 5, 261
Anrich, Ernst, 94
Anschütz, Gerhard, 17
Aristotle, 236, 237
Arndt, Adolf, 10, 228
Arnold, Karl, 219
Aron, Raymond, 258

Baden, Max von, 57
Bagehot, Walter, 168
Barth, Karl, 117, 165
Bauer, Otto, 256, 273
Beck, Ludwig, 120, 131
Becker, Max, 168
Bell, Daniel, 251
Bergsträsser, Ludwig, 164, 228, 240
Besson, Waldemar, 107, 110
Bethge, Eberhard, 112
Bismarck, Otto von, 7, 8, 32, 56, 73, 105, 178
Bloch, Ernst, 263
Blomberg, Werner von, 62

Blücher, Franz, 229
Bluntschli, Johann Caspar, 42, 47–8
Boas, Franz, 266
Bodelschwingh, Friedrich von, 165
Bolz, Eugen, 104, 107, 110–11, 131
Bonhoeffer, Dietrich, 112, 117–18, 122, 125–6
Boniface, 171
Bonn, Moritz-Julius, 174
Brandt, Willy, 154, 225, 226, 227
Brauer, Max, 227
Braun, Otto, 54
Brecht, Arnold, 63, 76, 174
Bredow, Ferdinand Eduard von, 120
Brentano, Heinrich von, 198, 207
Brentano, Lujo, 34
Brüning, Heinrich, 54, 65, 69–79, 81, 84, 85, 110, 170, 281
Buber, Martin, 172
Buchheim, Karl, 26, 175
Bülau, Friedrich, 35
Burckhardt, Jakob, 87
Burke, Edmund, 36
Buss, Franz Joseph, 34
Butte, Wilhelm, 35

Canaris, Wilhelm, 122
Chamberlain, Houston Stewart, 264

Churchill, Sir Winston, 181
Clausewitz, Karl von, 287
Conze, Werner, 69
Cornides, Wilhelm, 181
Cortes, Donoso, 15
Curtius, Ernst Robert, 89

Dahlmann, Friedrich Christoph, 30–48
De Gaulle, General Charles, 144–7, 154, 160, 255, 283, 285
Dehler, Thomas, 166, 168, 229
Delbrück, Johann Friedrich Ferdinand, 35
Deuerlein, Ernst, 76–7
Deutsch, Harold, 112
Deutsch, Karl, 261
Diederich, Niels, 242
Dogan, Matthei, 243
Dohnanyi, Hans von, 120, 122, 125
Döring, Wolfgang, 229
Drath, Martin, 13–14
Droysen, Johann Gustav, 34
Dulles, John Foster, 183, 187, 192, 195
Duverger, Maurice, 243, 244–6

Ebert, Friedrich, 16, 53, 55, 56, 58, 63, 64, 167, 280
Eden, Sir Anthony, 193
Ehler, Hermann, 127
Einstein, Albert, 95, 96
Eisenhower, Dwight D., 183, 187, 188, 195
Erhard, Ludwig, 205, 216, 219, 225, 227, 229
Erler, Fritz, 225
Ernst August, King of Hannover, 33
Eschenburg, Theodor, 16, 54
Eyck, Erich, 174, 176

Fallersleben, Hoffmann von, 175
Fanfani, Amintore, 148
Ferrero, Guglielmo, 276

Feuchtwanger, Lion, 98
Fichte, Johann Gottlieb, 10
Flechtheim, Ossip K., 246
Forsthoff, Ernst, 20
Fraenkel, Ernst, 107
Franck, James, 96
Frank, Hans, 19
Freisler, Roland, 111
Freund, Michael, 54
Freyer, Hans, 89, 94
Frick, Wilhelm, 82–3
Friedrich III, Emperor, 35
Friedrich, Carl Joachim, 28

Gablentz, O. H. von der, 7, 219
Gagern, Max von, 35
Gasperi, Alcide de, 148–9
Gentz, Friedrich von, 42
Gervinus, Georg Gottfried, 33, 34, 46
Glaser, Johann Karl, 34
Gneist, Rudolf, 12
Gobineau, Arthur, Count, 264
Goebbels, Joseph, 90, 158
Goerdeler, Carl, 109–10, 119, 121, 124, 125, 129
Gooch, George, 176
Gordon Walker, Patrick, 251
Görres, Joseph von, 42
Grimm, Jakob, 33
Groener, Wilhelm, 16, 74
Gross, Nikolaus, 111
Grotewohl, Otto, 186, 194, 203, 224
Gumplowitz, L., 265
Günther, H. F. K., 83

Haber, Fritz, 96
Hallstein, Walter, 195, 196, 201, 206, 208
Hammerstein, Kurt von, 85
Harnack, Adolf von, 165
Haubach, Theo, 111, 124
Hegel, Georg Wilhelm Friedrich, 6, 34, 42, 161

Heidegger, Martin, 92, 93
Heinemann, Gustav, 154, 187
Helfritz, Hans, 19
Heller, Hermann, 17
Henning, Leopold von, 34
Hennis, Wilhelm, 130
Hermens, F. A., 243
Hertz, Heinrich, 96
Heuss, Theodor, 28, 103, 156–77, 229
Hilferding, Rudolf, 273
Himmler, Heinrich, 90
Hindenburg, Oskar von, 77, 84
Hindenburg, Paul von, 11, 16, 64–7,
    72–3, 74–81, 84, 85, 167, 280, 281,
    282
Hirsch, Siegfried, 34
Hitler, Adolf, 13, 15, 19, 56, 64–6, 70,
    78, 83–5, 90, 92, 93, 98, 101, 106ff,
    113, 119–27, 135, 162, 167, 172, 176,
    178, 254, 256, 265, 271, 275, 276,
    279, 281, 282
Hobbes, Thomas, 15, 24, 25
Hobson, John A., 273
Hoffmann, Peter, 112
Hölderlin, Friedrich, 159
Huber, Ernst Rudolf, 24, 31
Huber, Kurt, 126
Hugenberg, Alfred, 64, 65, 81–3, 85,
    90, 108, 110
Husserl, Edmund, 92

Innitzer, Cardinal, 118

Jäckel, Eberhard, 107
Jahn, Friedrich Ludwig, 10
Jasper, Gotthard, 21
Jaspers, Karl, 128, 184
Jellinek, Georg, 13
Joos, Joseph, 78
Joseph II, Emperor, 34
Jünger, Ernst, 89

Kass, Ludwig, 75, 78

Kahrstedt, Ulrich, 101
Kaisen, Wilhelm, 227
Kaiser, Jakob, 171
Kant, Immanuel, 294
Kästner, Erich, 98
Kaufmann, Karl, 101
Keil, Wilhelm, 169
Ketteler, Wilhelm, 165
Key, V. O., 243
Khruschev, Nikita, 203
Kipling, Rudyard, 270
Kirchheimer, Otto, 25, 251, 252
Kleist, Heinrich von, 31
Koellreutter, Otto, 19
Kohn, Hans, 11
Kolb, Eberhard, 16
Kolping, Adolf, 165
Kopf, Hinrich, 227
Kosselleck, Reinhart, 24, 25
Krieck, Ernst, 94
Krieger, Leonard, 6
Krippendorf, Ekkehart, 248
Krockow, Graf von, 23
Krüger, Herbert, 12, 20

Lasalle, Ferdinand, 9
Lavau, George E., 243, 244, 246
Leber, Julius, 126
Lehmbruch, Gerhard, 21
Leibholz, Gerhard, 26, 27, 249
Lemmer, Ernst, 228
Lenin, 256, 273, 274
Leopold III, King of the Belgians, 149
Lepsius, M. Rainer, 11
Liebholz, Gerhard, 242
List, Friedrich, 35
Litt, Theodor, 52
Lübbe, Hermann, 11
Luther, Martin, 171
Luxemburg, Rosa, 273, 274

MacKenzie, Robert, 243

Maier, Hans, 23
Maier, Reinhold, 169, 229
Mann, Thomas, 8, 9, 71, 98, 131
Martini, Winfried, 285
Marx, Karl, 9, 256, 273, 275
Meinecke, Friedrich, 17, 32, 66, 87, 173
Meissner, Otto, 66, 74, 84
Mende, Erich, 229
Mendès-France, Pierre, 146
Mergenthaler, Christian, 110
Meyer, Conrad Ferdinand, 172
Meyerhoff, Otto, 96
Michels, Robert, 240, 245
Miller, Max, 110
Mohl, Robert von, 12, 35, 42, 51
Moltke, Helmut James von, 111, 124–125, 126
Montesquieu, Charles de Secondat, 12, 36, 237
Morgenthau, Hans, 261
Morsey, Rudolf, 17, 110
Müller, Christian, 112
Müller, Hermann, 75
Murr, Wilhelm, 110
Mussolini, Benito, 78, 148

Napoleon I, Emperor, 7, 270, 271, 276, 279
Narr, Wolf-Dieter, 246
Nasse, Erwin, 35
Naumann, Friedrich, 8, 160, 170, 172
Neumann, Franz L., 16, 276
Neumann, Sigmund, 241, 243, 246, 287
Niebuhr, Barthold Georg, 32
Niemöller, Martin, 119
Nipperdey, Thomas, 246

Oertzen, Peter von, 16
Ollenhauer, Erich, 171, 224, 225, 227
Oster, Hans, 120, 122–3, 125

Ostrogorski, M. I., 240, 245

Papen, Franz von, 13, 56, 64, 65–6, 70, 76, 79, 80–5, 281, 282
Parri, Ferrucio, 148
Pascal, Blaise, 41
Pechel, Rudolf, 80
Pfleiderer, Karl-Georg, 187
Pinder, Wilhelm 93
Pius XII, Pope, 118
Planck, Erwin, 111
Plato, 236
Plessner, Helmut, 11, 88
Polybius, 12
Preuss, Hugo, 16, 58, 59

Radbruch, Gustav, 17, 19, 72, 81, 212
Ranke, Leopold von, 42
Rapacki, Adam, 193
Raumer, Friedrich von, 34
Reichhardt, Hans J., 115
Reichmann, Eva, 53
Reichwein, Adolf, 124
Rein, Adolf, 92
Reuter, Ernst, 224, 227
Riedel, Adolph Friedrich, 34
Ritter, Gerhard, 112, 275, 289
Roon, Gerd van, 112
Roscher, Wilhelm, 34, 35
Rosenberg, Alfred, 93, 264
Rosenberg, Arthur, 16, 54
Rothfels, Hans, 86, 112
Rotteck, Karl von, 34, 42
Rousseau, Jean Jacques, 237
Russell, Bertrand, 296
Rust, Bernhard, 99

Sauer, Wolfgang, 16
Sauerbruch, Ferdinand, 93
Savigny, Friedrich Karl von, 42
Schacht, Hjalmar, 79, 82
Schattschneider, E. E., 243

Scheel, O., 229
Scheler, Max, 10
Schemm, Hans, 91
Schiller, Karl, 84
Schirach, Baldur von, 97
Schleicher, Kurt von, 64, 66, 73–4, 77, 81, 84, 85, 120
Schmid, Carlo, 164, 168, 181, 207, 227
Schmitt, Carl, 15, 17, 19, 23–5, 61, 92–3, 169, 285
Schmitthenner, F. J., 34
Schnur, Roman, 24
Scholl family, 103, 126
Schröder, Gerhard, 225
Schumacher, Kurt, 157, 167, 169, 187, 220, 223, 224
Schuman, Robert, 146
Schumann, Hans-Gerd, 246
Schumpeter, Joseph, 275
Schuschnigg, Kurt Edler von, 279
Schweitzer, Albert, 296
Seebohm, Hans-Christoph, 199
Seeckt, Hans von, 16, 62, 120
Seeley, Sir John Robert, 270
Severing, Carl, 54
Siegfried, André, 243
Sieveking, Kurt, 207
Smend, Rudolf, 86–7
Sontheimer, Kurt, 15
Spengler, Oswald, 19, 89
Spranger, Eduard, 92
Stadelmann, Rudolf, 45
Stahl, Friedrich Julius, 15, 42
Stalin, Josef, 178, 182, 184, 185, 188, 273
Stauffenberg, Claus Graf Schenck von, 112, 125, 126, 127
Stein, Karl, 32
Stein, Lorenz von, 12
Strauss, Franz-Josef, 201, 225, 257
Streicher, Gauleiter Julius, 101

Sturm, C. G. 35
Sturm, Ernst, 96
Sulzbach, Walter, 2, 54
Sybel, Heinrich von, 35

Tellkampf, Johann Ludwig, 34
Thoma, Richard, 18, 19
Tito, Josip, 184
Tocqueville, Alexis de, 42
Toynbee, Arnold, 276
Treitschke, Heinrich von, 34, 35, 39, 44, 46
Treviranus, Gottfried, 69, 74
Troeltsch, Ernst, 17
Tucholsky, Kurt, 98

Ulbricht, Walter, 203, 207

Varain, Heinz-Josef, 246
Verba, Sidney, 5
Vollgraff, Karl Friedrich, 35

Waitz, Georg, 34
Wassermann, Jakob, 98
Weber, Max, 16, 18, 28, 42, 59, 90
Weber, Werner, 20
Wehner, Herbert, 225, 227
Weisenborn, Günther, 115
Welcker, Karl Theodor, 34, 35, 42
Weyer, Willy, 229
Wichern, J. H., 165
William II, Emperor, 8, 9, 77
Willms, Bernard, 24
Windischmann, Carl Joseph, 35
Wolf, Ernst, 116
Wright, Quincy, 289, 293, 294

Zehrer, Hans, 84
Zeller, Eberhard, 112
Zinn, Georg-August, 227
Zweig, Arnold, 98
Zweig, Stefan, 98

General Index

absolutism, 6, 7, 12, 38, 43, 77, 105, 144
Abwehr, 120, 122, 125
academics and intellectuals, *see* universities
administration, 9, 18–27, 55–6, 62, 138, 250
Africa, 248, 254, 257, 260, 266, 272
Albania, 255
Allgemeine Deutsche Waffenring, 100
Anti-revolutionary Party (Netherlands), 150
anti-semitism, 46, 87, 89, 95, 97, 98, 116, 117, 118–19, 128, 265, 267–8
Arab nationalism, 255
aristocracy, 36, 60, 124
army, militarism, 61, 202; military opposition to state, 113, 114, 115, 120–1; nuclear weapons, 188, 192, 196, 201–2, 205–6, 225, 292; rearmament, 120, 180–2, 186–8, 191–2, 202, 209; *see also* Bundeswehr; Reichswehr; Wehrmacht
Asia, 248, 254, 256, 257, 266, 272
Association for Political Science, 156, 174
Austria, 118, 136, 186, 191, 256, 279
authoritarianism, 60ff, 72, 75, 81, 88, 104

autocracy, 237

Bad Godesberg, 223, 225
Balkans, 279
Basic Law, 20ff, 25, 49, 60, 68, 83, 153, 157, 160, 163–8, 171, 180–2, 220, 242, 247, 249, 278, 283
'Basic Rights of the German People', 59
Bavaria, 159, 220
Bavarian Party, 165, 214
Bavarian Peasants' League, 66
Belgium, 149–50, 257, 283; *see also* Benelux
Benelux, 146, 149–50
Berlin, 171, 176, 185, 194, 195, 198, 200, 201, 203–4, 219, 225, 261
Berlin Technical High School, 96
Berlin University, 95, 98, 101
BHE, *see* Refugees' Party
Bonn Treaties (1952), 185
Bonn University, 31, 35, 43, 44, 174
books, confiscation and burning, 93, 98
bourgeoisie, 9, 45, 63, 98, 115, 121, 146, 197
Brazil, 267
Breslau, 98, 117

Breslau University, 34, 96
Bundesrat, 56, 165, 166, 167, 168
Bundestag, 166, 167, 212
Bundeswehr, 175, 192, 201-2, 205, 284; *see also* rearmament
Bundeswehr Academy, 173, 175
bureaucracy, 9, 18-26, 55-6, 62, 138, 250

Canada, 283
capitalism, 141, 219, 273, 274-6
Catholic Church, 112, 114, 115, 118-19, 220
CDU, *see* Christian Democratic Union
Central Europe, 8, 11, 137, 139, 202
Central Labour Union, 56
Centre Party, 17, 57, 58, 60, 72, 75, 78, 81, 84, 110, 111, 214, 218, 220, 222, 241
China, 207, 255, 256, 272, 273, 275
Christian-democrat Students' Association (RCDS), 222
Christian Democratic Union (CDU), 146, 152, 159, 164, 168, 169, 187, 207, 212-14, 216, 218-24, 226-30
Christian-historical Union (Netherlands), 150
Christian-socialist Union (CSU), 165, 218
churches, opposition to the Nazis, 112-14, 116-19, 121; and party politics, 165-6, 218-19; and war, 296
civil servants, 108, 120
civil war, 121, 294
Coal and Steel Community, 145, 151, 180, 191, 205
coalitions, 61, 139, 141, 220; *see also* Great Coalition
Cold War, 137, 143, 163, 215, 218, 219, 222, 224, 287, 295

Colleges' Association, 92
Cologne, 219
Cologne University, 96
colonialism, 8, 271-2; *see also* imperialism
COMECON, 184, 260, 295
Common Market, *see* European Economic Community
communications media, 26, 47, 261
communism and communist parties, 64, 65, 82, 114, 115, 139, 140, 142, 255, 256
Communist Party (DKP), 230
Communist Party (KPD), 113, 211, 214, 230, 247
Communist Party (France), 145
Communist Party (Italy), 148, 149
concentration camps, 107, 115, 173
Confessional Church, 116, 117, 119
conformism, *see* Gleichschaltung
Congo, 266
Congress Party (India), 248
conservatism, 14, 108, 115, 116, 119, 146, 211, 220
Council of Brothers (Confessional Church), 117
Council of Europe, 180, 181, 295
CSU, *see* Christian-socialist Union
Cuba, 256, 261
currency reform, 194
Czechoslovakia, 142, 255, 261, 272, 291

DC, *see* Democrazia Cristiana.
DDP, *see* German Democratic Party
defence, *see* army; European Defence Council; NATO; peace and war
democracy, and emergency legislation, 278-86; and state, 3-29, 57, 60, 67, 136, 161, 167, 177; and political parties, 235-52; *et passim*

democratization, 7, 10, 19, 57, 105, 112, 217, 235

Democrazia Cristiana (DC), 148

Denmark, 283

Deutsche Studentenschaft, 97

DGB, *see* Trade Union League

dictatorship, 15, 79, 80, 89, 106, 109, 122, 128–9, 257, 279ff; *see also* president

disarmament, 193, 203–5, 225, 290–1

DKP, *see* Communist Party

DP, *see* German Party

DRP, *see* German Right Party

Düsseldorf, 219

East Europe, 4, 9, 125, 136ff, 142, 151, 184, 201; *see also* Soviet Union

East Germany, 27, 125, 128, 143, 171, 178–9, 183, 185–6, 191, 193–6, 199, 201–4, 206–9; *see also* partition and reunification

East-West confrontation, 136, 142, 143, 145, 154, 178ff, 255, 261

East-West *détente*, 201ff, 215

economic crises, 62, 64, 66, 73, 86

economic functions of the state, 28

economic recovery, post-war, 142, 152, 182, 197

EDC, *see* European Defence Community

Eden Plan, 193

education, 16, 17, 60, 91–2, 126, 162, 165; *see also* students; universities

EEC, *see* European Economic Community

EFTA, *see* European Free Trade Association

Egypt, 256

elections (1919), 58; (1920), 63; (1930), 65; (1932), 82; (1933), 83, 106; (1949), 212, 216; (1953), 212, 216; (1957), 197, 212, 216; (1961), 212, 216, 229; (1965), 212, 216, 229; (1969), 212, 216, 229

emergency legislation and powers, 3, 21, 29, 51, 59, 64, 65, 76, 83, 278–86

émigrés, 33, 46, 115, 174

Enabling Law (1933), 76, 78, 282

enlightened absolutism, 6, 7, 12

Essen, 84

ethnic state, 9, 254

Euratom, 191, 205

Europe, division into blocs, 136–7, 143, 145; *see also* East-West confrontation

European Defence Community (EDC), 145, 170, 185, 186, 188–90, 295

European Economic Community (EEC), 144, 145, 147, 151, 154–5, 180, 185, 191, 205, 260

European Free Trade Association (EFTA), 205, 295

European Union, 189

euthanasia, 117

Evangelical Church, 117, 119

'Evangelical Workers' Circle', 220

extermination policies, 117

extremism, 61–2, 63, 64, 65, 76, 102, 215, 216

fascism, 135, 141, 148, 247, 273

FDP, *see* Free Democrat Party

Federal Constitutional Court, 182, 231, 242, 247, 281

Federal Convention (1949), 167–9

Federal Council, *see* Bundesrat

Federal Republic, 3, 20, 21, 22, 49, 50, 68, 127, 128, 138, 146, 150ff, 156ff; *et passim*

federalism, 56, 125, 251, 270

finance, party, 22, 26, 231

Finland, 136

flag, national, 60, 64, 82

Flemings, 149–50

Foreign Minister's Conference, Berlin (1954), 189, 193

foreign policy, 7, 8, 10, 20, 27, 46, 73, 74, 124, 125, 143, 182ff, 185, 198ff, 222, 265; see also imperialism

formalism, 18

France, 7, 23, 143, 205, 243; communist and socialist parties in, 139, 140, 145–6, 147; defeat by Hitler, 123; and defence and rearmament, 180, 181, 190, 203; imperialism, 147, 270, 271, 272; liberalism and democracy, 14; nationalism, 253, 254; post-war, 144–7, 160, 283; revolutions in, 6, 50, 105, 237, 271, 279, 289; and Soviet Union, 185

franchise, 51, 57–8, 83; see also elections; proportional representation

Frankfurt University, 88, 95

Free Corps, 61

Free Democrat Party (FDP), 152, 169, 170, 187, 205, 209, 213, 219, 228–9

Free University, Berlin, 173

freedom of the individual, 6, 22, 23, 39–41, 47, 59, 67, 88–9, 105

Freiburg University, 34, 92, 96

French Revolution, 6, 50, 271, 279, 289

Führer cult, 62, 275; see also dictatorship

gaullism, 144–7, 255, 293, 295

Geneva Summit Conference, 1955, 193

German Association for Political Science, 156, 174

German Communist Party, see Communist Party

German Democratic Party (DDP), 57, 58, 156, 229

German nationals, 58, 63, 65, 66, 82, 83

German Party (DP), 214, 230

German People's Party, 58, 63, 66, 83

German Right Party (DRP), 230

German Students' Association, 97

'German Students' Day', 97, 98

German Students' Union, 99

'Germany Plan' (1959), 205, 208–9

Gestapo, 115

Giessen University, 34

Gleichschaltung, 18, 56, 64, 83, 86–103, 104, 114, 116, 118, 237, 281, 282; in East and Central Europe, 142, 179, 184

Goslar, 220

'Gottingen Seven' (1937), 31, 33, 41, 43, 48, 88

Göttingen University, 32, 33, 34, 86, 96

Graz, 97

Great Britain, and Berlin, 204; constitution, 36–7, 38, 45; democracy in, 5, 6, 7, 12, 14, 21, 23, 25, 154, 239, 284; emergency governments, 284; European defence, 181, 185, 189, 203; and European Economic Community, 147, 154; freedom in, 105; and German rearmament, 180, 181; imperialism, 270, 272, 290; monarchy, 140; nationalism, 253, 254; parliamentary opposition, 252; party system, 152, 159–160, 228, 243, 251; post-war Labour Party, 140, 142; relations with France, 145, 147; socialism in, 237

Great Coalition (1928/30), 64, 65, 74, 84; (1966/69), 21, 154, 217, 229, 278

Greece, 137, 283

Greece, Ancient, 36, 236–7

Halle-Wittenberg University, 34–5

Hallstein doctrine, 195, 196, 201, 206, 208
Hamburg University, 96
Hannover, 33, 37
head of state, see dictatorship; monarchy; president
Heidelberg University, 35, 95
Herrenklub, 84
High Court, 27
history, relationship with politics, 31ff
Hitler Youth, 100
Hochschule für Politik, Berlin, see Institute for Political Science, Berlin
Holland, see Netherlands
Holstein, 31, 32
human rights, 6, 21, 22, 39–41, 67, 129, 160–1, 164, 170, 283; see also freedom
Hungary, 204, 255, 256, 261

imperialism, 6, 8, 11, 14, 39, 73, 140, 263, 270–7
Independent Social-democrat Party (USPD), 57, 58, 66
India, 257, 291
Indo-China war, 145, 146, 189
industry and industrial society, 8, 14, 16, 17, 138, 222, 226, 239, 248, 249, 271, 287
inflation, 53, 86
influence, use of, 26
information and advisory services, 26
Institute for Political Science, Berlin, 17, 95, 156, 169, 241, 242, 249
international co-operation, 139
internationalism, 124, 253–63
Israel, 128, 172, 173, 254; see also anti-semitism; Jews
Italy, 5, 14, 139, 140, 141, 146, 147–9, 189, 247, 254, 272, 279, 283

Japan, 135
Jena University, 35, 83
Jews, 267; see also anti-semitism; Israel

Kellogg Pact (1928), 296
Kiel University, 98
Königsberg, 98
Korean war, 182, 185, 189
Kösen Students' Society, 100
KPD, see Communist Party
Kreisau Circle, 112, 114, 121, 124, 125–6
Kulturkampf, 105
Kuratorium, 171

Labour Party (Great Britain), 140, 142
Labour Party (Netherlands), 150
labour service, student, 99
Länder, 21, 56, 59, 92, 106, 157, 159–160, 163, 165, 167, 279, 280
Latin America, 248, 254, 256, 257, 260
League of Nations, 135, 139, 259, 294, 296; see also United Nations
legal positivism, 14
Leipzig, 93
Leipzig University, 35, 46
Liberal Party (Netherlands), 150
liberalism, 6ff, 14, 15, 30–48, 57, 67, 88, 105, 108, 116, 156, 211, 213, 228, 241, 245, 259
loyalty, to the state, 104–31
Luxemburg, 283

Marburg University, 35
Marshall Plan, 139, 142, 151, 184
marxism, 18, 28, 226, 270, 273, 274
mass demonstrations, 60, 61
meritocracy, 138
Middle East, 128, 201, 291
militarism, 61, 202

military opposition to the state, 113, 114, 115, 120-1

military rearmament, 120, 180-2, 186-8, 191-2, 202, 209; *see also* nuclear weapons

minorities, 28

monarchy, 8, 15, 39-40, 63, 72, 74, 140-1, 148

Mouvement Républicain Populaire (MRP), 146

Munich, 126

Munich Conference (1938), 121

Munich University, 91, 173

National Assembly (1919), 54, 55, 56, 58-60, 64

'National Opposition', 61, 64

National-socialists (NSDAP), 5, 24, 50, 211, 293; Brüning and, 74, 78; and democracy, 19-20; electoral support, 63, 64, 222, 281-2; evolution from Weimar Republic, 19-20, 49-68, 281; Heuss and, 172; imperialism, 271, 273, 275, 276; in post-war positions, 182; Papen and, 81, 82-3; and the party system, 240, 241, 247, 248; racialism, 257, 265, 266, 268; Reichswehr and, 62; resistance to, 104-33; *see also* Third Reich

nationalism, 3, 6, 10-11, 39, 87, 105, 124, 130, 179, 202, 253-8, 264, 274

nationalization, 141

NATO, 137, 139, 145, 150-1, 181-2, 188-9, 191, 204-5, 255, 260, 295

Nazism, *see* National-socialists

neo-Nazis, 127, 216, 230, 257-8; *see also* New German Party

Netherlands, 7, 122, 150, 283; *see also* Benelux

neutralization, 179, 184ff, 191, 202, 209

New German Party (NPD), 25, 127, 216, 227, 257, 258

Nigeria, 266

Norway, 283

NPD, *see* New German Party

NSDAP, *see* National-socialists

nuclear weapons, 188, 192, 196, 201-202, 205-6, 225, 292

Nuremberg Laws, 117, 268

Oberkommando der Wehrmacht (OKW), 120

Oder-Niesse line, 128, 153, 186, 196, 198, 200, 207-8

opposition parties, 23, 25, 252

opposition to the state, 41-1, 104-31, 219

ownership of property, 59

Papal Council, 118

Paris Treaties (1954), 189, 194

Parliamentary Council, 20, 49, 147, 158, 168, 170

parliamentary procedure, 26

parties, banning of, 21, 214, 247; and democracy, 235-52; in Federal Republic, 152, 160, 211-32; financing, 22, 26, 231, 247; in foreign countries, 139, 142, 145ff, 219; opposition, 23, 25, 252; *see also* individual parties; *et passim*

partition and reunification, 151, 153, 154, 171, 178-9, 181, 183-91, 193-6, 198, 200-10, 215, 216, 222

patriarchal state, 20-5, 54, 61-2, 72, 88, 105, 106, 113, 130, 217, 239, 292

Paulskirche-Parlament, 31, 35, 46, 160

peace and war, 26, 117, 287-96

Peace Conference (1843), 296

People's Party (Netherlands), 150

People's Republic, *see* East Germany

perfectionism, 16, 27, 237-8, 285

planning groups, 26

plebiscites, 21, 58, 59–60, 144, 160, 168

Poland, 136, 198, 206–8, 255, 279

Portugal, 137, 279, 285

Pour le Mérite, 174

Prague *coup*, 142, 158

president, 16–17, 50, 59, 64ff, 68, 76, 166–9, 170, 173, 279ff; *see also* emergency legislation

press, 26, 47

'Professors' parliament' (Frankfurt), 88

proportional representation, 21, 51, 57, 83, 159, 212

Prussia, 7, 8, 37, 39, 56, 68, 222, 281, 282, 292

public hearings, 26

public opinion, 26, 28, 53, 73, 179

racialism, 93, 96, 257, 264–9, 272; *see also* anti-semitism

Rapacki Plan, 193

Rapallo policy, 178, 206

RCDS, *see* Christian-democrat Students' Association

Realpolitik, 7–8, 89, 103, 187, 257, 269, 290, 295

rearmament, 120, 180–2, 186–8, 191–192, 202, 209; *see also* nuclear weapons

referendum, *see* plebiscites

refugees, 199–200, 202

Refugees' Party (BHE), 199, 214, 230

Reich concordat, 78, 119

Reich Union, 99

Reichslandbund, 85

Reichsbanner, 61, 81

Reichschaft, 99

Reichstag, 56, 59, 63, 65, 75, 78, 105, 212, 279–81

Reichswehr, 16, 17, 62, 74, 82, 106, 108, 110, 120

Resistance (French), 145, 146

Resistance (Italian), 148

resistance to the state, 40–1, 94, 103, 104–31, 219

reunification, *see* partition and re-unification

revisionism, 16, 73, 199–200, 202

revolution, 6, 7, 25, 41–2, 44, 105, 119, 129, 130; (1848), 67, 73, 88; (1918), 21, 52ff, 71, 72

rights of the individual, 6, 21, 22, 39–41, 67, 129, 160–1, 164, 170, 283; *see also* freedom

Roman empire, 12, 36, 270, 271, 275, 279

romanticism, 6, 12, 39, 43, 89, 173

Rostock University, 96

rule of law, state based on, 13, 14, 19, 79, 129, 131

Rumania, 255, 272

Russia, *see* Soviet Union

SA, 61, 81, 98, 99

Saar, 118, 190

Saxony, 222

Scandinavia, 38, 63, 140, 179–80, 275

Schleswig-Holstein, 31, 32

science, Nazification of, 91ff

science and politics, 30–1, 33, 47, 101, 103, 126

Scientific Council, 174

SDS, 225

Second Reich, 9, 68, 88, 128

Security Council, 204, 256

SED, *see* Socialist Unity Party

'Senior School', 93

Slavs, 128

social clauses, 45, 63, 130, 138–9

Socialist-democrats (SPD), 82, 152; and the Bonn party system, 212, 214, 216, 220, 222, 223–7, 228, 229, 231; defence policy, 181, 209; and

Socialist-democrats (*contd.*)—
the election (1919), 58; elections (1949–69), 212, 216; elections (1957), 197, 212, 216; 'Germany Plan', 205, 208–9; Heuss and, 164, 165, 169; leaves the coalition (1920), 63; and the 1918 revolution, 55; nuclear weapons, 205; and the reunification, 179, 208–9; and the rise of the NSDAP, 75, 113; and the Weimar Coalition, 57, 60

socialism, 108, 140–1, 146, 151, 197, 241, 274, 289; *see also* individual socialist parties

Socialist Reich Party (SRP), 214, 230, 247

Socialist Unity Party (SED), 224, 230, 249

South Africa, 266, 267

Soviet Union, 123, 135, 143, 215, 216, 257, 290; annexation of Baltic States, 136; and China, 255, 273; division of Europe, 136, 139; East-West confrontation, 136, 142, 143, 145, 154, 178ff, 255, 261; East-West *détente*, 201ff, 215; Eastern Europe under, 140, 142, 184; *Gleichschaltung* policy, 142, 179, 184; imperialism, 271, 272, 273, 275; and reunification of Germany, 182–209; support for Egypt, 256; and West Germany, 179, 180, 182–209

Spain, 137, 279

SPD, *see* Socialist-democrats

'Spiegel' crisis, 225

SRP, *see* Socialist Reich Party

SS, 123

Der Staat, 23

Staat und Recht, 27

stab-in-the-back legends, 16, 52, 78, 88, 121, 122, 126

Stahlhelm, 61, 66, 81, 82

state, and democracy, 3–29

Strasbourg, 180

student unions and associations, 97–100

students, 89, 93, 97–100, 126, 216, 262

Students' League, 97, 99

subordination of the individual, 90; *see also Gleichschaltung;* rights of the individual

Sudan, 266

Sudeten, 117, 199

Suez crisis, 204, 261

Sweden, 136, 283

Switzerland, 136, 160, 166, 254, 275, 283

Tatkreis, 84

Third Reich, 49, 66, 67–8, 84, 87, 101, 103, 106, 153, 172, 182, 218; *et passim; see also* National-socialists

Third World, 201, 236, 254, 272

Thuringia, 82

totalitarianism, 61ff, 89, 104, 247

Trade Union League (DGB), 219

trade unions, 8, 55, 84, 106, 113, 120, 146, 150, 205, 218, 219, 286

traditionalism, 27, 144, 295

treason, 114, 122

Treaty of Versailles, 52, 58, 60, 62, 66, 67, 73, 74, 86, 89, 90, 116, 120, 124

Tübingen University, 35, 96

Turkey, 283

Ulm, 110

UN, *see* United Nations

'underground', 107, 108, 115, 119

unemployment, 64, 66, 76

UNESCO, 267

United Nations (UN), 136, 187, 195, 256–7, 259, 266, 294, 295, 296; Security Council, 204, 256

United States of America, 105, 135, 203, 204, 237; confrontation with Soviet Union, 136, 142, 216; see also East-West confrontation; constitution, 161; containment of communism policy, 139, 142; democracy in, 5, 6, 7, 11, 12, 14, 21, 23, 25, 166, 283; dependency of the Federal Republic on, 195–6; and European defence policy, 180, 185, 189–90; imperialism, 272, 290; party system, 152, 159–60, 228, 239, 240, 242, 243, 252; presidential system, 59, 166; racial problems, 266, 267; relations with France, 145
universities, 15, 17, 34–6, 47, 86–103, 125; see also students
USPD, see Independent Social-democrat Party

Vietnam, 256, 261, 272, 291
völkisch policies, 87, 92, 94, 97
Volksgemeinschaft, 10, 62

Walloons, 149–50
war, 287–96
Warsaw Pact, 191, 260
Wehrmacht, 119–20, 122
Weimar Coalition, 56–60, 220

Weimar Republic, 88, 109, 116, 146, 154, 156, 181, 218, 225; constitution, 13, 17, 49–68, 106–7, 157, 158, 161, 212, 279; crises and failure of, 49–68, 69–70, 81, 113, 152, 153, 215; emergency powers, 51, 59, 64, 65, 279, 282, 283, 285; in retrospect, 49–68; party system, 56ff, 186, 211, 214, 241; president in, 50, 59, 64ff, 68, 166, 173; state and democracy in, 13, 15–16, 19, 21, 22, 23, 24, 49–68, 77, 129, 160, 161, 166, 217; and the Treaty of Versailles, 52, 58, 62, 67, 73
Western Alliance, 137, 158, 184ff, 192, 197, 216
'White Rose' leaflets, 126
Wismar, 31
women, emancipation, 97
working classes, 8, 58
World War I, 5, 9, 38, 49, 52–3, 68, 71, 72, 88, 105, 135, 153, 272
World War II, 121ff, 178, 254, 261, 272
Württemberg, 104, 110

Youth Union, 222,
Yugoslavia, 136, 207, 208, 255, 256, 272